Arguing until Doomsday

CIVIL WAR AMERICA

Peter S. Carmichael, Caroline E. Janney,
and Aaron Sheehan-Dean, EDITORS

This landmark series interprets broadly the history and
culture of the Civil War era through the long nineteenth
century and beyond. Drawing on diverse approaches
and methods, the series publishes historical works that
explore all aspects of the war, biographies of leading
commanders, and tactical and campaign studies, along
with select editions of primary sources. Together, these
books shed new light on an era that remains central to
our understanding of American and world history.

Arguing until Doomsday

Stephen Douglas, Jefferson Davis,

and the Struggle

for American Democracy

Michael E. Woods

The University of North Carolina Press

CHAPEL HILL

This book was published with the assistance of the
Anniversary Fund of the University of North Carolina Press.

Designed by Kristina Kachele Design, llc
Set in Miller Text with Directors Gothic 210 display
by Kristina Kachele Design, llc

Cover art: portraits of Stephen Douglas and Jefferson Davis by Julian Vannerson,
photographer, 1859, Library of Congress Prints and Photographs Division; (background)
U.S. map by Rufus Blanchard, 1856, Library of Congress Geography and Map Division.

Library of Congress Cataloging-in-Publication Data
Names: Woods, Michael E., author.
Title: Arguing until doomsday : Stephen Douglas, Jefferson Davis,
and the struggle for American democracy / Michael E. Woods.
Other titles: Civil War America (Series)
Description: Chapel Hill : The University of North Carolina Press, 2020. |
Series: Civil War America | Includes bibliographical references and index.
Identifiers: LCCN 2019044427 | ISBN 9781469656397 (cloth) |
ISBN 9781469679211 (paperback) | ISBN 9781469656403 (ebook)
Subjects: LCSH: Douglas, Stephen A. (Stephen Arnold), 1813–1861. | Davis, Jefferson,
1808–1889. | Democratic Party (U.S.)—History. | Slavery—History—19th century—
Political aspects—United States. | United States—Politics and government—1845–1861. |
United States—History—1783–1865.
Classification: LCC JK2316 .W74 2020 | DDC 973.7/11—dc23
LC record available at https://lccn.loc.gov/2019044427

This project is being presented with financial assistance from the West Virginia Humanities Council, a state affiliate of the National Endowment for the Humanities. Any views,
findings, conclusions, or recommendations do not necessarily represent those of the
West Virginia Humanities Council or the National Endowment for the Humanities.

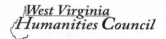

For Beth

Contents

Figures

Arguing until Doomsday

Introduction

Alfred Iverson was sick of congressional gridlock. The Georgia senator had endured four years of divisive votes, bombastic speeches, and violent disturbances. Now, in February 1859, as two fellow Democrats bickered away a Wednesday afternoon, his patience ran out. Other senators had tried to gain the floor, but even when David Broderick of California succeeded on his sixth attempt, the combatants kept sparring. As winter twilight settled over the capital city, Iverson urged the presiding officer, Florida senator Stephen Mallory, to enforce the rule that limited senators to two comments per topic. Normally, said Iverson, he would cheerfully allow the loquacious senators to wrap up, but one of them had spoken "at least six or eight times on this subject" and his adversary nearly as much. "If we permit these gentlemen to go on bandying arguments with each other," Iverson warned, "we shall never come to the end of the question. . . . They can go on here arguing against each other from this until doomsday."[1]

Iverson drew laughs, but the situation was deadly serious: Stephen A. Douglas of Illinois and Jefferson Davis of Mississippi had spent three hours clashing over property rights, democracy, and the future of the American West. Their battle had erupted over a seemingly routine matter. The previous day, the Senate had taken up House Bill 711, an appropriations bill to fund the federal government through June 1860. Debate remained comfortably dull until New Hampshire Republican John P. Hale proposed an amendment seeking repeal of an older provision to delay the Kansas Territory's statehood until its population reached the minimum required for one congressional representative. Stunned, other senators demanded to know why Hale would broach this fraught subject with the session nearly over and much work still undone. But Hale's amendment was relevant: H.B. 711 earmarked $20,000 for a territorial census. So, senators wrangled over Kansas for the rest of the day, proving only that no one knew how many people lived in the distant, bloodstained territory.[2]

The fireworks began Wednesday when the Senate returned to Hale's amendment and dropped all pretense of discussing anything but slavery. Mississippi's Albert Gallatin Brown opened with a blistering demand that Congress enact a federal slave code if territorial legislatures failed to safeguard slaveholders' property rights. He swore that if the North, "by mere force of numbers," denied slaveholders their rightful protection, then "the Constitution is a failure, and the Union a despotism," and he would support secession.[3]

This was too much for Stephen Douglas. After glancing around the new Senate chamber, in use for little more than a month, and finding no fellow northern Democrat willing to respond, the "Little Giant" from Illinois raised his rotund, five-foot-four-inch frame to reply. He first sought common ground with Brown, agreeing that slaves were property and that citizens could carry property into the territories. But that was the end of their agreement. Brown wanted to give slaveholders special federal protection; Douglas demurred. Slaves were subject to local regulation like any other type of property, he insisted, and if masters needed federal help, it was their "misfortune" and none of his own. According to Douglas's pet doctrine of popular sovereignty, property rights did not trump territorial self-government. After parrying counterattacks from Brown and Alabama's Clement Clay, Douglas threw down the gauntlet: no slave code crusader could call himself a Democrat, for such an agenda violated the "Democratic creed." Glancing ahead to next year's presidential election, he added that no Democrat who favored proslavery federal intervention could win a single northern state.[4]

With that, Jefferson Davis plunged into the fray. Maintaining a stiff military bearing despite the neuralgic pain searing his face, Davis hurled back the threat of excommunication, wishing Douglas "God-speed and a pleasant journey" if he insisted on popular sovereignty. The Constitution, Davis insisted, *did* recognize slaves as a unique form of property. Congress, he proclaimed, *was* duty-bound to safeguard masters' property rights in the territories. And if Democrats split over the status of "a few

Africans," Davis wanted it known that he condemned Douglas's apostasy.[5]

Davis and Douglas fenced for hours. Against Douglas's "heresy" of "squatter sovereignty," Davis argued that not all property was created equal and that slaveholders required special public support. Douglas retorted that any property, from enslaved people to dry goods, could be barred from Kansas by local legislation. In the heat of battle, senatorial courtesy yielded to spite. Davis charged Douglas with "catering to the prejudice" of antislavery northerners. Douglas condemned Davis for denying hardy pioneers the "great rights of self-government." At a time when congressional brawls had become distressingly routine, the threat of violence hung in the air: rumors of plots against Douglas's life had swirled in January, and Davis had rushed at him in previous debates.[6] This time, however, the senators exchanged nothing but verbal blows, and after several rounds of oratorical sparring, Iverson intervened, Broderick gained the floor, and doomsday drew nearer.[7]

Though less renowned than the great congressional debates of 1850 and less notorious than Preston Brooks's 1856 caning of Charles Sumner, Davis and Douglas's February 23, 1859, encounter illuminated forces that were fracturing the Democratic Party and destabilizing the Union. As leaders of sectional factions, Douglas spoke for northern Democrats when others remained mute, while Davis championed a hardline southern position on territorial policy. Loyal lieutenants rallied around them: Brown and Clay covered Davis's flanks, while George Pugh of Ohio accused southern Democrats of betraying their northern brethren.[8] Party unity was melting in the crucible of sectionalism. Davis and Douglas both detested Hale's antislavery creed, but they did not combine against the Republican who provoked their quarrel. And while both longed to suppress the slavery issue, neither would yield any ground. When Douglas and Davis debated on center stage, other speakers and issues languished in the wings.

The action of February 23 distilled the Davis-Douglas rivalry into its toxic essence. The hair-trigger debaters battled to claim the Democratic mantle and define party doctrine. Transfixed by visions of western empire, they expounded upon constitutional law, historical precedent, party tradition, and national purpose, and their voices echoed across the continent. Mississippians monitored this "Great Debate" closely, with one ranking Davis among the "great men of the age" and gloating that the "corrupt, revolutionary and dangerous" Douglas had "wholly alienat[ed] every true Southern man from him and his Squatter Sovereignty doctrines."[9] Meanwhile, an Indianan likened Davis's "detestable doctrine" to the Alien and Sedition Acts and vowed that it would never "be engrafted into the Democratic creed."[10] Seeking to give Douglas the last word, supporters circulated his remarks in pamphlet form.[11] Privately, one told Douglas that if southerners refused to relent, "you must certainly drive them to the wall."[12]

★ ★ ★

Davis and Douglas's rivalry crested on the eve of civil war, but its roots ran much deeper and its consequences changed the arc of American history. This book uses their parallel lives and intertwined careers to trace the long history of the Democratic Party's collapse. They were born five years apart in the first two states created after the original thirteen: Douglas's Vermont was admitted in 1791, Davis's Kentucky in 1792. Both buried young wives and children in an age of rampant disease and perilous childbirth, and both remarried well-connected and politically savvy women. Both joined a surging tide of western migration and built their careers in Mississippi Valley states admitted in 1817 (Mississippi) and 1818 (Illinois). Benefiting from upward mobility through westward migration, both envisioned breathtaking future expansion. Both were stalwart Democrats, relentless campaigners, and hard-nosed legislators who sacrificed physical health for political success. They entered the House of Representatives in the mid-1840s, elected from Whiggish portions of reliably Democratic states, and ascended to the Senate in 1847. Both championed Manifest Destiny, cheering for Texas annexation and war with Mexico, and by the early 1850s both were prominent party leaders. Except for a period in which Davis left public office and then joined Franklin Pierce's cabinet, both remained in the Senate until 1861, when Davis departed to preside over the Confederacy and Douglas, after rallying northern Democrats to the Union, went to an early grave.[13]

In the political history of the Civil War era, both men are understandably dwarfed by Abraham Lincoln. Studies pairing Lincoln with Davis and with Douglas are illuminating, but they can skew our perspective. Some Davis-Lincoln studies trace them back to their Kentucky origins, but most focus on the war years.[14] Davis's antebellum career, however, was not merely a prelude to his role as Confederate president. A formidable politician, Davis led a generation of Deep South Democrats who continued John C. Calhoun's proslavery crusade after 1850.[15] Davis figured prominently in the crisis of 1850, the presidential elections of 1852 and 1856, and mounting conflicts over slavery in the territories, American expansion, and the African slave trade. In the most creative chapter of his career, he wielded considerable power as secretary of war. The protracted intraparty struggle with Douglas underscores Davis's antebellum significance. With Douglas in the picture, we can better understand Davis's efforts to validate the Democratic Party's proslavery credentials and force the party to redeem his promises. Davis's quest to make his party and country safe for slavery tore them both apart.

This book also seeks to reinterpret, though not to vindicate, Stephen Douglas, the most polarizing antebellum Democrat. Now best known as Lincoln's opponent in the 1858 Senate election, Douglas is easily cast as the foil whose racist demagoguery and southern connections accentuate Lincoln's rugged decency and defiance of the Slave Power. Insightful studies of their storied debates remind us that Douglas, who was far more famous in the 1850s, was more than a speed bump on Lincoln's road to greatness.[16] Now it is time to reconsider Douglas from an entirely fresh perspective. The point is not to exalt Douglas by emancipating him from Lincoln, or to revive an antiquated narrative in which Douglas heroically resists antislavery extremism, but to reevaluate him as a national political figure. Interpreting Douglas through an intrastate rivalry can distort his career by placing him on a truncated political spectrum. Lincoln and Douglas were sharply opposed, but Illinois was not a microcosm of the country: without a Cotton Kingdom, the state lacked a cadre of planter-politicians, like Davis, who deemed slavery a positive good and sought to make its preservation a national priority. Only when contrasted with Davis can we understand why Douglas aroused so much loathing among southern Democrats. Only through a cross-sectional rivalry can we comprehend why some southerners called for secession, whether Lincoln or Douglas was elected in 1860. Only with a cotton state politico in the picture can we explain why Lincoln and Douglas joined forces against Davis's southern republic. The Lincoln-Douglas rivalry ended in an amiable alliance; the Davis-Douglas rivalry spiraled into disunion and war.[17]

Davis, Douglas, and their contemporaries recognized the importance of this simmering struggle. Personally, the men despised each other, with special animus on the Mississippian's side. Davis publicly threatened to hang Douglas alongside Lincoln and privately called him "our little grog drinking, electioneering Demagogue."[18] Varina Davis shared her husband's disdain for the "dirty speculator and party trickster" from Illinois.[19] But their rivalry captivated public attention because it was more than merely personal. Admirers saw both Democrats as leaders of factions warring for the party's soul. An Ohioan (who named his daughter for Douglas's wife) prayed that Douglas would triumph over the "Jeff Davises of the South" who sought to shackle the Democracy to a proslavery platform.[20] A Davis partisan denounced Douglas as "an abolitionist in disguise" and pressed Davis to "show him no quarter."[21]

The rancor outlived the Little Giant and shaped Davis's postwar campaign to mold public memory. Given the Civil War's ferocious course and revolutionary consequences, he might logically have fixated on Lincoln. But when Davis, who had just weeks to live, wrote a final autobiographical sketch in 1889, he zeroed in on Douglas. Reflecting on his early Senate career, Davis recalled his "active part in the debates on the Compromise measures of 1850, frequently opposing Senator Douglas, of Illinois, in his theory of squatter sovereignty." And when recounting the late antebellum years, Davis blamed Douglas for fracturing the Democratic Party and the Union. He mentioned Republicans and abolitionists only briefly, placing primary responsibility for the war on the Illinois Democrat, whom he still resented for having "insisted upon the rights of the first immigrants into the territory" to establish or prohibit slavery. From this sacrilege "arose a dissension which finally divided the Democratic party, and caused its defeat in the Presidential election of 1860." Waxing poetic, he concluded, "And from this empty, baseless theory grew the Iliad of our direst woes."[22] Davis went to his grave cursing Douglas.

By weaving two remarkable lives into a study of their times, this book revisits antebellum America's breathless optimism, restless expansionism, and self-destructive sectionalism. Thus, it offers both less and more than a traditional dual biography. By tracing Davis's and Douglas's connections to broad unofficial constituencies ranging from their home states across much of the West, it features a far more varied cast of characters. Many were active in office holding or electioneering; others, including soldiers, farmers, and merchants, offered valuable local intelligence. All shaped antebellum politics by influencing Davis's and Douglas's understanding of home-state developments and the burgeoning American West.[23] Equally important is what this approach reveals about how Davis and Douglas were perceived by their contemporaries. Both cultivated reputations as nationally minded statesmen who could unite a divided country behind the Democratic Party, but, by the late 1850s, both were widely regarded as champions of antagonistic sections. This grassroots perspective illuminates the popular pressure that shaped Davis's and Douglas's efforts to promote the Democracy back home.

The book culminates in the spring of 1861 with Douglas's death and the outbreak of civil war and only briefly sketches Davis's wartime activities, which have been ably covered elsewhere.[24] It does not chronicle every detail of Davis's and Douglas's lives. Rather, it foregrounds them in the narrative of a growing nation and an ascendant political party breaking apart. By contextualizing both men in their states and regions, the book uncovers the deepest sources of their motivations and ideals. It examines their beliefs, actions, and reputations to illuminate their growing influence as leaders of Democratic factions, which became increasingly sectionalized over time. Because the division and final rupture of the Democratic Party was an important prelude to secession, this approach follows two individuals down a path that led, although they willed otherwise, to disunion.

This approach yields three interlocking stories: personal, partisan, and national. As a collective political biography, this is the story of two men who moved west, planted roots near the Mississippi River, and visualized it as the heart of a sprawling empire.[25] Despite their shared party identity and racial prejudice, they developed distinctive visions for the future. Douglas imagined an extensive, decentralized empire of self-governing entities linked by material bonds of infrastructure and commerce. This web of flourishing white settler colonies would serve as an exemplar of republican self-rule while channeling trade toward Chicago and votes toward the Democratic Party. Davis, postbellum paeans to state sovereignty notwithstanding, pictured a tightly controlled empire in which a muscular central power protected masters' property rights and extended the Cotton Kingdom's reach to the Pacific. Douglas would make the hemisphere safe for white men's self-government; Davis would make it safe for slavery.

Neither agenda appeals to most modern eyes, and at first glance they might appear compatible. In practice, they were not. By tracing Davis's and Douglas's efforts to maintain a nationally cohesive Democratic Party that could prevail in their home states, this book underscores the challenges inherent in American federalism. Historians have noted that antebellum sectional strife cannot be understood without attention to the interplay between state and national politics, a dynamic that appears clearly in Davis's and Douglas's careers.[26] Both men revered the Democracy as a vehicle for advancing their respective policy programs, but they had to prove to critics back in Illinois and Mississippi that the party was trustworthy. To this end, they pulled the Democracy in different, ultimately opposing directions. It was a risky game of tug-of-war. When the rope broke, the Democracy collapsed and the Union crumbled.

On the partisan level, then, this is a story of Democrats wrestling with thorny questions about property rights, democracy, race, slavery, and freedom. By focusing on relentless internal conflict, this book reinterprets the antebellum Democratic Party. Some historians cast the Democracy as an inherently proslavery force cemented by commitments to white supremacy and states' rights.[27] They demonstrate the disturbing prevalence of racism and anti-abolitionism, but emphasizing Democratic solidarity leaves much about the party's chronic intramural tensions, and even more about its 1860 rupture, unexplained. Some opponents may have felt beset by a monolithic Democratic foe, but intraparty strife, as Abraham Lincoln and other shrewd critics understood, was vitally important. Indeed, antislavery activists were not passive observers of Democratic infighting but actually exacerbated these conflicts by refusing to allow Democrats to dodge divisive questions about slavery. In turn, the party's 1860 rupture marked a critical milestone on the road to secession: it sundered a national political party, prevented Democratic candidates from credibly claiming broad national appeal, and bolstered secessionists' arguments that slavery was no longer secure in the Union.

A second group of historians have identified a vibrant antislavery element within the Democracy's northern wing. Since many adherents became Republicans in the mid-1850s, however, these accounts often conclude several years before secession in 1861, precisely when simmering conflicts between northern and southern Democrats reached their boiling point.[28] This book thus shares most with a third body of scholarship on the Civil War–era Democratic Party, one that stresses internal diversity and disagreement, foregrounds northern Democrats who were neither embryonic Republicans nor proslavery "doughfaces," and explores both what held Democrats together and what tore them apart.[29]

Rather than try to pin down the Democracy as fundamentally proslavery or antislavery; inherently northern, southern, or western; or definitively progressive or reactionary, I view the party as a dynamic institution whose membership and ideals were constantly contested. Like most American political parties, the Democracy was an unwieldy coalition often sustained more by negative partisanship than by ideological uniformity. By outlining the party's increasingly sectionalized internal conflicts, I trace how Davis and Douglas tore it to shreds. Centripetal forces like racism and party affinity failed to maintain cohesion in the face of conflicting material interests and ideological commitments, which were pulling the Democracy apart.

Specifically, a deep-rooted conflict between guardians of slaveholders' property rights and champions of white men's majority rule created an irrepressible conflict within the Democratic Party. Tensions between property rights and democracy are familiar to political historians in many fields: scholars of the Constitutional Convention and founding era have explored them in depth, and comparable work exists on the Jacksonian era, the Gilded Age, and the New Deal.[30] With some notable exceptions, however, students of antebellum sectionalism have not given questions of property rights and majoritarianism as much attention.[31] This conflict lay at the heart of Davis's and Douglas's struggle to steer the Democracy according to the interests and demands of their constituents. Strident appeals to white supremacy or party fealty could not paper over basic questions about balancing slaveholders' peculiarly fragile property rights with popular self-government. Like most Democrats, Davis and Douglas rejected abolitionists' efforts to invalidate property rights in human beings. But as Matthew Mason has shown, antebellum sectionalism was not a binary struggle; opposition to one end of the political spectrum did not automatically align Davis and Douglas on the other.[32] We know much about the conflict between Republicans and proslavery southerners. We know far less about the related but not identical conflict that split the Democratic Party and ensured that Lincoln and Douglas, for all their substantial disagreements, closed ranks against Davis when the shooting started in 1861.

Davis and Douglas's rivalry was combustible because the Democratic Party's oft-cited proslavery pillars—racism and states' rights—did not adequately safeguard slavery in an increasingly hostile world. Both men recognized that slaveholders needed more than racist neighbors and a weak federal government to maintain control over enslaved people. Masters demanded active help from whites nationwide and from a central government empowered to advance their interests.[33] Building on this important reinterpretation of slaveholders' politics, I argue that "proslavery" was a moving target, not a fixed position, and that as Davis and other southerners escalated their demands for public support, restive northern Democrats, led by Douglas, set clear limits on what they would accept. When protection of slaveholders' property rights threatened white men's vaunted self-rule, conflict among antebellum Democrats raged out of control.

On the national level, therefore, this is a story of irony and failure. Davis and Douglas cherished the Union, but their efforts to govern it ended disastrously. Most modern Americans are grateful that neither Davis nor Douglas triumphed; neither plays a heroic role in most narratives of Civil War causation. But their rivalry was serious and their experiences are instructive. By failing to distinguish between partisanship and patriotism, quietude and harmony, obstinacy and courage, Davis and Douglas inadvertently aided their common foe, the avowedly antislavery Republicans. For Douglas, this meant electoral defeat and the outbreak of a war he had insisted was avoidable. For Davis, it meant taking a revolutionary gamble to escape an existential threat. Yet Jefferson Davis and Stephen Douglas did not simply argue until doomsday overtook them. They were not characters in a tragedy; they were not voices of reason in an age of passion; they were not giants of a more heroic past. Nor were they part of a blundering generation, though they did live at a moment when generations of bullheadedness caught up to a country that had flouted its noblest ideals. Davis and Douglas were politicians determined to have it all—victory for self, party, section, and ideology. Pursuing these aims with all the energy they could muster, they hastened their own doom.

Western Men

"There is a power in this nation greater than either the North or the South," proclaimed Senator Stephen Douglas, "a growing, increasing, swelling power, that will be able to speak the law to this nation, and to execute the law as spoken. That power is the country known as the great West—the Valley of the Mississippi." Sprawling from the Great Lakes to the Gulf of Mexico and from the Appalachians to the Rockies, this heartland empire would save the Union from suicidal sectionalism.[1] Delivered in March 1850, Douglas's prophecy was a timely one: Americans' mental geographies were adjusting to the conquest of northern Mexico, and sectional strife was glowing white-hot. Skeptics might have warned that expansion would inflame, not dampen, sectional quarrels over slavery's extension. Perhaps the West was the problem, not the solution. But Douglas had long since made western development the central theme of his career, and his "swelling power" speech transmuted his fondest desires into surefire guarantees.

Senator Jefferson Davis was a westerner, too. His Mississippi plantation was over a hundred miles west of Douglas's Chicago home, and as a young army officer, Davis had forayed onto the Great Plains, farther west than Douglas ever traveled; more recently, his Mexican War service had burnished his credentials as an agent of Manifest Destiny. A year after Douglas's speech, Davis self-identified as "an inhabitant of the valley of the Mississippi" and "a western man."[2] But his regional affiliation was complicated. Davis's admiration for John C. Calhoun, his calls for southern solidarity, and his vision of slavery's unbridled expansion all suggested that the South came first. He dreamed of the West as a powerful appendage to his native region, not as an antidote to sectional strife. Yet hindsight should not obscure Davis's western ties or elide his vision of a slaveholding sunbelt that stretched to the Pacific. Like his Illinois rival, Davis gazed westward with ambition, confidence, and passion born of personal experience and political aspiration. Both men enjoyed the upward mobility that white Americans associated with westward migration and saw the Mississippi Valley as the key to continental hegemony. As Democrats, Davis's and Douglas's western dreams drew them together and tore them apart. To understand their rivalry, we must situate both men in the dynamic river valley that they envisioned as the nucleus of a growing empire with enticingly imprecise borders.

This burgeoning domain was also riven by sectionalism. The monolithic "West" that Douglas imagined as the Union's mainstay was, even in his youth, splintering into northwestern and southwestern sections. True, Illinois and Mississippi had much in common. Hugging the eastern bank of the grandest western river, they shared a colonial past (which included exploitation of slave labor), a rugged self-image, and economic dependence on the global trading hub of New Orleans. Their citizens' commitment to commercial agriculture bred a voracious appetite for land, zeal for Indian removal, and esteem for Andrew Jackson. But Illinois and Mississippi began drifting apart even before they gained statehood in the nationalist afterglow of the War of 1812. Mississippi was maturing into the Cotton Kingdom's richest province, while slavery died fitfully in Illinois amid an influx of free migrants from the Northeast and abroad. By the 1830s, the two states were linked by the valley of the Mississippi and the party of Jackson, but demographic, economic, and political changes were dividing them. These divergent societies bred two titans who never agreed on what it meant to be a westerner, a Democrat, or an American.

★ ★ ★

The Civil War cemented Davis's image as a southerner, but Douglas's association with the West is unshakable. Renowned by contemporaries as "The Giant of the West," "The Giant Intellect of the West," and "the foremost of Western Democrats," Douglas's western persona endured long after his death.[3] But what did contemporaries mean by "the West"? Regional definitions are inherently unstable, but mid-nineteenth-century Anglo-American conceptions of the West centered on the Mississippi River. Even after U.S. sovereignty reached the Pacific, easterners imagined the West in terms of hydrological networks, with the Mississippi and its mighty tributaries veining one cohesive region. In 1860, Mississippi historian J. F. H. Claiborne eulogized the "vast empire of the West, stretching along the Ohio, the Missouri, and the Mississippi," as "the backbone of our Union" and the "citadel of our national strength."[4] He imagined the West as both a geopolitical center *and* a region thankfully peripheral to North-South conflict. Connection with the Mississippi River was therefore a source of pride. Davis heartily identified with those who "live on that great highway of the West—the Mississippi river," while Douglas boasted that "we" of the "great Mississippi Valley" constituted "the heart and soul of the Nation and the continent."[5]

Contemporaries associated the West with material bounty as well as with national strength. The Mississippi River cut a deep channel into eastern imaginations during the "flush times" of the 1830s, when the valley's booming economy attracted migrants and admirers. Many easterners encountered the region through the writings of publicists like Robert Baird. A Pennsylvanian who graduated from Princeton Seminary, Baird was an unlikely western promoter, but in 1832 he published a western guidebook whose title, *View of the Valley of the Mississippi, or the Emigrant's and Traveller's Guide to the West*, reinforced the identification of the river with the region. Writing roughly a year before Douglas reached Illinois and three years before Davis settled on his Mississippi plantation, Baird explained how to thrive on the frontier. Meticulous research into everything from transportation timetables to start-up costs informed his advice on where to go, how to travel, and what to plant. The Princetonian also dabbled in boosterism. Defining his subject as everything between the Alleghenies and the Rockies (which he called the "Oregon" mountains), Baird exulted that the "Valley of the Mississippi" encompassed 1.3 million square miles of incomparably bountiful real estate. The valley "surpasses all others in the richness and variety of its soil. . . . In beauty and fertility it is the most perfect garden of nature; and by means of its thousand streams, wonderful facilities are extended to every part of it for commercial intercourse." Like many contemporaries, Baird thought in terms of transport, agriculture, and geopolitical power. Blessed on all three accounts, the Mississippi Valley would soon control "the destiny of this nation," making "the West an object of the deepest interest to every American patriot."[6]

Surveying the Mississippi from its headwaters to the Gulf, Baird appraised each adjacent state and territory from the perspective of a potential migrant, revealing that the valley was not a single economic or geographic unit. Take his implicit comparison between Illinois and Mississippi. After enumerating the Prairie State's "exceedingly productive" (if stubbornly compact) soil, navigable rivers, and budding commercial capital of Chicago, Baird proclaimed that Illinois had "the finest situation of all the western states." For those who could afford $1,080 in start-up costs, Illinois was ideal.[7] Baird also attended to Mississippi but offered little specific advice. Instead, he warned of the sickly summer months and noted that cotton "absorbs almost the whole attention" of the locals, although they could raise corn, wheat, and cattle as well. Growing cotton, Baird conceded, "is by no means a difficult operation," at least not for his presumably free readers, because the "tedious" harvest work was done "by slaves, who go along with a basket, and gather all that they can pick out." Just a few enslaved laborers could run a paying plantation.[8] The lessons were clear: Illinois was a healthy place, in every sense, for smallholders; Mississippi was a riskier proposition, but the owner of human chattels could prosper. Emigrants who shared Baird's worldview would likely head northward. Baird tipped his hand when he calculated that the West contained enough land for four million farms of 160 acres each. A generation later, that magic number would taunt migrants whose dreams withered on arid western quarter-sections, but in 1832, it betrayed Baird's affinity for northern family farming over southern plantation agriculture.[9]

Yet Baird recognized that not all migrants shared his perspective, and his analysis of migration patterns indicated that the West would succumb to sectionalism. Addressing easterners trying to imagine life in the Mississippi Valley, Baird noted that migrants tended to move directly from east to west: New Englanders to the Great Lakes, Virginians to Kentucky, and South Carolinians to Mississippi. Thus, western communities were arranged in a pattern familiar to denizens of the Atlantic Coast. "If one knows what are the peculiarities of the several states east of the Allegheny Mountains," Baird explained, "he may expect to find them . . . in the corresponding parallels in the West." This included the most peculiar peculiarity of all: "Slavery keeps nearly within the same parallels."[10] Years before Davis and Douglas established western homes, sectionalism was already perceptible in the West. Easterners might imagine the Mississippi Valley as a homogeneous frontier where pioneers subdued a wilderness with rifle and ax, but as the West developed into a hothouse of commercial agriculture, sectional divisions reappeared. Davis and Douglas inhabited very different Wests.

★ ★ ★

For all intents and purposes, Jefferson Davis was a Mississippian. His Kentucky birth, not far from Abraham Lincoln's, makes for a satisfying coincidence, but it meant little to Davis's life. Even his birth year is clouded by doubt; many scholars accept 1808, as recounted in an autobiographical sketch, but others favor 1807.[11] Either way, Kentucky made little impression on the infant. In 1810, his father, Samuel, relocated the family, first to Louisiana and then to Woodville, Wilkinson County, in Mississippi's southwestern corner. There, Davis recalled a lifetime later, "my memories begin."[12] His neighbors' memories often began there, too. In 1859, a Vicksburg friend exulted over the political renown won by Davis, "a native Mississippian."[13] Davis noticed that "the old people about Woodville very frequently have spoken of me as a native of that neighborhood."[14] He relished this because he was a Mississippian by upbringing and by choice. After years away for school and military service, Davis elected to return to Mississippi to raise a family and pursue a political career. For a well-connected white male, it was a smart move. Contrary to the image of the Old South as a world frozen in amber, Davis's Mississippi was a dynamic place. Not long before his birth, it was an isolated backwater, but a combination of gumption and avarice, cunning and brutality, and private enterprise and government coercion transformed it into one of the world's richest cotton-growing regions.[15] Davis rose with Mississippi to the pinnacle of power.

The Davises arrived just as Mississippi was poised for an economic boom. A generation earlier, while Georgia-born Samuel fought in the Revolutionary War, Anglo-American migrants trickled into the area, usually avoiding the Choctaw and Chickasaw communities to the north and gravitating toward Natchez, a Mississippi River town some forty miles north of Woodville. Established in 1716, Natchez passed between French, British, and Spanish overlords until Spain relinquished it to the United States in 1798. Colonial-era planters had exploited slave labor to grow tobacco and cotton in the Natchez District, but in the late eighteenth century, plantation agriculture was confined to a small area. Many early American arrivals lived very much like their counterparts in frontier Illinois, including the hardy souls who settled upriver in Warren County, Davis's future home. Few owned slaves or large estates, and most lived rough, simple lives as subsistence farmers, raising hogs, planting

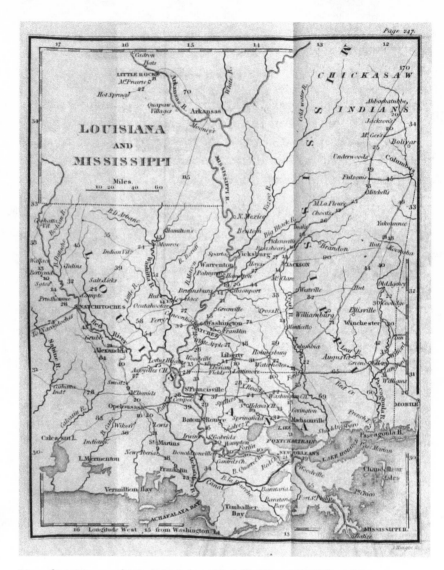

Map of Louisiana and Mississippi, from [Baird], *View of the Valley of the Mississippi*, 247. (Courtesy of Rare Book Collection, Louis Round Wilson Special Collections Library, University of North Carolina at Chapel Hill)

gardens, cutting wood, hunting game, and trading locally. They toiled to get by, not to get ahead. By the turn of the nineteenth century, however, some had started exporting cattle through New Orleans, a foreign (Spanish and briefly French) city until 1803, and purchasing slaves as a source of extra household labor. Many locals persisted as subsistence farmers, but a growing number had accumulated capital, acquired enslaved workers, and ventured into plantation agriculture. By the time Samuel and his toddler son reached Mississippi, it was primed for an economic revolution.[16]

When the takeoff arrived, it swept through Mississippi with the intensity of a gold rush. By the mid-1830s, Mississippi had become "the Mecca of American fortune hunters" whose dreams of quick riches anticipated California forty-niners or Texas oilmen.[17] Migration swelled the population by 175 percent between 1830 and 1840, when the total reached 375,000.[18] From every corner of the Union came young upstarts chasing material gain and professional advancement. When John A. Quitman, a wide-eyed New Yorker who later became Davis's neighbor, arrived in 1822, he kicked himself for having dawdled in Ohio before pushing on to Natchez. "No part of the United States holds out better prospects for a young lawyer" than Mississippi, he reported. Money was plentiful and attracted "the floating population of the whole West," bringing a mixture of sleaze and gentility, with "blackguardism and depravity" jostling alongside an elegant aristocracy. It meant brisk business for a hustling lawyer. With planters raking in $50,000 per year and 120 criminal indictments crowding the docket, Quitman liked his chances.[19] These, recalled another writer, were "the golden days of Mississippi."[20]

The rush was fueled by cotton. Ravenous British demand, coupled with Mississippi's long, hot growing season, created a bull market. In 1808, Natchez District planters exported around 5,000 bales of cotton, but output soared as cultivation spread across the state.[21] By 1830, Mississippi yielded around 100,000 bales, and the "flush times" were just beginning. When Mississippi passed Georgia to become the South's leading cotton producer in 1840, production exceeded 386,000 bales and reached 1.2 million twenty years later.[22] The western river counties, including Warren County, led the way. When Davis settled there in 1835, Warren County's soil was yielding some 30,000 bales per year, with its 32,000 bales in 1840 ranking second in Mississippi.[23] Notably, much of the state was beginning to resemble the older plantation zone of the southwest, as zealous planters acquired fresh land in the northern and eastern counties.[24] On the eve of the Civil War, small farmers predominated in the northeastern hills and southern piney woods, but much of Mississippi was cotton country. No longer confined to the Natchez District, King Cotton reigned statewide.

This economic explosion is often attributed to the cotton gin. Eli Whitney's Yankee ingenuity provided an important spark, but Mississippi's transformation depended on many factors. One was the use of new cotton varieties, including a Mexican strain, introduced around 1820, whose wide-open bolls were easier to pick.[25] Equally important was the state's mighty namesake. The river carries huge quantities of silt, which is periodically deposited on the floodplain, nourishing Mississippi's famously fertile riparian soils.[26] The river also linked Mississippi to the world. Towns like Natchez and Vicksburg existed to connect interior plantations to the river, which carried cotton down to New Orleans and on to global markets. The Louisiana Purchase, which secured U.S. control of the Crescent City, solidified the river's status as Mississippi's economic lifeline.[27] Traffic on this western highway multiplied after the advent of the steamboat, which quickened economic activity by providing two-way transportation and reducing shipping costs. Fewer than twenty steamboats operated on the Mississippi River in 1815, but more than two hundred plied its muddy waters in 1820, and over seven hundred by 1850.[28] Lacking a major seaport in their state, Mississippi planters relied on the river to keep King Cotton on its throne.

Jefferson Davis experienced this transportation revolution as a child. Samuel wanted his son to enjoy a better education than Mississippi offered, so in 1816 he enrolled him in St. Thomas College, a Dominican institution in Kentucky. Young Jefferson made the arduous outbound journey on a pony, accompanying an expedition led by War of 1812 hero Thomas Hinds and meeting Andrew Jackson along the way. Two years later, Davis cruised home to the recently admitted state of Mississippi aboard the *Aetna*, one of the earliest steamboats to ply the Ohio and Mississippi Valleys. The voyage thrilled the ten-year-old, who never forgot the names of the ship and its captain.[29]

Cotton growers also needed land, of course, and the federal government helped by wresting it from Native Americans. When Samuel Davis reached Mississippi in 1810, the northern half of the future state belonged to Choctaw and Chickasaw people. Eager to jump on the cotton bandwagon, covetous whites eyed their domain and demanded, as Reuben Davis (no relation to Jefferson) recalled with melodramatic conceit, that it be "rescued from savage tribes."[30] Andrew Jackson and Davis's onetime chaperone Thomas Hinds opened negotiations with the Choctaw, and in October 1820 they signed the Treaty of Doak's Stand, whereby the Choctaw ceded five million acres in exchange for land west of the Mississippi. Few left their homes, however, and it was not until now president Jackson convinced Congress to pass the Indian Removal Act in 1830 that the expropriation of Indian land gained momentum. In 1830 and 1832, Choctaw and Chickasaw representatives signed additional treaties, relinquishing their Mississippi lands and agreeing to relocate. By 1840 King Cotton's white courtiers had conquered their northern Mississippi estates, and Jackson's role in this redistribution of wealth cemented his place in the state's political pantheon.[31]

Federal policy and market forces nurtured the plantation system by funneling the richest lands to the wealthiest buyers. Idealists like Thomas Jefferson envisioned the West as a paradise for yeomen living on modest farms, and Mississippians who shared this dream asked Congress to sell land to actual settlers rather than to speculators. But the government needed revenue and often sold land at two dollars per acre, which favored wealthy buyers who accumulated the vast landholdings upon which plantation agriculture depended.[32] Large proprietors had another advantage when it came to using the flood-prone land near the Mississippi River, a "magnificent country" that, noted a Bolivar County planter, "is worthless without protection from levees."[33] Much like the enormous irrigation systems that made western deserts bloom—and promoted agribusiness over the yeoman ideal—flood control projects exceeded the means of family farmers.[34] It took battalions of enslaved laborers to construct and repair the levees that turned flood zones into plantations, and without slave labor, Mississippi Valley planters predicted in 1805, "the great river [would] resume its empire over our ruined fields and demolished habitations."[35] A northerner who visited the lower Mississippi Valley in 1835 vividly recalled the night when a levee failed: plantation bells clanged in alarm, and within thirty minutes, "several hundred negroes, with their masters," arrived to close the breach. When their work was completed, the observer mused, "the 'Monarch of rivers,' subdued by the hand of man, will be seen again moving, submissively obedient, within his prescribed limits, sullenly, yet majestically to the ocean."[36] The servile metaphor was apt: on Mississippi's riparian plantations, mastery of nature and mastery of labor were inseparably connected.

Among the lords of the riverfront realm was Joseph Davis, Jefferson's oldest brother and elder by twenty-four years. A lawyer with a lucrative Natchez practice, Joseph served in the state constitutional convention and established one of the first major plantations on the rich bottom lands in Warren County, just south of Vicksburg. He purchased thousands of acres of public land and bought out several small farmers to amass an 11,000-acre estate on a peninsula subsequently known as Davis Bend. When subsistence farmers sold out to the grandee, the local transition from western frontier to southern plantation society was complete. Joseph deployed more than 50 enslaved laborers to clear vegetation, plant cotton, and construct levees to protect the plantation eventually called Hurricane. By 1860, he commanded 345 unfree workers, making him one of nine Mississippians who owned more than 300 people.[37]

Joseph's career underscores the most important factor in King Cotton's rise: forced labor. The assumption that slavery was necessary for commercial agriculture in the lower Mississippi Valley prevailed at an early date and informed local whites' prickly opposition to abolition. Twenty years before statehood, Natchez planters petitioned Congress against abolishing slavery in the Mississippi Territory, claiming that without bound labor, their land "would be but of little more value to the present occupiers than an equal quantity of waste land."[38] As cotton cultivation spread along the river and then across the state, white Mississippians' hunger for enslaved workers became insatiable. The statistics are sobering. In 1801, there were fewer than 3,500 enslaved people in the territory; by 1810, there were over 16,000.[39] Steamboats, Indian removal, and the gold rush atmosphere pushed demand even higher: during the flush times of the 1830s, Mississippi's enslaved population grew by nearly 200 percent, and the state had a black majority from 1840 onward. By 1860, over 55 percent of Mississippians were property.[40] Most unfree Mississippians arrived through the interstate slave trade, as buyers and sellers shattered black people's families, communities, and lives to channel labor into the lower Mississippi Valley. A journey on the mighty Mississippi was a nightmare for enslaved people shipped "down the river" for sale in New Orleans or Natchez.[41]

Slavery was entrenched in the plantation counties where Davis spent most of his life. He was accustomed to living in areas where most people around him were not free and where he belonged to the ruling class of adult white men who totaled perhaps 10 percent of the population but controlled most of the property and all the formal political power.[42] When Samuel Davis arrived in Wilkinson County in 1810, enslaved people already made up over half the county population and would represent more than three-quarters by 1860.[43] Davis's adult home of Warren County swiftly caught up with the older plantation districts. It had a slave-majority population by 1830, and throughout most of the antebellum period, more than six in ten inhabitants were enslaved.[44] Raised to enjoy the legal, economic, political, and cultural privileges attached to white manhood, young Davis absorbed the ideology of mastery. Some scholars have emphasized the smallness of Samuel Davis's bound labor force, noting that he worked alongside his slaves.[45] But Samuel was no small-timer. By Jefferson's eleventh birthday, his father owned eleven people and was, as one historian aptly observes, "dedicated to the expropriation of black men's labor and to the notions of black inferiority and white supremacy."[46] Whatever his own work habits, Samuel taught Jefferson that some were born to labor, others to rule. Upon returning from Kentucky in 1818, Jefferson attended school close to home, and when he refused to complete an assignment he considered unfair, Samuel told him to decide "whether you will work with head or hands" and sent him out to pick cotton. Two days later, Jefferson concluded that "school was the lesser evil" and resumed his studies. Samuel wanted his son to resume his place as one "gently bred," and Jefferson got the message. He remembered being galled not only by the scorching sun and rough work but also by "the implied equality with the other cotton-pickers."[47] Education was a means of preserving inherited advantages of class and color.

White Mississippians' mastery was never entirely secure, however, and apprehension lurked just below their confidence. As Davis later discovered, even the stoutest levees sometimes succumbed to the river. An 1849 flood, the century's largest, inundated the valley for forty-eight days and devastated New Orleans, displacing 12,000 people. Only the desperate toil of Joseph and Jefferson's entire slave labor force saved Davis Bend from ruin.[48] The need for fresh soil also bred anxiety. Many planters treated land as a disposable commodity, and after a few years of intensive cultivation, they moved on, leaving "wild desolation" behind them: depleted topsoil, eroded hillsides, and a badly scarred landscape.[49] Not all planters were so profligate, but as a class they clamored for unspoiled acreage on new frontiers.[50]

Most worrisome of all was the control of labor. Surrounded by an enslaved black majority, whites lived under the constant threat of rebellion,[51] hence the paramilitary slave patrol system and the informal but "constant, habitual, and instinctive surveillance and authority of all white people over all black" noted by visitors.[52] Davis internalized these fears at an impressionable age when the War of 1812 exposed the fragility of a slave society, threatening to destroy Mississippi's nascent plantation system through British invasion, Indian assault, and slave revolt. Andrew Jackson's heroics at the Battle of New Orleans neutralized the foreign threat and removal eventually eliminated the Indian presence, but the internal enemy required constant vigilance. The discovery of wartime insurrection plots prompted territorial governor David Holmes to mobilize whites on the home front. He solicited weapons from the U.S. Army and opposed sending the local militia away for service in Louisiana. "In Slave Countries the Danger of insurrection always exists," he counseled, "and the Inhabitants should be prepared to meet the event."[53] Among them was one of Davis's older brothers who was, Jefferson later recalled, "prevented from being in the army" by the need to "retain a sufficient number [of white males] at home for police purposes."[54] Whites' mastery over slave labor, as over the environment, was precarious.

Nevertheless, Hurricane plantation remained a widely envied model of success, as a shared commitment to plantation agriculture linked whites across class lines. "A plantation well stocked with hands, is the *ne plus ultra* of every man's ambition who resides in the south," wrote one visitor in 1835. Whether they started as professionals or farmers, they all seemed to "catch the mania" for cotton. This, perhaps, was why few doctors or lawyers stayed long in practice; most followed Joseph Davis's example, quit professional life, and "turn[ed] cotton planter." "To sell cotton in order to buy negroes—to make more cotton to buy more negroes, 'ad infinitum'" was their mantra.[55] The cotton fever did not break. "'More negroes to make more cotton,' is as much the maxim in 1847 as it was in 1837," wrote another observer the year Davis entered the Senate.[56] When he started his own plantation in 1835, Davis reached the acme of achievement.

Slavery's centrality in white Mississippians' brightest hopes and darkest fears shaped their politics. As threats multiplied in the 1850s, the pressure to close ranks intensified, party competition diminished, and white Mississippians drifted toward what historian James Silver called a "closed society": resistant to change, intolerant of dissent, and prone to extremism.[57] But Mississippi's politics were complex. Voters divided over important issues like banking and fiscal policy, and partisan conflict between Whigs and Democrats raged during the 1830s and 1840s. Factions based on personality or geography rose and fell, and political power shifted across physical space and party lines. Davis inhabited an intricate political world where democracy for a small minority of voters coexisted uneasily with the subjugation of an enslaved majority and where debate churned within the confines of impervious orthodoxies.[58]

When Mississippi gained statehood in 1817, Natchez District was the locus of political power, with the territorial legislature housed variously in Natchez and the nearby community of Washington. Natchez aristocrats expected deference from residents of the sparsely populated northern and eastern portions of the state, but two developments eroded their authority. One was the seizure of Indian land and consequent cotton boom in north Mississippi. The other was the stunning rise of Andrew Jackson and his Democratic Party, whose egalitarian rhetoric, support for Indian removal, and populist style energized small farmers and striving planters who resented the stuffy aristocracy. An early portent came in 1821, when the state capital's relocation to the interior town of Jackson showed which way the political winds were blowing. The balance of power shifted further when the state constitution was rewritten in 1832. All property requirements for office holding and suffrage were removed, numerous appointed offices became elected, and lifelong tenure in office was abolished. Alarmed by the influx of Democratic state legislators from northern and eastern counties (which a Vicksburg paper compared to an Indian scalping raid), Natchez elites threatened to secede from Mississippi and either join Louisiana or make their own state. Many withdrew from politics. Although Whigs remained influential in many river counties, Democrats like Davis dominated state politics until the Civil War.[59]

Natchez's power was broken, but elites remained ascendant for the rest of the antebellum period. Planters had the time and education for office holding and the means to host barbecues, call in favors, and influence their neighbors' votes; thus, democratization often meant allowing voters to choose which slaveholder to support.[60] Poorer men had some chance to win local elections, but slaveholders controlled a disproportionate number of state and county positions.[61] The fifty-two men who represented the state in Congress between 1817 and 1861 owned an average of thirty-two people and their mean holdings increased over time, with those who served after 1839 owning nearly twice as many slaves as their precursors. Only two owned no slaves. Mississippi's congressmen also shared a history of migration; only three were born in the state, while another four, including Davis, moved there as children. The others relocated to Mississippi as adults, most coming from other slave states, though a handful migrated from the Northeast and one from Ireland.[62] Many of these arrivistes figured prominently in Davis's career: Jacob Thompson came from North Carolina; Henry S. Foote from Virginia; Robert J. Walker from Pennsylvania; Albert Gallatin Brown from South Carolina; and John J. Pettus from Tennessee. When they defended Mississippi in peace and war, they were not fighting for ancestral homes. Rather, they were relative newcomers who had made a killing on the Cotton Kingdom's western frontier and wanted to perpetuate that success.[63]

The blood and sweat of enslaved laborers defies descriptions of Davis's peers as self-made men, and certainly the term does not fit Davis. He was genuinely talented, but his path to success was smoothed by his brother Joseph, who became a father figure after Samuel Davis's death in 1824. "Without Joseph Davis," notes a perceptive biographer, "there never would have been a Jefferson Davis."[64] Joseph's influence was decisive at the turning points of Jefferson's life, including his matriculation to West Point, the establishment of his plantation, his second marriage, and his entrance into politics. Fraternal aid groomed Jefferson to join Mississippi's ruling cadre of planter-politicians.[65]

Davis's political ascent would have been more direct if he had followed his preferred path. In 1823, he began studying at the West's most prestigious educational institution, Transylvania University in Lexington, Kentucky. Nestled in the beautiful Bluegrass region, Transylvania rivaled Harvard and Yale and had already produced an impressive roster of alumni, including Stephen F. Austin and Francis P. Blair. Davis excelled at Transylvania, where he honed his talent for languages, history, and the humanities, and was selected as Junior Class Orator in honor of his rhetorical skill. He also cultivated a circle of close friends, some destined for political success; classmates David R. Atchison, Jesse Bright, and George W. Jones would all serve with Davis in the Senate. Transylvania also nurtured Davis's interest in the law, a traditional fast track into politics. But after little more than a year, Joseph surprised Jefferson with an appointment to West Point. In August 1824, Davis regretfully departed for New York.[66]

Davis was not a born soldier, and his deference to his oldest brother's wishes was reluctant and incomplete. Shortly before leaving Kentucky, Davis confessed that it was "no desire of mine to go on" to West Point, "but as Brother Joseph evinced some anxiety for me to do so, I was not disposed to object."[67] Despite this passive acquiescence, Davis clung to his hopes of studying the law. Years later, he recalled having "consented to go to the Academy for one year, and then to the University of Virginia" for legal training.[68] He was cagier in a letter to his sister, predicting that he would "probably" stay at West Point for the full four years, leaving open an unstated alternative.[69]

Davis hung on to graduate with the class of 1828, but his irregular performance placed him twenty-third in a class of thirty-three. He later enjoyed a reputation as a warrior, largely based on his performance in Mexico, which catapulted him into the Senate. This makes it tempting to overstate his martial predilections. Two historians are closer to the mark when they conclude that Davis "had a love-hate relationship with the military: he loved it most only when he was out of it."[70]

That vexed association began at West Point. Like many young men, Davis savored the trappings of military life: he maintained a soldierly bearing into old age and sparkled in drill and on parade. But he still gravitated toward the humanities, relishing courses on rhetoric and philosophy and idolizing his civilian instructor Chaplain C. P. McIlvaine. Unfortunately for Davis, antebellum West Point was primarily an engineering school, not a bastion of the liberal arts (or military science), and he struggled with many of his courses. (Tellingly, while secretary of war, Davis attempted to add a fifth year to West Point's curriculum to allow cadets to study humanities and law.) He also chafed against military discipline. Raised to command, not obey, Davis defied the Academy's strict regulations, earning 120 demerits in his first year and 137 in his last; 200 in a year could mean dismissal. Davis later extolled West Point, but it is doubtful that Cadet Davis would have seconded those nostalgic sentiments.[71]

Academy life highlighted two traits that shaped Davis's career. One was a nascent sense of sectional superiority. In 1825, Davis wrote to Joseph with a typical collegian appeal: send money. (The request violated Academy regulations.) Davis had hoped that his stipend would suffice, but he kept elevated company and needed cash. Scoffing that the "*Yankee part of the corps find their pay entirely sufficient*," Davis struggled to express how "*pittiful they generally* are."[72] He wrote as a broke teenager, not a fully fledged fire-eater, but still betrayed a penchant for sectional stereotyping and a budding view of northerners as déclassé. Northern critics would have seen shades of the Slave Power in these adolescent musings.

Cadet Davis also revealed his proclivity for splitting hairs, common among contemporaries who relished the parsing of legal points, and in a region whose leaders could pick nits ad infinitum. He should have been a lawyer. Davis showed his stripes when he faced expulsion for leaving a summer encampment to drink at Benny Havens's celebrated tavern. Davis's self-defense relied on technicalities, linguistic gymnastics, and indignant appeals. Other cadets had been caught drinking, but no one had actually seen him imbibe; he had not previously read the new regulations under which he was charged; wine and cider did not count as "spiritous liquors"; Benny Havens's place was not actually a "public house"; his judges should let a hundred guilty cadets escape rather than condemn one righteous man. These strained arguments were unavailing—Davis was convicted of all charges—but the Academy, hoping to avoid Davis's expulsion, secured his pardon.[73] Certain of his own rectitude, Davis tortured logic to prove his point and angrily wondered why others disagreed. It was a performance worthy of a senator.

Lieutenant Davis brought these habits into six years of army service, which carried him throughout the Mississippi Valley and onto the plains and left him with intimate knowledge of the West and a longing for a new profession. Davis spent much of his early army career along the northern stretches of the great river, shuttling between Jefferson Barracks, near St. Louis; Fort Crawford, located on the Mississippi in modern-day Wisconsin; Fort Winnebago, up the Wisconsin River; and the area around Galena, Illinois. His duties typically offered no more glory than could be squeezed from building blockhouses or managing supplies.[74] But the young lieutenant did have several experiences that informed his later views. In 1831, he confronted Illinois frontiersmen who had ventured into modern-day Iowa to mine lead, trespassing on territory reserved for the Fox and Sauk people. Davis dreaded evicting the interlopers by force but ultimately persuaded them to leave peacefully.[75] It was not the last time he sparred with proponents of squatters' rights. Davis also participated in Indian removal, which affected the northern end of the Mississippi Valley as well as the southern. He was home on leave for most of the 1832 Black Hawk War, which pitted Sauk leader Black Hawk, resisting his people's displacement from northwestern Illinois, against white soldiers and militia (including Abraham Lincoln). But Davis returned in time to guard the captured Black Hawk on his riverboat journey to Jefferson Barracks, from whence he was taken to Fortress Monroe in Virginia. Davis shielded Black Hawk from gawkers, evidently considering how he would feel in similar circumstances.[76] Perhaps Davis recalled this trip when he, too, was incarcerated in Fortress Monroe after losing a war against the United States.

Similarly memorable were two expeditions deep into the Trans-Mississippi West. The first began late in 1833, when Davis accompanied a column of dragoons on a miserable march from Jefferson Barracks to Fort Gibson in what is now eastern Oklahoma. For three weeks and five hundred miles, Davis and his comrades plodded through the bitter cold, only to find their new quarters bare of provisions. They depended on the Arkansas River as a supply line, but when it froze, they were cut off. A second mission, launched out of Fort Gibson the following summer, took Davis to the confluence of the Red and Washita Rivers in south-central Oklahoma. (Among Davis's companions was western artist George Catlin.) It was another logistical fiasco, with humans and animals tormented by heat, thirst, and disease, which killed more than 150 soldiers. Both journeys dramatized how distance and climate hampered military operations in the West and informed Davis's later efforts as secretary of war and chair of the Senate Committee on Military Affairs.[77]

Aside from the grueling routines of military life, Davis had personal reasons to want out. He continued to contemplate other careers, particularly the law. Writing from Fort Winnebago on his birthday in 1829, a homesick Davis pondered his future. "I cannot say that I like the army," he admitted to his sister, "but I know of nothing else that I could do which I would like better." He confessed that he was not a natural soldier, musing that his West Point education "made me a different creature from that which nature had designed me to be," and he resolved to explore other options. He would read widely to prepare for the legal profession or, if he remained in the military, a position as judge advocate.[78] Davis also still bristled at discipline. In early 1835, he faced a court-martial for absenting himself from reveille and responding insubordinately when ordered to appear for roll call. Davis's self-defense included a familiar mixture of extraneous detail and labored technicalities. This time, he was acquitted.[79]

The most compelling reason to leave the army was love. While stationed at Fort Crawford in 1832, Davis fell for Sarah Knox Taylor, the eighteen-year-old daughter of his commanding officer, Colonel Zachary Taylor. But Colonel Taylor refused to consent to their marriage, lest his daughter suffer the lonely fate of a military wife. Knox, as she was known, and Jefferson continued courting, however, and in early 1833 became engaged. When Davis left Fort Crawford that spring, he faced two years of exhausting campaigns as well as an agonizing separation from his beloved.[80] Davis wrote her from Fort Gibson in the dismal December of 1834, expressing himself through the prevailing epistolary conventions: he kissed her letters often and longed to "lay my head upon that breast which beats in unison with my own."[81] By the time he was court-martialed, Davis's mind was far from Fort Gibson and his heart was not in his career.

The year 1835 was a turning point. In March, Davis left Fort Gibson on furlough, having prepared his resignation in case he never returned. Within weeks, he decided to leave the army, marry Knox, and accept Joseph's offer to set him up as a cotton planter. Taylor relented, and Davis's dreams came true on June 17, when he and Knox wed in Louisville. They steamed down the Ohio and Mississippi Rivers for their honeymoon; ignoring the perils of the Deep South's unhealthy summertime conditions, Davis was impatient to tie the knot, introduce his bride to his family, and reenter civilian life.[82] Military service broadened his horizons, but Davis chose to return to Mississippi and the "gently bred" life his father had planned for him.

Mr. and Mrs. Davis settled down in a Mississippi where paranoia hung heavily in the humid air. Days after the wedding, an insurrection panic commenced in Madison County, a heavily enslaved plantation area north of Jackson and not far from Warren County, and radiated out through the western and central portions of the state. Witnesses claimed to have overheard slaves discussing an uprising, and on June 30, the suspects were seized and tortured until they divulged details of an Independence Day insurrection plot and named several fellow slaves and two whites as conspirators. The enslaved suspects were promptly lynched, while the whites were hauled before a committee of planters for summary justice. One admitted to following the notorious John A. Murrell, the "Great Western Land Pirate," who was suspected of stealing and selling slaves, and revealed a fantastical scheme to trigger an uprising from Maryland to Louisiana. The two men were hanged, but edgy whites continued to ferret out suspects as the contagion of terror spread to Hinds and Warren Counties. Vicksburg residents lashed out at transient gamblers, executing five. By July 13, when the governor inveighed against lynch law, at least a dozen whites, and many more blacks, were dead. Davis returned home just as the fragility of white mastery was laid bare.[83]

What Jefferson and Knox thought of this violent orgy is unknown, but they soon faced another scourge: disease. In August, they steamed downriver to West Feliciana Parish, Louisiana, to visit Jefferson's sister. It was a risky season for the journey and both contracted malaria. Jefferson recovered, but Knox died, in mid-September, at age twenty-one.[84] Discerning biographers surmise that Davis's repressed guilt later left him unable to accept criticism or admit his fallibility. To entertain doubt on any subject risked confronting his role in Knox's tragic death.[85] If so, this defense mechanism grew from an existing tendency to rationalize his own behavior, already visible in his West Point and army days. In any case, Knox's death opened a bleak period in Davis's life, from which he would emerge "a somber, brooding, serious, reserved, and demanding planter."[86]

Meanwhile, brother Joseph laid the financial foundation for Davis's political career by earmarking some 2,320 acres on Davis Bend for Jefferson's plantation, known as Brierfield. The older Davis retained title to the land and looked after things during Jefferson's frequent absences, but most contemporaries thought of Brierfield as belonging to Jefferson Davis. Its cotton output made him a wealthy man, and, like most antebellum Mississippi fortunes, Davis's was built on slave labor. Before planting, backbreaking work was necessary to clear the snarled thickets that gave Brierfield its deceptively idyllic name. It was done by enslaved people. In late 1835 or 1836, Joseph financed Jefferson's purchasing expedition to Natchez, where the younger Davis bought 16 people at the Forks in the Road, one of the nation's busiest markets in human beings. The investment paid off; within ten years, Davis's enslaved labor force had grown to 74 people, who produced over three hundred bales of cotton annually. He continued to reinvest his earnings in slaves and capital improvements, including a steam-powered cotton gin and a new dwelling, completed in 1849. By 1860, Davis owned 113 people, worth perhaps $80,000.[87]

Biographers often depict Joseph and Jefferson Davis as benevolent masters. In 1825, Joseph had chanced to meet Robert Dale Owen, the Scottish reformer who designed a model utopian community at New Harmony, Indiana. Intrigued by their conversation, Joseph implemented a radically modified Owenite system at his Hurricane plantation, where he afforded slaves a modicum of self-government, including the opportunity to hold trials for people accused of violating plantation rules. Jefferson introduced a comparable system at Brierfield. Of course, the laborers remained enslaved, and the innovative management scheme was designed to maximize productivity and eliminate dissent. When they had an opportunity to seek an alternative during the Civil War, scores of enslaved people from both plantations seized their freedom. Davis may not have been crueler than most cotton planters, but few historians who have lauded his kindness would envy the lives of those who toiled to make him rich.[88]

After Knox's death, Davis retreated into this plantation world for eight years. Since we know that he reemerged to enter politics, it is tempting to see Brierfield as a site of metamorphosis: into the cocoon went the grieving widower, out came the statesman. Certainly, Davis spent many hours reading and talking politics with Joseph. But he was not a hermit. Indeed, Davis's broad connections and correspondence revealed a man already possessed of considerable political knowledge and desire.[89] As will be shown in chapter 2, the Brierfield interlude was a time of recuperation, when Davis finally pursued long-deferred interests. Meanwhile, his Illinois rival was charting another path to power, following a much straighter and steeper line of ascent. From an early age, Stephen Douglas sensed that politics was his vocation, and he eagerly heeded the call.

★ ★ ★

During his 1858 debates with Abraham Lincoln, Douglas joked about an address he gave at Middlebury College: upon accepting an honorary doctorate in 1851, he had quipped that Vermont "is the most glorious spot on the face of this globe for a man to be born in, *provided* he emigrates when he is very young." Not surprisingly, Douglas had to explain this remark while running for president in 1860.[90] Still, Douglas's clumsy banter contained a kernel of truth: nineteenth-century Vermont produced many figures who gained fame elsewhere, including Mormon leaders Joseph Smith and Brigham Young, editor and intellectual Orestes Brownson, Republican titan Thaddeus Stevens, Chicago mayor John Putnam Chapin, and pioneering plow-maker John Deere. It was no coincidence that most of them moved west. Douglas joined a wave of Yankees who followed the sun to improve their prospects, and his success shaped his character and politics. Aptly described by a contemporary as "talented, ambitious, aspiring and reckless," Douglas embodied the virtues and vices of his milieu.[91] He thought he could read God's will on a map. He followed the pioneer spirit wherever it led, from spread-eagle expansionism to avid real estate speculation. He rejected some forms of bigotry and wallowed in others. Douglas personified the crude idealism of his adopted Northwest.

Douglas, noted a eulogist, "struggled into greatness."[92] He lacked Davis's affluent connections, and neither Douglas's background nor his upbringing foreshadowed his achievements. Born in Brandon, Vermont, in 1813, he entered a respectable family with an uncertain future. His ancestry was unpretentious but sturdy: one grandfather was a successful farmer, the other a pugnacious farmer-politician who served in the state legislature and defiantly professed the Methodist faith; his father was a Middlebury-educated physician. But when Douglas was two months old, his father died, forcing his mother, Sally Douglass,[93] to move with Stephen and his older sister, Sarah, to an adjacent farm owned by her brother, Edward Fisk. Douglas split his time between Fisk's hardscrabble fields and a local school, where his prodigious memory paid off. But this was not enough for the restless youngster, who by adolescence already exhibited the determination that would elevate him to the Senate. At fifteen, while Davis finished up at West Point, Douglas moved north to Middlebury and apprenticed himself to cabinetmaker Nahum Parker. Douglas honed his woodworking skills, read widely, and developed a fierce loyalty to Andrew Jackson (elected president that year) and the Democratic Party. After clashing with Parker over the terms of his apprenticeship, Douglas returned home and enrolled at Brandon Academy. When his mother remarried Gehazi Granger in late 1830, she moved to his upstate New York home, accompanied by seventeen-year-old Stephen, who entered Canandaigua Academy.[94] There, Douglas made lasting friendships rooted in mischief, including furtive poetry recitations enlivened by whiffs of nitrous oxide.[95] Academy life nurtured his love of masculine camaraderie, later a vital element of his political appeal.

Like Davis, young Douglas gravitated toward the law and soon discovered that geographic mobility was a shortcut to success in Jacksonian America. By 1833, Douglas had begun reading law full-time with two local attorneys, but he lacked the means to prepare for admission to the bar: New York required seven years of classical and legal education, and Douglas's mother could not afford to put him through four more years of school. Douglas's early life was hardly impoverished, but his family's limited resources left him with unsatisfied aspirations and a growing conviction that moving up would require leaving home. So, on June 24, 1833 (Douglas recalled the exact date five years later), with $300 in his pocket—all that his mother could spare—Douglas set out for "the 'great west.'" He had no specific destination in mind, but he knew the direction he wanted to travel.[96]

Douglas traversed the Northwest in fits and starts, stopping for several months in Cleveland, where he read law before contracting a serious illness. By the time he recovered that fall, he had only forty dollars left. Desire outweighed discretion, and Douglas, as he later admitted, "became reckless and adventurous" and kept moving. He drifted into the Mississippi watershed, cruising by steamboat down the Ohio River and on to St. Louis. Feeling unusually shy about lacking references, Douglas recrossed the Mississippi to find a new home. In late 1833, while Lieutenant Davis pined for Knox Taylor, Douglas entered Morgan County, Illinois.[97]

Jacksonian-era Illinois was a place where a half-educated twenty-year-old could be a lawyer. Naturally, it kindled in Douglas the same awestruck enthusiasm that Mississippi inspired in John A. Quitman. For up-and-coming easterners who felt stifled by hierarchy, convention, and entrenched interests, Illinois society seemed as open as the prairie; with the zeal of a convert, Douglas embraced the regional pride and booster spirit that shaped his politics. Six weeks after arriving, he channeled Robert Baird when he predicted that Chicago and Galena would soon outstrip the leading eastern cities, thanks to Illinois's productive soil and convenient transportation. "I have become a *Western* man," Douglas announced. "[I] have imbibed [*sic*] Western feelings principles and interests and have selected Illinois as the favorite place of my adoption, without any desire of returning to the land of my fathers except as a visitor."[98] Douglas was home.

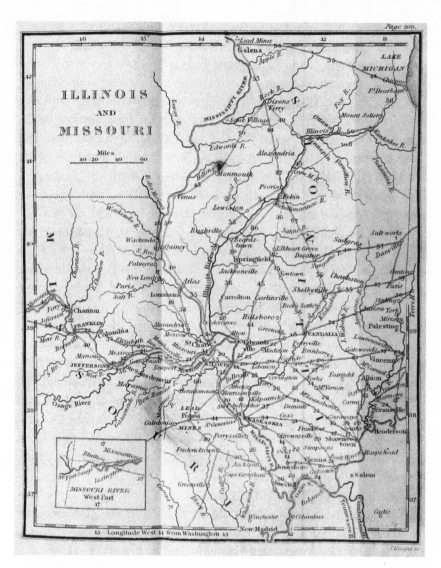

Map of Illinois and Missouri, from [Baird], *View of the Valley of the Mississippi*, 200. (Courtesy of Rare Book Collection, Louis Round Wilson Special Collections Library, University of North Carolina at Chapel Hill)

The flush times of the 1830s placed Illinois on a path very different from Mississippi's. French settlers had established colonial outposts in Illinois, but Anglo-Americans had been discouraged by its prairies (easterners assumed that scarce timber indicated poor soil) and the fierce resistance of indigenous people, particularly the Kickapoo. The War of 1812 shattered Kickapoo resistance, however, and Illinois's Anglo-

American population swelled as newcomers carved farms out of the densely wooded river bottoms. This influx, into southern and then central Illinois, hastened the transition from a frontier subsistence economy to commercial agriculture. Wheat, oats, corn, and livestock poured from the fields and pastures of what Douglas deemed "the best Agricultural State in the Union."[99] Upon achieving statehood in 1818, Illinois's 35,000 white residents were concentrated along the rivers that frame its western, southern, and southeastern borders. The Mississippi, Ohio, and Wabash facilitated migration and trade; much like their Mississippi counterparts, Illinois farmers relied on waterways for access to New Orleans and global markets, and where nature had not provided navigable waterways, they would demand artificial alternatives. Most of northern Illinois remained Indian land, controlled by Sauk and Foxes, but Anglo-Illinoisans turned rapacious eyes northward as Illinois grew. Its population swelled to over 270,000 by 1835, with most of the increase in the central region.[100] Crucially, most of the migrants settled in towns or on family farms; by 1860, the average Illinois farm was 122 acres. A few Illinoisans amassed large estates where they raised cattle, but the typical Illinois homestead contrasted sharply with the plantations that gobbled up prime Mississippi soil. High wages also enabled hired laborers to purchase land and set up for themselves. By the 1850s, tenant farming was on the rise as wealthy landlords rented to less fortunate folk, but Illinois's rural poor were not owned by their betters.[101]

Hardy yeomen dominate stories of how the Midwest was won, but town dwellers were equally important. Usually located on navigable waterways, towns provided economic, institutional, and infrastructural services to nearby farmers. These urban frontiers grew in tandem with rural areas and furnished professionals with opportunities unavailable in the hinterland. Among those hustling townsmen was Stephen Douglas, who embraced the booster spirit characteristic of western urbanites and eventually sought to spread their vision of progress to the Pacific. Douglas spent his formative Illinois years carving out a niche in the auspiciously named town of Jacksonville.[102]

Jacksonville, the seat of Morgan County, was blossoming when Douglas arrived in late 1833. Between 1825 and 1830, the county population tripled to nearly 13,000 residents and almost doubled again during the next four years; Douglas was among the estimated 25,000 Morgan Countians in 1834. Jacksonville, surveyed in 1825, grew apace, increasing from a handful of founding families to 446 souls by 1830. Among its amenities was an institution of higher learning. Boosters panting for rapid growth, allied with New Englanders eager to bring Yankee order and progress to the West, persuaded the American Home Missionary Society to establish Illinois College there in 1830. Inevitably, promoters dubbed Jacksonville the "Athens of the West." Accompanying the educational institutions (which also included Jacksonville Female Academy, founded in 1833) were sixteen stores, mills and manufactories, brickyards, boardinghouses, and a tannery. Some state legislators, keen to move the state capital out of stagnant Vandalia, ranked Jacksonville among the possible new locations. As a cultural and economic hub, Jacksonville's future looked bright.[103]

Illinois's growth was no more natural than Mississippi's; it was promoted by specific policies that fostered commercial agriculture. Farmers needed cheap land, access to markets, and easy credit, and usually got them. Smallholders purchased most of their land from the federal government, which sold a resounding two million Illinois acres in 1835.[104] Douglas tracked these sales and urged his eastern relations to buy land while it still sold for the rock-bottom price of $1.25 per acre.[105] The dark side of the real estate boom was Indian removal. Particularly in northern and western Illinois, as Lieutenant Davis discovered, conflict between whites and Native Americans crackled until it culminated in a process of dispossession often overshadowed by events in the South. A turning point came in 1832 with the Black Hawk War. Its roots stretched back to the 1804 Treaty of St. Louis, in which Sauk leaders of dubious authority ceded a swath of land between the Mississippi and Illinois Rivers, retaining usage rights until it was surveyed and sold by the federal government. When that procedure accelerated in 1828, conflicts erupted between Sauk inhabitants and white migrants. Some Sauk, led by Keokuk, chose to move west of the Mississippi, but others, including Black Hawk, vowed to resist the invasion. In early 1832, Black Hawk began raiding Anglo-American settlements in Illinois and the future state of Wisconsin, and army detachments, augmented by militias, mobilized in response. By August, Black Hawk had been defeated at the Battle of Bad Axe, where some of his people were massacred, and he was captured shortly thereafter. The war became the pretext for wider dispossession, as a series of treaties formalized the cession of Indian lands and the removal of Indian people, many of whom went to Kansas. Thereafter, northern Illinois attracted a new wave of white migration.[106] Shortly before Douglas reached Illinois, federal power had shifted the Indian barrier west to the Great Plains.

To rise above subsistence level, agriculturists also needed access to markets and cash to finance their operations. Initially, local and state governments worked with private contractors to facilitate transportation. Counties taxed residents to pay for local roads, while the state typically handled larger projects. Sometimes the legislature chartered private firms to build turnpikes or improve rivers by removing snags and dredging channels; in other cases, the state funded the work directly. By the mid-1820s, there was also talk of federally financed internal improvements, including a widely popular plan for a canal linking the Illinois River to Lake Michigan, completing the Great Lakes to Gulf of Mexico water route that nature had left undone.[107] The legislature also primed the pump by chartering a state bank. Despite the catastrophe of the first Illinois bank, which had suspended operations in 1823, the prosperity of the 1830s stoked popular demand for the increased money supply and flexible credit that a state bank could provide. Farmers needed currency to grease the wheels of commerce and speculators wanted easy loans, and even Douglas, usually critical of banks and their paper emissions, recognized these benefits.[108] Legislators gratified popular demand by chartering a state bank in early 1835, feeding the mania for land speculation and internal improvements.[109]

Breakneck growth provoked controversy, and, as in Mississippi, Andrew Jackson towered over Illinois politics. His record as an Indian fighter endeared him to northwesterners who ogled Sauk lands, and his rough-hewn image resonated with those who resented eastern elites. Illinois's state constitution allowed universal white male suffrage, and Jackson's common touch netted him hefty majorities in 1828 and 1832; in both elections, Jackson won over two-thirds of the state's popular vote. Yet to vote for Jackson in 1828 was not necessarily to identify as a Democrat or to accept the logic of a two-party political system. Early Illinois politics revolved around personalities and factions, not well-oiled partisan machines, and the Whig-Democrat party system was in flux when Douglas arrived.[110] There was no doubt about Douglas's position—he had embraced Jackson years before moving west—but there was considerable uncertainty about where candidates stood on the economic issues that agitated the 1830s. The internal improvements issue was especially dicey for Illinois Jacksonians. Could they rationalize Jackson's apparent hostility toward federally funded infrastructure when voters clamored for canals and river improvements? Politicians always juggle national party policy and local interests, and northwestern Democrats feared that rivals might beat them on economic issues dear to urban boosters and commercial farmers.[111] Douglas cut his political teeth championing a party that enjoyed a celebrity standard-bearer but had to tread carefully on pocketbook issues.

Slavery lurked in the shadows of Illinois politics. Theoretically, its fate was sealed by the Northwest Ordinance of 1787, which pronounced that "there shall be neither slavery nor involuntary servitude" in federal territories north of the Ohio River.[112] But congressional decrees did not permanently settle the question. Thus, while Davis's Mississippi background taught him that slavery was a vital interest to be safeguarded against internal and external threats, Douglas learned a different lesson in Illinois: slavery was alarmingly divisive and devilishly difficult to control from afar and should, if possible, be left alone. For Douglas, the politics of slavery was an upsetting distraction; for Davis, it was a matter of life or death.

The Northwest Ordinance notwithstanding, Illinois could have become a slave state. Slavery had existed there since French colonial days, and the United States did not emancipate slaves owned by French masters upon acquiring the territory in 1783. Some Illinoisans sought to broaden this toehold by petitioning Congress to repeal the antislavery provisions of the Northwest Ordinance. These frontal assaults failed, but the restrictions could be outflanked. Masters capitalized on loopholes that allowed them to bring indentured laborers into Illinois; the groundwork for an indenture system was laid in 1803, when Illinois was part of the Indiana Territory, and strengthened after Illinois became a separate territory in 1809. By 1814, the territorial legislature had explicitly affirmed masters' property rights in indentured laborers, who theoretically volunteered for service but in practice were slaves. They could be bound for ninety-nine years (effectively a lifetime of unfree labor) and sold or willed to new masters, and the indenture could pass from parent to child, exactly like servitude in the South and patently unlike the status of indentured whites. Many territorial slaveholders imported enslaved people to perform domestic labor, and masters in southern Illinois's salt-producing region depended on them to sustain their extractive industry.

Upon gaining statehood in 1818, Illinois rejected the examples of Ohio and Indiana, which had incorporated the Northwest Ordinance's free-soil provisions into their state constitutions. Instead, the state convention added an antislavery gloss to a constitution that shielded the highly adaptable quasi-slavery inherited from the territorial era. Unfree laborers could not be brought into the state, but masters of those already in Illinois retained their property rights indefinitely; the saltworks in Gallatin County were exempted from the prohibition on imports until 1825; and the children of current indentured laborers remained bound to their masters until adulthood. The number of masters and unfree laborers grew during the first few years of statehood until there were nearly a thousand indentured Illinoisans in 1820. Technically not a slave state, Illinois stretched the definition of "free state" to the breaking point.[113]

Illinois simultaneously established its reputation for virulent racism. In 1819, the first state legislature required free African Americans to have a freedom certificate, replicating the legal presumption of black servitude that prevailed in the South. Those without a certificate could be arrested and hired out for a year of forced labor. Thereafter, legislators regularly tightened the state's grip. An 1829 law obligated African Americans to post a $1,000 bond before moving into the state, and an 1848 referendum approved a ban on black immigration by a forty-point margin of victory. The crusade culminated in 1853, when the state legislature criminalized free black people's entrance into Illinois. Violators could be fined $500, and those unable to pay would be bound to labor until the debt was settled. Abolitionist opposition notwithstanding, these laws revealed the breadth and depth of racism among white Illinoisans. Many agreed with the state convention delegate who derided free blacks as "bold, thieving, restless, impudent, & indolent."[114]

Illinois voters and legislators proclaimed that free black people did not belong in the state; more controversial was the question of whether enslaved people belonged there. The constitution and early state laws safeguarded the indenture system and flouted the Northwest Ordinance, but some Illinoisans sought to make Illinois a full-fledged slave state. "For the first six years of Illinois' existence as a state," wrote historian Theodore Calvin Pease, "the question of slavery hung like a threatening storm over her politics."[115] The conflict had subsided by the time Douglas arrived, but the controversy molded his views of how questions about slavery should, and necessarily *would*, be answered.

Proslavery advocates sparked the debate while Illinois was recovering from the Panic of 1819. Leading the charge was Henry Eddy, who promised that an influx of slaves and masters would expand the salt industry, develop markets for local farm produce, and inject much-needed cash into the state's economy. In 1822, proslavery gubernatorial candidate Joseph B. Phillips narrowly lost to Edward Coles, an idealistic ex-slaveholder and former secretary to James Madison, who had moved from Virginia to establish his former slaves as free farmers. Undeterred, proslavery Illinoisans called for a new state convention, which they hoped would result in a proslavery constitution. In 1823 and 1824, heated debates over the convention served as proxies for arguments over slavery in Illinois. Partisans on both sides made wide-ranging claims. Some supporters of the convention extended Eddy's economic argument. Others recycled the "diffusionist" thesis: if slavery expanded, slaves' lot would improve along with the prospects for eventual emancipation. Still others stoked bigotry by declaring that only enslavement would bring the state's free black population under control. The equally varied counterarguments reflected the broad spectrum of antislavery politics. Governor Coles attacked slavery on moral, nationalist, and humanitarian grounds, denouncing it as sinful, contrary to America's founding ideals, and inhumane. Racists pointed out that legalizing slavery would darken the state's demographics. Populists warned that slavery would subject common whites to the rule of elite planters.[116] In this view, slavery was both a political and an economic issue; the choice was between democracy and aristocracy as well as between free and slave labor.[117] At the August 1824 election, Illinois voters defeated the convention and slavery, with 4,972 in favor and 6,640 opposed. The southernmost counties tended to support the convention, while those in the central portion of the state, including Morgan County, were strongly against it.[118]

Slavery continued to divide Illinoisans long after the convention debate, particularly as local abolitionists campaigned against both southern slavery and local prejudice.[119] Few provoked more white rage than Elijah Lovejoy, a transplanted New Englander who had absorbed far more of the region's reformist ardor than Douglas had. Born in Maine, Lovejoy moved to St. Louis in 1827, went east for ordination as a Presbyterian minister in 1833, and then returned to St. Louis to edit *The Observer*. Lovejoy attacked slavery and racist violence, calling for gradual emancipation in Missouri and condemning the lynching of Francis McIntosh, a mixed-race man burned to death in St. Louis for allegedly killing a law enforcement officer. Threats of mob retaliation drove Lovejoy from Missouri but also radicalized him; the more he was denounced for "abolitionism," the more he embraced it. He soon resumed publishing in Alton, Illinois, a Mississippi River town sixty miles south of Jacksonville and site of the final Lincoln-Douglas debate in 1858.

In late 1837, as Douglas settled into a new job as register of the General Land Office, Lovejoy paid for his activism with his life. That summer, Lovejoy had urged abolitionists to form the Illinois Anti-Slavery Society, and opponents demanded his silence. Lovejoy persisted, and the backlash grew more menacing. A mob attempted to tar and feather him. Several of his printing presses were destroyed. In October, he was dragged out of his mother-in-law's home and beaten. Undaunted, Lovejoy ordered his fourth printing press, which was delivered to an Alton warehouse on November

6. When irate anti-abolitionists tried to break in, one of Lovejoy's supporters opened fire, killing a carpenter named Lyman Bishop. Incensed, the attackers ignited the warehouse's roof, shot Lovejoy to death, and burst inside. In a deeply symbolic gesture, they smashed Lovejoy's printing press and threw the pieces into the Mississippi River, drowning an abolitionist voice in the waterway imagined as a bond of union between North and South. Lovejoy's death proved that neither fair skin nor residence in a free state guaranteed immunity from proslavery violence.[120]

These clashes invite us to view Illinois as a miniature of the Union. Disparate regional cultures did converge as New England Yankees poured into northern Illinois and upper South migrants predominated farther south. But Illinois was not a microcosm of the United States, and casting it as such risks distorting state politics by eliding several points. First, geographic origin did not determine political destiny. In 1823, antislavery forces rallied behind Edward Coles, a transplanted Virginian; a generation later, Abraham Lincoln of Kentucky led Republicans' effort to unseat Vermont-born Senator Douglas. Moreover, some southern migrants chose Illinois precisely because it was a free state, where they could avoid slavery and its attendant aristocracy. Writing to Illinois Republican Lyman Trumbull in 1857, Allen Persinger explained his antislavery stance as a product of his Virginia upbringing. "I was raised in Virginia until I was 26 years of age," he recalled, "and know all about the Institution of slavery." In the South, "the laboring white man is oppressed and but little better off than the rich mans Negro you need not wonder at me being a Republican for I would have remained poor and oppressed by the Slave Oligarchy."[121] Many of these migrants were bitterly prejudiced and wanted to bar black people as well as slave labor from Illinois, but so did many northern-born residents. Racist critiques of slavery hardly endeared them to suspicious masters, and loathing of abolitionists was compatible with resentment of slaveholders.[122] Moreover, the collision between northern and southern migrants can be overstated. After the Civil War, some local historians dramatically projected an irrepressible conflict back into the state's early history, but these hostilities waned as German and Irish immigration provoked new conflicts.[123] And as they settled in, white migrants formed a common western identity around many shared values, including racism, distrust of slaveholders, and commitment to free white labor.[124]

Finally, Illinois could not be a national microcosm because there was no local equivalent to the Cotton Kingdom. Illinois never contained counties where enslaved people represented 50, 60, or 70 percent of the population. It never elected a phalanx of planter-politicians whose economic, social, and political power depended on maintaining chattel slavery. Even the fiercest racists in southern Illinois's "Egypt" region (whose nickname's origins remain debated) tended to shrink from celebrating slavery as the foundation of an ideal society. Most of Illinois's southern-born residents hailed from the upper and border southern states, which followed a different political and economic trajectory than the cotton states farther south. Antebellum Illinois was more a microcosm of the North than of the nation.[125] Douglas's challenge would be to please these diverse constituents while maintaining alliances with cotton-state Democrats like Davis.

Douglas drew conflicting political lessons from life in Illinois. On one hand, the state's recent past revealed the limits of federal influence over western slavery. Historians have rediscovered that although the Northwest Ordinance was not a dead letter, local opinion was decisive in keeping slavery out of Illinois.[126] Douglas would regularly reiterate this point as he battled against proslavery and antislavery critics. On the other hand, violent clashes among Illinoisans suggested that slavery was no less divisive at the state or local level than it was in Washington. Political foes murdered each other in Illinois decades before they slaughtered each other in Kansas, proving that local self-rule did not guarantee peace. Confronted by Illinoisans' widely discrepant views on slavery, Douglas decided that the issue was simply too hot to handle.

Douglas could not avoid slavery, but he had other priorities as he settled down in Jacksonville. After teaching school for a winter, Douglas hung out his lawyer's shingle in early 1834. Not yet twenty-one, he received his law license after a perfunctory examination which ended with an admonition to study more.[127] But the fresh-faced attorney was rather indifferent about his practice; a neighbor remembered that Douglas preferred to be "out among 'the boys,' assuming the part of politician from the start, a germinating and budding Senator and President." Douglas's outgoing personality, memory for names and faces, and easy camaraderie endeared him to neighbors who relished the rough-and-tumble rituals of Jacksonian politics. He cultivated an "arm-in-arm intimacy, in street and saloon, with men . . . of the Jackson stripe."[128] He knew it was important "to mix with the crowd, to join the bar-room circle, to tell his story and sing his song, to smoke, and generally to conform to all those demands of pot-house oracles" required for political success.[129] A born politician, Douglas reveled in the hypermasculine political culture of a region where white men's egalitarianism was an ideological polestar. Even appointment to the state supreme court did not alter his jocular style. Douglas "took great pains to cultivate the acquaintance of every one, to shake them by the hand, to talk with them, and to please them," and he extended this familiarity into the courtroom. While attorneys addressed the jury, recalled an associate, "he would leave the bench go round among the listeners & spectators sit upon their knees and chat and laugh & joke with them," a display which paid lifelong political dividends.[130] Here was popular sovereignty in action: not a legal abstraction but a lived experience, the political equivalent of a boys' night out. When Douglas leveraged this personal esteem to launch his political career, he became the ideal type of an Illinois Jacksonian.

A quintessential westerner, Douglas also plunged into land speculation. Investors, not tillers of the soil, often reaped the richest harvests in the antebellum West, and Douglas regarded land with a gambler's eye. He avidly tracked land sales and town surveys and in an early letter to his brother-in-law anticipated windfalls from Indian removal: "The Lands in the upper part of the State are expected to be brought into market between this and next fall," he enthused, "then fortunes can be made easily."[131] Douglas excelled at salesmanship as well as electioneering, and his brother-in-law entrusted him with money for investment in Jacksonville real estate, which yielded a healthy profit. Even with his shoestring budget, Douglas scraped up funds to buy farmland and town lots in several counties.[132] This remained such a major part of Douglas's life that when Philadelphia editor John W. Forney, a key political ally, wrote his memoirs, he introduced Douglas not as a leading statesman but as a shrewd land speculator. Douglas "had an inspiration for land, and he delighted to tell his friends what his country must be in the course of years." Forney's only flutter with real estate came when Douglas convinced him to buy into a scheme based in Superior, in what is now Douglas County, Wisconsin. Confident that it would be the terminus of a railroad linking Lake Superior to the Pacific Ocean, Douglas cajoled Forney into purchasing a $2,500 share, which later netted him $21,000.[133] The episode illuminated Douglas's restive ambition, passion for northwestern development, and readiness to mingle finance, friendship, and politics. He savored the go-ahead society he found in Illinois and strove to extend it across the continent.

★ ★ ★

As Douglas and Davis planted roots in the Mississippi Valley, the foundations of a political alliance were clear, for their neighbors shared values widely regarded as western and Jacksonian: zealous expansionism, shrill racism, and strident nationalism.[134] The latter predisposed many

Mississippians and Illinoisans to reject South Carolina's nullification experiment. In 1833, Mississippi's legislature applauded Jackson's efforts to "preserv[e] the integrity of the Union" and denounced nullification as "contrary to the letter and spirit of the Constitution," and Illinois lawmakers did likewise.[135] Jackson's personal popularity bolstered this alliance. The personification of expansionism, Indian dispossession, and militant nationalism, Jackson handily won both states in 1828 and 1832. Indeed, he swept the Mississippi Valley in both years, except that in 1832, Kentucky backed favorite son Henry Clay.

The question was whether the Democratic alliance could outlive Jackson's presidency and endure the extensive changes wrought by the flush times of the 1830s. Well before 1840, it was absurd to refer to Mississippi and Illinois as parts of an undifferentiated western frontier. As smallholders poured into Illinois and cotton conquered Mississippi, locals' interests and ideals diverged. Omens of conflict appeared early. Nullification, for instance, attracted a vocal minority of Mississippi supporters, including John A. Quitman, who led a State Rights faction out of Mississippi's Democratic Party. By 1839, Quitman's radical cohort reentered the party fold, injecting an extreme proslavery strain into the Mississippi Democracy that was absent in Illinois.[136] Subtler warning signs also emerged. Would Mississippi Democrats support the costly internal improvement programs that appealed to many Illinoisans? Would Democrats continue to unite behind westward expansion, or would it drive them apart? Mississippians like Quitman fixated on Texas, which won independence from Mexico while Davis was settling down at Brierfield, and a considerable number moved there.[137] Illinois Democrats sympathized with Texans, but northwesterners were spearheading a separate wave of Anglo-American migration into the Oregon Country. As early as 1839, a group of adventurers departed Peoria, determined to drive the British out of Oregon and secure it for the United States. Their expedition disintegrated, but subsequent migration sustained Illinoisans' interest in the Pacific Northwest.[138] Dreams of Texas and Oregon were not incompatible, but could Democrats agree on how to prioritize them? Even the West's vaunted egalitarianism (for white men) reflected the divergence. Liberal suffrage laws attracted migrants to both states and boosted Jackson's political fortunes, but the politics of slavery played out differently on the ground. In Mississippi, universal white male suffrage gave poorer citizens a stake in the system, bolstering participation in slave patrols and stifling class hostility against planters. In Illinois, broad white suffrage fostered fiercely racist policies but also defeated the move to legalize slavery.[139]

Still, Democrats continued to proclaim unity. "The majestic Mississippi binds together, with a chain stronger than iron, the northern and southern portions of that part of the confederacy," insisted one editor, implying that economic geography would necessarily prevail over political discord.[140] But political decisions are made by people, not by flows of water or goods, and the people who governed Mississippi and Illinois, as Robert Baird knew, were already making very different decisions in the booming 1830s.

Indeed, the familiarity wrought by economic exchange and political interaction would eventually breed contempt. Consider the Illinois mechanic who traveled downriver to build cotton gins across from Davis Bend in Louisiana. When Louisiana seceded in January 1861, he was forced to flee so quickly that he abandoned his unpaid wages and his toolbox. Soon after, he enlisted in the 55th Illinois Infantry Regiment, part of the "Douglas Brigade," and trained at Camp Douglas in Chicago. The regiment's first commander was Colonel David Stuart, a former Democratic congressman from Michigan who moved to Chicago to work for the Illinois Central Railroad. As Federal forces closed in on Vicksburg in 1863, the blue-collar soldier revisited the plantation and recovered his tools; some said he also burned the cotton gin to the ground.[141] Outraged by rebellious Deep South planters, the Illinoisans transformed the Mississippi River into an avenue for invasion.

The Mississippi Valley's fragmentation into clashing sections was a political process propelled by slavery.[142] Despite the red flags visible in the 1830s, it was also a gradual process that accelerated in the 1840s and 1850s, coinciding with Davis's and Douglas's rise to national prominence. Ambitious and visionary, they wrestled for control of a badly divided party and nation. Underlying their struggle were questions about what it meant to be a Democrat, and what that meant for American democracy.

2

Jackson Men

In February 1859, W. A. Parker christened Stephen Douglas "the Ajax of the Democratic Party."[1] If this was a compliment, it was a backhanded one. Homer, Ovid, and Sophocles portray Ajax as an imposing warrior who repels Trojan counterattacks, fights Hector to a respectable draw, and battles alongside Odysseus to recover the body of Achilles. Then success sows discord: they quarrel over Achilles's magical armor, and when Odysseus prevails, Ajax comes unhinged. Mistaking a large ram for his rival, Ajax pummels the animal and then slaughters other livestock, which he thinks are the comrades who have spurned him. Upon recovering his wits, Ajax succumbs to shame and kills himself. Ajax, too mighty to be conquered by a foe, self-destructs after a scramble for the trophies of war.

Parker may have been so keen to flaunt his classical learning that he overlooked these implications, but perhaps the Texan meant exactly what he said. By 1859, Douglas had so thoroughly alienated many southerners that his career teetered on the edge of ruin. Thus, both of Parker's possible messages expressed important truths: Douglas *was* a pugnacious political warrior, and his Democratic Party *was* divided over the spoils of victory. Perhaps Parker was warning Douglas about the risks of conflict with erstwhile comrades, including Jefferson Davis, a rival for control of the Democracy's future.

Unlike the clash over Achilles's armor, however, Davis and Douglas's dispute did not erupt suddenly. The rupture of the Democratic Party has sometimes been explained as the product of short-term forces, including patronage squabbles, personal antipathy, or the latest developments in blood-soaked Kansas. The most detailed history of the breach, Roy Franklin Nichols's *Disruption of American Democracy* (1948), adopts this perspective with narrative flair and some analytical limitations. Nichols opens with the 1856 presidential election and devotes only four pages to the Democratic Party's previous twenty-eight years, thus isolating the party's final collapse from chronic divisions over interests and ideology.[2]

But Davis and Douglas's climactic struggle grew from conflicts that evolved over many years. Like every political party, the antebellum Democracy was a coalition of factions, cliques, and local machines, and their rivalries anticipated later historiographical debates.[3] Was the Democracy a stalking horse for slaveholders' interests? A working-class party rooted in the Northeast? A champion of western agrarianism?[4] Each of these latter-day interpretations resembles a vision cherished by some antebellum Democrats, whose enduring disagreements defy scholarly efforts to freeze the narrative at any single convention, election, or administration and pinpoint the genuine Democratic Party. No individual platform, speech, or bill can reveal the party's authentic values. Rather than try to distill the Democracy to its essence, this book studies the party in motion, as a shifting and perennially uneasy alliance among partisans striving to win elections back home while maintaining national power. By sketching these struggles from the Democracy's origins to Davis's and Douglas's entrance into national politics in the mid-1840s, this chapter excavates the roots of the clashes over property rights, majority rule, and expansion that wrecked the party in 1860.

Davis and Douglas plunged into this contentious political environment and dueled for leadership of a party long racked by sectionalism. Both believed that the Democracy best protected their constituents' interests and the Union's stability, but their divergent visions for its future sparked competition for ownership of the party's illustrious image. The Democracy's association with luminaries like Jefferson and Jackson, and with political polestars of liberty, self-government, and Union, raised the stakes in contests for the Democratic mantle. Davis and Douglas's clashes were magnified, not mitigated, by their shared Democratic loyalty; they prayed in the same partisan temple but professed different creeds. Their careers unfolded amid older and wider struggles over what it meant to be a "Jackson man."

★ ★ ★

Writing to Virginia editor Thomas Ritchie in 1827, Martin Van Buren called for a political partnership between the "plain republicans of the north" and the "planters of the South."[5] Over the next generation, this Democratic coalition won impressive victories: it elected celebrities like Andrew Jackson and obscurities like James Polk; demolished a national bank and conquered half of Mexico; and claimed to speak for "the people" against wire-pullers and wild-eyed radicals. But what did humble farmers and mechanics share with southern elites? In some contexts, the alliance was sound; in others, only naked partisanship could maintain it; in none was it entirely secure. Van Buren's own volatile career reflected the Democracy's fragile power.

Born in 1782, Van Buren rose through New York's ferocious political arena and served as state legislator and attorney general before reaching the U.S. Senate in 1821. He was an ardent Democratic-Republican who imbibed Jeffersonian ideals of limited government, popular rule, and antipathy for the Federalists, but he was no mere imitator, and he embraced political parties even as many contemporaries fantasized about faction-free governance. Convinced that parties were vital means for achieving worthy ends, Van Buren used the levers of patronage to build the Albany Regency into a formidable state machine. After backing William Crawford's failed presidential bid in 1824, he resolved to reconstruct the cross-sectional alliance that had underpinned Jefferson's Democratic-Republican coalition. Once revitalized, it could ease sectional tensions, curb federal authority, and reward the party faithful. This would require grafting a venerable ideology onto a novel party organization, complete with colorful candidates and electrifying campaigns.[6] As Davis endured West Point and Douglas tilled Vermont soil, Van Buren laid the foundation of their future partisan home.

Van Buren's use of the Democratic-Republican Party as a model made sense, given his Jeffersonian principles and the party's success in elevating Jefferson, Madison, and Monroe to the presidency. But slavery's perennially disruptive influence made the party a problematic prototype. Jefferson personified some of the tensions: he criticized slavery for enabling "unremitting despotism" by masters and demanding "degrading submissions" from slaves while he lived on the labor of the enslaved people whose bodies he exploited at Monticello.[7] Indeed, anyone asserting political descent from Jefferson would claim a paradoxical inheritance: co-opted by nullifiers and nationalists, fire-eaters and free-soilers, Jefferson was a cosmopolitan democrat and a Virginia aristocrat who clung to slavery's wolfish ears while declaring that all men are created equal.[8] Slavery, moreover, had plagued the Jeffersonian alliance from birth. Southern Jeffersonians needed northern allies but demanded that they accept proslavery policies. Northern Jeffersonians relied on southern associates but squirmed when Federalists denounced their sympathy for slaveholders. Some learned to tolerate slavery, but during the Missouri crisis of 1819–21, most northern Jeffersonians in Congress voted to block slavery's expansion. Despite racism, nationalism, and party affinity, therefore, the alliance was uneasy. Historian Padraig Riley notes that, pragmatically, "the accord between slavery and American democracy was clearly successful," as politics became more democratic (for white men) and slavery expanded westward. But ideologically, the alliance "remained tenuous, because slaveholder power could never be fully incorporated into a democratic ethos."[9] It would collapse if northerners concluded that slavery endangered democratic liberty, or if southerners decided that majority rule menaced their peculiar property.

Undaunted, Van Buren followed the Jeffersonian paradigm to build a new party, cultivating southern allies by affirming his fidelity to states' rights, decentralization, and strict construction of the Constitution. Fiercely opposed to John Quincy Adams's nationalist administration, Van Buren searched for a candidate who could topple the incumbent in 1828. Despite earlier doubts about Jackson, he ultimately embraced the rough-hewn hero and began fashioning a national coalition to elect him. Eager to recruit southern disciples of John C. Calhoun and William Crawford, Van Buren penned his letter to Thomas Ritchie.[10]

The infamous epistle offered considerable aid and comfort to slaveholders. Van Buren warned that "prejudices between free and slave holding states" would fester unless his party quelled the antislavery "clamour" that had erupted during the Missouri crisis. His cross-sectional coalition would provide "a complete antidote for sectional prejudices" by prompting northerners to view antislavery attacks "as assaults upon their political brethren."[11] Jackson's resounding 1828 victory, in which he and running mate Calhoun, both major slaveholders, swept the South and most of the free states outside New England, realized Van Buren's dream. Given its conception and birth, some scholars regard the Democracy as intrinsically proslavery and its architect as the original "doughface": a northern Democrat beholden to the South.[12]

But Van Buren had constructed a fickle partnership, not a smooth-running proslavery machine. He sought to exclude slavery from political debate in order to preserve party and national unity, not to perpetuate bondage as a positive good. Like many northerners, he regarded antislavery activism as a Federalist ploy to set Democrats at each other's throats.[13] The line between anti-abolitionism and proslavery crusading was blurry, but it was southerners who defined "proslavery" politics, and their demands often outpaced northern concessions. Crucially, southern leaders were not content with limited government. Convinced, as a Mississippi secessionist later proclaimed, that slavery, "of all property in the world, most needs the protection of a friendly government," they developed an expansive federal agenda.[14] But since Van Buren pledged to uphold slaveholders' basic rights, not to satisfy their every whim, his coalition was racked by conflict from the start of Jackson's administration.[15]

Jackson's presidency revealed that southern fidelity to Van Buren's alliance was conditional. Indeed, by the end of Jackson's second term, southern defections had made the Democratic Party quite different from the coalition that first elected him.[16] Some wealthy planters, for example, bolted the party over Jackson's war on the Bank of the United States.[17] More ominously, the showdown over South Carolina's effort to nullify a federal tariff law in 1832–33 pitted Jackson against his own vice president, turning Calhoun's acolytes into Old Hickory's enemies. Jackson worked to perpetuate a decentralized Union in which states' rights safeguarded majoritarian self-government. Calhounites would use states' rights to preserve the property of an affluent minority against hostile majorities and worried that Jacksonian nationalism might be abolition's Trojan horse.[18] A group of South Carolina nullifiers predicted an "exterminating *war*" on slaveholders' property rights: "All the property we possess, we hold by their boon," they warned, "and a majority in Congress, may, at any moment, deprive us of it and transfer it northward, or offer it up on the bloody altar of a bigot's philanthropy."[19] Jackson's fame and the primacy of Indian removal kept most Mississippi Democrats in the fold, but local nullifiers toasted Calhoun as the "inspired apostle of State Rights and State Remedies."[20] It was unclear whether Mississippi's political future pointed toward Jacksonian nationalism or Calhounian sectionalism.

Even stridently proslavery measures disappointed southern critics. When the American Anti-Slavery Society mailed thousands of abolitionist publications to the South in 1835, for instance, Calhoun demanded a vigorous federal response. But Jackson's proposed ban on the distribution of abolitionist materials through the mail did not pass muster. Instead,

Calhoun backed a bill that would forbid delivery of materials that violated state law; by braiding state regulations into a federal statute, he would empower slave states to quash incendiary publications with national authority. The bill failed because northern statesmen feared a civil libertarian backlash at home, confirming Calhoun's distrust of national parties. White southerners, he concluded, could not rely on northern allies who had to appease antislavery sentiment and instead must rely on "ourselves and ourselves only for safety."[21] Like-minded southerners ditched the Democracy and followed Calhoun into the nonpartisan wilderness; others became Whigs. Certainly, the Democracy retained significant southern support, but many slaveholders eyed Van Buren's coalition warily. Beset by Whig and Calhounite rivals, southern Democrats struggled to prove their party's dependability.

Calhounites drifted unpredictably as the major parties crystallized during the 1830s. Calhoun endorsed many Democratic positions, including free trade, but his antidemocratic ideology echoed that of conservative northern Whigs who shared his dread of majority rule. Northern Democrats' calls for "the DEMOCRACY OF NUMBERS" to "maintain the ascendency against the power of individual and ASSOCIATED WEALTH" did not charm slaveholders.[22] Elitist Whigs, on the other hand, embraced economic policies that Calhoun despised. Thus, neither party offered an ideal vehicle for the proslavery ideology that was intensifying in the 1830s as southern politicians insisted that slavery was a "positive good," discarded Revolutionary-era egalitarianism, and embraced reactionary doctrines derived from Federalists and European aristocrats.[23] Unmoored from a partisan berth, Calhounites would float into and out of the Democratic Party. Conflict between devout southern Democrats and fire-eating Calhounites shaped regional politics through the secession crisis.[24]

Underlying this tension was white southern anxiety over the threats to slavery that multiplied during the Democratic Party's formative years. The Cotton Kingdom boomed within an increasingly hostile political context, sharpening southern intramural debates over strategies for self-defense. Abroad, British abolitionism seemed rampant after passage of the Slavery Abolition Act in 1833.[25] Domestic antislavery activism also flourished. After David Walker's blistering *Appeal to the Coloured Citizens of the World* appeared in 1829, the drumbeat sounded steadily: William Lloyd Garrison began printing *The Liberator* in 1831, the same year as Nat Turner's rebellion in Virginia; the American Anti-Slavery Society organized in 1833; abolitionists churned out pamphlets and antislavery petitions in 1835; the Anti-Slavery Convention of American Women met in 1837; and by decade's end, the Liberty Party girded for the 1840 presidential contest.[26] Facing formidable opposition, proslavery politicians demanded federal protection and placed heavy burdens on northern allies.

Meanwhile, although most northern Democrats denounced abolitionism, their ideals contained antislavery potential. Slaveholders remembered the Missouri crisis, when many northern Jeffersonians backed gradual emancipation in Missouri.[27] Some northern Jacksonians appeared equally untrustworthy, particularly the labor activists who seemed hell-bent on subverting property rights, and the Democracy's southern critics took notice. As Congress wrangled over abolitionist mailings, Palmetto State nullifier Waddy Thompson informed "property-holders of the North" that they had as much to fear from "lawless insurrection" or the "equally terrible process of the ballot-box" as southern planters did.[28] This bid for cooperation between southern and northern elites repudiated Van Buren's coalition. Ely Moore, a New York trade unionist turned Democrat, struck back, resenting Thompson's insulting insinuations about the "laboring classes, the back-bone of the democracy of the country." He bristled at the implication "that Government ought to be founded on property . . . and that the minority should govern," a doctrine that "strikes at the very root of free government." Thompson, declared Moore, was on the wrong side in the timeless struggle between "the democracy and the aristocracy."[29] Eventually, clashes between property rights and majoritarianism would prompt masses of northern Democrats to bolt the party and inject Jacksonian ideals into the burgeoning antislavery movement.[30] These defections would increase southern clout within the Democracy, but they also enabled fire-eaters to argue that northern allies were inherently untrustworthy.

Van Buren's presidential hopes collided with southern anxieties. After replacing Calhoun as vice president for Jackson's second term, Van Buren's succession seemed secure.[31] But even before Van Buren was nominated for president in May 1835, his northern background provided grist for proslavery rumor mills, as southern Whigs and Calhounites set a lasting precedent in southern politics: win votes by blasting rivals' northern friends as unsound on slavery.[32] The proliferation of antislavery organizations in New York, Van Buren's ties to abolitionists like Arthur and Lewis Tappan, and the domestic life of his running mate Richard M. Johnson—a Tennessean who lived openly with an African American mistress—inspired demagogic attacks.[33] Especially extravagant was the two-volume novel *The Partisan Leader*, published in 1836 by Beverley

Tucker, a Virginia Calhounite. Set in 1849 with a tyrannical Van Buren still seated on the "presidential throne," the novel lionized secessionist guerrillas battling to propel Virginia into a southern confederacy.[34] Van Buren responded by denouncing abolitionism; he was not the last northern Democrat to walk the fine line between assuaging southern fears and alienating northern voters.[35] Van Buren defeated the badly divided Whigs, but his performance in the South was lackluster: he lost Kentucky, South Carolina, Georgia, and Tennessee, and while Jackson had won nearly 80 percent of the Deep South's popular vote in 1832, Van Buren received only a bare majority. In Mississippi, he edged out Hugh White by five hundred votes; four years earlier, Jackson had won every ballot cast in the state.[36]

The Panic of 1837 ensured that economic issues dominated Van Buren's presidency, but slavery remained divisive. He gratified cotton planters by displacing the Cherokee and warring against Seminoles who sheltered runaway slaves, but he disappointed southern expansionists by balking at the annexation of Texas. Some controversies were unavoidable. After enslaved Africans seized the Spanish slave ship *Amistad* and reached Long Island in 1839, the forty-two survivors were charged with murder and piracy. Sympathetic to Spain's demand for the captives' rendition, Van Buren hoped the district court would order their return; instead, it vindicated the slaves' right to resist kidnapping and ordered their repatriation to Africa. The administration appealed to the Supreme Court, but the original ruling was reaffirmed, leaving Van Buren defeated but also vulnerable to charges of pandering to the Slave Power.[37] By 1840, he had no reason to recant the irritated outburst he scribbled to a southern friend in 1835: "I have been stigmatized as the apologist of Southern institutions, & now forsooth you good people will have it . . . that I am an abolitionist."[38] Even for its creator, preserving the Democratic coalition was a vexing challenge.

In 1840, Van Buren fell under the juggernaut unleashed by the Whigs and their presidential candidate, Virginia-born war hero William Henry Harrison. Turning the tables on the Democrats, Whigs hailed Harrison's combat record and tarred Van Buren as an out-of-touch dandy. In the South, they recycled old charges against the New Yorker while trumpeting Harrison's southern birth, efforts to legalize slavery in the Indiana Territory, and support for Missouri's admission as a slave state. Southern Whigs also lauded Harrison's running mate, John Tyler, an ex-Jacksonian who excoriated Old Hickory's response to nullification.[39] A Mississippi Whig crowed that "Harrison and the slave holding States acted together," while Van Buren acted "with the abolitionists."[40] Southern Whigs played their strong hand shrewdly, winning the White House by capturing 54 percent of the southern popular vote and carrying the former Democratic strongholds of North Carolina, Louisiana, and Mississippi.[41]

The worst was yet to come, for in 1844 Van Buren was beaten by fellow Democrats. Van Buren initially liked his chances for redemption, since Harrison was now dead and "His Accidency" Tyler had alienated his own party, but a potent blend of expansionist ardor and proslavery intrigue dashed his hopes. Behind it all was John C. Calhoun. Gratified by Van Buren's economic policies, Calhoun had led his adherents back into communion with the Democracy in 1837. Now seeking to transform it into a southern party and make himself president, he brazenly asked Democrats to embrace a proslavery ideologue who "regarded majoritarian democracy as a sham."[42] The Democracy was vulnerable, with party bonds frayed after sixteen years of rough service. Northeastern Van Burenites, eager to recommit the party to egalitarianism and reform, eyed Calhounites warily, while northwestern expansionists hoped to promote what would soon be called Manifest Destiny. Prior to the national convention in Baltimore, most delegates favored Van Buren, but Calhoun and Mississippi senator Robert J. Walker contrived his downfall. Their secret weapon was Texas. Walker stoked annexationist fervor by arguing that acquiring Texas would benefit the entire country: northern manufacturers would snag a lucrative market; southern planters would secure their western flank against meddling British abolitionists; and white supremacists nationwide would gain an outlet for African American migration into the tropics.[43] Meanwhile, proslavery leaders sensed an opportunity to unite the South, smash the Van Burenites, and place the federal government squarely in slavery's corner. Annexationism resonated in Mississippi, whose legislature (site of the nation's first-ever legislative debate on Texas annexation) loudly championed acquisition of the Lone Star Republic.[44]

With southerners clamoring for Texas and northern Democrats divided among themselves, Van Buren's nightmare had come true: battles over slavery and expansion were splintering the Democracy. Like many of his supporters, Van Buren viewed Texas annexation as a proslavery ploy. In April 1844, he penned a fateful letter to Mississippi congressman William Hammett, agreeing to accept Texas if the public demanded it while censuring President Tyler's expansionist intrigues and warning that annexation would provoke war with Mexico.[45] Outraged Mississippi congressmen urged that no anti-annexationist be nominated for president. As insurance, southern Democrats seized veto power over the nomination by reviving the two-thirds rule at the convention. Ultimately, Democrats nominated James K. Polk of Tennessee, a fervent expansionist who won the presidency by sweeping the Deep South and most of the Northwest. Shortly before Polk took office, Congress voted to annex Texas.[46]

Resentful Van Burenites retaliated in 1848 by building a coalition of dissident Democrats and antislavery Whigs into the Free-Soil Party. Calling for the divorce of federal power from slavery's support, Free-Soilers nominated Van Buren for the presidency, won 10 percent of the popular vote, and injected antislavery into mainstream American politics.[47] Many Free-Soilers later became Republicans, but for others, old party loyalties remained strong. Even those most embittered by memories of 1844 could gravitate back to the Democracy: Van Buren returned in 1852, belatedly endorsed the Kansas-Nebraska Act, and voted for Douglas in 1860.[48] He spent his final years advocating for the Union and the Democracy until secession shattered both.

Van Buren's career underscored the intricacies of antebellum Democratic politics, which defy simple reduction to proslavery racism. His party was beset by quarrels among the planters and plain republicans who claimed the Democracy as their own. These rivalries, coupled with partisan warfare within North and South, created a political environment in which Van Buren and other northern Democrats could be simultaneously assailed as abolitionists and doughfaces. At the party's center were northerners and southerners who believed that despotism over blacks could coexist with white democracy.[49] But they faced opponents in both sections who doubted whether slaveholders' property rights were compatible with majority rule. Northern critics, from Whigs and abolitionists to Democratic dissidents, denounced Democrats for truckling to the Slave Power. Southern critics, including opportunistic Whigs and reactionary Calhounites, branded northern Democrats as false friends and questioned whether slavery could survive in a majoritarian political system that forced southerners to rely on northern allies.

Antebellum Democrats thus confronted a challenge that was both structural and contextual. The federal system forced them to convince plain republicans and planters alike that the Democracy worked for them, a difficult task since Jefferson's presidency. Developments during the Jacksonian Democracy's formative years made it even more daunting: flush times in the Cotton Kingdom, vocal abolitionist activism, and the rise of aggressive proslavery ideology buffeted Van Buren's coalition. Bolstering their positions at home required northern and southern Democrats to tug the party in divergent directions, increasing the strain that threatened to destroy it. This dynamic worsened after territorial expansion rattled American politics in 1844. Thereafter, conflict between property rights and majority rule would inflame debates over the future of a growing republic and baffle efforts to promote unity through expansion. Between 1828 and 1844, sectionalism had infected the Democratic coalition and now was poised to grow more virulent. As rising stars in Illinois and Mississippi, Douglas and Davis participated in many of these early debates at the grassroots level. When they entered national politics in the mid-1840s, these striving Democrats would inherit a treasured but fragile party.

★ ★ ★

To say that Stephen Douglas lived and breathed politics is to make apt use of a stale cliché. He scheduled his wedding for the narrow window between the 1856 election and the opening of a new session of Congress—after courting Adele Cutts from the campaign trail. Alongside professions of love and updates on his health, Douglas enumerated the speeches, parades, and railroad journeys that filled his exhausting itinerary. He even scrawled one letter on the hustings, hastily closing when it was his turn to speak.[50] Of course, he was stumping for the Democratic ticket. "It is almost needless to remark that Judge Douglas has from boyhood been a Democrat," averred an 1852 campaign biography, adding that his "youthful enthusiasm was first awakened by the name and achievements of Andrew Jackson."[51] Devoting his life to politics meant giving his heart and soul to the Democracy.

Douglas idolized Jackson from boyhood, honed his political skills in clashes ignited by Old Hickory's polarizing presidency, and marked each stage of his meteoric rise with professions of the Jacksonian creed. He developed his combative rhetorical style in debates at the Canandaigua Academy, where he won first prize from a Whiggish panel of judges for arguing that Jackson was "a greater soldier, statesman and hero than Napoleon Bonaparte."[52] He brought his Democratic faith to Illinois, settling in a town named for his idol where, ironically, Whigs were ascendant under the leadership of John J. Hardin, a nephew of Henry Clay. Days after opening his law practice in 1834, Douglas won local notoriety with a feisty defense of the Bank War.[53] Ten years later, in his first speech in Congress, Douglas defended Jackson's imposition of martial law during the Battle of New Orleans.[54] According to Democratic sources, when Douglas visited the Hermitage later that summer, he was (for once) left speechless when Jackson personally thanked him for the effort.[55] Regardless of its authenticity, the story affirmed the bona fides of an aspiring young

Democrat. After Jackson died the following year, Douglas carefully filed a funeral invitation among his papers, where it remains.[56]

Douglas had many like-minded neighbors in Illinois. After praising its fat cattle and bountiful fields in an 1835 letter to his stepfather, Douglas enthused that the "people of this country are more thoroughly Democratic than any people I have ever known." Egalitarian in spirit and meritocratic in rewarding talent, they always gave "Gen Jackson and his administration a warm and enthusiastic support," and he predicted that they would give Van Buren an even larger majority next year. These promising political conditions, he admitted, "had a great influence on my mind in inducing me to remain here."[57] Fertile soil lured farmers to Illinois, but Douglas dreamed of reaping political harvests.

But Democrats faced a test in 1836: could their party survive Jackson's retirement? Given Illinois's chaotic political environment, this was an open question. Personal factions were fading, but party lines remained blurry, and Jackson's undisciplined supporters often ran against each other, enabling anti-Jackson candidates to win with mere pluralities. Convinced that Democrats enjoyed a natural majority in Illinois, Douglas reasoned that control over nominations was vital for party success and majority rule. Indeed, he equated Democratic ascendance with majoritarianism because he viewed opponents as elitist usurpers. In a published appeal, Douglas opined that American politics inevitably had two parties: Democrats, "the advocates of the rights of the People," and Federalists or Whigs, "the advocates of the privileges of property."[58] To defeat the latter, Douglas promoted a convention system in which freshly elected delegates would gather to write platforms and select candidates. Accordingly, he met other delegates in Vandalia to nominate pro–Van Buren electors in early December 1835. A few weeks later, Douglas signed (and probably drafted) a message to Illinois Democrats defending the convention against critics who derided it as un-republican. The appeal insisted that the convention reflected the popular will. It stressed the need for "concert of action" to prevent wily enemies from "rid[ing] into power against the will of a majority." It endorsed Indian removal and the Bank War, denounced the "dangerous doctrines of nullification," and called for united effort to elect Van Buren.[59] Subsequent county conventions chose candidates for state and local offices, including Douglas for the state legislature.[60]

The convention system was not universally popular, with Democrats in northern Illinois accepting it more readily than those farther south, but its results were compelling. Van Buren won the presidency and carried Illinois, even as Indiana and Ohio went Whig. Democrats nabbed all three of Illinois's seats in Congress and triumphed in Morgan County, capturing five of its six seats in the state House of Representatives; only Hardin's election prevented a sweep. Impressed, Democrats statewide began holding conventions, and Whigs eventually flattered their rivals by following suit.[61] Thus commenced a new era of party regularity and local campaigns shaped by national issues. For Douglas, the elections also confirmed a connection between Democratic discipline and majority rule, which he would advocate for the rest of his life.

Douglas was among the Morgan County Democrats elevated to the state legislature in 1836. The canvass was, he recalled, "a very spirited one, conducted almost solely upon national politics and party grounds," but he was prepared for the challenge.[62] Despite his inexperience, he had been named state's attorney for the First Judicial District in early 1835. Trying cases across eight west-central Illinois counties required him to travel widely, size up local affairs quickly, and argue before juries comprising farmers and artisans. These duties, which resembled a hard-fought election campaign, sharpened his debate skills and increased his visibility.[63] Thus, when Douglas ran for the legislature, he was well known and inured to campaigning's hardships. Indeed, he relished the West's exhausting style of canvassing, particularly the head-to-head debates. "I find no difficulty in adopting the Western mode of Electioneering by addressing the people from the Stump," he bragged. He had met Hardin in a "a number of pitiched [sic] battles" and "came out conqueror."[64] Victory validated his decision to settle in Illinois and his devotion to majoritarianism; he could hardly question the vox populi when it cheered him so loudly.[65]

When Douglas arrived in the state legislature in December 1836, conflicts over economic issues glowed white-hot. Douglas toed the Jacksonian line on the Bank War, collaborating with John A. McClernand on a vigorous defense of Jackson's course.[66] Internal improvements were even more important, however, and Illinois Democrats had to be careful: Jeffersonian purity and Jacksonian frugality were rhetorically appealing, but Douglas recognized that the "current of popular feeling" ran so strongly in favor of infrastructure "that it was hazardous for any politician to oppose it."[67] Early in the session, he proposed state-financed completion of the Illinois and Michigan Canal, to connect Lake Michigan to the Illinois River and thence to the Mississippi; construction of a railroad from the canal's Illinois River terminus to the Ohio River, and another from the Mississippi River town of Quincy to the state's eastern border; and improvements on the Illinois and Wabash Rivers. This program would accelerate development of central and northern Illinois, including Morgan County.[68]

Douglas's plan disappointed legislators solicitous of their own pet projects, and after a more extensive bill was reported out of committee, representatives raced to tack on amendments, creating what Douglas derided as a "mammoth bill." But his constituents instructed him to vote for it, so Douglas joined the majority, which passed the bill in early 1837.[69] Work commenced on a multitude of projects, only to be derailed by the Panic of 1837, which brought the good times to a screeching halt and saddled Illinois with a $10.5 million debt.[70] Dismayed, some Illinoisans resolved to seek federal aid for infrastructure, while others moved west. Douglas would champion both constituencies in the future.

When the panic struck, however, Douglas had already moved on to a position as register of the General Land Office in Springfield. The town was originally called Calhoun, but locals adopted the Massachusetts-derived moniker in 1832, thus inscribing the Democracy's nullification-era rupture on the map.[71] Springfield did not become the state capital until 1839, but Douglas's position as register was immediately profitable. Ever the speculator, he monitored railway construction, which would raise the value of lots in adjoining towns, and reaped the consequent windfalls.[72] Douglas's public duties also expanded his social network, and he cultivated new contacts with finesse. An acquaintance later recalled his "wonderful power . . . of recognizing" everyone "at a glance" and "calling 'Cap,' and Dick and John and Patrick each by his proper name on the instant" while making it look "as spontaneous as breathing." Humble folk felt that Douglas was "the frank, personal friend of each one of them."[73] For Douglas, his Land Office labors were democracy in action, a lively mixture of speculation, bonhomie, and strategic socializing.

Douglas also remained keen to reenter electoral politics. In 1838, as he approached his twenty-fifth birthday, he was tapped to run against John T. Stuart, Abraham Lincoln's senior law partner, for a seat in the U.S. House of Representatives. Douglas campaigned on a Jacksonian platform of white men's egalitarianism and hostility to entrenched privilege, zeroing in on national banking issues. He championed President Van Buren's proposed Independent Treasury, designed to prevent inflation by limiting the supply of paper currency and to depoliticize banking by keeping federal deposits out of private banks. Although some voters worried that this would strangle credit markets and stifle economic growth, Douglas insisted that there "should be a Divorce granted between the Banking system and the Government."[74]

Douglas and Stuart fought a running battle across the sprawling Third Congressional District, which encompassed northern and central Illinois. They campaigned from March until Election Day in August, speaking six days a week and holding numerous debates. Douglas breathed fire in these joint appearances, particularly in Springfield, where he provoked Stuart to violence. The enraged Whig dragged his diminutive opponent around by the head until Douglas bit his thumb so hard that it left a permanent scar. This bloody spectacle notwithstanding, the candidates addressed serious issues, with Douglas decrying a national bank and calling for preemption laws that would enable squatters to gain title to land they worked. Stuart countered by denouncing Douglas as weak on internal improvements.[75]

The contest roared to a nail-biting finish. Early reports bade fair for Douglas, who ran well in the counties along the Illinois and Michigan Canal, where he courted Irish laborers; in Chicago, which he carried by a two-to-one margin; and among poor farmers who loved his land policy. But the final tally gave Stuart the election by 35 votes out of some 36,000 cast. As rumors of fraud trickled in from across the district, Douglas asked Jacksonian titans Thomas Hart Benton and Francis Preston Blair for advice on contesting the outcome. In March 1839, after Stuart received a certificate of election, Douglas proposed establishing a commission to review the ballots or, alternatively, holding a fresh election; either way, "a majority of the people should rule." Partisan bickering dragged on, with Democrats insisting that Douglas votes had been undercounted and Whigs complaining of Irish voter fraud. By year's end, with no prospect of reversing the official result, Douglas tacitly conceded, and Stuart went to Washington.[76]

Defeat reveals at least as much about a person as victory, and Douglas's loss was illuminating. It highlighted his tenacity, remarkable even in an age full of political brawlers, and his emergent constituency, a coalition of Chicago boosters, hardscrabble farmers, and immigrant laborers. Douglas was closely associated with central and northern Illinois, and not just because he resided in the Third District; he dominated in Chicago and among immigrants, and Whigs took heed. One griped that Douglas's idea of democracy was himself "mounted upon the shoulders of two Irishmen, addressing a Chicago rabble upon the glorious privilege of a free country, and the right of unnaturalized foreigners to control the elections of Illinois."[77] Historians have emphasized the bigotry of these remarks, but the geography also matters: as immigrants flocked into Illinois's burgeoning central and northern regions, Douglas's future looked bright.

Douglas held no office upon resigning from his register position in March 1839, but he remained politically active. In Illinois, as across the country, Whigs had matched Democrats' campaign spectacle and were already mobilizing for the 1840 presidential election. Douglas organized local and state Democratic conventions, served on the state central committee, and spent most of 1839 and 1840 campaigning for Van Buren, exhorting fellow Democrats not to "relax our exertions because we feel confident of success."[78] In hindsight, his most notable clashes were public debates with Abraham Lincoln.[79] The campaign also underlined Douglas's violent temper and dubious judgment. Amid a running feud with Whig editor Simeon Francis, Douglas publicly attacked him with a cane, but the strapping Francis grabbed Douglas's hair and threw him against a market cart. Lincoln exulted that everyone was laughing about it—except Douglas.[80] These efforts produced bittersweet results: Van Buren carried Illinois and Democrats won the state legislature, but Whigs captured the presidency.[81]

With Democrats still ascendant at home, Douglas's star continued to rise. In November 1840, he was appointed secretary of state for Illinois and then elevated to the state supreme court the following February. Two years on the Fifth Circuit, which covered nine western Illinois counties, earned him the lasting sobriquet "Judge Douglas" and revealed the breadth and limitations of his sense of justice. Douglas exuded egalitarianism, descending from the bench to chat, shake hands, and sit on laps.[82] On cases involving white people, the substance of his judgments matched his style. He issued important rulings in favor of Joseph Smith and the Mormons, who had settled in western Illinois after being expelled from Missouri. Their presence became a partisan issue, with Whigs wooing anti-Mormon voters and accusing Democrats of pandering to Smith and his coreligionists. But Douglas befriended Smith and maintained close ties to the Latter-day Saints long after Smith's death in 1844 and Mormons' trek to Utah two years later.[83] In the late 1850s, a Mormon admirer presented Douglas with an enormous bound volume containing five years of the *Deseret News*.[84] These rulings reflected a lifelong dedication to freedom of conscience. When his Catholic fiancée later worried that their marriage might hurt him politically, Douglas wrote that "religion is a matter between each person and his God and that no one else has a right to interfere with them. If the people don't like your religious faith I cannot help it."[85] Douglas sacrificed much for political advantage, but he would not cater to religious prejudice.

Douglas's broadmindedness collided with the color barrier, however, and his ruling on a fugitive slave case reflected his view of democracy as a means for whites alone to determine policy. In early 1843, he heard the case of Richard Eells, a physician and Underground Railroad operative. Defense counsel argued that Illinois's fugitive slave law was unconstitutional in light of the recent U.S. Supreme Court decision in *Prigg v. Pennsylvania*, which made rendition of runaway slaves strictly a federal matter. Douglas disagreed. He held that the Illinois law was designed to preserve internal order and that every polity could make police regulations necessary to keep the peace. This was an early example of his insistence that local lawmaking prevail on questions about slavery and that white majorities should rule on race. This racially circumscribed egalitarianism reflected Democratic orthodoxy.[86]

When the state supreme court upheld Douglas's ruling, he had already moved on. Rapid population growth boosted Illinois's congressional representation, and by 1843, the Fifth Congressional District had been carved out of the west-central portion of the state. Democrats nominated Douglas to run for the seat against Orville H. Browning, a Kentucky-born Whig, in a special election that August. Like Douglas's first run for Congress, the grueling contest focused primarily on national economic issues. Douglas denounced Whigs' plans for a national bank, criticized tariffs, and urged that public lands be sold cheaply to encourage property ownership and westward migration. He won by 461 votes out of 17,000, joining a Democratic wave that captured six out of Illinois's seven House seats.[87]

★ ★ ★

As Douglas prepared to begin his term in December 1843, several new issues were beginning to supplant the economic questions he had debated with Browning; all would shake the upcoming Congress, and some would resonate for the rest of his career. The most immediate was the looming presidential election: Washington buzzed with wheeling and dealing as president making intersected with westward expansion. The beleaguered John Tyler, estranged from the Whigs, hoped to lead a bipartisan crusade for Texas annexation, while Calhoun and Walker conspired to make Texas a Democratic party test and deny Van Buren the nomination.[88]

Illinoisans, meanwhile, focused on Oregon, which the United States and Great Britain had occupied jointly since 1818. Glowing accounts of this "New El Dorado" spread Oregon fever, particularly after 1838, when returning missionary Jason Lee stopped in Peoria while en route to Washington with a petition urging Congress to end joint occupancy and establish a territorial government. Lee praised the Willamette Valley's rich resources and salubrious climate and inspired the Peoria Party to launch its doomed expedition to liberate Oregon from British tyranny.[89]

More level-headed Illinoisans recognized Oregon's potential; an Alton editor proclaimed that if the U.S. reached the Pacific Ocean, "nothing but the power of Omnipotence could prevent the United States from becoming the leading nation of the world."[90] Oregon also appealed to humbler folk reeling from the Panic of 1837. As grain prices plunged, demoralized Illinois farmers saw Oregon as a place to start afresh.[91] In the spring of 1843, while Douglas canvassed the Fifth District, the first major wave of emigrants set out on the Oregon Trail.[92] Thereafter, Douglas regularly received appeals to bring Oregon under U.S. control.[93] It was an auspicious time for an expansionist northwestern Democrat to stride onto the national stage.

No stranger to upward mobility through westward migration, Douglas grafted expansion onto his existing platform to create a sweeping plan for western development. Combining Democratic initiatives for broad-based land ownership and territorial aggrandizement with Whiggish infrastructure policies, this agenda would inform northwestern Democratic politics for years to come. To help Illinois, Douglas would seek federal aid for river and harbor improvements and railroad and canal construction. To promote western migration, he would annex Texas and secure the Oregon Country, give pioneers public land and military protection, and connect them to markets with internal improvements. Illinois would become the gateway to a wider western empire that American settlers were extending into the Willamette Valley. Viewing Illinois's development as inextricably linked to a Greater Northwest stretching from Lake Michigan to Puget Sound, Douglas resolved to make the Democracy its champion.[94]

Douglas pursued this dream during his first session in Congress. Determined to prevent sectional discord or strict constructionism from upsetting his plans, he emerged as both a western spokesman and a sectional mediator. When he endorsed a bill to fund harbor improvements, Douglas urged westerners to form a "solid phalanx" behind it while promising that every region would benefit from "the protection of commerce on the Western waters."[95] He also admonished Democrats not to reject the bill for ideological reasons, claiming that Jackson himself supported reasonable river and harbor improvements. Tellingly, Douglas specifically defended appropriations for the Illinois River, which lay within one state; since it was part of a hydrological network connecting the Atlantic to the Gulf of Mexico, he argued, its improvement was crucial for national commerce.[96] But South Carolina Democrat Robert Barnwell Rhett countered with a classic slippery slope argument: funding internal improvements would transform Congress into a "Parliament like that of Great Britain," which would wield "a giant's power."[97] Aligning the Democracy behind Douglas's program would not be easy.

Debate on the improvements bill revealed troubling divisions among Illinois Democrats as well. On April 20, 1844, the bill was amended to remove funds for the Illinois River project. Douglas decided that half a loaf was better than none and voted for the bill, which financed other key projects on the Mississippi River and Chicago's harbor. Democrats from northern Illinois, including Joseph P. Hoge of Galena and John Wentworth of Chicago, joined Douglas in the affirmative, as did John J. Hardin, the state's lone Whig. But the Democrats from southern Illinois—Orlando B. Ficklin, John A. McClernand, and Robert Smith—voted no, citing constitutional objections.[98] Douglas was a rising star in a deeply divided party; even among Illinois Democrats, his agenda was not universally popular.

Douglas continued to promote his western program during the brief 1844–45 session, and Illinoisans looked to him for leadership. As one admirer wrote, Douglas's "position at Washington" was "of paramount influence & importance" for Illinois "& indeed the West generally."[99] Another predicted that Douglas would eclipse Henry Clay: "It will shortly be—Stephen A. of the west, instead of Harry of the west."[100] Eager to fulfill these grand expectations, Douglas secured a federal land grant to finance completion of the Illinois and Michigan Canal, setting a precedent for subsidies later given to railroads.[101] He tried and failed to pass an Oregon territorial bill in which the U.S. would have claimed the entire Oregon Country, not merely the portion south of the forty-ninth parallel, which some colleagues were willing to accept as a compromise.[102] Hoping to change their minds, Douglas introduced a bill to purchase copies of a book recently published by State Department employee Robert Greenhow that urged Americans to claim all of Oregon, even at the risk of war.[103] (His wife, Rose O'Neal Greenhow, later became a Confederate spy, and his niece was Adele Cutts, Douglas's second wife. The nineteenth-century world was tiny.) Amid domestic and diplomatic controversies over Oregon, Douglas was so zealous to protect overland migrants that he backed legislation to establish military posts in both Oregon and the nonexistent territory of Nebraska.[104] And, anticipating his most infamous legislative triumph, Douglas also introduced a bill to organize the Nebraska Territory in December 1844, only to have it die in the Committee on Territories.[105] The freshman lacked the power to enact his program, but his vision for federal development of the prairie-to-Pacific corridor was already clear.

Douglas's rise from defeat in 1838 to his first term in the House was illuminating. Determined to accelerate the development of his home state by harnessing it to a burgeoning western empire, Douglas crafted an agenda that merged expensive internal improvement policies with spread-eagled expansionism. This program was not universally palatable, and it quickly collided with southern Democratic scruples. Also evident was a pattern that has been obscured by Douglas's rivalry with Lincoln. Students of the famous 1858 debates associate Douglas with "Egypt," the portion of southern Illinois dominated by southern-born emigrants, an alignment often entwined with the depiction of Illinois as a microcosm of the nation. But this interpretation elides the regional affiliation that shaped Douglas's politically formative years. At every step of his path to Congress, Douglas was associated with central and northern Illinois: it was there that he lived, campaigned, and held office; there that his convention system was most readily accepted; and there that his stance on internal improvements was most widely shared.

Douglas appealed to the hopes, class tensions, and ethnic conflicts that pervaded Illinois's most dynamic regions. His constituency included Irish immigrants, struggling farmers, urban boosters, and prospective western migrants. He refined his political skills on Jacksonian era economic issues but soon devised a more ideologically flexible program to make Illinois the gateway to the West. This, however, moved him and his party into perilous waters. Once expansion catapulted slavery to the political forefront, it was unclear how Douglas's constituents would respond. Plain republicans might swallow the sham populism of white supremacy, but their hostility to entrenched elites could turn them against southern planters. This, of course, lay in the unknowable future in 1845, when Douglas was joined in the House by another exuberant expansionist with very different notions of Democracy.

★ ★ ★

Jefferson Davis was a crafty politician, tireless campaigner, and staunch Democrat and has received little credit for it. For conflicting reasons, Davis's hagiographers and detractors have distanced him from the messy intrigues of partisan politics. Varina Davis depicted him as a high-minded statesman repulsed by political chicanery. He "did not know the arts of the politician," she insisted in her memoirs, and would not have used them if he had.[106] Alternatively, Richmond journalist Edward A.

Pollard, among other critics, blamed Davis's political obtuseness for Confederate defeat.[107] Although one offered praise and the other censure, they followed similar logic: working backward from the Confederacy's collapse, they concluded that Davis was averse to nineteenth-century mass politics. Many scholars have echoed these evaluations, contrasting Davis's cold pedantry against Lincoln's political acumen.[108]

Most Davis scholars focus on the Confederate years, but bringing Davis's antebellum career out from the Civil War's shadow illuminates the diligence, skill, and ambition that propelled his political ascent. Varina's memoirs, for instance, actually reveal a dedicated partisan who ran himself ragged on the campaign trail and in Congress.[109] Davis's stump speeches show his readiness to resort to loyalty politics and demagoguery. Private correspondence demonstrates that Davis sought office as actively—if covertly—as his contemporaries, who habitually feigned reluctance while ambition burned within. Davis's path to power also paralleled Douglas's: both rebounded from defeat to reach Congress; engaged with economic issues and then swiftly embraced expansionism; learned to balance principle with pragmatism by operating in Whiggish regions of Democratic states; and strove to make the Democracy serve regional interests. No political naïf could have enjoyed the success Davis had before the Civil War.[110]

Army life diverted Davis from the legal and oratorical pursuits that he savored in his youth, but he resumed them after his bride Knox's death in 1835. Some biographers characterize the next eight years of Davis's life as a period of monkish seclusion and study.[111] Certainly, Davis capitalized on his brother's library and the leisure time afforded by slave labor to learn political economy from Locke and Smith, law from Blackstone and Kent, and literature from Shakespeare and Scott. But he also followed politics through newspapers, the *Congressional Globe*, and conversations with Joseph, who molded Davis's worldview. Many of their neighbors were Whigs, and the precise origin of the Davis brothers' Democratic allegiance is unclear, but Jefferson later wrote that to Joseph, "materially, as well as intellectually, I am more indebted than to all other men."[112] The younger Davis, who had enjoyed a childhood meeting with Andrew Jackson, shared Joseph's diehard loyalty to the Democracy.[113]

Davis's education was practical as well as theoretical because he kept in touch with prominent politicians. "I am living as retired as a man on the great thoroughfare of the Mississippi can be," Davis wrote in 1840.[114] This was not very retired at all; that Davis penned these words in a letter to a Democratic senator from Ohio reveals the breadth of his political correspondence. It also highlights how the Mississippi River, the muddy artery of the Cotton Kingdom, connected Davis with a global marketplace of goods and ideas. Varina Davis recalled welcoming arriving steamboats by sending fruit and flowers to their captains, since "'the boat' meant ice, new books, and every other luxury New Orleans could furnish or their purses command."[115] They also brought mail, through which Davis swapped political intelligence. From a New York in-law, Davis learned about popular interest in the Independent Treasury.[116] From Joseph, he received a lively account of Whigs' electioneering in 1840.[117] And in his replies, Davis analyzed political affairs. In 1839, Davis claimed to be "out of my element" while perceptively critiquing Van Buren for dividing Democrats by softening his stance on banking.[118]

In fact, politics was so much Davis's "element" that he ended his brief period of true seclusion in the winter of 1837–38 by traveling to Washington.[119] Davis left home in November and visited relatives in New York before reaching the capital, where he reconnected with George W. Jones, a Transylvania University chum who represented the Wisconsin Territory in Congress. Jones introduced Davis to influential associates, including President Martin Van Buren and Franklin Pierce, then a young senator from New Hampshire. The visit coincided with the Senate's debate over proslavery resolutions introduced by John C. Calhoun, which Davis may have attended.[120] Calhoun's six resolutions outlined his theory of state sovereignty, denounced abolitionism as dangerous to the South and harmful to the Union, insisted that the federal government provide "increased stability and security" to slavery, and condemned as unconstitutional efforts to abolish slavery in Washington or any territory.[121] Calhounites pilloried their critics as abolitionists and forced five of the resolutions through the Senate; only the final resolution, which censured any refusal to acquire new territory on the grounds of slavery's legality, was tabled.[122] The debates dramatized slavery's disruptive influence and sketched an aggressive proslavery agenda, which Davis would make his own.

★ ★ ★

Davis lacked Douglas's experience in state and local office holding, but both used party conventions to enter the political arena, and in 1840 and 1842, Davis served as a delegate to the Democratic state convention in Jackson.[123] The following year, he was tapped to run for the state legislature. It was an irregular nomination, as Warren County Democrats had chosen another candidate but switched to Davis shortly before the election, seeking to avoid a likely defeat. Despite the long odds, Davis jumped at the opportunity, displaying his political zeal and party fidelity; a good

Democratic soldier, he would make the desperate charge. Hailing Davis as a "sterling Democrat" with "unsullied private character, talents of a superior order, [and] extensive political information," Democrats hoped he could prevail in a Whig bastion.[124]

Like Douglas's early campaigns, Davis's first canvass hinged on economic debates inflamed by the Panic of 1837. Most divisive was the question of state debts. Mississippi voters, like their counterparts in Illinois, loved easy credit, and the legislature issued bonds to capitalize state-chartered banks, including the Planters' Bank in 1830 and the Union Bank in 1837. The latter institution quickly failed and forfeited its charter. Led by Governor Alexander McNutt, Democrats sought to repudiate the bank bonds, claiming that they were unconstitutional and had been sold fraudulently. The issue dominated the 1843 contests between Democratic repudiators and Whigs, who held that the state was honor-bound to pay its debts. Caught in between was Davis, a Democrat running in a Whig stronghold. Characteristically, he sought the middle ground: he agreed that the bonds were unconstitutional but would allow the courts to decide if they were valid debts; if binding, they must be paid. Startled, Democrats suppressed Davis's statements so that voters would assume he backed repudiation. (The taint lingered; during the Civil War, Unionists reviled Davis as an unreconstructed repudiator to dissuade Europeans from lending to the Confederacy.) Davis lost by some 170 votes out of nearly 1,200 cast but profited from the failure. He gained experience backing a party that was powerful statewide but weaker in the river counties, and he won Democrats' gratitude for faithful service in a lost cause.[125]

Davis's ambitions were undiminished as he entered the pivotal year of 1844. Just before Christmas in 1843, he had met Varina Banks Howell, the teenage daughter of a prominent Natchez Whig. She found him proud and overbearing but conceded that, for a Democrat, he was "refined and cultivated," an underwhelming first impression that reflected her sense of Davis as a political animal.[126] A few weeks later, Davis addressed the Democratic convention in Jackson, where he reluctantly followed instructions to endorse Van Buren's nomination while giving a rousing speech for Calhoun and Texas annexation, a measure "of vital importance to the south."[127] A faithful southern Democrat, Davis worked within the party to set it on an avowedly proslavery course; this strain between sectional and partisan loyalty persisted until secession. He spent 1844 campaigning for Varina's heart and the Democracy's soul.

As a Democratic elector, Davis dove into the presidential race knowing that the party needed a candidate who could carry the South. Van Buren's stock was dropping, and Davis was not eager for the New Yorker to win the nomination. In March, he sent Van Buren a pointed letter asking his views on tariffs, Texas annexation, and congressional power over slavery in Washington, D.C.[128] Slavery and expansion were central to partisan conflict within the South, and Davis worked to place Mississippi Democrats on the strongest possible ground.

Davis recognized that Texas was a winning issue with Mississippi voters, who regarded the Lone Star Republic much like Illinoisans viewed Oregon: a place to make, or remake, fortunes. White Mississippians had keenly followed the republic's violent birth in 1835 and 1836, convening public meetings to advocate Texas independence, vilify Santa Anna, and raise money and recruits for the Lone Star cause.[129] Enthusiasm for Texas swelled after the Panic of 1837, when droves of Mississippians tacked notes reading "G.T.T." (Gone to Texas) to their doors and headed west, seeking fresh land and sanctuary from creditors.[130] Varina Davis vividly recalled "the poor fellows who were ruined by their speculating proclivities" who moved to Texas "by the thousand to wipe off the long score against them and begin anew."[131] Those left behind remained interested in Texas, whose annexation would fortify the South's position against abolitionists by swelling the region's political power. Slavery, averred Hinds County petitioners, "is cherished by our constituents as the very palladium of their prosperity and happiness," and they urged their representatives to press for annexation.[132] By 1844, the "Texas question" seemed "destined to overrid[e]" every other issue, and when Whig candidate Henry Clay waffled on annexation, Mississippi Democrats smelled blood in the water.[133]

Thanks to the Calhounites and the two-thirds rule, Van Buren's candidacy imploded and Democrats nominated James K. Polk, a Tennessean whose ardent annexationism resonated in Mississippi, where he owned a cotton plantation.[134] Mississippi Democrats campaigned on annexation, stressing the importance of adding a new slave state and keeping Texas out of British abolitionists' clutches.[135] Davis stumped for Polk, addressing at least seventeen rallies between June 13 and November 2. Texas was his main theme, and his rhetorical efforts impressed onlookers throughout Mississippi.[136]

Stephen Douglas supported Polk with equal zeal, but not for identical reasons. Initially, he had favored Van Buren, but by early 1844, the New

Yorker's tepid support for expansion left Douglas hoping for a different standard-bearer, preferably a northwesterner like Lewis Cass.[137] Polk would do, however, and by June 1844 Douglas was campaigning for him on the floor of Congress, promising that Polk would secure America's lawful claim to all of Oregon, a territory valuable for its trans-Pacific connections and "inexhaustible natural resources . . . fertile soil and genial climate." Douglas also pressed for Texas, mixing Anglophobia with the dubious claim that the U.S. had already purchased Texas along with Louisiana in 1803 to argue for "reannexation" before Britain snatched it away. Douglas closed with a rousing cry for Polk and Democracy, with "Oregon and Texas, democracy and freedom, inscribed upon our banner."[138] The order in which Douglas listed the coveted territories was portentous, but in a hard-fought campaign, expansionism offered a platform broad enough for northern and southern Democrats to stand together. Indeed, after Congress adjourned, Douglas stumped for Polk in the South as well as in Illinois, visiting Nashville (and the Hermitage) and St. Louis.[139] Clay won Tennessee, but Davis's and Douglas's labors paid off in their home states, which both backed Polk by healthy margins. Expansion resonated in the Northwest, where Polk won every state save Ohio, and in the South, where Democrats reversed their Van Buren–era decline by sweeping the cotton states for the first time since 1828.[140]

Election season brought Davis private joy as well as public triumph. One month after meeting Varina Howell, Davis proposed, and they soon secured her family's permission to wed. Davis's arduous campaigning separated them for much of 1844, but they corresponded regularly, and Davis, like Douglas, wove politics into love letters, including one that mocked Clay's prevarication on Texas.[141] On February 26, 1845, six days before Polk's inauguration, they married in Natchez and then cruised to New Orleans for a six-week honeymoon.[142] The union was not always happy, but it lasted for the rest of Jefferson's life.

Politics swiftly intruded into their marriage. Four months after the wedding, Davis attended his county Democratic convention, which appointed him a delegate to the state convention and endorsed him to run for Congress. Even before being formally nominated, Davis plunged into the contest by giving a eulogy to recently deceased Andrew Jackson at a meeting in Vicksburg. Varina gloomily recalled that the summer and fall of 1845 introduced her to "the bitterness of being a politician's wife," including "long absences, pecuniary depletion from ruinous absenteeism, illness from exposure, misconceptions, defamation of character; everything which darkens the sunlight and contracts the happy sphere of home."[143]

Whatever her claims about Davis's aversion to the politician's craft, she knew he was part of the guild. Despite recurring illness, Davis canvassed relentlessly, denouncing banks and praising states' rights. In November, Democrats swept Mississippi's four congressional elections, with Davis winning the second-highest vote total.[144] "Our State," reveled a Democratic editor, "will be ably and faithfully represented in the next Congress."[145]

★ ★ ★

Texas was almost moot when Davis took his seat in December 1845, as Congress had acted on annexation the previous winter. Annexationists prevailed by passing resolutions (which needed bare majority approval) rather than by ratifying a treaty of annexation (which required a two-thirds vote in the Senate). Several House Democrats offered annexation resolutions, but Douglas's dominated the debate because it seemed most likely to silence critics. Douglas held that Congress must accept Texas into the Union because it had acquired the territory through the Louisiana Purchase and could not reject Texans' request for annexation. This fishy argument allowed northern Democrats to sidestep slavery by insisting that the Missouri Compromise had resolved the issue: Texas would be a slave state, although any states formed out of its territory lying north of the 36° 30′ line would be free. By February 1845, both houses had passed resolutions that resembled Douglas's proposal. All Illinois Democrats voted for annexation, while Hardin, the lone Whig, voted no; Mississippi's four Democrats voted unanimously in favor. President Tyler signed the annexation resolution on March 3, his last day in office.[146]

Annexation seemed to cement the alliance between Davis's and Douglas's wings of the Democracy, but their first session together signaled trouble. The immediate cause, ironically, was expansion. For Douglas, Texas was the first step of a larger expansionist program, and he expected Oregon would be next, as he had indicated in January 1845 in the peroration of his speech on Texas. Rejoicing that American self-government was "admirably adapted to the whole continent," he urged Congress to "drive Great Britain and the last vestiges of royal authority" from North America, "extend the limits of this republic from ocean to ocean," and make the U.S. "an *ocean-bound republic*."[147] Two days after voting on Texas, Douglas demanded passage of an Oregon bill "without delay."[148]

The bill stalled, so Oregon remained a leading issue in the Twenty-Ninth Congress, Davis and Douglas's first shared session. Watching from the galleries, Varina Davis reported hearing "nothing but Oregon."[149] Initially, the session augured well for northwestern expansionists. Douglas was appointed to chair the House Committee on Territories and worked to fast-track Oregon bills.[150] Moreover, there were indications of southern support; the previous September, Davis had endorsed acquiring both Oregon and California.[151] But many southerners were unwilling to hazard war with Britain to acquire a distant domain where slavery was unlikely to flourish. "For Texas I would fight the world," wrote a Georgian, "but for Oregon north of 49, I would not quarrel."[152] Others were more blunt. "I don't [care] a fig about *any* of Oregon," spat Georgia representative Robert Toombs. "The country is too large now, and I don't want a foot of Oregon or an acre of any other country, especially without 'niggers.'"[153] Northerners smelled treachery, and Douglas heard from several who feared that southerners, led by Polk, would settle for the area south of the forty-ninth parallel. "Mr Polk's course in offering to settle at 49. is to me inexplicable," wrote a New Yorker who felt betrayed, since "the grand issue" upon which Polk was elected "was *Oregon* and Texas."[154] Oregon fever burned in Illinois, where 3,000 people attended an August 1845 meeting to denounce any equivocation on America's claim to the whole territory.[155]

Douglas channeled this zeal in December 1845, when he introduced a resolution insisting that the U.S. title to "any part of the Oregon Territory south of 54° 40' of north latitude is not open to compromise."[156] Soon after, he challenged southerners to be as "brave and fearless in looking Great Britain in the face" as they had been with Mexico on the Texas question.[157] Sometimes he called out individuals, including South Carolina Democrat Isaac E. Holmes, for "dodging" the Oregon issue.[158] Constituents relished this boldness. "The speech of Judge Douglas is to the point, and pointed," wrote an editorialist from north-central Illinois. "It gives to the south a very clear intimation of what they may expect at the hands of the great west if they betray us on the Oregon question, after we have stood by them so firmly for Texas."[159] So much for the harmony of western and southern interests or the affinity between plain republicans and planters: on Oregon, Douglas championed a Northwest aggrieved by southern duplicity.

Westerners had good reason to worry. In his first major congressional speech, Davis urged precisely the compromise that Douglas deplored. Unwilling to fight Britain for the sake of Democrats' 1844 platform, which implied that U.S. claims extended to 54° 40', Davis counseled against war and argued that the area south of 49° was enough to sustain national interests and honor. Defending "southern men" against charges of deserting Oregon, he insisted that Texas had been completely different, as the U.S. had borne more "insult and outrage" from Mexico than it ever would receive from Britain. Yet Davis understood the Democracy's fragility, for he closed by saluting the "common agricultural interest" of the South and West and applauding "our natural allies, the Democracy of the North."[160]

Some biographers praise Davis's speech as a statesmanlike effort to cool northwestern war fever, while others accuse him of veiling a sectional position behind nationalist rhetoric.[161] These interpretations are not incompatible. Certainly, many northeasterners shared Davis's reluctance to confront Britain. Connecticut Democrat John M. Niles urged moderation, since the U.S. claim was "disputed by a great and powerful nation, who has been long in possession" of the contested territory.[162] But slaveholders had the most to lose from brinkmanship. In the last Anglo-American war, British coastal raids had liberated thousands of slaves, spread fears of insurrection, and forced one of Davis's brothers to stand guard at home.[163]

Davis's ode to agrarianism failed to quell the debate. In April, he sparred with Douglas, defending compromisers' patriotism and party fidelity against the Illinoisan's angry rebukes.[164] Ultimately, however, it was not up to the House to decide. When Polk settled for the region south of 49° in June 1846, he accepted a compromise that the former U.S. minister to Britain Edward Everett had proposed long before.[165] But the treaty also contradicted the 1844 Democratic platform, which trumpeted that "our title to the whole of the Territory of Oregon is clear and unquestionable," a statement Polk had endorsed in his inaugural address.[166] Inevitably, the settlement divided the Democrats. When the Senate ratified the treaty by a 41–14 vote on June 18, all the "no" votes were from Democrats, twelve of them from free states; half of those were northwesterners, including both Illinois senators.[167]

Some scholars have alleged that Polk broke a quid-pro-quo agreement on Texas and Oregon made at the Democratic convention.[168] Although most now believe there was no formal compact, what mattered in 1846 was northwestern Democrats' deep feeling of betrayal.[169] "Our Rights to Oregon," seethed an Ohioan, "have been shamefully compromised." He accused southern Democrats of relenting "not so much to avoid war as to permanently fix the boundaries of free territory," leaving northerners "hemmed in" between British tyranny and southern slavery. He wanted revenge: "It is time lovers of freedom should unite in opposing the common enemy by fixing bounds to their aggression."[170] Another Buckeye predicted that southern faithlessness would *"sour the Stomachs* of a great number at the North and West against the South and their slave policy."[171] One of Douglas's correspondents thanked him for having "fought the battles of freedom manfully" but lamented that "we have gained but half of Oregon."[172] Candid southerners conceded that "the Southern democracy have not redeemed their pledges to their Northern allies."[173] After their boisterous campaign rhetoric subsided, Democrats learned that the devil of Manifest Destiny was in the details.

Internal improvements exacerbated these sectional quarrels. The same southerner who validated northerners' Oregon grievances accused them of forsaking "cardinal measures of the Democratic party" by supporting a rivers and harbors bill.[174] Northwesterners regularly clamored for federally financed infrastructure, but its political prominence grew in June 1845 when Illinoisans convened in Springfield to prepare for a larger Memphis convention scheduled for July. Douglas offered resolutions endorsing federal projects, including the long-delayed Illinois and Michigan Canal. For him, internal improvements were entwined with Oregon since they would facilitate transcontinental transportation and boost America's readiness for war with Britain. This link between expansion and infrastructure would persist throughout his career. Douglas was appointed a delegate to the Memphis convention, although it was rescheduled for November and he did not attend. Seeking to cement a southern-western coalition, the Memphis convention did host John C. Calhoun, who endorsed federal investment in western infrastructure. A memorial passed at the gathering was presented to the Twenty-Ninth Congress.[175]

The resulting congressional debate on a rivers and harbors bill aggravated the feud over Oregon. In March, Douglas endorsed the bill, which would aid Illinois by providing $12,000 for Chicago's harbor and $40,000 to improve the St. Clair Flats, a treacherous waterway between Lake Erie and Lake Huron and a key link in the northwestern transportation network.[176] Exasperated by Democratic strict constructionists, Douglas snarled that "there were some powers in this Government that, by this time, ought to be conceded" and insisted that Madison, Monroe, Jackson, and Van Buren had supported improvements to navigable waterways. He was incensed by southern Democrats' charges of apostasy, including Alabama representative William Lowndes Yancey's derisive reference to northwesterners as "pretended Democrats." Douglas retaliated by raising the sore subject of Oregon: southerners who would surrender American soil were "at least equally obnoxious to the charge" of infidelity as westerners who wanted to facilitate commerce.[177] Three days later, Davis, who had pursued improvements for Mississippi, blasted the rivers and harbors bill for financing projects of purely local interest and singled out the

Chicago harbor provision. He also again denied that the 1844 platform precluded Democrats from accepting "a fair and equitable settlement of the Oregon difficulty."[178] Three months into their first shared session of Congress, Davis and Douglas were battling to define the Democracy's core principles.

Voting on the improvements bill clarified the conflict. Most Illinois representatives supported it, with Douglas joined in the affirmative by the lone Whig (Edward D. Baker) and the Democrats from northern and central Illinois, John Wentworth and Robert Smith. (Joseph P. Hoge of Galena did not vote.) But the Democrats from southern Illinois, John McClernand and Orlando Ficklin, voted no, along with the uniformly Democratic Mississippi delegation. Once again, Egyptian Democrats aligned with southerners against infrastructure spending, while Douglas joined Whigs and northern Illinois Democrats in support.[179]

Polk disappointed many northerners when, citing constitutional scruples, he vetoed the rivers and harbors bill. In response, Douglas praised Polk's ideals but insisted that the bill did not violate them. He hoped it would be revised and passed again, but the bill died, and Douglas was left empty-handed.[180] Twice in one session, southern Democrats had derailed his plans for the Greater Northwest. Douglas pledged to continue promoting internal improvements, vowing that "his southern friends . . . could not drive him from it."[181] The question was how many of these conflicts his career—and his party—could endure.

★ ★ ★

With a quarter century of hindsight, New York editor Horace Greeley observed that "in the Democratic triumph of 1844 was the germ of future Democratic disasters and humiliations."[182] Even without this perspective, Democrats already fretted about party disunity. None was more anxious than Polk, who resented criticism from congressional Democrats and, ignoring the realities of constituent pressure, blamed it on their presidential ambitions. "My fear," he wrote in March 1846, "is that these factions looking to the election of my successor in 1848 will so divide and weaken the Democratic party by their feuds as to defeat my measures and render my administration unsuccessful and useless."[183]

Rivals coveted Polk's job, but he overlooked the deeper divisions in a party that was perpetually riven by quarrels. Democrats could rally around figureheads like Jackson and crusades like Manifest Destiny, a slogan coined by the *Democratic Review* the year Polk took office.[184] But Davis's and Douglas's early careers showed that the Democracy was not a solid phalanx. As they raised their constituents' expectations by promoting territorial growth, they rekindled old rivalries between plain republicans and planters. Expansion was already tugging them apart, as Davis exulted over Texas and Douglas sulked over Oregon.

Davis and Douglas had to prove that the Democracy could deliver for the folks back home, and by 1846, Douglas had several reasons for concern. Most immediately alarming was that he, like Van Buren, was clashing with antislavery and proslavery activists alike. Antislavery critics blasted him for Texas annexation, calling him "the subservient tool of the slaveholders."[185] Meanwhile, southern Democrats impugned Douglas's party loyalty and opposed his agenda, twice thwarting his efforts to develop Illinois and the Greater Northwest through territorial growth and investment in infrastructure. Douglas had staked his career on the Democratic Party's ability to realize his northwestern vision, but by 1846 he had only half of Oregon to show for it. It was uncertain whether Davis's and Douglas's efforts to align the Democracy with their constituents' demands would strengthen the party or destroy it.

Meanwhile, Polk led the nation into a war that would present Davis and Douglas with exhilarating opportunities even as it escalated intraparty conflicts. As Manifest Destiny raced onward, it would reveal serious discrepancies among Democrats over not only *where* to expand but also *how* to govern conquered territory. After 1846, expansion raised divisive questions about democracy itself, pitting Douglas's majoritarian instincts against Davis's dedication to slaveholders' property rights in a controversy that would shake the Democratic alliance to its foundation.

3

Manifest Destinies

Thomas Charles—twenty-eight years old and $15,000 in debt—needed a second chance. Bad luck and terrible decisions had nearly ruined his life. Born in 1824, the Illinoisan had drifted downriver to Mississippi, where he met Ellen McRaven. They married in 1848, but Charles soon began drinking and gambling with the ruffians who made river towns like Vicksburg notorious for debauchery. By 1852, he decided to start afresh in California. Charles knew that Ellen would never consent to the move, so he told her he was going to New Orleans and then lit out for San Francisco, leaving her in the dark until she received his first letter from the Pacific Coast. When she joined him several months later, Thomas vowed to reform: he would find honest work, shun the cardrooms, and, he promised Ellen's aunt, "make up for all of my unkindness to her."[1]

The couple struggled at first and Ellen, while battling chronic illness, took in boarders to make ends meet. Eventually, however, Thomas landed a job at the Customs House and saved enough to invest in a small ranch. "California and Oregon is bound to be a great Country," he exulted. "There is nothing like a new Country for poor folks."[2] He and Ellen raised three children, cheered the Democrats—Thomas preferred Stephen Douglas for president in 1856 but celebrated James Buchanan's victory—and lived comfortably. Their story humanizes the bombastic oratory of contemporaries like Indiana Democrat Andrew Kennedy, who envisioned "the inhabitants of the great Mississippi Valley" reaching westward across the Pacific and eastward across the Atlantic and "grasping the trade of the civilized earth."[3] For Thomas and Ellen Charles, the West was a place to rebuild their lives, not fulfill a cosmic plan.

Yet high politics did touch their humble household. Thomas's employment depended on Democratic victories, hence his relief when Buchanan succeeded Franklin Pierce. Meanwhile, Ellen, raised in a slaveholding home, often thought about slavery. En route to San Francisco, she glumly remembered that "California is a free state," which meant that "I will have all my own work to do." She expected it would "go very hard with me at first, but I hope I will soon get used to it," for servants' wages were beyond her means.[4] Thereafter, relatives reminded her of the costs and benefits of mastery. In 1853, her sister recounted the hanging of an enslaved girl who had attempted to poison a white family.[5] Two years later, Ellen's brother offered $800 for her slave Mandy; Ellen resided in a free state, but her title to human property in Mississippi remained intact.[6] Eventually, the Civil War severed family ties until Thomas, a widower for two years, heard from a sister-in-law in 1865. She lamented the social revolution wrought by emancipation and yearned to restore bonds of kinship: "Dear brother let not the *link* that *bound us* be *broken*."[7] Thomas did move back east, but he resettled in St. Louis, not Mississippi.

Thomas and Ellen Charles's lives reflected wider national trends. Married the year that Anglo-Americans conquered California, they joined a torrent of migrants who transformed expansionist ideology into reality. Ellen's misgivings about California, however, paralleled the crisis that convulsed the Union at midcentury. She and Thomas cooperated, but their regional roots remained visible: Ellen struggled to keep house on free soil, and Thomas never returned to his wife's southern home.

Propagandists spoke of one Manifest Destiny, but the Union, and the Democratic Party that spearheaded its expansion, was as divided as the far-flung Charles family. As a result, the conquests of the 1840s unleashed sectional strife within both party and country. Democrats had long debated federal responsibility for safeguarding slavery in the South, so acquisition of a sprawling western empire raised dangerous questions: What property rights did slaveholders enjoy in federal territories? Would those rights be subject to majority control? Because so many Americans defined territorial growth as progress, the stakes in these debates were enormous.

Empire building proved rewarding and perilous for Stephen Douglas and Jefferson Davis. They fought zealously to extend the republic to the Pacific, and their triumphs earned them Senate seats. But they also clashed over reconciling white men's democracy with slaveholders' prerogatives, a perennial challenge for Democrats who traditionally opposed both abolitionism and concentrated wealth. The rift widened until by 1850 they were at each other's throats, as Douglas insisted on territorial self-government and Davis strove to shield property rights from western majorities. Even a troubled truce in 1850 failed to ensure party and national unity. Plain republicans and planters chased conflicting destinies in the antebellum West.

★ ★ ★

In hindsight, the U.S. declaration of war on Mexico in May 1846 marked a milestone on the road to civil war. But at the time, it rallied westerners by masking sectional and partisan divisions behind the pageantry of patriotism. Throughout the Mississippi Valley, Democrats, and many Whigs, flocked to the colors. Seizing the opportunity, Davis and Douglas rode wartime triumphs into the Senate.

Douglas joined his state's originally bipartisan prowar movement. Congressman Abraham Lincoln later challenged Polk's justification for the war—that Mexico had spilled American blood on American soil in southern Texas—but many Illinois Whigs initially supported the conflict. In June 1846, John J. Hardin, Douglas's old Whig rival and reputedly Illinois's first volunteer, expressed his zeal while soliciting Douglas's aid in securing a military commission: "This war ought to bring some other fruit besides that of thrashing the Mexicans," he opined, deeming California a worthy prize.[8] Hardin would command one of Illinois's four regiments. Goaded by journalists who labeled Mexicans "reptiles in the path of progressive democracy," Illinoisans volunteered in such numbers that half had to be turned away.[9]

Among those eager to "slay a Mexican," as one recruit coarsely put it, was Stephen Douglas, who sought an officer's commission.[10] Polk, however, convinced him to remain in Congress, expressing reluctance to appoint congressmen to positions created by their own votes.[11] Propriety aside, Polk needed Douglas's political support: Douglas had already endorsed Polk's rationale for war and, despite his dismay at the president's course on Oregon and internal improvements, remained a staunch administration ally.[12] Polk also valued Douglas's advice on sensitive issues, including creating a lieutenant general's position, governing conquered territory, and drafting his 1847 message to Congress.[13] By the end of his term, Polk ranked Douglas among his "most ardent and active political supporters & friends."[14]

Douglas coasted to reelection in 1846 on a wave of militarism, but he was keen on a Senate seat. Since state legislatures chose senators, Douglas campaigned principally through letters. He worried that Democratic challengers would surface after he returned to Washington and was especially concerned about John A. McClernand, a powerful rival from southern Illinois. After shoring up his support in that region known as Egypt, Douglas departed for Washington; soon after, the legislature voted 100 to 45 to send him to the Senate, commencing in December 1847.[15]

Davis pursued a different path with equal savvy. War fever burned across party lines in Mississippi, where aspiring volunteers chafed at Polk's initial call for only one regiment. According to John A. Quitman, they feared missing a war that was the South's to fight and win. "We were foremost in the cause of [Texas] annexation," he proclaimed in a public letter that belied Polk's efforts to isolate the war from slavery. "We look upon this as our own quarrel. . . . We want no aid from the abolitionists."[16] Mississippi's 2,400 volunteers placed it eleventh nationwide.[17]

Davis shared this enthusiasm and jumped at the chance for a field command. He was elected colonel of the First Mississippi Rifles after rival Alexander B. Bradford insisted that the first ballot, on which he beat Davis by fifty votes, was not decisive; Davis won on the second.[18] Despite having promised not to volunteer, Davis accepted the post without telling Varina, provoking a bitter quarrel that is conspicuously absent from her memoirs.[19] Davis was solicitous of his constituents' feelings, however, and as he departed for Mexico on the auspiciously named steamer *Star Spangled Banner*, he penned a 2,700-word public letter explaining that he had left Washington only after safeguarding Mississippi's interests, including by voting for the Walker Tariff, which lowered import duties.[20]

Colonel Davis ensured that his exit from politics was temporary. He was not a reluctant officeholder rushing back into uniform but a skilled politician keeping his options open. Rather than immediately resign from Congress, Davis entrusted his resignation letter to his brother Joseph, who withheld it until October, in case the war ended in time for Davis to return to Washington in December.[21] While away, Davis communicated with leading Mississippians, including Treasury Secretary Robert J. Walker, and with Joseph, who forwarded political intelligence. Davis's

continued attention to minor patronage matters underscored his dedication to civilian affairs.[22] In turn, commanding the First Mississippi Rifles
was the wisest political investment Davis ever made. As Zachary Taylor
and Winfield Scott could later attest, fame was among the war's most
valuable spoils. This brought out the best and worst in Davis, who exhibited cool-headed leadership under fire but indulged in unseemly quarrels
with fellow officers. Unlike his West Point education or his plantation,
Davis's military laurels were his achievements alone, and he fought hard
for them.[23]

After arriving in northeastern Mexico in August 1846, the Rifles were
assigned to John A. Quitman's brigade in the Army of Occupation, commanded by Davis's former father-in-law, Zachary Taylor.[24] They tasted
combat at Monterrey in September, where Davis led a climactic attack
on a fortified Mexican position called La Tenería, and they helped turn
the tide at the Battle of Buena Vista the following February. After other
regiments fled, the Mississippians repelled a furious attack at the cost of
forty-one killed and fifty-two wounded. Among the injured was Colonel
Davis, struck in the foot by a bullet that drove pieces of his boot and spur
deep into his flesh, inflicting a nasty wound that kept him on crutches for
two years.[25] (John J. Hardin was killed in action.) Taylor's report lauded
Davis and the Rifles, and the regiment jubilantly returned home in June
1847. Guests at a New Orleans reception held in their honor included Mississippi governor Albert Gallatin Brown, a Democrat destined to shape
Davis's career.[26]

Monterrey and Buena Vista earned Davis an enviable reputation. Hungry for heroes, newspapers praised him and his regiment to the skies.
"The Mississippi Regiment, Commanded by Davis, was . . . the bravest
of the brave at the dreadful seige [sic] of Monterrey," one reported. "They
have shown themselves to be among the best soldiers in the world."[27]
Towns named for both battles dotted the map from Alabama to Oregon,
while amateur poets, including William Faulkner's great-grandfather,
enshrined American valor in verse.[28] Davis's subordinates parlayed their
prestige into public office; junior officers won county and state elections,
and Major Alexander Bradford later went to the Confederate Congress.

But Davis regarded fame as a scarce resource and nursed several bitter feuds. Shortly after Monterrey, he sparred with the commander of a
Tennessee regiment over who first pierced the Mexican lines and asked
Quitman to support him.[29] Quitman decided that Davis was not such a
"generous and noble hearted man," and their friendship suffered.[30] Controversy over Buena Vista, site of American cowardice as well as courage,

later reached Congress and nearly provoked a duel between Davis and Illinois Democrat William H. Bissell.[31] Bissell bragged that the "'Chivalry' attempted to exalt the heroism of 'Southrons' and disparage the North," but his response sowed "confusion and mortification" among them.[32]

Davis need not have worried: Taylor's glowing report made him a celebrity, and prominent Mississippians were already considering him to replace recently deceased senator Jesse Speight.[33] In August 1847, Governor Brown offered Davis the seat as "tribute" for "heroic deeds of disinterested patriotism" and cited his knowledge of Mexicans' "weaknesses & follies," which would help him meet the challenge of governing conquered peoples.[34] Davis quickly accepted and prepared to join Douglas in the Senate four months later.[35]

★ ★ ★

Davis and Douglas entered a Senate poised to confront the consequences of Manifest Destiny. Among their first major duties was to discuss the Treaty of Guadalupe Hidalgo; ratified in March 1848, it confirmed U.S. possession of Texas and brought another 500,000 square miles under the Stars and Stripes. Well before ratification, it was clear that expansion would aggravate sectional strife. As Davis warned, "We have drawn near to that which has been for many years my dread, a division marked not by opinions, but by geographical lines."[36]

Dread notwithstanding, Senator-elect Davis put the South's interests, as he defined them, first, and he already anticipated a party rupture. "It might become necessary to unite as southern men, and to dissolve the ties which have connected us to the northern democracy," he advised Vicksburg merchant Charles J. Searles in September 1847. He euphemistically hoped northern Democrats would respect "southern institutions and southern rights" and proposed to test them at the next year's national convention, where they must accept "the equal rights of the south"—masters' property rights—in the territories. But if they evinced a "spirit of hostility," then southerners should bolt the convention. "We shall then have reached a point at which all party measures sink into insignificance under the necessity for self-preservation."[37] Resentful northern Democrats might have interpreted this as a vow to rule or ruin, but it also reflected southern Democrats' ongoing struggle to maintain national alliances while proving the party's reliability back home. Davis would scuttle the party if necessary but preferred to use it to safeguard slavery. Whether northern Democrats would cooperate remained unknown.

Meanwhile, Douglas's top priority remained Illinois and the Greater Northwest. Along with elevation to the Senate, 1847 brought major changes to Douglas's life that informed his politics. In April, he married Martha Martin, the cousin of his close friend David Settle Reid, a North Carolina congressman, and daughter of Robert Martin, a wealthy planter. The day after the wedding, Martin offered Douglas a cotton plantation in Lawrence County, Mississippi. Wary of constituent backlash, Douglas politely refused, professing ignorance about managing a slave-labor enterprise, so Martin gave the property to his daughter, stipulating that Douglas would receive one-third of the profits. When Martha died six years later, the plantation passed to their sons, Robert and Stephen, for whom Douglas discreetly managed the property until his death. He visited the plantation only three times, preferring to work through overseer James Strickland and commission agents in New Orleans, but rivals periodically denounced his investment in slavery.[38]

More politically significant was Douglas's relocation to Chicago. The city was booming when the Douglases arrived in mid-1847, having swelled from 50 inhabitants in 1830 to some 17,000. Real estate speculation had run wild in the 1830s, driven by anticipation of the Illinois and Michigan Canal. The Panic of 1837 postponed completion, but it would be finished in April 1848 and, along with harbor improvements, promised to make Chicago the capital of a vibrant regional economy. Surrounded by flourishing farmland, it was already a hub for finance and transportation, with wheat shipments increasing almost fourfold between 1842 and 1845. Chicago was also on the cusp of an even greater boom sparked by railroads. In 1848, only ten miles of track radiated from the city, but within a decade, Chicago would be the nexus of a colossal rail network that was poised to reach the Pacific. Douglas arrived just as the "opening of new channels of communication," as one editor wrote, was beginning to "change the condition and prospects of our City; increase its population; introduce capital to operate in our staples, produce, provisions, lumber, &c; [and] enlarge every avenue of commerce."[39]

Chicago's rise was not inevitable: it depended on infrastructure, including harbor improvements. In 1833, Congress spent $25,000 to cut a channel through the harbor's sandbars and invested another $200,000 over the next five years, but the bars returned to strangle shipping in 1839. Additional federal funds arrived in 1843 and 1844, but another bar formed in 1847. The Sisyphean work of harbor upkeep meant that setbacks, like Polk's veto of the 1846 river and harbor bill, painfully underlined Chicago's dependence on federal largesse. In July 1847, outraged Chicagoans hosted the Northwestern Rivers and Harbors Convention to express formally the indignation that had already inspired them to nickname the obstructions

"Polk bars." Douglas, a staunch advocate of internal improvements, had carried Chicago handily in previous elections, but since locals blamed his party's southern wing for the veto, he would have to prove that Democrats could deliver regular federal aid.[40]

Nevertheless, the dazzling prospect of future improvements fueled another real estate boom. Douglas fit in with the city elite, mostly northeastern-born merchants who bought up town lots and worked to increase their value by attracting infrastructure. In 1848, they organized the Chicago Board of Trade, an agricultural commodities exchange, and commenced an ambitious railroad-building program.[41] Douglas dove in, buying 160 acres around 31st Street and Cottage Grove Avenue, near where he is now buried, and eventually thousands more acres close to Lake Calumet and around the modern-day University of Chicago.[42] His fortunes would rise or fall with those of his vibrant new home.

Chicago's future, in turn, also depended on events far beyond its limits, since local boosters envisioned it as the heart of a region stretching from the Great Lakes to the Pacific Northwest. In his brilliant history of nineteenth-century Chicago, William Cronon explores how the railroads that penetrated Wisconsin forests, prairie farmlands, and Great Plains grazing areas made Chicago a gateway between eastern industry and western raw materials; the city thrived on and facilitated capitalist development of the West.[43] This process represented the realization of Douglas's massive dreams, for although students of antebellum politics typically focus on Kansas and the Southwest, the Greater Northwest captured his imagination. Already in 1845, he imagined a federally financed railroad stretching from Chicago to the Pacific that would "subdue[e] the wilderness, and peopl[e] it with a hardy and industrious population, who would soon have a surplus produce" to exchange for eastern goods. The railroad would develop "a continuous line of settlements from the Mississippi to the Pacific" and make Chicago the hub of a continental economy.[44]

Douglas could not attain this goal by securing internal improvements for Illinois alone; the whole West must be transformed by organizing new territories and states, giving migrants land and military protection, and building infrastructure. If successful, this program would be triply rewarding: Douglas's property would appreciate, his city and state would flourish, and his Democratic Party would triumph. But there were two potential obstacles. One was sectionalism: could northern and southern Democrats cooperate to develop the West? The other was the imbalance of power created by a curious feature of U.S. politics. For all the paeans to western pioneers, the fact was that upon moving from a state to a terri-

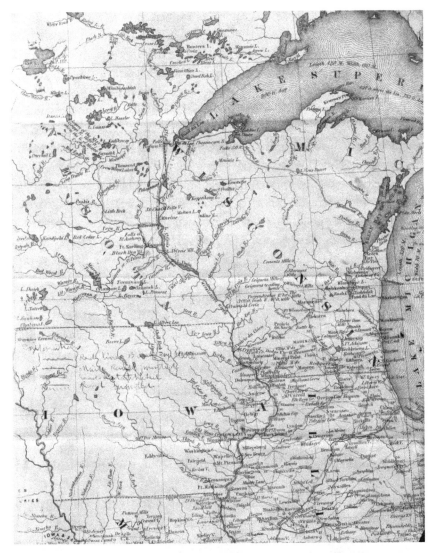

Map of Iowa, Wisconsin, and northern Illinois. (Box 41, folder 14, Stephen A. Douglas Papers; courtesy of Special Collections Research Center, University of Chicago Library)

tory, citizens lost voting representation in Congress (territorial delegates could speak but not vote) and the chance to participate in presidential elections. Thus, western voices could easily be drowned out by thunderous eastern disputes over slavery.

Acutely aware of both hazards, Senator-elect Douglas undertook to represent an extended constituency, which included Illinoisans and white residents of a wider western empire. Confident that a rising tide would float all boats from Lake Michigan to San Francisco Bay, Douglas resolved to promote regional development.[45] As what one supporter called "the acknowledged representative and advocate of the interests and principles of the people of the North West," Douglas would become a western gadfly, pressuring Congress to address the region's urgent needs.[46] This strategy shaped Douglas's political calculations. Scholars typically foreground his position on slavery, viewing him as impartial or amoral depending on whether they see sectional conciliation as noble compromise or shameful appeasement. But Douglas's priorities were different; for him, the West was not a battleground between slavery and freedom but a region with its own pressing interests. Ignoring this outlook distorts Douglas's career. Admirers, for instance, have lauded Douglas as a Union saver, obscuring the point that Douglas resisted sectionalism because it diverted attention from his western constituency.[47] For Douglas, sectional compromise was not an end in itself but a means to advance other goals.

When Davis and Douglas arrived in the Senate, they sought to harness the Democracy to two vast regions that transcended their home states. The southern sentinel would safeguard slaveholders' current and prospective domain, while the western gadfly would empower pioneers to harvest the fruits of empire. Their collision would swell disputes over property and democracy to continental proportions.

★ ★ ★

Davis and Douglas's encounters in the Thirtieth Congress exposed antagonisms that boded ill for their party and country, particularly with a presidential election looming. Despite the triumph over Mexico, neither the Democracy nor the Union seemed secure.

Douglas quickly began promoting the Greater Northwest. He presented a petition from Illinoisans seeking homestead legislation; it was buried in the Committee on Public Lands.[48] He tried to organize the Nebraska Territory; like his prior effort in the House, the bill went nowhere.[49] Convinced that political organization would encourage migration and economic growth, Douglas also attempted to create new territories of Oregon and Minnesota and to admit the state of Wisconsin.[50] Frustrated by delay and alarmed by the violent aftershocks of a massacre at the Whitman Mission in modern-day Washington State, Douglas rebuked sluggish senators. "If we adjourn without establishing the Territorial Governments," he scolded, "we shall be responsible for the blood of men, women, and children, which shall be shed."[51]

Douglas's agenda stalled amid sectional animosity, which swelled when several dozen enslaved people attempted to escape from Washington,

D.C., on a schooner named the *Pearl*. After recapturing the fugitives, pro-slavery rioters assailed abolitionist newspaper editor Gamaliel Bailey, whose press was rescued by District police. Disgusted, New Hampshire's staunchly antislavery senator John P. Hale, an ex-Democrat who left the party over Texas annexation, sought to make the District responsible for damages. His bill polarized senators along sectional lines.[52] Speaking as a southern sentry, not a concerned nationalist, Davis excoriated the escape plot and proclaimed himself ready for civil war.[53]

Douglas rebuked extremists in both sections but aimed his sharpest barbs southward. "It is the speeches of southern men ... breathing a fanat-icism as wild and as reckless as that of the senator from New Hampshire, which creates abolitionism in the North," he asserted. This prefigured his oft-repeated claim that proslavery radicalism and antislavery radicalism were two sides of the same coin, but here he singled out southern leaders. Bluntly rejecting John C. Calhoun's claim that congressional proslavery crusaders acted in self-defense, Douglas accused them of blowing the *Pearl* incident out of proportion and aggravating the tumult on which abolitionists thrived.[54]

While Douglas sparred with southerners, Calhoun yielded leader-ship of the proslavery phalanx to younger hands, and Davis raced to the fore.[55] Aware that his outrage might be attributed to fear of revolt, Davis repeated an old litany: slaves were "happy and contented"; he had "no more dread of our slaves than I have of our cattle"; and he resented abo-litionists only for being insulting.[56] These remarks reflected Davis's flu-ency in an increasingly strident proslavery idiom. Whether he read much proslavery theory, including a recently published book by fellow Missis-sippian Matthew Estes, is not clear, but Davis championed slavery as a positive good.[57]

Douglas replied from his own sectional position. Speaking as a north-ern moderate trapped between "abolitionism" and "that extreme [pro-slavery] course . . . which is akin to abolitionism," he chided southern-ers who baited abolitionists and then expected northern allies to rescue them. There were limits to what plain republicans would do for planters. Douglas would defend their basic rights but would never "take the posi-tion that slavery is a positive good—a positive blessing." Northerners had chosen free labor and if "slavery be a blessing," he concluded in an implicit response to Davis, "it is your blessing; if it be a curse, it is your curse."[58] The divide between a moderate "us" and proslavery "you" illuminated the widening rift among Democrats. Certainly, Douglas opposed antislavery protest, belying Varina Davis's later accusation that he took Hale's side.[59]

But he also rejected southerners' bid to make proslavery dogma into party orthodoxy. Defining slavery as neither a positive good nor an intolerable evil, Douglas assumed a tenuous position that appeared amoral to anti-slavery activists and inadequate to proslavery ideologues.

Meanwhile, sectionalism hamstrung Douglas's efforts to organize the Oregon Territory. In 1843, Anglo-American migrants had crafted a provisional government and legal code, including a ban on slavery, only to languish in political limbo. Disputes over the Southwest are better remembered today, but contemporaries regarded Oregon as an import-ant precedent, and southern congressmen resisted any legislation that might hamper slavery's extension.[60] Between 1846 and 1848, the north-ern-dominated House of Representatives passed several territorial bills that upheld the local slavery prohibition, but southerners squelched them in the Senate. Calhoun held that Congress must not exclude slavery from the territories, which were the common property of the states, although he endorsed extension of the Missouri Compromise line, which would secure slavery in most lands likely to be seized from Mexico.[61] The result was congressional gridlock. By 1848, five years after the onset of major Anglo-American migration, Oregon still lacked a recognized territorial government. Frustrated but undeterred, Douglas introduced his fourth Oregon bill that January.[62]

Later that summer, Oregon dominated Senate business. Alarmed by Douglas's bill, which legitimized the provisional government's slav-ery prohibition, Davis counterattacked in a two-hour speech on July 12. Scholars rightly stress the importance of this address, in which Davis, worried that failure to hold the territorial line would imperil slavery across the South, extolled slavery's benevolence and warned of disunion.[63] He defined the controversy in terms of property rights versus majority rule and sought ironclad safeguards for the former. Disclaiming any desire to "force slavery into the Territory of Oregon," Davis denied that the federal government could prohibit slavery by validating territorial legislation and demanded protection for "those rights of property which existed before the Constitution, and which were guarantied by it." This anticipated a doctrine that would flourish after the 1857 *Dred Scott* deci-sion: the Constitution recognized masters' primordial property rights throughout its jurisdiction. To allow Oregon's motley missionaries and mountain men to bar slavery was to submit property rights to the whims of western adventurers. Thus, Davis was not defending localism against centralization; rather, he would empower governments to protect, but never infringe, masters' prerogatives. Neither local nor national majorities could despoil the ancient right of property in man.[64]

Meanwhile, Douglas hustled for votes. Initially, extending the Missouri Compromise line seemed a promising solution, so he amended the Oregon bill to justify the slavery prohibition by virtue of the territory's position north of 36° 30′. But since this might also settle the pending dispute over the Mexican Cession, it alienated northern congressmen who wanted to exclude slavery from the Southwest. They preferred the House's Oregon bill, which extended the Northwest Ordinance's slavery ban and affirmed the territorial prohibition.[65] Just before adjourning in August, the Senate narrowly voted to recede from Douglas's amendment and pass the House version. All twenty-five nays came from southerners, including Davis, while Douglas joined the chiefly northern majority.[66]

Douglas had his Oregon bill, but his agenda's future looked grim. Whatever unity they derived from racism, anti-abolitionism, and Manifest Destiny, northern and southern Democrats could not agree on how to govern. In the key vote on Oregon, northern Democrats unanimously (15–0) supported the House bill, while southern Democrats were solidly (16–2) opposed. Without help from northern Whigs, Douglas would have failed again. This boded ill for the Democracy's long-term unity and Douglas's prospects of enlisting the party behind his western program. The controversy left two other legacies. First, Douglas had abandoned the Missouri Compromise principle and embraced local control to break the logjam. Second, slavery's fate in the newly conquered southwestern empire remained unsettled. As the 1848 presidential canvass heated up, this issue battered both parties and threatened the Union.[67]

★ ★ ★

With party unity cracking under sectional pressure, Whigs and Democrats scrambled to contain the territorial controversy. Slavery expansion roiled American politics throughout the conflict with Mexico, and by war's end in 1848, four distinct positions had crystallized.[68]

At one extreme was the call for "free soil": Congress must ban slavery from every territory. Proponents rallied behind the Wilmot Proviso, an amendment to an appropriations bill offered by Pennsylvania Democrat David Wilmot in August 1846 that would outlaw slavery in all conquered Mexican lands. Born of intraparty rivalry and endorsed by many northern Democrats frustrated by Polk's administration, the proviso repeatedly passed the House but never the Senate.[69] In mid-1848, advocates organized the Free-Soil Party, which demanded removal of federal support for slavery and adopted elements of Douglas's agenda, including river and harbor improvements and homestead legislation. With Martin Van Buren atop their presidential ticket, Free-Soilers exhorted northerners to unite against the slave power.[70]

Davis and Douglas both opposed the free-soil movement but for different reasons. Like many southerners, Davis believed that its moderate veneer concealed a radical core. Slavery's foes, he argued, had many names—"anti-slavery men, non-extensionists, emancipationists, liberty party, freesoil party, &c."—but belonged to "one family, differing somewhat in their mode of attack, but not at all in the final purpose of it." By excluding slaveholders from the territories, they would seize "the unchecked power of a three-fourths majority" and abolish slavery by constitutional amendment.[71] The proviso also violated slaveholders' property rights, which Davis often framed in sectional terms: since the territories belonged to the whole country, "the South" must have access to them. He echoed southern threats that adoption of the proviso would justify secession.[72]

Douglas did not regard free-soilism as an existential threat, but he did fear its impact on party and national unity. Most Illinois representatives opposed the proviso in 1846, but Chicago Democrat John Wentworth, a key ally on internal improvements, voted for it, and on a subsequent vote in 1847, northwestern Democrats divided, 57 percent favoring the proviso and 37 percent opposing it.[73] Back home, some editors urged Democrats to unite behind Wilmot. The Democratic sheet from Douglas's old hometown of Jacksonville, the *Prairie Argus*, vigorously opposed "extension of slavery over countries which we may acquire and in which it does not exist."[74] Ottawa Democrats concurred, denouncing the "monstrous heresy" that masters could take slaves into any territory and demanding that Oregon and the Mexican Cession remain "the common property of the freeman."[75] By January 1849, Free-Soilers controlled the state legislature and instructed Douglas to support legislation barring slavery from the Mexican Cession. Some predicted he would resign in protest.[76]

Douglas retained his Senate seat and his hostility to free soil, but his logic differed from Davis's. He neither denounced the proviso as a plot against property rights nor denied Congress's authority to pass it. Instead, he deemed it impolitic and unnecessary. Douglas argued that slavery could never flourish in the Mexican Cession: it was already illegal there because of Mexican laws; the land would not support plantation agriculture; locals and likely migrants favored freedom. As he told a Springfield audience in October 1849, the cession "would forever remain free under all circumstances, by the decree of the people themselves," no matter what Congress did. Thus, while the proviso could do no good, it could cause harm by alienating the South. For foes of slavery expansion, "non-interference was the true doctrine" because it would yield free soil without igniting conflict.[77] Douglas's early critique of the proviso envisioned similar results through subtler means, a point that southern rivals would turn against him.

By 1850, Douglas also stressed that free-soilism violated "the great principle of self-government." Rebuking Davis, Douglas held that prohibiting slavery in a territory "is no violation of the rights of the Southern states" because no state or section had any inherent claim to western lands.[78] Rather, it was territorial voters who would be wronged by the proviso. Thus, while Davis rejected the proviso for subverting southerners' property rights, Douglas assailed it for infringing the rights of western majorities. The ramifications of this divergence would develop over time, but it was already evident that free soil's opponents did not march in lockstep.

Free soil's polar opposite was the dogma that slavery followed the flag into every territory. Outlined by Calhoun in February 1847 and honed during the Oregon debate, the "common property" doctrine held that since the states jointly owned the territories, Congress, as their agent, must safeguard slavery in each one, essentially extending state law into the territories by federal fiat.[79] Proponents often conflated masters' property rights with southern sectional rights, thus transmuting individual liberties into regional prerogatives.

Davis's and Douglas's critiques of free soil informed their conflicting views of the common-property doctrine. Douglas rejected it for the same reason that he opposed the Wilmot Proviso: it violated western self-government in the name of a nonexistent sectional right.[80] But most southern Democrats endorsed Calhoun's bid to shield masters' property rights from hostile majorities.[81] In his 1847 letter to Searles, Davis insisted upon "the equal right of the south with the north in the territory held as the common property of the United States" and never wavered.[82] The doctrine quickly gained traction in Mississippi. In his January 1848 message to the legislature, Governor Brown rejected the power of "an anti-slavery majority in Congress" to "exclude slavery from a territory." A "citizen of Mississippi," he proclaimed, "may settle with his slave property in the territory of the United States, with as little constitutional hindrance as a citizen from any other state may settle with any other species of property."[83] Mississippi voters concurred in public meetings, with Canton residents declaring that violation of the common property doctrine would "subvert the Union itself."[84]

Between these extremes were two possible compromises. One was to divide the West between free and slave territory by extending the Missouri Compromise line to the Pacific. Davis and Douglas both endorsed this idea during the Mexican War, Douglas viewing it as a pragmatic solution and Davis regarding it as a reasonable, if constitutionally dubious, method to safeguard slavery in most of the Mexican Cession.[85] In mid-1848, Polk urged Congress to extend the 36° 30′ line and settle the matter.[86] That August, Douglas and Davis voted with a Senate majority for such a measure, but antislavery northerners, determined to stop slavery's expansion, defeated it in the House.[87] The venerable compromise could not close the ragged wound ripped open by Manifest Destiny.

More promising was a fourth option known as "non-intervention," "squatter sovereignty," or "popular sovereignty." The diverse meanings attached to the doctrine's sundry names reflected its malleability, but essentially popular sovereignty would shift decision-making from Congress to the territories. Deference to territorial self-government was not new; for half a century, Congress had allowed voters in areas where slavery was not banned by federal law (south of the Ohio River and the Missouri Compromise line) to allow or prohibit slavery, correctly anticipating that they would sanction an institution already present there.[88] The novelty was applying popular sovereignty to areas, like the Mexican Cession, where slavery previously had been illegal. The political calculus was complex: many northerners recoiled from opening free territory to slavery, while many southerners doubted that local control would foster slavery in places where it lacked a foothold. But northern Democrats like George M. Dallas, Daniel S. Dickinson, and Lewis Cass offered popular sovereignty as an antidote for sectionalism.[89] In a famous December 1847 letter to Tennessee Democrat Alfred O. P. Nicholson, Cass opined that Congress should create territories and then leave "the people . . . in their respective local governments" free to "regulate their internal concerns in their own way."[90] This raised more questions than it answered. When and how could territories decide on slavery, and what was its status until then? Was popular sovereignty a principled policy or a cowardly dodge? Was it a proslavery ploy, an antislavery swindle, or truly impartial? Historians have debated these issues almost as fervently as antebellum Americans did, producing a rich literature on popular sovereignty's relationship to slavery, expansion, and partisanship.[91]

Davis's and Douglas's responses to popular sovereignty's rising prominence illuminate several crucial points. Davis's reaction highlights the sometimes-neglected proslavery critique of the doctrine.[92] Because most historians sympathize with slavery's foes, it is easy to adopt their criticism of popular sovereignty as a proslavery perversion of democracy.[93] But this obscures Davis's vehement hostility to the antislavery wolf he saw lurking in the doctrine's fleecy garb. On December 25, 1847, one day after Cass wrote to Nicholson, Davis confronted colleague Henry S. Foote at a Christmas party and berated him for defending popular sovereignty. When Foote barked back, Davis dropped his crutches, leaped on Foote, and beat him until onlookers pulled them apart. Davis wanted to settle things with pistols but agreed to dismiss the fracas as a "Christmas frolic."[94]

If Davis was ready for a yuletide brawl with a fellow Mississippian, he was not likely to pull punches against popular sovereignty's northern promoters. Predictably, he denounced those who insisted that popular sovereignty empowered territorial legislatures to ban slavery, a policy he regarded as equivalent to the Wilmot Proviso. Since Congress could not prohibit slavery in the territories, Davis argued, neither could the territorial governments that Congress created. The notion that territories could block slavery was a "northern" creed that was "absolutely wrong."[95] Davis clarified his views in 1850, when he sought to amend a territorial bill to "restrict the territorial legislature from action hostile to property, but not from making necessary provisions for its protection."[96] Local majority rule must be circumscribed to make the West safe for slavery. Other southern Democrats agreed that the northern version of popular sovereignty would inevitably yield free soil across the West. In 1848, North Carolina's James C. Dobbin, who later served with Davis in Franklin Pierce's cabinet, insisted that territorial legislatures had "*no right* to pass a law to prohibit slavery," for this would "practically exclude the slaveholder forever."[97] This logic would lead proslavery southerners down an antidemocratic path as they likened popular sovereignty—often derided as "squatter sovereignty"—to mob rule. Lincoln loathed popular sovereignty for subordinating morality to majoritarianism, but Davis assailed it for subjecting property rights to the whim of "King Numbers."

Meanwhile, Douglas climbed on the popular sovereignty bandwagon. Most immediately, he hoped it would reunite Democrats in the 1848 presidential election, and he offered some of his earliest public statements about the doctrine during the canvass.[98] Control over slavery, he proclaimed, "belongs entirely with the State or Territory." Each one may "determine upon what system or basis its institutions and society shall be organized," and federal intervention would be a "flagrant usurpation." This, he declared, was the "democratic creed."[99] He implicitly equated state and territorial authority, suggesting that both could establish or prohibit slavery at any time. Douglas spent the next decade cultivating this interpretation of territorial self-rule, but its seeds were already germinating. By defining his position as party dogma, moreover, Douglas risked alienating southern advocates of the common-property doctrine. He and Davis rejected the Wilmot Proviso, but their alternatives were already starkly opposed.

Douglas's deepening commitment to popular sovereignty reflected several important corollary beliefs, some of which were anathema to Davis. One was Douglas's assumption that popular sovereignty would produce free states. Arguments about Douglas's innermost thoughts on slavery have sometimes elided his predictions, echoed by other northern Democrats, about freedom's future in the West.[100] Douglas told northern audiences that the Wilmot Proviso was unnecessary because local majorities would oppose slavery, and he made similar claims on the Senate floor. In March 1850, he envisioned seventeen new states in the West, all of them "free States, whether Congress shall prohibit slavery or not."[101] These forecasts, which unwittingly validated charges that popular sovereignty was a cloaked Wilmot Proviso, alienated southerners. Perhaps for this reason, Douglas later stopped making them, even in situations, such as his 1858 Senate campaign, when they might have rallied northern support.[102]

The second was Douglas's belief that popular sovereignty conformed to the lessons of Illinois history. He often contradicted Free-Soilers by arguing that it was local lawmaking, not the Northwest Ordinance, that had preserved the Northwest for freedom. "We tried slavery once in Illinois," Douglas remarked in a typical 1848 speech. "It did not suit our circumstances or habits, and we turned philanthropic, and abolished it."[103] Douglas regularly reiterated this point, insisting that the ordinance was "practically a dead letter" and that the northwestern states "became free . . . by virtue of their own will, solemnly recorded in the fundamental laws of their own making and execution."[104] He challenged Free-Soilers by denying the efficacy of federal legislation and casting local self-rule as a means for slavery's restriction while mollifying southerners by presenting local determination as unavoidable; popular sovereignty, Douglas suggested, made a virtue of inevitability.

Douglas's historical argument was both pragmatic and astoundingly naive. His doubts about federal influence over distant territories were plausible, and recent scholarship echoes his emphasis on the practical limits of national power.[105] But Douglas trusted that a conflict that defied compromise in Congress could be resolved smoothly at the territorial level. He assumed that it would be easy to divine the popular will and that local minorities would acquiesce to majority decisions. If Anglo-American settlers had been angels, popular sovereignty might have worked this way. Reality was devilishly different.

Third was Douglas's confidence that popular sovereignty was valuable for reasons that transcended slavery. It was, for one, eminently compatible with his political instincts. As historian Martin H. Quitt has shown, Douglas's enthusiasm for local majoritarianism long predated 1848 and shaped his thinking on issues from suffrage requirements to legislative apportionment.[106] Popular sovereignty also promised to loosen the sectional gridlock that impeded his western agenda. Westerners often complained about federal neglect and blamed sectionalism for problems like inadequate military protection and nonexistent infrastructure.[107] Frustration encouraged separatism: according to one Californian, westerners despised Congress's "snail like pace" and might well secede over the lack of "prompt action in matters of legislation and improvements."[108] Correspondents from Minnesota to California regularly solicited Douglas's aid, recognizing that his chairmanship of the Territorial Committee made him an invaluable advocate.[109] Entreaties from these unofficial constituents, including one who dubbed him "the champion of the Territories," reinforced Douglas's resolve to use popular sovereignty to circumvent sectional stalemate.[110]

Thus, popular sovereignty appealed to Douglas because it could reduce western dependence on federal power by reconfiguring the relationship between federal and territorial authority. Although often remembered as a model of Jeffersonian foresight, the territorial system's undemocratic features grated at western sensibilities: Congress controlled the financing and planning of internal improvements and could nullify territorial laws; presidents appointed territorial officers; and territorial voters lacked voting representation in Congress and any voice in presidential elections.[111] One critic insisted that the territories fared worse than Ireland under British rule.[112] The case of Oregon in the early 1850s is instructive: in a largely Democratic territory, appointment of local officers by Whig president Millard Fillmore felt oppressive. To make the system *"tolerable,"* stressed an Oregonian, voters must have the right "of *electing* their own officers."[113] Even the prospect of Democratic victory in 1852 only reminded Oregonians that they were "silent spectators" of national politics. "How," one asked, "does a man lose his capacity or rights in a journey from the States to Oregon?"[114] Any policy that expanded territorial autonomy was bound to be popular in the West.

Douglas channeled these grievances into his case for territorial self-rule, including in debates against southern Democrats seeking to limit local power over slavery. If citizens were "capable of self-government" before moving west, Douglas proclaimed, they were certainly not less capable upon arrival.[115] He directed similar arguments against Free-Soilers, who would grant territorial authority over every issue save slavery. Spiking his rhetoric with racism, Douglas blasted "Abolitionists" for allowing westerners to govern everything except "a few miserable negroes."[116] Entwined with Douglas's bigotry was impatience with sectionalism and a desire to unlock federal support for western development.

Popular sovereignty's growing prominence widened the rift among Democrats. For Douglas, it was a means to sidestep congressional controversies and empower his extended constituency. For Davis, it was a threat to property rights, which must be circumscribed by the common-property doctrine. With clarity of hindsight, Republican James G. Blaine recalled that the "Democratic doctrine of the North and the Democratic doctrine of the South were . . . in logic and in fact, irreconcilably hostile."[117] The 1848 election, and the two tumultuous years that followed, exposed the severity of Democrats' irrepressible conflict.

★ ★ ★

The 1848 presidential contest revealed the resilience of partisan allegiances and the feebleness of popular sovereignty as a unifying principle. Davis, the good soldier, remained loyal despite the Democracy's stance on territorial self-government, while Douglas campaigned as zealously for popular sovereignty as he did for the party's nominee. Both senators kept their states in the Democratic column but faced a disappointing defeat nationwide.

Internally divided and anticipating a Whig ticket graced by a war hero, Democrats girded for what Douglas predicted would be "a fearful struggle" to retain the presidency.[118] A few Illinoisans, including Free-Soil congressman John Wentworth, advocated Douglas's nomination, but the muffled boom quickly subsided.[119] Still, Douglas welcomed the results of May's national convention, which aligned the Democracy behind popular sovereignty by nominating Lewis Cass. One incident clouded the proceedings: alarmed by the affirmation of popular sovereignty, Alabama delegate William Lowndes Yancey tried to place Democrats on record denying that Congress or a local legislature could bar slavery from a territory; when his motion was crushed 216 to 36, Yancey, a fellow Alabamian, and the entire Florida delegation stormed out.[120] Coupled with a revolt among antislavery Democrats, who helped launch the Free-Soil Party that summer, Yancey's bolt highlighted the precariousness of the platform on which Cass and Douglas wanted to perch.

Douglas denounced free-soilism and advocated popular sovereignty throughout the contest. Back home, damage to the Illinois Democracy was mitigated by Wentworth's adherence to the regular ticket. Meanwhile, Douglas stumped for Cass on a southern tour from North Carolina to Louisiana, in which he praised popular sovereignty as the only pragmatic solution to the territorial controversy.[121] From Mississippi, he reported to Cass that southern Democrats would support him, although he also warned against writing public letters; the less Cass said about territorial policy, the better.[122]

But all was not rosy in the South, where Cass's northern background inspired withering Whig attacks on the nominee and his apostles. One Whig paper condemned Douglas's presence at North Carolina's Democratic convention, calling him an "abolition intruder."[123] Whigs' nomination of Zachary Taylor, a Mexican War hero and wealthy Louisiana planter, burnished their sectional credentials. The previously apolitical soldier had little relevant experience and no deep-rooted party ties, but his ownership of more than 100 people reassured many southern voters unsettled by two years of alarm.[124]

The election placed Davis in a quandary. He felt little hostility to the Whig ticket: Taylor was a fellow southern planter and, as Davis's former commanding officer and father-in-law, was bound to the Mississippian by class, camaraderie, and kinship. They had maintained a politically candid correspondence throughout the war.[125] Meanwhile, the Democratic nomination stirred scant enthusiasm in Davis, who complained privately that Cass was too Whiggish on internal improvements and held "unpalatable" views on slavery.[126]

Davis adapted by scorning popular sovereignty and campaigning for Cass on a Calhounian platform. In Mississippi, he denounced Democratic turncoats—southerners who voted for the Oregon bill and northerners allegedly tainted by antislavery—more loudly than he praised Cass. He rejected territorial control over slavery as "palpably wrong and exceedingly contemptible" and emphasized Cass's willingness to veto the Wilmot Proviso.[127] Some speeches read less like partisan oratory and more like sectional war cries, as Davis deprecated northern plans to monopolize the West and abolish slavery.[128] These themes coexisted uneasily with Davis's endorsement of a northern-led ticket and suggested that he was looking past the election to rally southern voters against a hostile northern host. In late October, he blended sectional and partisan appeals in a public letter that denounced congressional or territorial prohibitions of slavery as "absolutely wrong," urged "unanimity" in slavery's defense, and exhorted Mississippians to vote Democratic.[129] Seeking to unite southern voters behind the Democracy, Davis advanced a territorial doctrine that the party had rejected at the national convention. Davis and Douglas's tug-of-war over Democratic dogma intensified during the 1848 canvass; united only by party loyalty and opposition to Free-Soilers, they lacked a common philosophy.

Cass's rickety campaign creaked along to defeat. Nationwide, Democrats' share of the popular vote dropped from 49.5 percent in 1844 to just 42.5 percent, and while Taylor and Cass both won fifteen states, Taylor carried the Electoral College, 163–127. Cass ran well in his home region, sweeping the Northwest and returning Ohio, which Polk had lost, to the Democratic column. But the Free-Soil Party's strength was unmistakable; in Illinois, it garnered nearly 13 percent of the popular vote and ran particularly well in and around Chicago's Cook County, formerly a Democratic stronghold. Southern returns were equally disquieting: Cass and his vulnerable territorial policy lost eight out of fifteen slave states, including two in the Deep South (Georgia and Louisiana) that had backed Polk. A majority (52 percent) of southern voters supported Taylor. Cass won by a nose in Mississippi, but his 50.6 percent of the popular vote fell far short of Polk's 57 percent.[130]

Election postmortems foreshadowed future difficulties. Mississippi Democrats blamed the nominee, noting how easily Whigs spread rumors that Davis hated his party's standard-bearer.[131] Some even admitted voting for Taylor. One, who self-identified as "a democrat a whole democrat & nothing but a democrat," confessed his inability to support Cass, "a very exceptional specimen of democracy to say the least."[132] Meanwhile, Illinois Democrats, unnerved by free-soilism, hoped to settle the territorial question with popular sovereignty.[133] Thus, northern Democrats would depend upon the very doctrine that had hobbled their southern counterparts. Intended to harmonize a discordant party, popular sovereignty exposed Democrats to antislavery and proslavery criticism without resolving their internal conflicts. With the Mexican Cession still roiling national politics, they ended 1848 defeated and divided.

★ ★ ★

The United States paid for the national sin of slavery in the Civil War, but the conflict's cost might also be added to the bill for westward expansion. Tempted by new territory, Democrats discovered, as historian Frederick Merk remarked, that Manifest Destiny was a "bomb wrapped up in idealism."[134] Following Cass's defeat, many Democrats hoped to dispose of the Mexican Cession quickly, lest prolonged debate shatter brittle party ties. Instead, political war raged for two years before Douglas brokered an armistice.

Disturbed by party infighting and fearful that irate Californians might secede and take Oregon with them, lame-duck president Polk urged rapid action.[135] Early in Congress's 1848–49 session, Douglas, who shared Polk's concerns and westerners' impatience, proposed bypassing the territorial stage by admitting the Mexican Cession as one enormous state. Polk preferred a separate government for New Mexico but liked the basic plan, which would allow local decision-making on slavery.[136] He threw his waning influence behind it, courting congressional support at dinner parties and private meetings.[137] In the Senate, Douglas demanded passage of any bill to provide a government for gold-crazed California. The western gadfly cared little about details, so long as Congress tightened the fragile bonds of a continental Union.[138]

These efforts collided with northern free-soilism and southern mistrust. In the House, northerners pressed for a federal ban on slavery throughout the Mexican Cession. Meanwhile, southern senators recognized that Douglas's plan would produce a free state, since few slaveholders had moved to the Southwest. After defending local control where it would yield proslavery outcomes, they now rejected territorial self-rule and immediate statehood as free-soil stratagems. By referring it to the southern-dominated Judiciary Committee rather than to Douglas's Territorial Committee, proslavery senators killed the California bill.[139]

The seething controversy nudged southern Democrats closer to Calhoun. In February 1849, Davis and the entire Mississippi delegation joined a total of forty-eight southern senators and representatives in signing Calhoun's "Southern Address," a manifesto that blamed antislavery aggression for thirty years of strife, from the Missouri crisis to clashes over Oregon and California. "The great body of the North is united against our peculiar institution," Calhoun warned, and emancipation would condemn the South to "disorder, anarchy, poverty, misery, and wretchedness." United resistance was vital, for northerners would relent only when convinced of white southern resolve to safeguard slavery at all costs. Partisanship had distracted southern voters, but if they subordinated everything to slavery's defense, they could protect themselves, in the Union or out of it.[140]

At a sectional caucus early in the session, Calhoun exhorted southern colleagues to endorse his address, but skeptics regarded it as another ploy to build a southern party and become president. Georgia's Howell Cobb privately grumbled that it would be a "national blessing" if the Lord called Calhoun "home."[141] He did not sign the address. Since only 48 of 124 southerners approved it, some historians regard the episode as a case of moderation defeating extremism.[142] But the address resonated with many Democrats; while only 2 of 48 southern Whigs signed Calhoun's credo, 46 of 76 southern Democrats endorsed it. In the crucible of territorial debate, much of the southern Democracy was melding with Calhoun's fire-eating phalanx.[143]

Davis's support for the address requires careful analysis. Contemporaries and scholars have identified him as Calhoun's political heir; one Vicksburg paper dubbed him "the Calhoun of Mississippi."[144] But he was less Calhoun's disciple than a fellow traveler, and this had fateful consequences for the Democratic Party. Certainly, Calhoun had given Davis vital support, particularly at a Vicksburg reception where Davis launched his congressional career in 1845.[145] In turn, Davis had favored Calhoun for president in 1844 and championed the common-property doctrine; after Calhoun's death in 1850, Davis would escort his remains to Charleston.[146] But Davis sometimes defied Calhounian orthodoxy. Although he loathed Andrew Jackson's response to the Nullification Crisis, Davis questioned a state's right to nullify federal laws, suggesting it should secede instead.[147] Calhoun recoiled from extensive Mexican conquests, fearing sectional turmoil and the incorporation of free, nonwhite masses into the Union, while Davis tried to amend the Treaty of Guadalupe Hidalgo to grab additional territory.[148] Most importantly, Davis and Calhoun divided over the Democratic Party. Deeply suspicious of national parties and determined to unite southern voters, Calhoun refused to endorse any candidate in 1848, accusing both parties of pandering to the antislavery northern majority.[149] Davis, a staunch partisan, had swallowed hard and stumped for Cass, deeming a southern party unnecessary because he believed the Democracy could be the vehicle for proslavery politics.[150] He would achieve Calhounian ends using Jacksonian means, forging sectional unity by honing the national Democratic Party into a proslavery weapon. The strategy was fraught with danger, not least because it would require northern Democrats to accept a frankly proslavery party line.

While Davis charted his risky course, Douglas labored on his western agenda. On the first day of the 1848–49 session, Douglas announced his intention to create new territories of Nebraska and Minnesota and handle the Mexican Cession.[151] This legislative package, promised his Springfield mouthpiece, would foster western development without promoting slavery, which was unlikely to enter the projected territories.[152] Sidetracked by debate over the Southwest, Douglas failed again on Nebraska but did pass a Minnesota territorial bill in March, thus sealing his bond with the Minnesotans in his unofficial western constituency.[153] Thereafter, Douglas zealously sought appropriations for the territory whose development—driven by urban boosterism, commercial agriculture, and federal aid—followed his blueprint for the Greater Northwest. Minnesotans regularly expressed their gratitude; one deemed Douglas "the Guardian in Chief of all northwestern interests."[154] The investment paid partisan dividends in 1858 when Minnesota achieved statehood with a Democratic governor and congressman and two Democratic senators, including Henry M. Rice, who lived next door to Douglas on I Street, on what Washingtonians called "Douglas Row" or "Minnesota Row."[155]

★ ★ ★

By 1850, territorial controversy had unleashed a political tempest that battered the Democracy and the Union. The antagonism between Davis's and Douglas's wings of their party lingered long after the midcentury crisis, from which they drew dramatically divergent lessons.

Political storm clouds thickened over Mississippi in 1849 as voters met to denounce free-soilism and prepare for a statewide convention in October.[156] Encouraged by this activity, Calhoun reached out to key Mississippians, including Collin S. Tarpley, a Hinds County lawyer, Democrat, and staunch Davis ally. In early July, Calhoun suggested that the October convention call for a regional meeting where delegates could dictate terms to the North and prepare for possible secession.[157] Mississippi's October convention followed suit, endorsing the common-property doctrine and summoning a sectional conclave to meet at Nashville the following June. Soon after, in state elections, Mississippi voters overwhelmingly backed hardline proslavery Democrats. The state's congressional delegation would be uniformly Democratic, large Democratic majorities would control both houses of the legislature, and firebrand John A. Quitman won 70 percent of the votes in the gubernatorial contest.[158] In his blistering inaugural, Quitman praised "the domestic slavery of an inferior race" and denounced efforts to exclude slavery from the "common territory" as part of an abolitionist "war of extermination."[159]

Davis joined the chorus of protest. In May 1849, he counseled resistance to antislavery aggression and insisted that slavery was indispensable to developing sparsely populated western lands. Although he cautioned against rashness, Davis predicted that southern secession would desolate the northern economy and exhorted white Mississippians to fight if their demands were rejected.[160] Subsequently, he condemned popular sovereignty, averred that slaveholders were entitled to federal protection of their property rights, and spoke of exploiting slave labor in California gold mines.[161] He also corresponded privately with proslavery theorist Samuel A. Cartwright. After vindicating the African slave trade and extolling cheap slave-grown produce as a boon for the world's poor, Davis reiterated his faith in sectional solidarity as a deterrent against northern aggression.[162] His position was clear: slavery's expansion must be guaranteed for the sake of southern security and global prosperity. Proslavery activism in Mississippi convinced him that he spoke for that dominant minority of its inhabitants often called "the people."

Meanwhile, Douglas concentrated on western development. Early in the first session (1849–50) of the Thirty-First Congress, he introduced a bill to grant 160 acres to settlers who cultivated public lands for four years, although his insistence that homestead legislation served national interests proved unavailing.[163] Despite objections from Davis and other southerners, however, Douglas notched a momentous victory by securing a land grant to finance construction of the Illinois Central Railroad. When the Illinois portion was completed in 1856, it fueled the state's booming economy from Galena and Chicago to Cairo. Needing southern votes and keen to stiffen cross-sectional ties with railroad iron, Douglas also extended the projected line south to Mobile. Thus, the bill reflected Douglas's preferred style of lawmaking: compromise converted enough southern skeptics to pass a measure that would foster western economic development and national unity while netting Douglas a profit on Chicago land he later sold to the railroad.[164] One Illinoisan rejoiced that Douglas had "*pioneered* the way in the great work of internal improvements in the *West*" and made Illinois "among the best States of the Union."[165]

Slavery expansion dominated the session, however, so Douglas slid into the role of Union saver while Davis remained the southern sentinel. In late January, Kentucky's venerable Henry Clay presented a compromise package that addressed the Mexican Cession and other delicate topics, including slavery in Washington, D.C., and the recapture of fugitive slaves. After quotable commentary from fading luminaries like Calhoun and Daniel Webster and from rising stars like William Seward, Clay's bill imploded under pressure from Free-Soilers and Calhounites, who despised it for different reasons. Exhausted, Clay departed for Rhode Island's cooler clime and Douglas took over. After dividing compromise legislation into separate bills, which each garnered support from one sectional bloc and moderates of both regions, Douglas shepherded them through Congress and on to Millard Fillmore, who became president after Taylor's death in July. By late September, the Compromise of 1850 was completed through the passage of six bills: California became a free state; the New Mexico and Utah Territories were organized under popular sovereignty, their legislatures tacitly authorized to decide on slavery; Texas assumed its modern borders and the U.S. assumed its debts; a stringent Fugitive Slave Act was passed despite heated objections from northern states' righters and civil libertarians; and slave trading was restricted in the nation's capital.[166] Sometimes obscured by the oratory, Douglas's floor leadership was decisive, though the grueling effort left him afflicted by a gruesome abscess on his hip.[167] "If any man has a right to be proud of the success of these measures," remarked Davis, "it is the Senator from Illinois."[168]

The crisis widened the gulf between Davis and Douglas, who regularly clashed in floor debates, particularly after Calhoun died on March 31 and Davis, described by a foreign observer as "a young man of handsome person and inflammable temperament, who talks violently for 'Southern rights,'" took command of the proslavery vanguard.[169] Few southerners resisted Clay and Douglas's compromise efforts more vehemently, and none more loquaciously; Davis's remarks filled over fifty densely printed *Congressional Globe* columns.[170] If Douglas was the architect of compromise, Davis led the sappers laboring to undermine it.

The conflict confirmed that popular sovereignty was a flimsy foundation for unity. In his major speech against Clay's proposal, Davis wove Calhoun's territorial theory and positive good proslavery ideology into a strident defense of slavery's westward expansion. Opening on February 13, Davis proclaimed that slavery predated written laws and that its modern renaissance had blessed Africans with the enlightening influence of Christian masters. "Through the portal of slavery alone," he claimed, have Africans "entered the temple of civilization." Benevolence aside, Davis insisted that the federal government must protect slaveholders' property rights throughout its jurisdiction. Neither Congress nor "any territorial community" could bar slavery from the territories, so the Wilmot Proviso and popular sovereignty were equally unsound, although Davis provocatively claimed to prefer the former, blasting Douglas's assertion that the proviso was "wholly unnecessary" to check slavery's growth. At least Free-Soilers sought to "rob me of my rights, whilst acknowledging them," thundered Davis; Douglas denied their existence. Douglas interrupted to reiterate that he opposed the Wilmot Proviso as a violation of self-government, underscoring the political distance and personal antipathy between them.[171]

Continuing the next day, Davis shifted from the abstract to the concrete, envisioning a bright future for slave labor in southwestern gold mines and irrigated farms.[172] Given enslaved workers' prominence in North Carolina's 1820s and 1830s gold rush, the long history of communal labor in irrigated western agriculture (reminiscent of work on Mississippi levees), and unfree labor's prevalence across the West, Davis was not just whistling Dixie.[173] In a militant conclusion, he deemed northern insults "just cause for war," praised the Nashville Convention (slated to meet in June), and announced that the South, with its cotton monopoly and rock-solid social structure, was prepared for anything.[174] Davis made northern acquiescence to proslavery policy, including the common-property doctrine, the price of union.[175]

Douglas replied one month later, opening with a paean to the great western valley that would save the country from sectionalism. Then he tackled the territorial issue, rejecting Davis's transmutation of property rights into southern entitlements: "It is no violation of southern rights to prohibit slavery, nor of northern rights to leave the people to decide the question for themselves." Popular sovereignty would safeguard western majority rule without invading anyone's rights, a thesis consistent with both Douglas's abhorrence of sectional extremism and his racism. Lauding the Oregon territorial bill that Davis had criticized for two years, Douglas praised the "great Democratic principle, that it is wiser and better to leave each community to determine and regulate its own local and domestic affairs in its own way." Douglas then confronted his free-soil opponents, insisting that local action had kept slavery out of the Old Northwest and predicting that the trend toward freedom would continue. "We all look forward with confidence," he declared in a prophecy not likely to thrill Davis, "to the time when Delaware, Maryland, Virginia, Kentucky, and Missouri, and probably North Carolina and Tennessee, will adopt a gradual system of emancipation." He projected that local majoritarianism would operate similarly west of the Mississippi, yielding seventeen free states. Calhoun's calls for perpetual balance between slave and free states would be doomed by liberty's westward march under the banner of majority rule.[176]

Douglas's predictions confirmed proslavery crusaders' darkest suspicions about popular sovereignty, but they could not reject it out of hand. Southern leaders, notes historian William Freehling, promised that masters' "dictatorship over blacks" would not corrupt "majoritarian government for whites."[177] Thus, when proslavery politicians concluded that local self-government would not shield slavery in New Mexico or California, they were compelled to oppose it without appearing elitist. Davis found the answer in racism: by deriding westerners as a motley rabble, he channeled a defense of property rights into an attack on people deemed unfit for self-rule. In 1848, he had judged it "palpably wrong and exceedingly contemptible" to leave slavery's status up to the "mongrel population of our Mexican territories."[178] By 1850, this was a regular talking point. Davis condemned California's constitution as the product of "a few adventurers" conspiring with "a herd as various in color and nearly as ignorant of our government, as Jacobs cattle," to cheat slave owners out of "equal participation in the common property of the states."[179] In his February address, Davis refused to defer to the "will of the conglomerated mass of gold-hunters, foreign and native," swarming in California.[180] He quoted himself a week later, castigating popular sovereignty for empowering "a conglomerated mass from every quarter of the globe" to wrest sovereignty from the United States.[181] Davis wielded racism, a central ingredient of Manifest Destiny and Democratic demagoguery, against Douglas's territorial policy.

Equally noteworthy was Davis's assertion that slaveholders' property required special federal protection. Enslaved people were "the most delicate species of property," he argued, and must be held "under special laws and police regulations" to make them "useful or profitable to the owner" and not "injurious to the community."[182] Aware from childhood of slaveholders' peculiar fears, Davis maintained that "non-intervention" in the territories must never undermine masters' authority.[183] The full implications of this point would emerge years later, but Davis already contended that the right to take slaves into a territory obligated "the Federal Government to provide the necessary means to secure the enjoyment of that right."[184] He backed amendments to the Utah and New Mexico bills that would prohibit their legislatures from infringing masters' property rights while empowering them to pass laws necessary for safeguarding them.[185] From each government according to its authority, to each property owner according to his needs.

Douglas's opposition to one such amendment triggered a revealing debate. Introduced by Maryland Whig Thomas Pratt, the amendment would forbid territorial legislatures from "introduc[ing] or exclud[ing] slavery" while authorizing them to pass laws to uphold property rights "of every kind."[186] Douglas objected to its violation of popular sovereignty's promise that territorial governments could legislate on any subject, including "African slavery," and warned that it might force slavery upon unwilling territorial residents. Davis promptly countered that westerners must wait for statehood to decide on slavery.[187]

Douglas's reply illustrated the divergence between their views about majority rule. He contended that as soon as they were numerous enough to require a territorial government, local voters could "enact their own laws" on any issues. "Why except African slavery?" Douglas queried, using his pet argument for territorial autonomy. If western voters were "competent to govern themselves upon all other subjects, and in reference to all other descriptions of property," from banks to whiskey, why tie their hands on slavery? Seeking to maximize the scope of territorial legislation, Douglas denied that "to exclude any species of property by law from any territory is a violation of any right to property." He refused to disavow Congress's power to exclude slavery from the territories but urged that it be delegated to territorial legislatures. Thus, he would cede federal authority to the territories, which might well bar slavery, while Davis would require positive protection from both.[188]

This showdown dramatized the broader crisis roiling the Democratic Party. Vigilant southern Democrats saw erstwhile northern allies as alarmingly unreliable. "God deliver me," prayed a furious Alabamian, "from such friends as the northern Democrats!"[189] Meanwhile, northern Democrats grew increasingly impatient with their southern counterparts. Their private correspondence reveals fear of disunion, frustration at southern intransigence, and little fealty to the Slave Power. In early January, Illinois representative Timothy R. Young warned that "our party is in a very bad fix, divided and rent asunder by this slavery question."[190] Thereafter, Illinois Democrats bemoaned southern obstinacy. One mocked "Calhoun men who turned up their chivalrous noses" at northerners, castigated "ultra southern fanatics," and vowed to make California a free state, proslavery "outrages" be damned.[191] Another rebuked "fanatical" southerners for plotting secession.[192] William H. Bissell, who narrowly avoided dueling with Davis, pronounced southern congressmen "insolent, overbearing & bullying beyond all endurance."[193] An Illinois colleague blasted delegates to the Nashville Convention as "propagandists of treason."[194] Several representatives armed themselves with knives and pistols and one urged Governor Augustus C. French to mobilize the state, lest civil war sever commercial ties with the Gulf of Mexico.[195] They focused on admitting California and organizing new territories, expecting popular sovereignty to yield free soil. Bissell pledged to support the Wilmot Proviso if it were necessary for preventing slavery's expansion; thus far, however, he believed it was not. He also rejected the "Southern idea" that slavery followed the flag and speculated that its adherents longed to secede and conquer Mexico.[196]

Passage of compromise legislation did not heal these wounds. Scholars have stressed that the Compromise of 1850 was largely a Democratic venture, but it was, specifically, a *northern* Democratic measure also supported by many southern Whigs. Four senators voted for all six compromise bills: two were northern Democrats, one was a border-state Whig, and the fourth was Texas maverick Sam Houston, later ousted from the governor's chair for opposing secession. Seven senators voted for five of the six bills; all, save a Delaware Whig, were northern Democrats. Similar patterns prevailed in the House, where twenty-four of twenty-eight representatives who voted for every bill were northern Democrats, including four from Illinois.[197] Southern Democrats, especially from the cotton states, overwhelmingly rejected the compromise. Mississippi's unanimously Democratic delegates cast only three of twenty-six possible votes for compromise measures other than the Fugitive Slave Act. Two, Albert Gallatin Brown and Winfield S. Featherston, supported the fugitive law but opposed every other compromise bill.[198]

Davis and Douglas fit this pattern. Douglas voted for every compromise bill except the Fugitive Slave Act; ostensibly, a private financial transaction in New York kept him from the Senate vote.[199] Davis backed the fugitive law and the Utah bill, abstained on New Mexico, and opposed all the rest. Thus, he and Douglas aligned on only one of the six bills, a divergence reflected among Senate Democrats generally. Northern Democrats voted 11–3 to organize Utah; southern Democrats supported it 13–0 but with five abstentions. Northern Democrats endorsed the New Mexico bill 10–3, while half of southern Democrats abstained from endorsing popular sovereignty. The other compromise bills were more polarizing. Northern Democrats voted unanimously for California statehood; southern Democrats opposed it 14–2. The Texas bill won eleven northern Democratic votes, with two opposed and two abstaining; only five southern Democrats backed it, while ten opposed and three abstained. Save one abstention, northern Democrats voted as a bloc to limit slave trading in Washington, D.C., while southerners opposed it 12–2, with four abstentions. Still more divisive was the Fugitive Slave Act: northern Democrats offered three yeas, three nays, and nine abstentions; southern Democrats backed it 15–0, with three abstentions.[200]

The midcentury crisis also revealed party disunity within both sections. Northern Democrats with free-soil inclinations, like Chicago's John Wentworth, opposed many of the compromise measures; Wentworth voted against all but the California and slave trade bills.[201] Conversely, a handful of southern Democrats, including Davis's colleague Henry S. Foote, embraced the compromise. Foote helped Douglas steer the bills through the Senate and urged southerners to accept them, although even

he opposed California statehood.[202] By 1850, the Democracy was fragmenting along three axes, with minority factions in both sections defy-
ing regional trends while Davis's and Douglas's majority factions butted
heads. Since neither Davis nor Douglas would bolt the party, it was in
danger of being torn apart.

Passage of compromise legislation did not quell this infighting, in part
because Davis refused to surrender. On the day that the Senate approved
the California bill, Davis and nine southern colleagues (eight Democrats
and one Whig) issued a widely reprinted protest. They reiterated the
common-property doctrine and resented California's "odious discrimination" against slave property. Statehood, they warned, invited westerners
to exclude fifteen slave states from the growing empire. They closed by
inveighing against a free-soil onslaught that, unchecked, could provoke
disunion.[203] On his deathbed four decades later, Davis defiantly recalled
"opposing Senator Douglas . . . in his theory of squatter sovereignty"
and resisting the "threatened usurpations of the Federal Government"
embedded in the compromise.[204] Varina Davis shared his bitter memories, referring in 1890 to Douglas's "so-called compromise."[205]

Both Davises would have questioned claims that the compromise
entailed appeasement of slaveholders.[206] Jefferson Davis spent the next
year proclaiming that the compromise "trampled the rights of the South
in the dust" and branding its southern apologists as "traitors."[207] California statehood was a "*fraud* upon the South," the District slave trade law
was "utterly unconstitutional," and popular sovereignty was "an odious
doctrine" that flouted property rights and screened northerners who were
"hostile to the institution of slavery."[208] He endorsed the Fugitive Slave
Act but doubted its utility, reminding Mississippians that it mainly benefited border-state masters whose slaves were far likelier to reach a free
state. Convinced that the act had seduced border-state delegates into
supporting a raw deal, he accused them of abandoning the Deep South on
the territorial front.[209] Davis was not appeased.

Thus, it is difficult to view the Compromise of 1850 as a victory for proslavery extremists. Rather, it empowered southern moderates to stem the
rising tide of Calhounism, which had swept up much of the Democracy's
southern wing. Moreover, since neither section was monolithic, the compromise triggered intraregional debates, which challenged Davis and
Douglas to vindicate themselves back home.

★ ★ ★

Homeward bound in October 1850, Davis passed the spot where the
steamboat *Jeff Davis* had recently sunk, an ill omen for an embattled sen-

ator.[210] As national officeholders with state constituencies, he and Douglas faced harsh scrutiny upon returning from Washington. Douglas's success in deflecting public criticism proved intoxicating, while Davis's failures sent his career off the rails. Lessons from these desperate days would shape their thinking for years.

Douglas's antislavery critics focused primarily on the Fugitive Slave Act, and although he had not voted for the brutal law, he did defend it. Ominously, the epicenter of the backlash was Chicago. On October 21, 1850, Chicago's Common Council decried the act as unconstitutional, enjoined city police not to enforce it, and compared its northern advocates to Benedict Arnold and Judas Iscariot.[211] Two days later, Douglas responded to an indignant crowd at City Hall. Observing that the compromise was simultaneously being assailed as an abolitionist outrage and a proslavery coup, he insisted that it was neither. Douglas then lauded the California, Utah, and New Mexico bills for promoting self-government and reiterated that if western voters could legislate "for the government of white men," they were "competent to legislate for the negro." Predictably, he insisted that local control, not federal fiat, had kept slavery out of the Northwest Territory and, now, California. Moving to the main charge, Douglas defended the Fugitive Slave Act against the council's resolutions, which he compared unfavorably to South Carolina's nullification-era rhetoric. He conceded that the law should have done more to protect free blacks but argued that it was vital for executing the Constitution's fugitive slave clause and closed by offering counter-resolutions pledging fealty to the sacred bargain of 1787. Apparently persuaded, the council recanted its criticism and adopted Douglas's resolutions.[212]

Douglas's victory was dampened by a subsequent meeting of Chicago antislavery activists who renewed the attack on the Fugitive Slave Act and shouted down a Douglasite who tried to speak.[213] But his City Hall performance highlighted his persistent strength in Illinois, and his vindication seemed complete when the legislature rescinded its instructions to support the Wilmot Proviso.[214] Moreover, Douglas's stock was soaring across the West. As an expensive token of thanks for his "deep devotion to the interests of our Territories and younger States," California subscribers bought him a jewel-encrusted gold watch bearing the slogan "California knows her friends." When Douglas accepted the gift in March 1851, he gave a brief speech in which he described "the great West and the Pacific coast" as the "theatre for new and wonderful events" and urged construction of a Pacific railroad.[215] As a western measure, the Compromise of 1850 was just the beginning.

Davis's reckoning unfolded more slowly but culminated in a harrowing defeat. In late 1850, he returned to a Mississippi where secessionism seemed rampant but internal divisions ran deep. Citing the "recent acts of Congress" that "virtually excluded" southern citizens from the Mexican Cession, Governor Quitman summoned the legislature to respond and, if necessary, "assert [Mississippi's] sovereignty."[216] Privately, he argued that antislavery sentiment controlled the government and secession was imperative. Otherwise, slavery was "doomed," for it required "a fostering government" for protection against the "prejudices of the age."[217] Davis moved more cautiously but denounced the compromise and suggested that another southern convention should make demands and, if rebuffed, dissolve the Union. He indignantly denied sponsoring secession, even as he described scenarios in which he would support it.[218] Moderates like Henry Foote condemned his extremism and organized a pro-compromise Unionist countermovement.[219] Thus, while most white Mississippians loathed California statehood, restrictions on slave trading in Washington, and popular sovereignty, they divided over how to react.[220]

By 1851, this intramural debate had thrown political parties into chaos. Most Mississippi Democrats and a handful of Whigs supported Davis's defiant position, although radicals like Quitman and Albert Gallatin Brown embraced the final resort of secession more eagerly than Davis did. Meanwhile, most Whigs, joined by a few Democrats and led by Democratic senator Foote, defended the compromise. Anticipating two major elections—a September 1851 contest for delegates to a November state convention and the regular November elections for state offices—both groups adopted new names: Davis's faction became the Democratic State Rights Party, while Foote's supporters formed the Union Party.[221] Similar realignments occurred in South Carolina, Georgia, and Alabama, and firebrands in all four states coordinated their efforts, with South Carolina taking the most extreme position.[222] As secessionist ardor cooled in the spring and summer of 1851, however, Mississippi radicals scrambled to respond, and Davis became their primary spokesman. After the brief 1850–51 session of Congress, he hastily apologized to Varina for his absence and, despite battling a painful eye inflammation, launched another exhausting speaking tour.[223] He still counseled resistance and declared that if forced to choose between secession and "degradation," he would support the former. But for now, Mississippi should work with other slave states to secure their rights, resist antislavery aggression, and support South Carolina.[224]

Davis also appealed directly to nonslaveholders, whose preponderance among Mississippi whites controverted his habitual conflation of masters' property rights with the rights of "the South." In repudiating claims that nonslaveholders would naturally support the Union Party, Davis revealed his skill in the unsavory art of demagoguery. "Negro slavery . . . is necessary to the *equality* of the *white* race," he argued. Poor whites needed slavery because they owned little more than the wages of whiteness: "Their all is suspended upon their *superiority* to the *blacks*."[225] As war darkened the horizon, Davis exhorted yeomen to the defense of slaveholders' property, a project that would continue for fifteen years.

By late summer, however, the campaign to tar Davis's party as disunionist was gaining traction. In the September special election, the Union Party won 57 percent of the vote and elected over two-thirds of the delegates to the November convention. Low turnout among Democrats reflected reluctance to support the Whig-dominated Union Party and lack of enthusiasm for Davis's movement.[226] Anticipating disaster in the November elections, State Rights Democrats turned to Davis as a last-minute replacement for Quitman, whose candidacy for governor seemed likely to alienate voters, particularly after he was pummeled in debates (the last of which devolved into a brawl) against Union Party candidate Henry Foote. Davis, they hoped, would attract chary Democrats to the polls.[227] It was a desperate move, but Davis accepted the call on September 17, averring that his "whole political life has been devoted to the Democratic cause."[228] Then he resigned from the Senate and squared off against an old nemesis.

The race allowed Mississippi voters to choose between the senator who opposed the Compromise of 1850 and the one who supported it. The four years since their Christmas fisticuffs had not warmed relations between Davis and Foote. Rising from his sickbed and donning goggles to protect his ailing eyes, Davis hit the campaign trail in late October.[229] Fire-eaters hailed his leadership of a movement that could culminate in secession; South Carolina's Robert W. Barnwell thanked Davis for his "noble effort" and promised to help him "rally the broken forces of the South."[230] But the campaign was, Davis later recalled, a "forlorn hope."[231] Davis parried Foote's charges of disunionism by denouncing him as a "submissionist," a loaded term among those who sanctified black and female subordination while glorifying white masculinity, but failed to convince enough voters that the compromise was an emasculating insult. Foote won by 999 votes (1.7 percent of the total), a marked decline from the Union Party's 7,000-vote margin of victory in September's elections.[232] Davis narrowed the gap by putting a moderate face on a radical cause.

Still, it was a stinging defeat. Campaigning on patriotism and compromise, the Union Party nabbed the governor's chair, sixty-three out of ninety-eight seats in the state legislature's lower house, and a majority of contested seats in the upper house.[233] Davis had misread his constituents and was now involuntarily out of office for the first time in six years, having learned, as two historians aptly put it, a painful lesson about "the majesty of public opinion."[234] Some admirers believed Davis would recover swiftly and become president, but for now he had nowhere to go but Brierfield.[235]

★ ★ ★

Davis's and Douglas's experiences in the midcentury crisis could hardly have been more dissimilar. Douglas savored his ability to rally support for the compromise he had guided through the Senate. Confidence soaring, he concluded that popular sovereignty was the key to unlocking western development, and he forged ahead with his ambitious agenda. Meanwhile, Davis licked his wounds after failing to defeat the hated compromise or to align Mississippi voters behind him. Always wary of majority power, Davis saw California as proof that Douglas's doctrine endangered the South. But he had outpaced public sentiment and lost to one of Douglas's few southern Democratic allies.[236]

As historian Brian R. Dirck has noted, Davis was understandably alarmed by the compromise and its aftershocks. Particularly unnerving was the rise of Douglas, a Democrat who "bartered away the slaveholding rights of other Democrats," a northerner who "endorsed a compromise inimical to the rights of Southerners," and "an American whom Davis believed was engaged in trimming the constitutional rights of other Americans."[237] Davis shared Douglas's racism, anti-abolitionism, and expansionist zeal, but they had skirmished for years before the midcentury crisis ripped them apart. Assailed by critics back home, they continued on opposite courses, and while the Union seemed safe, the Democracy was badly torn.

Yet Davis remained committed to bringing the State Rights faction back into the national Democracy even as northern Democrats struggled to satisfy their own constituents.[238] Champions of white men's majoritarianism had defeated the guardians of property rights, but both were determined to control the Democratic Party's illustrious name and powerful machinery. Hobbled by disunity at home and a growing chasm across sectional lines, northern and southern Democrats sought to reunite while pursuing manifestly disparate destinies.

4

Down to the Crossroads

Samuel Ashton was the kind of operative no antebellum politician could do without. Long before opinion polling, agents like Ashton monitored public sentiment by mingling in the taverns and courthouses where political beliefs were made, swayed, and paid for. His letters to Stephen Douglas offered a seasoned perspective on Chicago politics. When German immigrants burned Douglas in effigy to protest the Kansas-Nebraska Bill, Ashton penned a detailed report.[1] When locals endorsed Douglas for president two years later, Ashton rejoiced that the city was "redeemed."[2] Naturally, he expected compensation in the currency of nineteenth-century politics: patronage. In 1855, he coveted a vacant army captaincy, and other confidants urged Douglas to secure it for him. "Sam Ashton is with you utmost this time," advised *Chicago Times* editor James W. Sheahan. "Do get him [the] captaincy if you can."[3]

The path to the appointment ran through Secretary of War Jefferson Davis. Douglas rarely wrote to him, but the quest for Ashton's commission provoked their most extensive correspondence, beginning when Douglas recommended several Illinoisans for army posts in March 1855. Davis inquired about their military experience but then filled the vacant positions before receiving a response. Douglas complained that one of the two commissions credited to Illinois had gone to a Virginian, George Pickett (later of Gettysburg fame), and that Ashton and other "worthy & gallant" hopefuls had been ignored.[4] Davis, always prickly about protocol, responded at length. He dismissed several candidates' Mexican War records as "not particularly distinguished" and noted that a thorough investigation revealed "no trace" of Ashton's "alleged services."[5] Douglas did wangle a commission for another Illinoisan, but he never reported for duty; in one of his last acts as secretary of war, Davis pressed Douglas to explain.[6] Alas, Ashton, the wire-puller of dubious martial prowess, never got his commission.

Ashton's appointment was a relatively minor matter, but, like a seismograph needle, it tracked powerful forces shaking the political landscape. It revealed that the Compromise of 1850 had not handed the government to antislavery zealots and that southern Democrats were more formidably entrenched than ever.[7] Indeed, the central story of late antebellum politics was not southern resistance to federal overreach but northern reactions to minority rule. Direct defiance of the Slave Power, particularly free soil's renaissance in the Republican Party, is best remembered. Less familiar are the responses of northern Democrats who eschewed confrontation and refused to bolt their party. "Doughfaces" among them bowed to southern masters, but most strove to satisfy constituent demands while maintaining sectional and party harmony. Thus they confronted the question embedded in the Ashton episode: How could a northern politician deliver for northern voters while working within a southern-dominated party?

Proslavery southerners' surging power reshaped the Davis-Douglas rivalry. After the 1852 presidential election, Davis recovered from his earlier disaster and seized new opportunities as secretary of war. In this, the most dynamic phase of his career, Davis labored to solidify southern power over national policy. Meanwhile, Douglas fenced with southern Democrats over internal improvements and western development. Caught between constituent pressure and southern clout, Douglas reached a political crossroads, where he made a fateful bargain to advance his agenda under Democratic auspices. This time, however, he could not mollify the folks back home. Instead, he propelled his party toward disintegration and his country toward a bloody reckoning with its gravest sins. By 1856, Davis neared the zenith of his antebellum power while Douglas struggled to stay afloat.

★ ★ ★

Democrats' most pressing task in 1852 was to mend fences before the presidential election. In Mississippi, this meant reconciling the minority of Democrats who backed the Unionist movement with recently defeated hardliners who still constituted a majority of the party. Hostility between the factions ran deep. One Union Democrat tried to correspond with a relative who favored the State Rights bloc, "but we differed so much about the 'Compromise Bills of 1850,' and lashed one another so severely about them," that his kinsman stopped writing.[8] Parties were less jumbled in Illinois, but relations between Democratic regulars and Free-Soilers were frosty. One Illinoisan praised "true democrats" for resisting the "torrent of free soilism" but admitted to courting antislavery support at the polls.[9] Party reconstruction demanded considerable dexterity.

Mississippi's State Rights faction rebuilt the Democracy on its own terms. Unionists hoped to maintain the partisan alignment of 1851, but State Rights leaders appealed to Democrats' deepest loyalties. Arguing that the Compromise of 1850 was a dead issue, they called for Democratic solidarity against the Whigs, and when the latter held their own state convention in the spring of 1852, it was clear that the old alignment was returning. Still worse for Union Democrats, the State Rights wing remained adamant on slavery and secession. Reunion did not mean moderation, and the dominant force in the Mississippi Democracy was the stridently proslavery element, which resented the compromise and its defenders.[10]

Davis remained politically active, and in a key speech to the Democratic state convention in January 1852, he offered Union Democrats an olive branch without abandoning his previous position. Provocatively, Davis defended the right to secede, repudiating November's Unionist-controlled state convention, which had deemed secession "utterly unsanctioned by the Federal Constitution."[11] He also outlined his vision for the Democracy's future: Union Democrats would fall into line under the State Rights banner and adhere to Democratic principles, like state sovereignty, which remained vital for southern self-defense. The 1851 election had signaled acquiescence to the compromise but not the defeat of Democratic ideals, and he urged Union Democrats to return to their partisan home. After castigating Whig president Millard Fillmore, Davis encouraged Mississippi Democrats to retake the White House.[12]

Davis's dream was realized by the end of 1853. Mississippi's overwhelming support for 1852 Democratic presidential nominee Franklin Pierce, who won nearly 61 percent of the popular vote (the fifth-highest proportion among thirty-one states), showed that the wounds of 1851 were healing.[13] Then came the 1853 state elections, which Davis regarded as the most important contests in recent memory.[14] He continued to preach party cohesion on a State Rights platform, while Whigs seethed as their erstwhile Union Democrat allies flocked back into the Democratic fold.[15] Critics kept attacking Democrats as secessionists; one waggish pamphlet, titled *Chronicles of the Fire-Eaters of the Tribe of Mississippi*, dissected state politics in an Old Testament idiom, mocking "Jefferson of Brierfield's" 1850 battles against "the nation of the Squatters."[16] But Democrats triumphed, winning the governorship and large majorities in the state legislature, and sealed their victory in January 1854 by electing Albert Gallatin Brown to the Senate over Henry Foote. Embittered, Foote departed for California, taking his moderating influence with him.[17] Democrats dominated the state for the rest of the decade. Ominously for the national Democracy, Davis hereafter faced more pressure from radical rivals like Brown than from moderates like Foote.[18]

Meanwhile, Illinois Democrats reckoned with free-soilism. When some dissenters sought to return to the party, Democrats across the North divided over whether to welcome them back; in New York, the dispute between forgiving "Softs" and vindictive "Hards" grew severe.[19] Well into 1853, New Yorkers warned of "a war full of bitterness" erupting from this three-sided conflict, and Illinoisans worried it would spread to their state.[20] Loath to proscribe potential allies, Douglas embraced prodigal Democrats, even those who did not endorse the Compromise of 1850. He reconciled with John Wentworth by helping the former Free-Soiler win reelection to Congress in exchange for Wentworth's support for the presidency in 1852.[21]

Douglas's presidential ambitions energized his efforts to repair the Democracy. He had previously favored renominating Lewis Cass, but by June 1851 he decided to seek the nomination himself.[22] Douglas had reason for optimism: throughout that year and into the next, editors and private correspondents clamored for his nomination.[23] Most hailed from the Northwest, with a smattering from the upper South and California, but congenial letters from the Deep South, including from Horatio J. Harris, Davis's Vicksburg confidant, made his prospects even more tantalizing.[24] Douglas, who turned thirty-nine in April 1852, inspired a rising generation of Democrats who identified as "Young Americans." They shared Douglas's zeal for internal improvements, hunger for territorial expansion, and sympathy for foreign democratic crusaders, particularly Louis Kossuth, the Hungarian revolutionary whose 1851–52 American tour prompted Douglas to hail the United States as an exemplar of democracy and hint at overseas intervention.[25] For Young Americans, Douglas was an energizing alternative to "old fogies" who refought Jacksonian battles while a steam-powered world sped into the future.[26]

Douglas's brassiest spokesman was George N. Sanders, a Kentucky-born adventurer who purchased the *Democratic Review* in order to champion Douglas's nomination and hasten global republican revolution. Sanders regarded 1852 as a tipping point in human history and urged Democrats to field a candidate who understood the decisive role that his party and country must play in the denouement. Brazenly, he ordered older Democrats to yield and allow a "new generation of American statesmen" to lead.[27] Sanders followed with slashing attacks on Douglas's rivals that even the pugnacious Little Giant considered "impolitic & unjust," and possibly a "fatal mistake."[28] As the June 1852 national convention approached, cool-headed Douglasites worried that this bluster would backfire.[29]

The convention results validated these fears. For forty-eight grueling ballots, Douglas dueled with James Buchanan, Lewis Cass, and William Marcy, peaking at 92 votes, far shy of the 197 needed for nomination. The lack of solid northwestern support beyond the Illinois delegation hurt him, but also critical was Douglas's failure to kindle much enthusiasm in the South. On no ballot did more than 40 percent of Douglas's votes come from southerners, and over two-thirds of his roughly 2,440 aggregate votes came from free-state delegates.[30] As delegates braced for a party split, the Virginians offered Mexican War veteran and former New Hampshire senator Franklin Pierce as a compromise candidate.[31] Democrats balanced the ticket with Alabama's William R. King, though some had considered Davis for the vice presidency.[32] Their platform denounced abolitionism, endorsed the Compromise of 1850, and rejected a national bank, protective tariffs, and a "general system of internal improvements."[33]

Southern Democrats heartily applauded the ticket. In Mississippi, Albert Gallatin Brown pronounced Pierce "as reliable as Calhoun himself" and "far above *all* suspicion" on slavery, and Benjamin F. Dill rejoiced that State Rights and Union Democrats alike were "well satisfied and pleased" with him.[34] Northern Democrats, especially New Englanders, also lauded the nomination, but some had doubts. One of Pierce's confidants warned that northwesterners resented his past opposition to river and harbor improvements.[35] Others lamented the Democracy's southward tilt. One Young American considered the party essential for "the advance of freedom throughout the world" but regretted that the "influence of the South is preponderant," for the Democracy would "depend upon the votes of the northern and western states" for victory.[36] An Illinoisan deemed Pierce and King "good sound Democrats" but confessed that he could not campaign with "such a zeal" as he would have done for Douglas.[37]

As in 1848, Davis and Douglas both canvassed energetically, but now Davis brimmed with unreserved enthusiasm. Douglas spoke mainly in the North, where he tarred the Whigs as abolitionists and nativists, promised that Pierce would restore American global power, and hinted at expansion into Latin America.[38] In Mississippi, Davis campaigned ardently for Pierce, a close friend since 1838 and a "trust-worthy and reliable" Democrat of the "Jeffersonian school." Characteristically conflating regional identity, proslavery politics, and party loyalty, Davis urged Mississippi voters to embrace the Democracy as slavery's only safeguard, promising that Pierce would quash antislavery agitation. He also denounced popular sovereignty as dangerously vague and unlikely to spread slavery.[39]

The result was a ringing Democratic victory. Democrats solidified their power in the House of Representatives, and while Pierce won a bare majority of the popular vote, he carried all but four states (Vermont, Massachusetts, Kentucky, and Tennessee). In Illinois, he received nearly 52 percent of the ballots, while the Free-Soil Party's share of the popular vote declined by half. The election was even more decisive in the South. Zachary Taylor's strong showing in 1848 and moderation's triumph in 1851 had boosted southern Whigs' confidence, but 1852 brought disaster: Whig nominee Winfield Scott won just 35 percent of the Deep South popular vote, down from half in 1848, and lost thirteen of the fifteen slave states. In Mississippi, Pierce ran eleven points better than Cass had done. Few southern Whigs defected to the Democrats, but thousands, dismayed by antislavery sentiment among their northern counterparts, stayed home. The catastrophe continued in the 1853 congressional elections, when Whigs won only twenty-two seats from southern states. Opposition to the Democracy did not cease, but 1852, notes historian Sean Wilentz, "marked the beginning of the creation of a nearly solid Democratic South."[40] Davis inched closer to making the Democracy a proslavery machine, although his strategy could work only if the national party survived the transformation.

★ ★ ★

Enraptured by Pierce's election, Vicksburg attorney Horatio J. Harris cribbed a line from Jesus to celebrate: henceforth, the Democracy would "be a rock, against which the gates of whiggery, abolitionism and hell cannot prevail."[41] It was also a victory for Harris's friend Jefferson Davis, who had been politically active but unemployed since 1851. Davis's personal ties to Pierce, coupled with the president-elect's strategy for unifying his party, would restore the Mississippian to the highest circles of national power.

Like all incoming presidents, Pierce had to distribute the loaves and fishes of patronage without upsetting party unity. With loyalists hungering for offices after four lean years, multiple factions jockeying for advantage, and discontent among southern radicals and northern Free-Soilers still festering, he faced a daunting task. Ultimately, Pierce's efforts to placate dissidents offended mainstream Democrats nationwide. Did recent loyalty atone for past treachery? How could he reward deserters who had opposed the Compromise of 1850, which the party was bound to uphold? Why, for instance, had so many jobs in northern Illinois gone (with Douglas's blessing) to Wentworth's free-soil friends? Pierce's bid for harmony unleashed latent jealousies within the ostensibly ascendant Democracy.[42]

The controversy swelled with Pierce's selection of Davis as secretary of war. A month after the election, Pierce solicited Davis's advice about cabinet personnel and hinted about a place for the Mississippian.[43] Their correspondence was confidential, but rumors spread, and by February 1853 Mississippi Democrats proclaimed that Davis's appointment would strengthen the southern Democracy by signaling Pierce's determination to "faithfully maintain the rights, the interests and the honor of the South."[44] Varina implored him to decline, but he accepted the War Department portfolio, although he reserved the right to resign if elected to the Senate.[45] Intensely ambitious and keen to erase the stain of 1851, Davis constantly monitored his senatorial prospects until the state legislature gratified him in January 1856.[46]

Davis's appointment delighted proslavery hardliners who anticipated his influence over Pierce. "The whole State Rights party of the South look to you as the exponent and defender of our faith," wrote South Carolina's James Gadsden. Fearful that Secretary of State William Marcy might corrupt Pierce's administration, just as Martin Van Buren had done to Andrew Jackson's, Gadsden welcomed Davis's presence at Pierce's elbow.[47] Harassed by "distrust of the Northern Democracy," Gadsden hoped that Davis could "restore the Democracy as a unit, to the principles of the Jeffersonian school."[48] Mississippians also relished Davis's appointment.[49]

But some northern Democrats and southern moderates bristled at Pierce's decision. A New Yorker warned that Davis, "a rigid adherent of the doctrine of secession," would be among "the master-spirits of the administration."[50] A southern critic blasted Pierce for appointing a "secessionist" to high office.[51] Whether thrilled or disheartened, however, observers agreed that Davis had been chosen to placate the Democracy's radical proslavery element. "Davis," wrote a Navy Department employee, "was the selection of the fire-eaters generally." He hoped that Pierce would now co-opt them into the Democratic mainstream.[52]

Davis, however, saw his secretaryship as an opportunity to do precisely the opposite: to make the Democratic Party a proslavery instrument. For years, his clashes with southern rivals, who saw national parties as inherently unreliable, forced him to prove that the Democracy could safeguard slavery in a hostile world.[53] He reiterated this strategy in a letter written just before the 1852 election. Sanguine about Pierce's chances, Davis hoped that Democratic victories would make secession unnecessary. Like the fire-eaters, he sought sectional unity; unlike them, however, Davis would align southern voters behind a national party that promoted sectional interests. Proslavery southerners "have the best chance of security through the democratic party," he wrote, candidly adding, "Let us use it as we may" and "sustain a sound party at the north to extract whatever we can from party organization for the security of our constitutional rights."[54] A Machiavellian plan, but one consistent with Davis's partisan identity and political interests. Now ensconced in the cabinet, he was well positioned to carry it out.

Davis faced two potential obstacles. One was resistance from northern Democrats, whose response to escalating southern demands would either fulfill Davis's hopes or smash the party and push him toward secession. The other was the tangle of troubles facing him as secretary of war. The United States was still digesting over one million square miles it had swallowed in the mid-1840s, and the army's primary mission was to facilitate the process by subjugating Native Americans and fostering Anglo-American migration. Congressional budget hawks had slashed military spending, leaving the army shorthanded and under-equipped. With perhaps 10,000 soldiers on duty, Davis, who was both a conscientious federal administrator and an ardent southern sectionalist, faced a daunting assignment.[55]

Despite unseemly quarrels with senior officers, Davis provided the War Department with innovative leadership. Military spending rose by nearly two-thirds during his tenure, and the army's effective strength increased to around 15,000. Secretary Davis provided new equipment, outlined a new strategic doctrine for warfare against Plains Indians, oversaw preparation of an infantry tactics manual, and directed renovation of the Capitol Building.[56]

His signal achievements, however, wielded federal might to promote a western slaveholding empire.[57] Davis had long envisioned exploitation of slave labor in mines and on irrigated farms, and, even after the Compromise of 1850, slavery's prospects in the Southwest remained bright. Hundreds of enslaved laborers toiled in California gold mines for years after statehood, and passage of a fugitive slave law in 1852 bolstered masters' authority with the coercive power of an ostensibly free state. Coupled with the elevation of transplanted southerners, like William M. Gwin of Mississippi, to political offices, slavery's persistence in California disproved two widely shared assumptions: that nature barred slavery's expansion to the Pacific Coast and that California statehood doomed the South to political vassalage.[58] New Mexico, where bound labor had long shaped indigenous and colonial societies, also seemed promising. Despite popular support for a free-state constitution drafted in 1850, the increasing power of southerners over the territorial government facilitated the adoption of a territorial slave code in 1859.[59] Davis monitored southwestern developments through contacts in San Francisco and Santa Fe. In 1856, James J. Deavenport, a Mississippian who presided over New Mexico's territorial supreme court, reported that the Americanization of local "Mexicans" was proceeding nicely: they were "opposed to abolitionism" and "safe upon all the questions of the day."[60]

The model for proslavery expansion was Texas, which by the 1850s marked the cutting edge of slavery's march toward the Pacific. Texas cotton production skyrocketed from 58,000 bales in 1850 to 431,000 in 1860, a rate of increase twice that seen in Mississippi during the 1830s.[61] Soaring output stimulated an insatiable hunger for forced labor: the slave population nearly doubled between 1846 and 1850 and again between 1851 and 1855, reaching 182,000 in 1860, when nearly one-third of Texans were enslaved.[62] Demand remained high as new cotton and sugar land came under cultivation; in 1858, an Austin editor projected that Texas could employ 2 million slaves.[63] Nor did aridity seem an insurmountable barrier. Already, small slaveholders exploited unfree labor on cattle ranches, and they appeared poised to carry slavery across the dusty reaches of west Texas.[64]

Human agency, not natural limits, posed the greatest challenge to Texas slaveholders. For years, southern expansionists had worried that the West's multiracial population might hinder slavery's extension, hence Davis's hostility toward California's diverse constitution-makers, and prospective migrants' concerns about Indian and Hispanic neighbors. While traveling near Davis's boyhood home of Woodville, Frederick Law Olmsted met a Mississippian who was interested in ranching but worried that "negro property isn't very secure" in Texas.[65] Texas slaveholders shared these suspicions and blamed Indians and Hispanics for aiding runaway slaves.[66] This anxiety was rooted in both prejudice and reality: escapes were common in Texas, with most fugitives fleeing to Mexico, where they built new lives in border towns like Piedras Negras.[67]

Proslavery Texans responded by raiding these free black communities, petitioning Mexico to return fugitives, and calling for new conquests to push the border south to the more easily policed Sierra Madre.[68] They also attacked internal enemies. For Texans who regarded "Mexicans" as "vermin," safeguarding slavery meant using government power and mob violence to crush Hispanic dissent.[69] In 1854, whites denounced "peons" for meddling with slaves and resolved to expel them from Guadalupe County; by 1856, whites in Austin as well as Colorado and Matagorda Counties had banished most Hispanics from their midst.[70] These expulsions relied on local or extralegal authority, but white Texans enjoyed federal support in their campaigns against Indians, including those, like Seminole leader Wild Cat, whom they accused of abetting slave escapes. Secretary Davis contributed by urging Texas officials to establish Indian reservations on the Brazos River and creating two cavalry regiments to assail Indians who refused to live on reservations or leave the state. The battle for west Texas would continue for many years, but by 1860 the central and eastern regions were secure enough for slavery to sink deep roots into Texas soil.[71]

As both observer and participant, Davis drew a compelling lesson from Texas history: southern migration and state-sanctioned violence could make the West safe for slavery. Thus, one key to slavery's expansion was to improve transportation between the South and the West. In an illuminating December 1855 letter to Mississippi Democrat William R. Cannon, Davis outlined his plan for western "colonization," which would restore southern "equality in the Senate" by producing new slave states. He urged concerted southern settlement in Kansas, New Mexico, and the West Coast. "The country on the Pacific is in many respects adapted to slave labor," Davis asserted, and "many of the citizens desire its introduction." The only reason why slaveholders had not already seized California and Oregon was lack of transportation, since the easiest emigrant route was by ships that sailed from northern ports. "If we had a good railroad and other roads" from Texas to New Mexico and southern California, southern migration would swell, westerners would appreciate bound labor, and their antislavery "prejudice" would "yield to the persuasion of personal interest." New slave states would bloom like desert flowers.[72]

This vision inspired several of Secretary Davis's most famous projects, including his diligent work on a Pacific railroad.[73] For years, his correspondence with western surveyors had piqued his interest in a wagon road and railroad running from the lower Mississippi to California via the Gila River valley in modern-day southern New Mexico and Arizona.[74] During a speaking tour a few months after joining Pierce's cabinet, Davis endorsed a federally constructed Pacific railroad, rebuffing constitutional objections by arguing that it was necessary for defense of the West Coast.[75] Discussions of its route and eastern terminus, however, inflamed sectional jealousies, particularly among southerners who sought to boost regional power by linking the railroad to Vicksburg or New Orleans.[76]

Davis gained tremendous influence over route selection in March 1853, when Congress appropriated $150,000 for a War Department study of the optimum path from the Mississippi to the Pacific. He maintained an air of impartiality, disbursing the funds among teams he dispatched to explore four routes: a northern expedition (St. Paul to Puget Sound) led by Isaac Stevens; a central survey from St. Louis to San Francisco initially headed by John W. Gunnison; a south-central mission under Amiel W. Whipple, which followed the thirty-fifth parallel to Los Angeles; and a southern survey directed by John Parke and John Pope, which traced Davis's favorite line through the Gila River valley to San Diego. The surveys compiled mountains of data but failed to identify a clearly superior route. Davis, already dead-set on the southernmost option, placed his thumb on the scales. In his final report, written in early 1855, he emphasized the drawbacks of competing routes (including cost, weather, and terrain) and minimized those of his favorite; the Gila River route's aridity, for instance, could be mitigated by drilling artesian wells. Not coincidentally, he had recently directed John Pope to study the feasibility of artesian wells in the Southwest, and the order's urgency suggests that Davis wanted Pope to find the correct answer in time for his year-end department report.[77] Historians disagree over the depth of Davis's bias, but he strengthened the southern position in the route debate.[78]

Davis also intervened by supporting the purchase of a swath of Mexican land south of the Gila River, thus removing a geopolitical barrier to U.S. railroad construction in the valley. Named for negotiator James Gadsden, the South Carolinian who hailed Davis's cabinet appointment and dabbled in western proslavery schemes (including carving a slave state out of southern California and pressuring Mexico to return fugitive slaves), the Gadsden Purchase did more than round out the modern borders of the lower forty-eight states.[79] Signed in December 1853 and ratified by the Senate in April 1854, the treaty secured nearly 30,000 square miles of land and promised to tilt the railroad rivalry in the South's favor.[80] Many northerners regarded it as another example of the Slave Power's mastery over federal policy. A Bostonian bitterly charged "'Southern State Rights' and 'Strict Construction' Democrats" with raiding the public purse "for a strip of Mexican desert, and a Southern Route to the Pacific."[81]

First, however, the United States had to solidify its sovereignty over a vast region still dominated by Native Americans. Secretary Davis's desire to enhance the army's tactical performance and logistical support in southwestern campaigns inspired his most famous project: the camel experiment. Typically regarded as a whimsical western tale or an example of Davis's visionary leadership, the camel episode had sinister ties to a global proslavery network.

For several years, Davis had studied camels' use by other armies, including French forces in North Africa.[82] This fascination was not unique: after the war with Mexico, novelists, explorers, diplomats, and scientists predicted that camels would provide transportation across the arid empire conquered in 1848, and venture capitalists chartered corporations to import camels for public and private use.[83] Thus, when Davis first sought congressional funding for a military camel experiment in 1851, his was not an isolated voice. But the Senate rejected his proposal (Douglas voted nay) and laughed at him; the derision appears in the congressional record.[84]

Elevation to Pierce's cabinet boosted Davis's authority, though, and in early 1855 he convinced Congress to invest $30,000 in camel research. He coordinated with the navy to organize a purchasing expedition, led by army major Henry C. Wayne, a longtime camel aficionado, in the eastern Mediterranean. Wayne bought dozens of camels and hired five experienced handlers before unloading thirty-four animals at Indianola, Texas, in April 1856. The next January, a second expedition brought back forty-one more. Military trials looked promising at first: Wayne lauded the camels' performance and suggested commencing a breeding program to expand the herd. But when James Buchanan became president in 1857, his secretary of war, John B. Floyd, focused strictly on testing the existing stock. Between 1858 and 1861, the army dabbled in additional camel projects in California and Texas. The Civil War interrupted them, however, and by March 1866, the army, convinced that railroads had mooted the experiment, liquidated its camel caravans. Circuses and mining companies purchased some of the beasts, while others were simply released into the desert. It was an inglorious end to an ambitious program.[85]

The camels marched into western folklore, but the tale has an insidious connection to the Atlantic slave trade. Davis's project triggered a train of events that underscored the grim consequences of slaveholders' far-reaching power.

The connection was Major Wayne. Born and raised in Savannah, Wayne believed that camels could do valuable service on cotton plantations. He was not alone: southern journalists tracked the experiment and reported that camels could haul several bales of cotton, measuring their utility in terms of the South's signature crop.[86] In November 1858, Wayne ignited a camel craze by penning a public letter to Washington's *National Intelligencer*. Writing as "a Southern man, from a cotton, corn, and rice growing section," he deemed camels superior to horses and mules, pictured them at work on plantations, and opined that enslaved laborers could manage them. The letter was reprinted in planters' periodicals like *Southern Cultivator*, and within two months a Georgian responded with a portentous question: "Who's Got a Camel for Sale?"[87] By 1859, camel trials were afoot in Alabama and drew crowds at the state fair in November.[88] Dallas County planter Benjamin C. Woolsey exuberantly reported that the animals pulled plows and carried massive burdens at a fraction of the expense required for mules.[89]

Thus far, the camel project had simply identified an unexpected civilian application for government-funded military research. But it also fostered a brutal connection to the illicit slave trade. Indeed, the conceptual link between camel and slave importations was there from the start. As one letter to the *Southern Cultivator* crudely put it, cotton planters needed cheap labor and work animals, and West Africa offered both: "Let 'Cuffy' come and his appropriate co-laborers the Camel. . . . Let us have the Camels right off, and then defy the world to prevent our getting as many of the wool bearing bipids [*sic*] as we may need."[90] The author referred, of course, to the importation of enslaved Africans, which continued despite the U.S. ban imposed in 1808. By the 1850s, planters' interest in African chattels surged along with cotton prices, and some proslavery radicals demanded repeal of the prohibition.[91] The repeal movement failed, but smuggling expanded: one historian estimates that 60,000 Africans were imported annually in the late 1850s, and while that figure is questionable, illicit trading did occur.[92]

Geography and economics made Texas a hotbed for human trafficking. Its coastline is dotted with bays, islands, and sandbars that for decades had attracted slave smugglers who brought captives to remote coastal camps and then sold them in Louisiana.[93] As cotton cultivation boomed in the 1850s, Texas itself became the primary market for smuggled laborers.[94] Texas newspapers openly advertised illicit auctions, such as the sale of four hundred Africans "lately landed upon the coast."[95]

At the crossroads of the Wild West and the Cotton Kingdom, Texas was where camel capers became entangled with slave smuggling. Slave traders had means and motive to enter the camel business: they had contacts with African merchants, could transport living cargoes across the Atlantic, and needed alibis. To identify slavers, British naval patrols looked for giveaways like water tanks, overabundant food stores, and the stench of excrement. In response, slave smugglers posed as palm oil merchants or whalers in order to justify carrying large tanks, and many did transport legitimate wares along with hidden captives. Others concealed food supplies under false decks and used chemicals to eliminate foul odors.[96] In the duel between slavers and their pursuers, camels offered ideal cover. Available in West Africa, they consumed tons of food and water and produced copious waste and could be routed to American buyers through familiar Texas ports.

The link was forged in October 1858, when the schooner *Thomas Watson*, accompanied by the smaller *Lucerne*, docked in Galveston and unloaded eighty-nine camels owned by a passenger named Mrs. Watson. The local British consul quite literally smelled trouble and urged U.S. officials to investigate. A federal attorney agreed that the camels probably had been used "as a cloak for slaves" but, lacking concrete evidence, refused to intervene. By early 1859, the *Thomas Watson*'s owner, John A. Machado, arrived from New York City to complain about the holdup. The *Thomas Watson* sailed away shortly after, leaving the camels to varied fates: some were slaughtered and eaten, others wound up on Lieutenant Governor Francis Lubbock's ranch, and many went with Watson to New Orleans for sale to planters across the South. Galvestonians were left with a colorful tale that lingered in living memory into the 1930s.[97]

Both principals in the Galveston caper were veteran slave traders. Portuguese American merchant John A. Machado directed legal and illegal commerce between Sierra Leone and the Americas from his Wall Street office, and the *Thomas Watson* had made several slaving expeditions, posing as a whaler, and was briefly detained by British authorities in 1857. Later, it would be commandeered for use by the Confederate government before running aground near Charleston, South Carolina, in 1861. Machado continued his criminal enterprises until the Lincoln administration cracked down on human trafficking. After being indicted in early 1863 and released on bail, Machado vanished.[98]

Mary Jane Watson was one of Machado's closest conspirators. She frequently captained the *Thomas Watson* and purchased the ship outright in 1860. In 1858, she had likely procured captives and camels in Sierra Leone and then used the *Lucerne* to ferry the human cargo ashore at a lonely spot on the Texas coast; several Texans later said they bought Africans smuggled in with camels, and one mentioned Watson by name.[99] Then, carrying only camels, the *Thomas Watson* docked at Galveston and Watson departed to dazzle journalists while peddling the camels to planters in New Orleans and Alabama. Like her ship, however, Watson met a miserable end, apparently dying drunk in a Madrid hotel in 1862.[100] Little is known about most of the camels, but one probably became the mascot of the 43rd Mississippi Infantry, the "Camel Regiment," before being killed at Vicksburg. The Mississippians named it Old Douglas.[101]

Davis did not set out to shield slave traders, but the camel experiment had unintended consequences that illuminate the Slave Power's global reach.[102] Usually regarded as a conspiracy among southern politicians and their northern allies, the Slave Power included a wider constellation of agents who shared a commitment to slavery's growth. Rather than a finely tuned conspiracy, they formed a network of public officials and private citizens who collaborated on a range of schemes, from slave smuggling to political activism. Although not monolithic, the Slave Power was insidious: Davis did not collude with Machado and Watson, but his projects dovetailed with their ugly entrepreneurship. More generally, the camel episode revealed the breadth of southern power over federal policy, power that shaped the context in which Stephen Douglas pursued his own agenda.

★ ★ ★

For Douglas, 1853 brought tragedy. In January, Martha Douglas died after childbirth, and their infant daughter passed away weeks later, searing him with the sorrow shared by Davis and many other widowed contemporaries. The grieving senator sailed to Europe for a high-profile tour complete with republican critiques of Old World monarchy.[103] Upon returning home that fall, Douglas faced a familiar challenge: unifying the Democracy. His efforts nearly wrecked his career, his party, and his country.

Douglas hoped to align Democrats behind his agenda of internal improvements, a Pacific railroad, and territorial organization of the vast expanse between the Missouri River and the Rocky Mountains, believing that development of this interior empire would infuse the party with badly needed energy.[104] Based on the letters and petitions flooding his desk, moreover, constituent pressure to fulfill these old promises was mounting. A Chicago alderman demanded internal improvements; Cook County petitioners wanted to make the mouth of the Calumet River into Lake Michigan's premier harbor; the St. Louis Chamber of Commerce sought Mississippi River improvements; correspondents from Washington, D.C., to Utah pressed for a Pacific Railroad; and anxious pioneers, including one auspiciously named for Thomas Jefferson, admonished Douglas to pass his long-delayed Nebraska bill.[105] Failure could be ruinous: in September 1853, one observer warned that Young Americans chafed at Douglas's "want of boldness & progress in what pertains to the spirit of the age."[106] Democratic strength in Illinois had facilitated his reelection to the Senate in January 1853, but now that Democrats controlled the presidency and Congress, Douglas had to deliver.[107]

Dynamic growth and rising regional consciousness stoked northwestern impatience. Thanks to emigration from abroad and from the Northeast, Illinois's population doubled in the 1850s, making it the fourth most populous state by 1860. Northwesterners craved infrastructure and often got it—Illinois's railroads expanded from around 100 miles in 1850 to over 2,800 by 1860—but they wanted more, along with homesteads and territorial organization. Democratic editors credited the party for regional progress, and many northwesterners did, too, but they also blamed southern Democrats for setbacks, a persistent theme since the complaints about Chicago's "Polk bars."[108] Party strength and constituent satisfaction depended on Douglas's ability to meet their needs.

Douglas's previous efforts had produced mixed results. He had watched a southern Democrat veto an infrastructure bill, repeatedly failed to organize the Nebraska Territory, and gotten nowhere on homestead legislation. Southern opposition had regularly thwarted him.[109] During his latest effort to organize Nebraska in March 1853, the Senate voted 23–17 to table his bill, with southerners siding overwhelmingly (18–2) with the majority. Only Missouri's senators broke ranks.[110] Sectional strife, which Douglas regarded as a distraction from constructive lawmaking, also stymied him. In 1852, he interrupted an animated debate over the Fugitive Slave Act to demand consideration of bills to protect overland emigrants and build a Pacific railroad. The Senate, he fumed, must prioritize "practical matters of legislation" over efforts to "fan the flames of discord."[111]

On the other hand, Douglas had organized the Oregon and Minnesota Territories and in his banner year of 1850 established the Utah and New Mexico Territories and secured a land grant for the Illinois Central Railroad. Popular sovereignty was the winning formula in the southwestern territories, while a classic logrolling technique had passed the railroad bill. These triumphs, along with the apparent pacification of Illinoisans who loathed the Fugitive Slave Act, convinced Douglas that he could win sufficient southern support without alienating too many constituents.

A recent struggle over internal improvements clarified Douglas's problem and pointed to a possible solution. In early 1851, Davis began marshaling southern Democrats against a new rivers and harbors bill, urging its defeat at a February 27 party caucus, where he spoke on behalf of what one correspondent called "the ultras of the South, constituting the majority of the party in many of the Southern States." Illinois Democrat James Shields bristled at Davis's remarks, but Douglas, eager to align the party behind his ambitions, was cagier. He regretted the tendency for "hair-splitting among our Southern friends" but promised "to do anything reasonable to please them."[112] Unmoved, Davis assailed the bill on the Senate floor, singling out Chicago's harbor appropriation and labeling federal infrastructure investment a "deadly contagion."[113] The session ended without further action on a bill, which nearly left the Democracy "demoralized, dissolved, annihilated for the next twenty years."[114] Chicagoans blamed southern Democrats for depriving them of $15,000 for their sand-choked harbor.[115]

No Illinois Democrat could sanction Davis's scathing attack, but Douglas was determined to satisfy his constituents without disturbing party unity. Buried in Davis's speech was a possible compromise: Congress could authorize states to finance internal improvements by taxing goods in transit.[116] These taxes, known as tonnage duties, met Davis's constitutional standards, and Douglas, always more interested in results than theories, embraced them. Tonnage duties could win broad Democratic support for northwesterners' pet projects, and since they shifted decision-making away from a fractious Congress, they might liberate states from dependence on unreliable federal aid. By accepting tonnage duties as the price of fulfilling his agenda and removing a divisive question from Congress, Douglas followed a path on internal improvements that paralleled his journey to popular sovereignty.[117]

During the next session of Congress, Douglas endorsed both tonnage duties and land grants as practical means for building infrastructure without the delay and discord associated with federal outlays.[118] He pressed these points for years, most notably in a January 1854 public letter to Illinois governor Joel Matteson, in which he hailed tonnage duties as more economical and reliable than any alternative.[119] But westerners were skeptical. Some warned that Douglas's plan would break the Union into a constellation of rival principalities bristling with customs houses; others vilified it as part of John C. Calhoun's "nullification creed."[120] Later, Republicans would cite the tonnage duties scheme as proof that Democrats were too beholden to slaveholders to support internal improvements.[121] These frosty responses showed that not all northwesterners would pay the same price for southern support.

Sectional rivalries also dogged Douglas's efforts to promote a Pacific railroad. One of the project's earliest congressional supporters, he was the only Illinois congressman who responded publicly to an 1845 Pacific railroad proposal offered by merchant Asa Whitney. Douglas preferred to finance the road through land grants to states and territories but heartily endorsed the idea of fostering white settlement from the Mississippi to the Pacific.[122] Public support grew quickly, and Douglas's correspondence shows that popular pressure for the railroad flourished even during the secession crisis.[123] As a presidential aspirant who represented an economically diverse state, however, Douglas had to finesse the route question; unlike Davis, he could not sponsor one pet plan. Many observers associated Douglas with the northernmost route, from the Great Lakes to Puget Sound.[124] Selection of this route would have elated residents of the Greater Northwest, and Douglas collaborated as closely with its surveyor, Isaac Stevens, as Davis did with sponsors of the Gila River route. Stevens visited Douglas before departing and corresponded with him during and after the expedition, which convinced Stevens of the route's superiority.[125] Douglas praised the route in an 1858 Senate speech, enumerating its plentiful water, grass, and timber resources.[126] But although single-minded advocacy of Stevens's route might have curried favor in Minnesota and Oregon, it would have cost Douglas support in southern Illinois, which lay within the economic orbit of St. Louis, a likely eastern terminus for a central line. This pushed him toward a more agnostic stance on routes, such as a central trunk branching into three prongs terminating at Chicago, St. Louis, and Memphis.[127]

In late 1853, however, the prospects for all of the central and northern routes dimmed as Davis's southern route emerged as a frontrunner. The Compromise of 1850 had created an unbroken line of territories and states across the Southwest, and the Gadsden Purchase would soon secure the Gila River region. Sensing victory, southern editors predicted that lines from Vicksburg, Memphis, and other southern cities would converge in Texas and form the trunk of the Pacific railroad.[128] The stakes multiplied as treasure flowed from California gold mines, and southerners, thanks in part to their well-placed cabinet spokesman, enjoyed a commanding lead. When Douglas returned to Washington in December 1853, he had every reason to press his agenda with hot haste.[129]

★ ★ ★

Tellingly, the law conceived as the Nebraska bill and christened the Kansas-Nebraska Act was often referred to as the "Douglas Bill," the "Douglas measure," or "that Douglas project."[130] The Illinoisan encouraged this view, boasting that "I passed the Kansas-Nebraska Act myself. I had the authority and power of a dictator throughout the whole controversy."[131] For Douglas, a skilled parliamentarian who, fortunately, never wielded despotic power, the bill was a response to multiple pressures: constituent impatience, sectional railroad rivalries, the clout of southern Democrats, and the need to align his party behind his sputtering western agenda. A biographical perspective on lawmaking, however, must not allow the life to overshadow the times, since the final version of the act, which repealed the Missouri Compromise's venerable ban on slavery in the newly organized territories, was the work of many hands. For Douglas, the Kansas-Nebraska Act was, in its final form, less a Pyrrhic victory than a cyanide pill.

Historians have scrutinized Douglas's motives for introducing the Nebraska bill and accepting repeal of the slavery prohibition, sometimes conflating the two issues.[132] Some scholars, echoing Douglas's northern critics, view the act as the fruit of conspiracy between slaveholders and their northern pawns and charge Douglas with pandering for southern support for his next presidential bid.[133] Wary of this argument's partisan roots and overeager to debunk slavery's political salience, others claim that Douglas simply wanted to secure a Chicago terminus for the Pacific railroad.[134] This interpretation's insistence on compartmentalizing western development and sectionalism limits its persuasiveness, but other scholars seek to situate the Nebraska bill within Douglas's broader regional agenda. Some look beyond the Pacific railroad to argue that Douglas sought to promote political and economic development across the West, an interpretation favored by many specialists in western history.[135] Other scholars argue that Douglas strove mainly to advance the principle of popular sovereignty. This interpretation echoes many of Douglas's western contemporaries, who welcomed the Kansas-Nebraska Act as an omen of increased self-government.[136] Whether focused on economics or politics, these narratives present Douglas as a spokesman of the West rather than a tool of the South. Of course, he was also a diehard Democrat, and other scholars stress the partisan goals—unite the Democrats and reignite conflict with the Whigs—driving Douglas's actions.[137]

Examining the Nebraska bill as Douglas imagined it, not as a precursor to civil war but as the next step in his program for Democratic-sponsored western development, illuminates the complexity of his position. A nationally prominent politician who championed a broad western constituency but answered to voters in a state with diverse interests, Douglas always had multiple motivations. He had been introducing Nebraska bills into Congress for a decade, and his clamorous constituents shared his impatience. Popular pressure and the brightening prospects of a southern railroad to the Pacific added to Douglas's urgency by 1854, but there was nothing fundamentally new in his desire to organize Nebraska and then tackle complementary projects like railroads and homestead legislation. In light of his wider career and the immediate context, Douglas's zeal for a Nebraska bill was overdetermined.

Since Douglas did not write, revise, and pass the Kansas-Nebraska Act by himself, some scholars look elsewhere to understand its evolution. Several studies foreground Senator David Atchison and the ferociously competitive arena of Missouri politics.[138] Others explore how a contingent of southern senators transformed the "Douglas Bill" into something very different than what the Little Giant had proposed, showing that Douglas's reasons for sponsoring the Nebraska bill cannot explain its final form.[139]

Why, then, did Douglas accept the revised Nebraska bill's inflammatory repeal of a decades-old ban on slavery? He recognized the risks, so why did he pay so high a price?[140] On their own, his motives for organizing new territories do not explain this. But here, too, there is continuity between Douglas's prior career and his actions in 1854. He had long balanced responsiveness to his constituents with partisan loyalty, striving to promote his western agenda under the auspices of a fractious Democratic Party. This tension shaped his stance on everything from harbor improvements (tonnage duties) and slavery expansion (popular sovereignty) to the Pacific railroad (multiple lines). Douglas's recent successes in brokering among sectional interests, and in convincing Illinoisans that he had not conceded too much to the South, emboldened him in 1854. Recent trends in party leadership, meanwhile, empowered southern Democrats to exact an exorbitant price in return. Douglas bargained them down somewhat, but not enough to appease northerners who believed that he had sold them out in the infamous deal he struck at the crossroads of his career.

★ ★ ★

When Douglas pressed for a Nebraska bill in 1854, he was reprising his role as western gadfly. Since 1844, he had offered bills to organize the territory, but colleagues hesitated even to discuss them. In his most recent attempt, Douglas sputtered that senators had "refused to hear a territorial bill" for two years and that for "two weeks past, I have sat here hour after hour endeavoring at every suitable opportunity to obtain the floor. I ask now that the Nebraska bill be taken up, and I mean to insist on the motion."[141] He scolded them for neglecting western needs and repeated his prophecy that the West Coast would secede unless "continuous lines of [white] settlements" linked the Mississippi to the Pacific via Nebraska.[142] Again, the Senate failed to budge; again, southerners were stubborn. Some expressed solicitude for Native Americans, but their prime concern was the Missouri Compromise's slavery prohibition, for they had little incentive to propel Nebraska toward statehood.[143] If slaveholders were barred from the territory, growled one Missourian, "I say let the Indians have it *forever*. They are better neighbors than the abolitionists, *by a damn sight*."[144] Douglas already recognized and resented these sectional considerations. Back in 1852, he had upbraided Congress for lavishing millions on southeastern coastal defenses while ignoring western migrants and accused southerners like Andrew P. Butler of "direct, open hostility" to the West.[145]

Still, Douglas needed southern help to organize Nebraska, and by late 1853, southern Democrats could demand much in exchange. Nearly half of Senate Democrats were southerners, and they controlled key offices, particularly members of the F Street Mess. Named for their shared Washington living quarters, these Calhoun-inspired Democrats included Virginians James M. Mason and Robert M. T. Hunter, who chaired the Foreign Relations Committee and Finance Committee, respectively; Butler of South Carolina, chair of the Judiciary Committee; and Missouri's David R. Atchison, Davis's school chum and the Senate's president pro tempore.[146] This scenario, in which Douglas needed favors from powerful southern Democrats, resembled the Samuel Ashton affair, but with far higher stakes. Yet Douglas did have reasons for optimism. Late in the previous session of Congress, his bill to organize the Washington Territory, in which slavery was prohibited by local enactments but not by federal law, had passed without controversy.[147] Moreover, growing grassroots pressure from Iowa and Missouri seemed likely to weaken congressional opposition to a Nebraska bill.[148]

By January 1854, Douglas's rising expectations propelled him toward a reckoning with entrenched southern strength, which would upend American politics. The resulting Kansas-Nebraska Act is often regarded as an unalloyed triumph for the Slave Power, but its legislative history reveals a more interesting story. The bill's twisting path through Congress underscored the might of the proslavery bloc as well as Douglas's determination to haggle down the price of southern support, and the outcome fully satisfied no one. As historian Robert R. Russel observed, northern Democrats "made great sacrifices of sentiment, interests, principles, and personal political advantage," but the law still "fell far short of meeting what the great majority of Southern congressmen thought were the South's just demands."[149] The Kansas-Nebraska Act was largely a victory for slaveholders, but it sowed suspicion among antislavery and proslavery critics alike. Its origins, like its bloody epilogue, aggravated conflicts over property and democracy and ravaged the Democracy and the Union.

Iowa Democratic senator Augustus C. Dodge opened the ball by introducing a Nebraska territorial bill, modeled after Douglas's proposal from the previous session, on December 14, 1853.[150] Initially, some southerners eyed it with mistrust. A *Richmond Enquirer* correspondent cautioned that Free-Soilers were plotting to "hasten on a territorial organization," exclude slavery from Nebraska, and leave Missouri exposed to abolitionists on three sides.[151] Southern fears were compounded by the fact that complementary items on Douglas's agenda, including a northern railroad to the Pacific and a homestead law, would facilitate nonslaveholders' westward migration.[152] Dodge's bill, moreover, left the existing restriction on slavery untouched. Shortly after the bill was referred to Douglas's Committee on Territories, David Atchison urged the Illinoisan to explicitly repeal the venerable ban.[153]

Douglas established a pattern by seeking to soothe southern apprehensions without sacrificing popular sovereignty. Shopping for southern support at a cut-rate price, he offered a new version of the Nebraska bill, along with an explanatory report, on January 4. Contrary to Atchison's wishes, neither document called for repealing the federal ban on slavery; instead, the existing prohibition would remain, and the territorial legislature could govern slavery unless courts ruled otherwise. Thus, while the Supreme Court could delimit the scope of territorial self-rule, the bill would empower Nebraska to authorize or prohibit slavery throughout its territorial existence, thereby establishing popular sovereignty as most northern Democrats understood it. Douglas's report likened the present situation to the midcentury quarrel over the Mexican Cession: both conflicts pitted an extant free-soil provision (Mexican law in New Mexico and Utah; the Missouri Compromise ban in Nebraska) against the common-property doctrine. In 1850, Congress had compromised by adopting popular sovereignty. Now, he argued, it should do the same on Nebraska.[154] The comparison between a foreign statute and the Missouri

Compromise was disingenuous, but the rationale seemed plausible to an impatient western gadfly.

Dissatisfied, Atchison pressured Douglas, perhaps with the offer of a coveted spot on the Committee on the Pacific Railroad (to which Douglas was appointed on January 9), to clarify his bill. Douglas obligingly added a twenty-first section, which reaffirmed that territorial citizens could settle questions about slavery, left legal questions surrounding slavery to the courts, and required enforcement of the Fugitive Slave Act in every territory. He insisted that the stray paragraphs had been omitted inadvertently from the original text, but Atchison probably had forced his hand, even if the new section squared with Douglas's views.[155]

Atchison liked the revised bill, but other southerners still smelled a rat. Since the federal ban on slavery remained, they declared, slaveholders would shun the territory and popular sovereignty would produce a free state.[156] Alabama Democratic congressman Philip Phillips mentioned this to the F Street Mess and worked quietly for outright repeal of the slavery prohibition by penning an amendment that would render "inoperative, void, and of no force and effect" all federal statutes that limited territorial voters' power over slavery.[157] Far noisier was Senator Archibald Dixon, a Kentucky Whig who on January 16 moved to amend Douglas's bill by providing that slaveholders "shall be at liberty to take and hold their slaves within any of the Territories of the United States, or of the States to be formed therefrom."[158] Dixon thereby injected the common-property doctrine into the Nebraska debate and offered one of the most brazen proslavery proposals ever introduced into Congress. It transcended Nebraska and applied to all territories, including those where slavery was possible under popular sovereignty (Utah and New Mexico) and those where it was already illegal (Oregon, Washington, and Minnesota). The reference to states "formed therefrom" suggested that slavery must continue after statehood, an interventionist policy that exceeded Calhoun's boldest schemes. Stunned northern Democrats suspected that the amendment was a Whig ploy to destabilize their party.[159] In fact, Dixon's proposal showed that party identities were yielding to sectional loyalty politics. As he put it, "Upon the question of slavery, I know no Whiggery, and I know no Democracy. I am a pro-slavery man. I am from a slaveholding State; I represent a slaveholding constituency; and I am here to maintain the rights of that people whenever they are presented before the Senate."[160] As southern Whigs and Democrats clamored for repeal of the slavery prohibition, a sectional bloc, which threatened both national parties, was beginning to coalesce.

Appalled, Douglas immediately urged Dixon, as a patriot and friend of the Compromise of 1850, to withdraw it.[161] Douglas also rebuked Dixon's proslavery pronunciamento by insisting that the Nebraska bill must never legislate slavery into a territory and pressing him to disavow any intention of doing so.[162] But Douglas's opposition to repealing the Missouri Compromise's free-soil provision was weakening. With southern Democrats determined not to be outdone by Whigs and southerners of both parties making vociferous demands, it was increasingly difficult to rally the Democracy. Douglas would have to stem the southern tide without drowning popular sovereignty in Calhounian dogma.[163]

Preparing to amend his bill again, Douglas entered a second round of negotiations with southerners, including both Phillips and Dixon. On an infamous carriage ride with the latter, Douglas vowed to support repeal "though I know it will raise a hell of a storm."[164] Meanwhile, southerners ratcheted up the pressure on the president. Pierce favored Douglas's original Nebraska bill and hoped to defer slavery-related questions to the Supreme Court, but Davis and James C. Dobbin of North Carolina, the secretary of the navy who shared Davis's hostility to popular sovereignty, insisted that Pierce endorse repeal. Southerners in Congress and the administration had set the price of organizing Nebraska.[165]

The turning point came at a meeting on Sunday, January 22, which highlighted southern power over federal policy. Accepting the necessity of repeal, Douglas sought administration support for another iteration of the Nebraska bill, which he would unveil the next day. But Pierce was a strict Sabbatarian, and only a close friend could finagle a political meeting on a day of rest. Enter Jefferson Davis, a trusted advisor who had tracked the Nebraska bill's progress and now fulfilled the hopes of southern ultras who had cheered his appointment. When Douglas arrived at the White House, accompanied by Phillips and most of the F Street Mess, Davis secured them an audience with the president. Reluctantly, Pierce agreed to make Douglas's bill a test of party fidelity. Having agreed to southerners' high price, he and Douglas staked the Democracy's future on a bill sure to provoke backlash.[166]

Douglas rolled the dice and reported his substitute bill on January 23. It provided for two territories, Kansas and Nebraska; left slavery's status up to popular sovereignty; and insisted that the Missouri Compromise restriction was "inoperative" because it had been superseded by the Compromise of 1850.[167] Douglas amended the bill several more times, including to declare the old slavery ban "inoperative and void" and to enhance territorial self-government by allowing legislatures to override gubernatorial vetoes and removing the requirement that territorial legislation receive congressional approval.[168]

Douglas had boosted western self-rule and parried Dixon's extreme demands, but the bill stirred up a hornet's nest. Debate raged in the Senate until early March and in the House until late May, producing memorable scenes, from the "Appeal of the Independent Democrats," a stirring call for northern unity against an "atrocious plot" to make the West "a dreary region of despotism," to Douglas's running press battle against antislavery clergymen.[169] Douglas's mail reflected public polarization: northern admirers commended him for defending popular sovereignty, southern enthusiasts added their praise, friendly observers warned of antislavery outrage, and critics rebuked him directly.[170] Months before becoming law, Douglas's bill had upended American politics.

Nevertheless, Douglas followed a familiar path even as political tremors shook the ground beneath his feet. He remained the western gadfly, pressing for debate on his bill just one day after introducing the heavily revised January 23 version. He acknowledged that many colleagues had not read it but complained that "my territorial bills" were always "crowded over by other business" and added that he hoped to pass other western bills as well.[171] Douglas also rehashed his vision of the "great West" as a wellspring of unity, proclaiming that the upper and lower Mississippi River valleys were "one and inseparable."[172] He continued to insist that local decisions, not the Northwest Ordinance, had kept slavery out of Illinois, provoking a sharp debate with former governor Edward Coles.[173] And despite his quest for southern support, Douglas predicted that popular sovereignty would yield free soil in Nebraska, arguing that "it is worse than folly to think of it being a slave-holding country."[174] Rehashing an idea he broached in 1850, Douglas again speculated that local self-government, which had made California a free state, might roll slavery back from states where it currently existed.[175] The continuity between 1854 and Douglas's earlier career suggests that he saw the Nebraska bill as the next step of his program, not a political turning point. But it also underscores his serious miscalculation about northern responses to the bill.

By the time Pierce signed the Kansas-Nebraska Act in late May, Douglas had magnified many problems he meant to solve. Instead of silencing protest, the bill triggered a wave of antislavery activism. Instead of promoting western development, the bill incited debate that swamped Douglas's agenda; Pacific railroad and homestead bills fizzled that session, and Pierce vetoed a river and harbor measure.[176] And instead of uniting Douglas's party, the bill splintered northern Democrats into pro- and anti-Nebraska camps, fostering sectional realignment rather than party cohesion.[177] The final votes in Congress made this clear. In the Senate, ten southern Whigs, twelve northern Democrats, and fifteen southern Democrats combined to pass the bill, while four northern Democrats, six northern Whigs, two Free-Soilers, and two southerners opposed it. Southerners were resolutely in favor, while cracks in northern Democratic unity were emerging.[178] Signals from the House were even more alarming: all but nine southerners voted for the bill, while northern Democrats split, forty-four in favor and forty-three against.[179] Douglas left the crossroads of his career with a hollow victory and a heap of trouble waiting back home.

★ ★ ★

Douglas recalled returning to Chicago in August 1854 "by the light of my own effigy."[180] He had paid a higher price for Nebraska than many northerners could stomach, and their outrage triggered a massive political groundswell. Douglas's inability to dispel their criticism contrasted sharply with his handling of constituent dissent four years before.

The difference was stark when Douglas attempted to stanch the torrent of indignation in Chicago. Anti-Nebraska newspapers, led by the *Chicago Tribune*, publicized Douglas's planned appearance and urged Chicagoans to turn out en masse to prevent another slick defense of a hated law. When Douglas mounted the speaker's platform in front of North Market Hall on the evening of September 1, he faced a fuming crowd 10,000 strong. "I come before you tonight to explain to you the provisions of the act of congress known as the Nebraska and Kansas act," he began, drawing groans and hisses. "The bill is framed upon the great principle of the right of the people to regulate their own government." Chicagoans would have none of it. Douglas struggled for two and a half hours but was shouted down by jeers, insults, and challenges. Beaten, he shook his fist and left. Alas, his oft-quoted valedictory, "It is now Sunday morning—I'll go to church, and you may go to hell!," is unsupported by contemporary evidence or the 1854 calendar, which shows that September 1 was a Friday.[181] Regardless, Douglas had failed to defuse popular ire.

The Chicago protest foreshadowed the wave of antislavery wrath that swept the free states. Editorialists denounced the Kansas-Nebraska Act as "a perfidious breach of compact" and an "unholy conspiracy against freedom," supported by "trucklers to the Slave power," which warped the nation into a "gigantic Confederacy of Crime."[182] Illinoisans agreed, branding Douglas an "ambitious and dangerous demagogue," the "tool of southern slave-drivers," and a "blemish upon the honor of the State of

Illinois."[183] These sentiments crossed party lines, as the typical anti-Nebraska meeting was "indiscriminately composed" of Whigs and Democrats. Douglasites tried to dissuade Democrats from attending by cracking the whip of party discipline, but their failure indicated that "the party screws cannot be applied with sufficient force to drive the people to an abandonment of the Missouri Compromise, and the approval of slavery in Nebraska."[184] As a result, Illinois Democrats, like their counterparts across the North, divided into pro- and anti-Nebraska wings. Anti-Nebraska Democrats like William H. Bissell and Lyman Trumbull hesitated to leave the party but opposed Douglas and his law, driving a wedge into the state Democratic organization, which foreshadowed future realignment.[185] "The Democratic party," wrote a Jacksonville resident, "is much broken up."[186] The act also aroused antislavery Whigs, including ex-congressman Abraham Lincoln, who condemned Douglas for abandoning the founders' policy of restricting slavery's expansion.[187] It would take several years for the Republican Party to blossom, but its seeds were planted by Douglas's bill and fertilized by bipartisan outrage.

Douglas scrambled to respond. To shore up support before the fall midterms, he recruited James W. Sheahan, a Maryland-born son of Irish immigrants, to take over the *Chicago Times*. Sheahan left his family in Washington and dutifully assumed the editorship in the summer of 1854.[188] In editorials and speeches, Douglasites proclaimed that the Kansas-Nebraska Act safeguarded territorial self-government and would not foster slavery's expansion. Thus, they sold popular sovereignty as a matter of justice to western voters and a practical free-soil policy. In a typical editorial, a Michigander argued that the "inalienable right of self-government" was "just as sacred to the republican citizens of the new territories" as to those of any state. Popular sovereignty would protect local majority rule from interference by pro- or antislavery meddlers. Nebraska voters, he concluded, would never endorse "negro bondage," for they had "too much foresight" to embrace the "curse" of slavery.[189] Territorial Democrats made similar arguments: Lafayette Grover cited Oregon's ban on both slavery and black immigration as proof that westerners favored free soil.[190]

Like his supporters, Douglas recognized that the midterms represented a referendum on the Kansas-Nebraska Act, so he launched another exhausting campaign tour. He insisted that territorial organization was imperative for maintaining the westward march of liberty, progress, and railroads; that popular sovereignty offered the only means to organize them; and that the doctrine simply recognized westerners' right to self-rule. He also assailed his opponents as an unholy alliance of fanatical abolitionists and bigoted nativists. Unwilling to acknowledge the sincerity of concerns about slavery expansion and slaveholders' power, Douglas blamed the backlash on the Know-Nothing (American) Party, which would ride hatred of immigrants and Catholics to victory in many state elections that fall.[191] But Douglas failed to satisfy northern critics, including disgruntled Democrats who charged him with surrendering to the South. Unlike the Compromise of 1850, the Kansas-Nebraska Act offered no clear counterbalance to the opening of previously free soil to slavery. And unlike the Fugitive Slave Act, whose constitutional basis was conceded even by many antislavery critics, including Lincoln, popular sovereignty stood on flimsy legal foundations.

The midterms eviscerated the northern Democracy. Entering the contest, Democrats held 93 out of 144 northern congressional districts; they retained only 22. Supporters of the Kansas-Nebraska Act fared even worse, with only seven of the forty-four free-state Democrats who voted for the act winning reelection. Similarly striking was the damage to the party's image overall, as only fifteen of the northern Democrats who had *opposed* Douglas's bill were returned to Congress. The backlash breached Democratic strongholds in the Northwest. Democrats had controlled all but one of Indiana's eleven congressional districts; after 1854, they held only two. Democrats took only four of Illinois's nine seats in Congress, carrying one by the smallest possible margin: one vote.[192] "Never before," admitted a Democratic editor, "have the democracy of Illinois been so completely vanquished."[193] Douglas was not up for reelection, but voters had dealt him a stinging blow. As a New Yorker observed, "No Senator of the United States ever before received such a withering repudiation."[194] Consolidating their victory, a coalition of Whigs and dissident Democrats elected anti-Nebraska Democrat Lyman Trumbull to join Douglas in the Senate. Typically remembered as a setback for Whig candidate Abraham Lincoln, Trumbull's election underscored the importance of Democrats in the emerging Republican coalition, encouraged other Democrats to break ranks, and rebuked both Douglas and the pro-Nebraska incumbent, James Shields.[195] Southerners took note: one Mississippian marveled at election returns from *"the State of Douglas,* to whose whistle the Clans, I fear, will never rally again."[196]

White southern responses to the Kansas-Nebraska Act were mixed. Many hailed it as a victory and Douglas as a champion of what they euphemistically called "southern rights." A North Carolinian assured Douglas that he stood "far ahead all of the statesmen of the present day, in the affections of our people."[197] One Mississippian envisioned a Douglas-Davis Democratic ticket in 1856.[198] Beyond repeal of the Missouri Compromise restriction, however, southerners bickered over what, if anything, they had won.[199] The act left "the people" of both territories "perfectly free to form and regulate their domestic institutions in their own way, subject only to the Constitution of the United States."[200] This language veiled Democrats' disputes over popular sovereignty by inviting a judicial resolution. Northerners, who rejected the common-property doctrine, insisted that territorial slavery bans were constitutional and likely to be imposed, while southerners promised that the Supreme Court would squash "squatter sovereignty" and shield masters' property until statehood.[201]

This ambiguity inspired southern doubts, which reflected enduring antipathy toward popular sovereignty. South Carolina's Laurence Keitt, for instance, carried Calhoun's torch in a scathing speech that berated northern friends of squatter sovereignty and demanded federal recognition of slaveholders' property rights in the territories.[202] Dissatisfied with Douglas's bill, Keitt abstained from voting on it. Equally revealing was the split within Mississippi's uniformly Democratic delegation. Senator Albert Gallatin Brown denied that territories could prohibit slavery and vowed not to vote for the Nebraska bill if it authorized squatter sovereignty.[203] In the House, Wiley P. Harris and William T. S. Barry sparred over Douglas's bill: Harris denounced it for embracing squatter sovereignty and scolded southerners who backed a measure that offered "little to commend it to their support," while Barry promised that it rejected squatter sovereignty and that the Supreme Court would strike down any territorial prohibition of slavery.[204] Mississippi editors echoed this debate, some swearing that the Kansas-Nebraska Act codified the common-property doctrine, others that it enacted squatter rule.[205]

These quarrels fueled a proslavery critique of the Kansas-Nebraska Act that mirrored northern criticisms. From the Appeal of the Independent Democrats to Lincoln's 1858 senatorial campaign, antislavery northerners accused Douglas of conspiring with the Slave Power to spread slavery.[206] Less famous are the conspiracy theorists who accused Douglas of duping southerners into supporting a free-soil measure. As early as April 1854, Albert Pike of Arkansas claimed that the Nebraska bill, like the homestead bill, would expand free soil in the West and secure for the North a "preponderance over the whole South!"[207] An Alabama editor urged that Douglas—"not the black-skinned [Frederick] Douglas[s], but the black hearted [Stephen] Douglas"—should be hanged.[208] A few weeks before his death in 1858, James Gadsden warned James Henry Hammond, "Beware lest another 'Kansas Fraud' is sprung upon the South," for Douglas was "again on the Frontier for expansion" and looking to organize new territories.[209] These suspicions were inflamed by northern Democrats' frantic pledges that the act would not expand slavery. When Douglas (falsely) claimed that repealing the Missouri Compromise restriction had opened to freedom areas formerly reserved to slavery, a Louisiana editor charged him with "representing the Nebraska bill as an abolition measure." "This," he concluded, "will be special news for his Southern friends."[210] Like Pike, the writer belonged to the anti-Democratic opposition and sought to sow dissension by insisting that Douglas had played southern Democrats for fools. This theory eventually entered southern historiography when Davis biographers debated whether Douglas had conned the Mississippian, who routinely denounced popular sovereignty as a cloaked Wilmot Proviso, into endorsing the doctrine in 1854.[211]

Southern suspicions were grounded in reality: the Kansas-Nebraska Act was *not* the Calhounian measure demanded by Dixon, and popular sovereignty *could* leave property rights exposed to majority rule. The most practical response was to recruit settlers to win the territorial race. Writing to Davis in September 1854, David Atchison resolved to vanquish "the Negro thieves in Kansas" and predicted that proslavery migrants "will be compelled to shoot, burn, & hang" their way to victory.[212] White Mississippians joined the crusade; residents of Hancock County called for emigrant associations to assist "vigorous and patriotic Southern men" in moving to Kansas, where they would defend slavery "lawfully at the ballot box, and, if necessary, with the cartridge box."[213] In the short run, southern misgivings encouraged the competitive migration that made Kansas bleed; in the long run, they primed proslavery partisans to view Douglas and northern Democrats as traitors.

Thus, even in the ostensibly triumphant year of 1854, the coalition that had written, revised, and passed the Kansas-Nebraska Act was not monolithic. Spring 1854 marked the peak of southern acquiescence to popular sovereignty, a doctrine that was temporarily useful for smiting the Missouri Compromise but generated little enthusiasm among proslavery politicians who loathed squatter sovereignty.[214] Simultaneously, northern Democrats chafed at southern denials that the act said what Douglas insisted it said: that territorial voters were free to choose.[215] Northern backers supported Douglas's bill *because* of its popular sovereignty provisions and *despite* its repeal of the Missouri Compromise restriction; southerners had done the opposite, accepting popular sovereignty as the price of repeal. This discrepancy mirrored previous cases in which Democrats were united primarily by what they opposed. Built on an unsteady foundation of hostility to free-soilism, the coalition that passed the Kansas-Nebraska Act would collapse amid struggles over what the Democracy supported. Festering divisions between local majoritarianism and elite property rights could not be ignored.

★ ★ ★

Davis and Douglas followed radically different trajectories after the midterms. Secretary Davis soared through 1855: early that year, Congress approved the creation of two cavalry regiments for southwestern service and appropriated money for camel research, and by year's end he had penned two reports endorsing the southern route for the Pacific railroad.[216] In January 1856, he won sweet vindication when Mississippi returned him to the Senate, to begin after he completed his cabinet service.[217] Mississippi Democrats also triumphed in the 1855 state elections, repelling a Know-Nothing challenge by convincing voters that the national Democratic Party was the South's only source of security.[218]

Meanwhile, Douglas's western agenda stalled. In early 1855, he introduced bills to construct Pacific railroads along northern, central, and southern routes and to admit Oregon as a state.[219] Both efforts fizzled out amid fierce debates over the Fugitive Slave Act and the Kansas-Nebraska Act, in which Douglas defended both measures against stinging criticism.[220] Intended to satisfy northwestern ambitions, the Kansas-Nebraska Act had sown a sectional whirlwind that swept Douglas's agenda from the Senate floor.

Events in Kansas pushed Douglas deeper into a corner. Had the territory barred slavery in 1855, Douglas's free-soil critics would have lost steam; instead, popular sovereignty devolved into fraud and violence. In March 1855, Missourians poured into Kansas to elect a legislature, which adopted draconian proslavery laws and criminalized dissent. In response, free-state settlers established a rival government at Topeka and pressed for statehood. At year's end, ongoing tensions sparked violence in the Wakarusa War.[221] Northern Democrats worried that this "monstrous perversion of the doctrine of popular sovereignty" would ruin Douglas, cripple the party, and split the Union.[222]

Desperate to defeat the "army of *isms*"—abolitionism and Know-Nothingism—opposing the Democracy, Douglas spent much of 1855 on the hustings.[223] Crisscrossing Illinois, he defended popular sovereignty, denounced abolitionists and nativists, and extolled the Democracy as the only national party. As if stumping for his own reelection, Douglas wore himself ragged and wound up bedridden in Terre Haute, Indiana. Physicians diagnosed him with bronchitis and inflammation of the throat and referred him to a Cleveland surgeon, who in December removed much of his uvula and lower palate. Douglas's confidants tried to conceal his infirmity while laying the foundation for his 1856 presidential run.[224] "No one . . . can represent the National Union sentiment, so strongly as Judge D," one wrote. "The Nebraska Bill and its principles must be sustained or there is a gloomy uncertainty before the country."[225]

As Pierce's presidency entered its fourth year, Davis and Douglas, like their respective wings of the Democracy, faced profoundly different prospects. Davis anticipated a triumphant return to the Senate, and back in Mississippi, Democrats celebrated Pierce's widespread popularity.[226] But the view from Douglas's sickbed was grim. Three years of Democratic ascendancy had ravaged the party's northern wing and provoked massive defections. A Chicagoan spoke for many dissidents when he wrote to Lyman Trumbull, "My affections . . . have been with the Democratic Party always, but when I look back upon its history for the past few years my gorge rises." He hated seeing no one among the party leadership "but Polks & Pierces, Jeff Davis's & renegade Cushings, Douglas's & Ike Cooks. . . . Can we stand it?" Certainly not when "our Slavocrat masters" blocked river and harbor legislation, deprecated public education, and rammed the Kansas-Nebraska Act through Congress. He urged Trumbull to teach the "Southern Chivalry" to respect the North.[227] By 1856, the Democracy was badly splintered and tilting southward, compounding the problems that had shaped Douglas's Faustian bargain two years before.

5

Wages of Whiteness

G. W. Armstrong could not believe what Stephen Douglas had done. The Memphis carpenter had revered "the embodiment [of] the Great head of Democracy" so much that he named his only son Stephen A. D. Armstrong. Now, that former esteem only magnified his dismay. In an emotional December 1857 letter, Armstrong recanted his support for Douglas's presidential aspirations, compared the senator to recreant Democrats like Martin Van Buren, and begged him to "be a man a patriot and a hero" and cut ties with the "Black Republicans." Armstrong expressed more grief than anger, but his outburst indicated a broader unraveling of the Mississippi Valley's political bonds.[1]

Armstrong was appalled by Douglas's opposition to the Lecompton Constitution, which, if accepted by Congress, would bring Kansas into the Union as a slave state. President James Buchanan, like Jefferson Davis and most southern Democrats, favored Lecompton, but Douglas and a coalition of northern Democrats and Republicans condemned it as a mockery of self-government. Controversy over Lecompton raged far into 1858 and foreshadowed the Democracy's 1860 rupture.

Far from an isolated squabble, the Lecompton battle heralded an escalation of chronic disputes among Democrats who rallied around white supremacy and anti-abolitionism but never agreed on how white men should govern. It marked an especially explosive confrontation between Douglas's majoritarianism and Davis's quest to shield slaveholders' property rights from nonslaveholding majorities. The struggle and its aftermath rattled a seemingly triumphant Democracy, revealed the fragility of racism and negative partisanship as foundations of party unity, and compelled Democrats to confront issues that had haunted them for decades.

Reverberations from the Lecompton battle quickly reached Illinois and Mississippi, forcing Davis and Douglas to prove that the Democracy advocated local interests. For Douglas, this meant defending his Senate seat against a formidable Republican foe who sought to brand him a traitor to northern values while simultaneously disrupting the Democracy. Meanwhile, Davis sparred with proslavery extremists who castigated him for courting northern allies. Davis and Douglas survived these assaults by adopting more overtly sectional positions, thus deepening the divide between them. By 1859, long-simmering contests over the Democracy and American democracy had reached a rolling boil.

★ ★ ★

The Lecompton quarrel fed on rising expectations. Democrats ended 1856 hopeful that the Kansas conflagration would soon be extinguished and that their darkest days were past. Much of the work that Democrats undertook that year remained undone, but their party had survived a serious test.

But Democrats could not wish away the Kansas imbroglio that dominated the first session of the Thirty-Fourth Congress. Party leaders defended popular sovereignty and blamed antislavery fanatics for territorial turmoil, but the conflict defied resolution. Republicans pressed for Kansas statehood under the Topeka constitution, which would exclude slavery and African Americans alike. Democrats worked to settle the dangerous controversy but refused to recognize the Topeka government, which Pierce deemed insurrectionary.[2] Instead, Douglas sponsored a bill authorizing Kansas voters to write a constitution and apply for statehood once the population reached the 93,420 threshold that would entitle them to a representative in Congress.[3] Blaming antislavery zealots for the violence, he defined Bleeding Kansas as a battle between Democratic champions of self-government and a meddlesome medley of Know-Nothings and abolitionists.[4] He also began crafting a constitutional foundation for popular sovereignty. Previously, Douglas had defended it as pragmatic and fair to westerners, but now he denied that Congress could establish or prohibit slavery in a territory, since this would deprive the nascent state of its equality with other states. Following a contemporary trend of transmuting policy questions into constitutional debates, Douglas took a large step toward eliding the distinction between states and territories.[5]

Douglas's bill flopped, but other plans remained in circulation. In June, Georgia senator Robert Toombs suggested permitting Kansas voters to select convention delegates under careful supervision intended to prevent the fraud and violence that had marred previous territorial elections. Most Democrats welcomed the Toombs bill and hoped it would boost their chances in the pending presidential race. Republicans defeated it in the House of Representatives, however, leaving Douglas fuming over their alleged desire to milk Kansas for partisan gain.[6] Nevertheless, he voted with Republicans and against most southern Democrats on several infrastructure bills, including one to improve the Illinois River and another, which failed, to construct a Pacific railroad.[7] These votes underlined the political disarray of the mid-1850s: partisanship dominated Kansas debates, while sectional alignments were forming on internal improvements. Douglas's agenda stalled because no single party would adopt it wholesale.

Meanwhile, 1856 devolved into the most sanguinary year in the Kansas Territory's bloodstained history. In late May, proslavery forces demolished the antislavery stronghold of Lawrence; shortly after, abolitionists led by John Brown killed five proslavery settlers in a grisly nocturnal sortie. The subsequent guerrilla war increased the body count and kept Kansas in national headlines. Even if reports were exaggerated, as skeptics have claimed, the bloodletting put Democrats on the defensive.[8] As a distraught Ohioan told Douglas, "A good many Democrats in this state are leaving our party, and becoming violent against you and the administration," because of the "present proceedings in Kansas." Peace might salvage the party's fortunes, but "if towns are sacked and burned, and men killed there, I fear a storm will rise at the North that can't be stayed by the most prudent statesman."[9]

The bloodshed also crept eastward, most infamously in the attack on Senator Charles Sumner, a Massachusetts Republican, by Preston Brooks, a Democratic congressman from South Carolina. On May 19 and 20, Sumner delivered a blistering speech in which he likened slavery expansion to rape and denounced the authors of the Kansas-Nebraska Act, deriding Douglas as "the squire of Slavery, its very Sancho Panza, ready to do all its humiliating offices."[10] Two days later, Brooks beat Sumner into unconsciousness with a gold-headed cane. Many Democrats agreed that Sumner got his comeuppance, but the disparate reactions of northern and southern Democrats are instructive. While listening to Sumner's speech, Douglas grumbled, "That damn fool will get himself killed by some other damn fool," a remark consistent with his self-identification as a moderate stuck between sectional extremists.[11] Some northern Democrats joined in public demonstrations of outrage against Brooks and condemned his assault on civility and free speech.[12] But southern Democrats closed ranks behind Brooks. Davis could not attend a South Carolina gathering held in Brooks's honor, so he published a letter expressing "high regard and esteem" for Brooks, a victim of "vilification, misrepresentation, and persecution."[13] While northern Democrats panned both Brooks and Sumner as fanatics, southern Democrats hailed the cane-wielding Carolinian as a sectional hero.

Amid the bloodshed, Democrats scrambled to unite for the 1856 election. Ahead of the national convention in Cincinnati (a nod to the burgeoning West), Democratic contenders jockeyed for the nomination, and Douglas was very much a candidate, even before supporters officially raised his name in February.[14] As in 1852, he received a flood of letters endorsing his nomination, mostly from the North and West, with a sprinkling from the South.[15] Among his rivals was Davis, whose friends began speculating about his own presidential prospects in 1853. An April 1856 *Democratic Review* article ranked him among the contenders, citing his bravery at Buena Vista as his primary credential.[16]

The Cincinnati convention exposed Democrats' serious divisions. Pierce remained popular in the Deep South, where many Democrats, including Davis, hoped to renominate him. Pennsylvania's James Buchanan, who as minister to Great Britain was relatively untarnished by the Kansas-Nebraska Act, had considerable northeastern support, while Douglas attracted westerners, Young Americans, and a smattering of southerners.[17] When balloting commenced on June 5, Buchanan and Pierce raced ahead of Douglas, with Lewis Cass a distant fourth. The next day, Douglas surged into second place thanks to rising support from the border and upper South, but after sixteen ballots, it was clear that he or Buchanan would have to yield. Illinois Douglasite William A. Richardson rose to read a letter from Douglas authorizing withdrawal of his name if Democrats could unite behind a strong candidate; shortly thereafter, Buchanan prevailed on the seventeenth ballot.[18] Democrats balanced the ticket with Kentuckian John C. Breckinridge and crafted a platform with an ambiguous territorial policy: congressional "non-interference" with territorial voters' right to enter the Union with or without slavery as they chose.[19] Democrats spent the next four years wrestling over the Cincinnati platform, which northerners read as an endorsement of squatter sovereignty and southerners as a confirmation of the common-property doctrine.[20] Southern Democrats knew that Buchanan would lose the slave states if he adopted "the old Cass heresy of squatter sovereignty."[21]

Bitterly disappointed, Douglas expected a reward for his party loyalty. He was only forty-three years old and had received assurances from Buchanan's backers that the Pennsylvanian would eschew a second term and endorse him in 1860. Many Democrats thought he deserved it; an hour after Buchanan's nomination, one delegate assured Douglas that the "hearts of the representatives of the Democracy melted at your magnanimity; and you are already determined upon as the successor of Mr. Buchanan in 1860."[22] Douglas also claimed victory on the platform and regarded the election as a referendum on the Kansas-Nebraska Act, so he campaigned tirelessly in Illinois while keeping tabs on the key swing state of Pennsylvania. Late in the canvass, Douglas liquidated some Chicago real estate and donated the proceeds to the party's Pennsylvania war chest, ultimately investing over $40,000 in Buchanan's campaign.[23]

Fear of disunion permeated the 1856 election and energized Douglas's efforts to defeat the Republicans. Their party had coalesced swiftly by drawing support from former Whigs, Free-Soilers, and anti-Nebraska Democrats and had nominated dashing frontiersman and former California senator John C. Frémont for president. Their platform decried slavery as one of the "relics of barbarism," demanded that Congress bar its expansion, and urged statehood for Kansas under the Topeka constitution.[24] Republicans had brought antislavery into the northern political mainstream, and some southerners called for secession in the event of a Republican triumph. "If Fremont should be elected President," announced a Mississippi Democratic editor, the slave states should "establish an independent Confederacy," peacefully if possible but "in war and blood" if necessary.[25] Jefferson Davis hoped that a Democratic victory would avert disunion but quietly advised that slave states should ready their militias.[26] Amid multiplying threats of secession, many southern votes for Buchanan reflected sectionalism rather than nationalism, since fealty to the Union was conditional upon the success of a southern-directed Democracy.[27] Southern ultimatums put northern Democrats in an awkward position, arming them with arguments about the dangers of Republicanism while tainting their party with prospective treason.[28]

Buchanan eked out a victory, winning 45 percent of the popular vote, carrying every slave state but Maryland (won by American Party candidate Millard Fillmore), and adding five free states—California, Illinois, Indiana, Pennsylvania, and New Jersey—to snag 174 electoral votes. Frémont took every other free state and a plurality of northern popular votes, cementing the Republicans as Democrats' chief rival in the North. Meanwhile, the Democracy kept tilting southward: Pierce carried all but two free states in 1852, but Buchanan won only five and received a majority of the popular vote only in Pennsylvania and Indiana.[29] Northern Democrats began to rebuild after the 1854 disaster, raising their congressional delegation from twenty-five to fifty-three. But Republicans won portentous victories, including the election of ex-Democrat William H. Bissell as governor of Illinois, whose triumph over William A. Richardson, Douglas's right-hand man, was a stinging blow.[30]

Southern Democrats had no reason for complacency, either. Indeed, shortly after the election, a Mississippian warned Davis that the future "is big with peril."[31] Buchanan won 56 percent of the slave-state popular vote and nearly swept the region, but the South was not monolithic; opposition parties remained active and fire-eaters still doubted that any national party could crush the Republican menace. When Davis returned to the Senate, he would need to demonstrate that Democrats could meet the rising expectations of white southerners who were alarmed by Republicanism and keen on a variety of proslavery projects.[32] Democrats would have to maintain party unity while governing a bitterly polarized nation.

★ ★ ★

Democratic infighting marred even joyful occasions, such as Douglas's marriage to Adele Cutts, a twenty-year-old Washington belle related to Dolley Madison and Rose O'Neal Greenhow. Following their campaign-trail courtship, the couple were married by a Catholic priest in late November 1856, during the brief interval between Election Day and the opening of a new session of Congress.[33] Douglas's admirers appreciated Adele's influence on her husband, whose slovenly appearance improved after the wedding. Enemies were less charitable: Varina Davis accused the "the dirty speculator and party trickster, broken in health by drink," of using "his first wife's money" to buy "an elegant, well-bred woman because she is poor and her Father is proud" and sneeringly hoped that Douglas "may wash a little oftener."[34]

James Buchanan shared this disdain, and from the start of his presidency, his hostility to Douglas's wing of the party stirred a personal, factional, and ideological quarrel. Since Douglas's withdrawal had secured

Buchanan's nomination, it would have been politic to reserve plum appointments for Douglasites, but the aging Pennsylvanian regarded the western upstart as a dangerous rival. So, he snubbed Douglas, threw northwestern patronage to Indiana's Jesse Bright, and stacked his cabinet with proslavery southerners and like-minded northerners.[35] These appointments tilted the party further southward, reflecting Buchanan's determination to "arrest . . . the agitation of the Slavery question at the North & to destroy sectional parties."[36]

Buchanan counted on the Supreme Court to derail antislavery activism, but in embracing its most infamous decision, he magnified sectional strife and Democratic discord. In his inaugural address, Buchanan alluded to a decision that would end the Kansas controversy and "speedily and finally" settle the question of timing—when could territorial voters decide on slavery?—which divided the Democracy.[37] The case was *Dred Scott v. Sandford*, in which an enslaved Missouri man sued for his freedom on the grounds of his longtime residence in Illinois and the Wisconsin Territory. Buchanan promised to abide by the decision, whatever it said; in fact, he already knew the outcome thanks to covert communications with several justices.[38]

Shortly thereafter, when the Court ruled 7–2 against Scott's bid for freedom, Chief Justice Roger B. Taney sought to chisel proslavery dogma into American jurisprudence. First, he rejected Scott's standing, not merely because of his enslavement but also because of his ancestry; in a grotesquely flawed historical argument, Taney insisted that African Americans could not be citizens, for they had always "been regarded as beings of an inferior order . . . and so far inferior that they had no rights which the white man was bound to respect." Gaining momentum, Taney held that the Missouri Compromise's free-soil provision, which covered one area where Scott had lived, was unconstitutional because Congress had no power to bar slavery from a territory. Echoing John C. Calhoun, he declared that Congress had only "the power coupled with the duty of guarding and protecting the owner in his rights." Finally, Taney addressed an issue that was not before the Court but provoked Democrats' intraparty disputes: whether a territorial legislature could prohibit slavery. Since Congress could not enact such a ban, he reasoned, neither could it delegate that power to territorial governments. In one swoop, Taney dismissed African American citizenship, gutted free-soilism, and smashed squatter sovereignty.[39]

Democrats hoped the case would settle the territorial controversy and upend the Republicans. Robert J. Walker promised Douglas that the decision "would give renewed confidence at home and abroad in the stability of our institutions, and insure another democratic victory in 1860."[40] Another correspondent celebrated Taney's racism, opining that although "the masses" knew little constitutional law, the vindication of white supremacy would resonate with even "unsound and ignorant" minds.[41] Douglas and Davis initially shared the enthusiasm. Speaking in Springfield in June 1857, Douglas defended the Court from the "poisonous shafts of partisan malice," parroted Taney's bigotry, and accused Republicans of advocating racial equality, while tiptoeing around questions about popular sovereignty.[42] In several Mississippi speeches, Davis eagerly seconded Taney's repudiation of squatter sovereignty.[43]

Thanks to Buchanan's election and Taney's ruling, the Democracy appeared harmonious, victorious, and firmly under southern control. But this was an illusion. Soon, the Kansas controversy and proslavery southerners' soaring expectations would rekindle a smoldering struggle within a badly divided party.

★ ★ ★

Taney's ruling did not cause the Democratic rupture but did expose its buried roots. Taney relied on two pillars of proslavery ideology: white supremacy and the sanctity of property. These dogmas coexisted uneasily and made proslavery politics, as historian Merrill Peterson observed, "a fantastic mixture of racist democracy and planter aristocracy."[44] The challenge for proslavery crusaders was to recruit white multitudes to defend property owned by a small minority; in an age of mass white male suffrage, elite interests needed popular appeal.

Elites often fear majoritarian assaults on property rights, but the uniqueness of slaveholders' property compounded the problem, since enslaved people's capacity for resistance made them uniquely dangerous chattels. Slave property, Davis acknowledged, was "the most delicate species of property" and "must be held under special laws and police regulations, to render it useful or profitable to the owner, or that it may not be injurious to the community under which it is held."[45] Thus, masters demanded far more from nonslaveholders than passive acquiescence. It was not enough to dissuade them from espousing abolitionism or abetting slave rebellions; they had to be reliable *supporters* of slavery and active *participants* in its maintenance. Slavery imposed a burden on all free people, who shared the risk of insurrection and the task of preventing it. As voters, slave patrollers, pursuers of fugitives, and suppressors of rebellions, nonslaveholding whites helped police slavery, an ongoing process that transcended the master-slave relationship. Slavery, noted Republican statesman and postbellum historian Henry Wilson, was "a social matter, and men were obliged to join hand in hand in its guilt, or to relinquish it altogether."[46]

Yet even within the South, masters could not take nonslaveholders' support for granted, particularly not when elite interests clashed with popular sentiments. After Nat Turner's 1831 insurrection, for instance, Virginia masters scrambled to prove that slaves were under control, lest panicked yeomen massacre valuable human chattels or embrace gradual emancipation.[47] Slaveholders' response to Hinton Helper's *Impending Crisis of the South* (1857) showed that mistrust of nonslaveholding majorities persisted a generation later. Appealing to racism and economic self-interest, Helper urged poor whites to rid the South of slavery and African Americans alike. Planter-politicians banned the book and denounced its author.[48] Outside the South, masters needed public help to recapture fugitives, conquer new lands, and fill federal offices with friendly occupants. At the local, regional, and national levels, therefore, maintaining mass support for slavery was an unending project with enormous stakes. If slaveholders could harness white men's democracy to their interests they could defy the world, but majoritarian backlash could ruin them.[49]

To transmute proslavery politics into a populist crusade, slaveholders turned to racism. Particularly as the proportion of white southerners who held slaves declined in the 1840s and 1850s, southern elites appealed to racism to smother class antagonism and enlist poorer whites in safeguarding a slaveholding society.[50] Rather than stratify wealth, they insisted, slavery lifted all white men into an aristocracy of color. "The presence of these laborers of an inferior race," Davis told Mississippians in 1857, "elevated the white man," liberating him from "humiliating discrimination and dependence among individuals of our own race," which would otherwise "leave but the name of political equality."[51] Like-minded northerners also insisted that whites' dignity, liberty, and equality depended on black subordination. White men, averred New York Democrat Daniel Dickinson in an attack on the Wilmot Proviso, would be "degraded" by competing with blacks for jobs.[52] Historians disagree as to how solidly whites in the South, let alone nationwide, were unified by racism, but some argue that this racist glue also cemented Democratic solidarity by aligning plain republicans with planters.[53]

Antebellum racism was pervasive and pernicious, but to conclude that it gave the Slave Power uncontested control over the Democracy elides several tensions that plagued the party and led to its rupture. These pressures intensified during the Lecompton debate and pitted Davis against Douglas in a ferocious struggle.

The first source of strain was the fact that racists do not always agree with each other, since white supremacy's defective logic can lead to conflicting conclusions. Antebellum racism bolstered support for conquering tropical provinces and keeping their dark-skinned inhabitants at arm's length; reopening the African slave trade and leaving it closed; spreading slavery westward and barring black people from western lands; protecting slavery indefinitely and abolishing it gradually; maintaining a vast enslaved labor force and colonizing freed blacks overseas.[54] The deplorably broad consensus that the United States must remain a white man's country splintered when whites had to make policy.

Historians rightly contrast Davis and Douglas's prejudice against Lincoln's comparatively enlightened views, but the two Democrats diverged on vital issues.[55] Historian James Oakes warns against assuming that a "racial consensus" stifled conflict in the nineteenth-century U.S., a point that the Davis-Douglas rivalry demonstrates quite clearly.[56] Davis defended slavery as a positive good, a divinely ordained boon to the enslaved, and the only system in which black and white people could coexist. He criticized southerners who apologized for slavery as a necessary evil and braided biblical and pseudo-historical arguments to argue that "the good of society requires that the negro should be kept in his normal condition" of slavery.[57] For Davis, maintaining white supremacy meant protecting slaveholders' property rights as the foundation of white domination.

Douglas was no egalitarian, but he denied that alleged racial inferiority mandated enslavement and envisioned a decentralized system in which white voters determined the fate of African Americans in their communities. Undemocratic by modern standards, Douglas's brand of white supremacy was anathema to Davis because it subordinated property rights to local majorities, authorizing whites of all classes to decide whether to shoulder the burden of slavery. Douglas also supported and served as a vice president of the American Colonization Society. Excoriated by abolitionists for its patently racist goal of whitening the country by deporting free African Americans, the society also drew fire from proslavery crusaders, including Davis, who believed it threatened slavery.[58] Douglas's northern admirers often echoed the society's aversive racism, and some even endorsed black self-government so long as it occurred outside the United States.[59] Davis and Douglas united against egalitarians, but their prejudices pointed in different directions. This would become clear in the Lecompton struggle's acrimonious aftermath.

Powerful southerners suspected that northern bigotry was poorly calibrated to sustain slavery, so they fostered overtly proslavery racism with help from local allies like John Van Evrie. A New York physician, author, and editor, Van Evrie published books, pamphlets, and a periodical, the *Day Book*, which *DeBow's Review* hailed as "a great engine for good."[60] Among his efforts was an anthology that included a scientific racist treatise by Samuel Cartwright, Taney's *Dred Scott* opinion, and an introduction in which Van Evrie hailed the case as the greatest event in North American history since the Declaration of Independence.[61] For a quarter of a century, Van Evrie hammered on one theme: slavery was "a normal condition, a natural relation . . . in harmony with the order, progress, and general well-being of the superior [race], and absolutely essential to the very existence of the inferior race."[62]

Davis appreciated Van Evrie's labors and became his patron. While secretary of war, Davis praised the forthcoming *Negroes and Negro "Slavery"* (1853) for exposing the "fallacy" of abolitionism, an endorsement that Van Evrie proudly printed in his book.[63] Davis later recommended Van Evrie for an Interior Department sinecure, which would support him while he finished another book, effectively a federal subsidy for proslavery propaganda, and John A. Quitman disseminated copies of Van Evrie's work during the 1856 election.[64] Vehement opposition to Douglas among Van Evrie's northern devotees reveals the friction between rival racist worldviews. In an 1860 letter to Davis, one of Van Evrie's Vermont aficionados mocked the "Douglas Democratic abolitionists."[65] In his own correspondence with the Mississippian, Van Evrie excoriated northern Democrats for favoring squatter sovereignty and free territories and pledged to repair the damage by propagating southern ideals.[66]

Nonslaveholders' racism notwithstanding, few masters wanted to leave their property rights up to a vote. Hence a second source of tension in the Democratic coalition: the sometimes veiled but always present antidemocratic thrust of proslavery politics.[67] Southern politicians boldly expressed these sentiments during the Lecompton controversy: they denied that rule by "the people" meant rule by "the majority" in Kansas; denounced an "absolute majority" as "the most cruel, rapacious, intolerant and intolerable of all tyrants"; and warned that defeat of the Lecompton Constitution would convert the United States into "a pure Democracy" ruled by "an irrepressible mob."[68] These ideas had thrived in proslavery thought for years. In his seminal 1832 proslavery text, Thomas Dew opined that "the exclusive owners of property ever have been, ever will, and perhaps ever ought to be, the virtual rulers of mankind," a sentiment approvingly quoted by southern writers into the 1850s.[69] Davis wholeheartedly agreed, recoiling from the prospect of slavery being subjected to "the paramount purpose of a reckless majority."[70] This antimajoritarian ethos bred hostility to popular sovereignty. As a Georgian wrote in 1856, "The *citizens* of a territory according to the Democratic creed may control the matter [of slavery], but not according to my doctrine. No number of *citizens* or *people* have a right to take away my property so long as we live under the Constitution." If "the free community steal or trespass on the property of the slave-owner . . . Congress is bound to protect it."[71] In polities where property rights undergirded racial hierarchy, reactionary critiques of democracy remained vibrant.

Southern statesmen acted on these impulses by reducing the power of local and national majorities. Southern Democrats used the two-thirds rule to maintain a minority check on presidential nominations, and during the 1850–51 crisis, Davis advocated imposing a similar rule on Congress to give the South a sectional veto.[72] From 1835 to 1844, southern congressmen shielded slavery from debate by gagging antislavery petitions.[73] They also worked within their own states to protect slavery from popular meddling. Mississippi's 1832 state constitution prohibited the legislature from emancipating slaves without masters' consent.[74] A generation later, a clash over Virginia's state constitution pitted westerners, who supported a one (white) man, one vote policy, against eastern planters, who defended property requirements for office holding and the incorporation of property into legislative apportionment, lest western schemes allow property "to be plundered at the discretion of the majority."[75] Virginia's comparatively egalitarian 1851 constitution provoked southern critics of universal white male suffrage to denounce government by "King Numbers" as "a thorough and complete absolutism."[76] Clearly, planter-politicians' efforts to garner mass support for slavery did not mean that they relished sharing power. Rather, they demanded exclusive control over slavery as well as public assistance for its maintenance, belying claims that slavery promoted white equality. There were some majority rights that masters did not feel bound to respect.

Tensions over race, property, and democracy eroded Democratic solidarity in three ways. First, they made racism a fragile foundation for party unity. Though sometimes regarded as a monolithic force, racism divided Democrats when they attempted to build concrete policies upon divergent beliefs. Douglas conflated white supremacy with white men's equality and would empower local white majorities to establish slavery, prohibit it, or outlaw black migration, as in Illinois. This collided with Davis's dedication to slavery's perpetual stability, grounded in masters' right to impose the burden of slavery on any community they chose. United by loathing of antislavery activists, Davis and Douglas could not agree on how white men should rule. Like anti-abolitionism and negative partisanship, racism rallied Democrats against common enemies but provided no single template for lawmaking.

Second, slaveholders' peculiar concerns compelled them to ask for far more than a weak government. Mere insulation from federal interference could not sustain a property regime that required so much collective effort to maintain. Northern Democrats resisted frontal attacks on slaveholders' property rights, but they quarreled with southern allies over how far to extend federal power to protect them. By the late 1850s, southern Democrats were primed to ask for even more from their northern counterparts. Since proslavery politics was a moving target, Democrats' relationship to slavery was subject to constant and rancorous renegotiation.

Finally, these tensions made territories likely settings for intraparty battles. Conflicts between popular sovereignty and the common-property doctrine had long divided Democrats, and the ongoing turmoil in Kansas, coupled with the *Dred Scott* decision, raised the stakes. A triumph for southern Democrats, Taney's ruling rendered local and national majorities impotent to bar slavery. But as events in Kansas and Congress stoked further conflict, it was an open question whether northern Democrats would acquiesce. The issues were not new, but the intensity of the debate prevented Democrats from papering over their disagreements.

★ ★ ★

Hoping to stanch the bleeding from the Democracy's self-inflicted wound, Buchanan named Robert J. Walker as the Kansas Territory's fourth governor in May 1857. Pennsylvania-born but deeply rooted in Mississippi and devoted to the Democracy, Walker seemed ideally suited to the task, and Douglas persuaded him to accept the appointment, arguing that honest execution of popular sovereignty would pacify Kansas and vindicate the Democratic Party. In a polarized political climate, however, Walker could not please everyone. Southerners who expected him to champion slavery detested his inaugural address for implying that Kansas was destined to be a free state and insisting that any state constitution be submitted for popular approval.[77] Mississippi legislators expressed "unqualified condemnation" of Walker, and Democrats across the Deep South denounced his perfidy.[78]

Proslavery partisans in Kansas tried to outflank Walker by expediting statehood. Because free-state voters had boycotted the June 1857 election of delegates to the latest convention, it was a proslavery conclave that met in Lecompton in October to write a state constitution. Alarmed by recent regular elections that ensured an antislavery majority in the next territorial legislature, Lecompton delegates were determined to achieve slave statehood before free-staters took power.[79] Accordingly, they wrote a constitution that embodied the antimajoritarian, proslavery ethos. Article 7 declared that "the right of property is before and higher than any constitutional sanction, and the right of the owner of a slave to such slave and its increase is the same and as inviolable as the right of the owner of any property whatever," echoing Davis's argument that paper constitutions merely recognized masters' primordial property rights. Other provisions barred legislators from emancipating slaves without masters' consent or preventing slaveholders' migration into the state. The constitution could not be amended until 1864, and "no alteration shall be made to affect the rights of property in the ownership of slaves." Crucially, the delegates ignored Buchanan's private entreaties and refused to submit the entire document to Kansas voters, instead allowing them only to decide on whether to include Article 7; even if it were rejected, "the right of property in slaves now in this Territory shall in no manner be interfered with." Either way, slavery would be embedded in Kansas.[80]

Douglas began receiving advice about the Lecompton Constitution months before it reached Congress in December. Kansas contacts advised that northern settlers were Douglas's true allies and that proslavery Democrats' obstinate opposition to a popular referendum would trigger a crisis. The alienation between northern and southern Democrats in Kansas was portentous.[81] Meanwhile, friends across the free states worried that proslavery trickery would cause the "utter destruction" of the northern Democracy.[82] By late fall, most northern Democrats concluded that the Lecompton Constitution would desecrate popular sovereignty and demolish their party. (Conversely, some southern Democrats believed that admitting a free Kansas would ruin the party in the South.[83] Democrats had made too many promises.) Three-quarters of Indiana's Democratic newspapers opposed Lecompton, as did all but one in Illinois and large majorities in Iowa, Michigan, Wisconsin, and Ohio.[84] Douglas remained undecided in late November but pledged to oppose Lecompton if it were the "act and will of a small minority, who have attempted to cheat & defraud the majority by trickery & juggling."[85] Two weeks later, driven by zeal for popular sovereignty and dread of popular backlash, he swore hostility to the "Lecompton Fraud."[86] Illinois Democrat Thomas L. Harris regretted Buchanan's support for Lecompton but boasted that "we will whip out the whole concern." "Douglas," he predicted, "will make the greatest effort of his life in opposition to this juggle."[87]

As Davis prepared to return to the Senate, he made his own position clear: the South must secure Kansas. Speaking in Mississippi, Davis vowed to abandon Buchanan if he opposed the Lecompton Constitution; denounced popular sovereignty and Walker; lauded slave labor as a boon to world civilization that could profitably be used to raise tobacco and hemp in eastern Kansas; and warned that if abolitionists captured Kansas, they would assail Missouri, Arkansas, and Texas. According to this domino theory, Kansas stood between the South and destruction by antislavery encirclement. Davis also advised that congressional rejection of Lecompton would confront the South with the question it faced in 1851: resistance or submission? He favored resistance and spoke of stockpiling arms and strengthening southern militias.[88] Eager to snag a new slave state and please their constituents before the fall 1857 elections, southern Democrats defended Lecompton's legitimacy.[89]

As Davis and Douglas sped toward a collision, Buchanan received divided counsel. Southern Democrats echoed Davis's threat to disown the administration, and some advocated secession if Lecompton were rejected.[90] But other powerful voices begged Buchanan to demand its submission to Kansas voters. According to Governor Walker, even proslavery partisans admitted that "a very large majority of the Settlers are for a free state."[91] Democratic public intellectual George Bancroft offered historically informed guidance, contrasting Andrew Jackson's battle against nullification with Pierce's timid administration, which had "died of Jefferson Davis" and other proslavery schemers who were now trying to dupe Buchanan. Allow Kansans to make their own government, Bancroft advised, and peace would prevail.[92] But Buchanan decided that Lecompton's passage would wreck the Republicans and unite Democrats behind his leadership. In his December 8 message to Congress, Buchanan endorsed the Lecompton Constitution and promised that "excitement" would "speedily pass away" after Kansas statehood. He had planted his flag in the southern camp.[93]

Congressional debate erupted immediately. After hearing Buchanan's message, Douglas brusquely rebuked its approval of the "proceedings of the Lecompton convention." Davis objected that it was "premature" to discuss the message but then did precisely that, concurring with Buchanan that no popular referendum on Lecompton was necessary.[94]

Douglas and Davis had sketched the basic arguments they would reiterate deep into 1858.

The next day, Douglas asserted that he was not merely feuding with Buchanan but battling for the Democracy's soul. Claiming ideological consistency, he insisted that the principles of the Kansas-Nebraska Act demanded that the entire Lecompton Constitution be referred to Kansas voters. Douglas cast the conflict in terms of majority versus minority rule by accusing Lecompton delegates of "disfranchis[ing]" voters who loathed the proffered constitution and would boycott the vote, "thus referring the slavery clause to a minority of the people of Kansas." He professed to "care not" how Kansans voted, emphasizing that he opposed Lecompton because it was undemocratic, not because it was proslavery. To tremendous applause, Douglas closed with a statement about party loyalty. He prized Democratic unity, "but if the party will not stand by its principles, its faith, its pledges, I will stand there, and abide whatever consequences may result from the position." He would resist the Lecompton Constitution "to the last" and defend "the great principle of popular sovereignty ... against assault from any and all quarters."[95] These comments revealed a shift in Douglas's thinking. Previously, he had seen antislavery dissidents like John Wentworth and Lyman Trumbull as the primary threats to the Democracy, but now the danger came from proslavery proponents of minority rule.

Douglas's defiance scrambled political alignments. In editorials, diaries, and letters, most northerners hailed his course. Conspicuous in their reactions was the image of Douglas as a northern paladin. Still committed to national party cohesion, Douglas did not identify as such, but many northerners, including some who formerly regarded him as a proslavery stooge, did. Four days into the debate, New York diarist George Templeton Strong mused that Douglas had "seced[ed] from the Administration and the South."[96] An Indiana Democratic editor hailed Douglas as "the giant of the North."[97] A Pennsylvanian praised Douglas's "noble stand" against "this nefarious outrage sought to be inflicted by the Lecompton Convention [and] by the fire eaters of the South."[98] Some admirers already imagined Douglas riding northern support to the White House; one predicted that "the North will rally [*sic*] around you for their standard bearer for 1860."[99] Once reviled as a pawn of the Slave Power, Douglas now appeared to be its enemy. A New Yorker vowed that if the "Southern fire eaters" provoked civil war, they would reap nothing but "death ... to them and their peculiar institutions." In any event, he enthused, "the slave Power will not govern this country but three years" longer.[100]

Many northern Democrats adopted this sectional outlook on the controversy, criticizing their southern counterparts and arguing that the party would collapse if it jettisoned popular sovereignty. An outraged New Jerseyan reported that his "blood boil[ed] with indignation" over southern Democrats' attacks on Douglas and their short-sighted zeal for Lecompton.[101] A Michigan Democrat hated to see the Cincinnati platform discarded by the "Administration and the Southern wing of the Party" and worried that the northern Democracy would be "blotted out."[102] Even bigots balked at endorsing minority rule. "Be not driven from the Democratic party by a set of nigger drivers aided by Northern party heads," exhorted a New Yorker. "The people will, ere long, see that in this last contest you was the true expounder of Democracy, and not your opponents."[103] Bracing for the worst, some vowed to follow Douglas out of the party, although most hoped to remain within the Democratic fold.[104]

The Lecompton conflict aggravated sharp ideological divisions that Democrats had repressed but never resolved, and Douglas's advocates recognized the struggle between white men's democracy and planters' property. One New Yorker contrasted Douglas's fidelity to majoritarianism against the South's only principle: "that of protecting & enhancing the value of its slave property."[105] An Illinoisan urged Douglas to persevere against an administration that debased the Kansas-Nebraska Act by "favor[ing] and assist[ing] a minority to do things repugnant to a large majority" of Kansas inhabitants.[106] Some predicted a showdown with Douglas's Mississippi rival: "Jeff Davis desires to break a lance with you," observed an Illinoisan who eagerly anticipated the battle.[107]

Republicans looked on with mixed emotions. Accustomed to deriding northern Democrats as lackeys of the Slave Power, prominent Illinois Republicans initially downplayed Lecompton's significance, but some reconsidered. In early December, Lyman Trumbull doubted that the "'Rumpus' among the bogus Democracy will amount to much."[108] Twenty days later, however, he granted that Douglas had "materially damage[d] his prospects with the South" and might become a Republican.[109] Some were torn between adopting Douglas as an ally and rebuffing him as an opportunist. William H. Herndon, Lincoln's law partner, accused Douglas of caring only about reelection; his motives were "as base as his base nature."[110] But the next day, Herndon admitted his willingness to support Douglas to serve a greater good: "Mr. Douglas will in due time become Republican and attempt to lead our forces," he informed abolitionist Theodore Parker, "and I may have to vote for the wretch—I will do so to kill a worse—Slavery."[111] Outside Illinois, many Republicans were readier to accept Douglas. "I say nothing about motives," declared Massachusetts senator Henry Wilson. "I leave motives to God." The Illinoisan was "of more weight to our cause than *any ten men* in the country . . . and I know that Douglas will go for crushing the Slave power to atoms."[112] These sentiments unnerved Illinois Republicans who considered Douglas an unworthy ally.[113]

But they also feared Douglas's appeal among the Republican rank and file. In a famous letter to Trumbull, Abraham Lincoln criticized New York editor Horace Greeley's pro-Douglas paeans, apprehending that his 10,000 Illinois readers might not "stand firm" against the Democracy.[114] If Lincoln had perused Douglas's mail, his anxiety would have increased, for it included numerous Republican endorsements. One Ohio Republican admitted having felt "deep bitterness" toward Douglas over the Kansas-Nebraska Act but now prayed that God would sustain him.[115] An Indianan who had never voted Democratic in his life vowed to support Douglas and circulate his speeches.[116] From Kansas came word that Republicans appreciated Douglas's defense of territorial self-rule.[117]

Many of these correspondents, moreover, were warming to popular sovereignty. A self-identified "Black Republican" from New York endorsed the policy so long as it was "fairly and honestly administered." He once suspected it was a "game to benefit the South," but Douglas's anti-Lecompton stance "did much to remove my prejudice."[118] Similarly, a Pittsburgh Republican belatedly accepted the Kansas-Nebraska Act, believing that popular sovereignty "is, perhaps, all we need" to make Kansas free. He predicted that if northern Democrats continued to defy the "aggressions of the Slave Power," they would sweep the North.[119] The dynamics of the Lecompton struggle encouraged Republican conversions, since southern hostility to majority rule suggested that popular sovereignty might really be a free-soil policy.[120] Thus, some erstwhile opponents decided that Douglas stood for freedom. "If the people of Kansas can be protected in their just rights against fraud," wrote one Free-Soiler, "all will yet be right, and Slavery with its unlimited demands will be kept out of that devoted territory."[121] Douglas seemed uniquely capable of persuading former foes, and Republicans rightly worried that he would disrupt their diverse coalition.

Particularly noteworthy was Douglas's magnetic effect on prodigal Democrats. "I had been driven to act with parties whose sentiments did not altogether suit me," wrote a Bay State correspondent, "because of the *downright dishonesty*" of many leading Democrats. Now he hoped northern Democrats would regroup behind the "principles of 'Squatter Sovereignty.'"[122] An Ohioan who had bolted the Democracy "because I thought it given over to the Slave Power" was now "willing to forget and forgive and extend the right hand of fellowship."[123] These defections alarmed Republicans who knew that dissident Democrats had long galvanized antislavery politics.[124] Historians have parsed crucial differences between Republicans and northern Democrats on issues ranging from slavery to gender norms, but late antebellum party affiliations were mutable, and Douglas's anti-Lecompton crusade ensured that movement between parties flowed both directions.

Partisan loyalties were flexible in Illinois despite leading Republicans' antipathy toward Douglas. From Carrollton came word that most Republicans "heartily approve[d]" Douglas's position.[125] In Chicago, "hundreds of Democrats" who had voted Republican while awaiting a "plausible excuse to return to the democratic fold" were ready to jump.[126] Statewide, erstwhile Republicans signaled acceptance of popular sovereignty if honestly executed, since they believed it would make Kansas free.[127] Some Republicans even endorsed fusion, reckoning that Douglas deserved their support for opposing the common-property doctrine.[128] Republicans' internal debate was not a geographic dispute between malleable easterners and Illinois purists; it was an ideological quarrel between those who would embrace Douglas and popular sovereignty and those who saw both as dangerous.

Douglas's most astounding admirer was Jonathan Blanchard, an Illinois abolitionist with unimpeachable credentials. Born in Vermont two years before Douglas, Blanchard had lectured for the American Anti-Slavery Society, studied at Lane Seminary, been a delegate to London's 1843 World Anti-Slavery Convention, and, since 1845, served as president of Knox College, a Galesburg institution that later produced a vocally Republican audience for the fifth Lincoln-Douglas debate. Blanchard had twice sparred with Douglas, once in an epistolary assault on the Fugitive Slave Act and once in a live discussion of the Kansas-Nebraska Act.[129] In May 1858, however, he praised Douglas for "boldly resist[ing]" the South and declared that God had placed him "on the side of freedom against all unconstitutional demands of the slave power." Blanchard backed Douglas's reelection to the Senate and hoped he would win the presidency in 1860.[130] This endorsement suggested Douglas might swallow the antislavery movement whole.

Douglas had no intention of switching parties or embracing abolitionism, but he did coordinate with Republicans, including in a mid-December strategy session with Congressmen Schuyler Colfax (Indiana) and Anson

Burlingame (Massachusetts). Colfax's meeting notes are instructive. Douglas accused Davis and other "Southrons" of contemplating secession and suggested that "the formation of a great Constitutional Union party" might be necessary to defeat them. He resolved to allow Kansans to write a new constitution, to advance his northwestern agenda by admitting Minnesota and Oregon as free states, and to place southern radicals in the position of "insurgents" so that the "Army & the power of the Nation would be against them" in case of war. Douglas and Colfax agreed that a temporary alliance was vital, even if new issues would soon divide Republicans and anti-Lecompton Democrats.[131]

This bipartisan cooperation handed Douglas's foes an inflammatory argument. After Douglas first repudiated the Lecompton Constitution, Albert Gallatin Brown sarcastically congratulated Henry Wilson on the "new leader of the Republican party."[132] A recent southern migrant to Illinois denounced Douglas as an "abolitionist in disguise" and the "bedfellow" of Charles Sumner, Salmon Chase, and William Seward.[133] Douglas's northern adversaries—acolytes of dough-faced James Buchanan, William Bigler, and Jesse Bright—echoed these indictments, with one Philadelphian blasting Douglas for backsliding into the free-soilism that had made him zealous for California statehood.[134] Southern critics made similar accusations. A South Carolina editor branded Douglas "a traitor to the South" and condemned him for being "frequently closeted with leading abolitionists." Boldly advocating southern primacy, he concluded, "The Democratic party, and particularly the Southern Democracy, (which is identical with what the national Democracy is, or should be,) needs no alliance with those who are polluted with the leprosy of Abolitionism."[135] Southern attacks reflected loathing of popular sovereignty; as Varina Davis recalled, this heresy, embraced by Democratic "abolitionists," was "eminently dangerous" to slavery.[136] Despite their rhetorical power, however, the "Republican" and "abolitionist" epithets obscured a vital point: Douglas resisted Lecompton from *within* the Democratic Party. Northern bolts, from the Barnburners of 1848 to the Republican exodus of 1854–56, had magnified southern power over the Democracy. But Douglas's resistance threatened the southern hegemony that slave-state Democrats cited as proof of the party's reliability. Lecomptonites tarred Douglas as an apostate, but his prestige among Democrats actually made him a deadlier foe.

Douglas's swelling popularity therefore emboldened fire-eaters who questioned whether the Democracy could deliver a slaveholding Kansas. Antislavery was rising like Mississippi floodwaters, warned John A. Quitman, and Lecompton's defeat would prove that northern Democrats had been swept away.[137] Nervous southern Democrats declared that congressional rejection of the Lecompton Constitution would justify secession. Davis vowed that the slave states would resist such "degradation" to the extremity of "pulling down . . . this grand political fabric of ours to its foundation," and similarly militant talk echoed in private correspondence and the southern press.[138] A Mississippi congressman urged constituents to prepare for war, for when "the sun of the Union sets, it will go down in blood."[139] With the Democracy and the Union's futures hanging in the balance, Davis and Douglas fought over Kansas and the deeper question of whether property rights would trump majority rule.

The battle raged throughout early 1858 and further alienated northern Douglas Democrats from the party's chiefly southern pro-Lecompton wing. Although often incapacitated by an excruciating eye ailment, Davis participated when able.[140] Meanwhile, Douglas, buoyed by Kansas voters' overwhelming rejection of the Lecompton Constitution on January 4, led the opposition.[141] Had northern Democrats all accepted Lecompton, it would have passed easily, for the party controlled 128 of 234 House seats and 37 of 62 in the Senate. But with much of the northern wing in revolt, southern Democrats struggled to force Lecompton through Congress; even if southerners voted as a bloc in the House, they still needed over two dozen northern votes.[142] The clash rattled southern Democrats because it exposed the limits of their power and weakened their argument for the party's soundness on slavery.

Debate intensified when Buchanan formally submitted the Lecompton Constitution to Congress on February 2. Douglas promptly countered with a protest petition from Kansas officeholders.[143] Six days later, Davis came from his sickbed to praise Buchanan, insist that Kansas needed slave labor, and accuse critics of opposing Lecompton for its slavery clause, thus impugning those, like Douglas, who professed indifference over slavery's future in Kansas.[144]

Douglas replied at length on March 22. He denied that Lecompton reflected the will of Kansas's free-state majority; hailed popular sovereignty as the galvanizing principle of the American Revolution; reiterated that it was Lecompton's antimajoritarian genesis to which he objected; and charged southerners with supporting Lecompton solely for slavery's sake. He also rebutted a series of editorials published in the Buchanan administration's mouthpiece, the *Washington Union*, which affirmed the Lecompton Constitution's elevation of slavery above state or territorial power. This doctrine, which sprouted from seeds planted by Calhoun and fertilized by Davis and Taney, would insulate slaveholders' property rights from local or national majorities. Appalled, Douglas warned that this would nationalize slavery and deliver "a death blow to State rights." The idea that slavery "goes everywhere under the Constitution . . . and yet is higher than the Constitution, above the Constitution, beyond the reach of sovereign power . . . will not be tolerated."[145] Democrats' efforts to contain the dispute failed because it touched issues far beyond Kansas. Douglas anticipated future conflict by pledging to defend the right of any state or territory to prohibit slavery.

As debate ground on, correspondents deluged Douglas with letters. Northern Democrats thanked him for rebuking a perversion of popular sovereignty.[146] Old Free-Soilers, including Jacob Brinkerhoff, one of the Wilmot Proviso's original proponents, hailed Douglas as an ally.[147] Admirers of all parties praised Douglas's defense of majority rule, and some Republicans applauded popular sovereignty.[148] Congratulations came from unlikely quarters, including the correspondent who, after hearing Douglas's March 22 speech, requested a donation to Wilberforce University, an African American institution named for a British abolitionist.[149] From the South came variations on an ultimatum: relent or face personal and national ruin.[150]

Buchanan launched a two-pronged campaign to force Lecompton through Congress and bring party rebels to heel. In Congress, he turned the screws on wavering northern Democrats, offering threats and inducements to change their votes. The administration resorted to outright bribery (one agent admitted spending over $30,000) and left a trail of corruption that Republicans uncovered and exploited in the 1860 election, another case of antislavery activists capitalizing on Democrats' internal battles.[151] Buchanan also wielded the patronage club against western Douglasites. In February 1858, Douglas complained that Buchanan was "removing all my friends from office & requiring pledges of hostility to me from all persons appointed to office."[152] The president struck hardest in Illinois and Ohio, dismissing recalcitrant postmasters from lucrative jobs in Chicago, Cleveland, and Columbus. Buchanan and Douglas had quarreled over patronage for a year, but these sackings clearly aimed to cow northern Democrats into submission; in fact, they only escalated intraparty conflict.[153]

Buchanan notched a preliminary victory on March 23 when the Senate voted 33–25 to accept the Lecompton Constitution. Davis was out sick, while Douglas predictably voted nay with the Republicans and three Democrats: Charles Stuart of Michigan, George Pugh of Ohio, and David

Broderick of California.[154] But the House, where the Douglasite-Republican coalition was stronger, passed a rival bill that would return the constitution to Kansas for amendment and a popular referendum.[155] Caught between their most popular leader and their president, some northern Democrats scrambled to cut a deal. William English of Indiana, a member of the conference committee tasked with reconciling the Senate and House bills, lent his name to a possible compromise. It would submit the Lecompton Constitution to Kansas voters with the stipulation that if they rejected it, they must wait until their population reached 93,420 (the minimum for one representative) to reapply for statehood; if they adopted Lecompton, Kansas would be admitted with a generous federal land grant of four million acres, although this was substantially less than the twenty-three million acres requested by the Lecompton convention.[156]

Contrary to a persistent misconception, the English Compromise did not offer extra land to bribe Kansans into sanctioning slavery. Rather, the *reduced* land grant was the pretext for referring the Lecompton Constitution to the voters; the bait was expedited statehood. The compromise addressed northern objections by returning the constitution to Kansas voters, while the acreage adjustment allowed southern hair-splitters to claim that land, not slavery, was at stake in the territorial referendum.[157] Douglas found it tempting, but a conversation with Broderick—who allegedly roared that, rather than acquiesce, Douglas "had better go into the street and blow out your brains!"—stiffened his spine.[158] He spurned the compromise for two reasons: it failed to refer the entire constitution to territorial voters, and it rigged the scales by postponing statehood if they voted no. He deemed this an insidious form of congressional intervention: with "inducements on one side, and penalties on the other, there is no freedom of election."[159] Douglas's opposition actually persuaded some southern holdouts to accept the English Compromise, and it passed the Senate on April 30. Once again, Douglas voted nay with Broderick, Stuart, and the Republicans, while Pugh joined southerners, including Davis, and pro-administration northerners like Bigler and Bright in the affirmative.[160] In the House, enough anti-Lecompton Democrats switched sides to pass the compromise bill and Buchanan signed it, lamely claiming victory. That August, Kansas's free-state majority rejected the Lecompton Constitution by a decisive vote: 11,300 to 1,788.[161]

The Lecompton conflagration exacerbated intraparty conflict in three ways. First, it cemented Douglas's place as the North's leading Democrat, embittering Buchananites and alarming southern Democrats who felt the reins of power slipping away. Second, Douglas's improved standing among a startlingly wide range of northerners encouraged a perceptible, though always incomplete, convergence between northern Democrats and Republicans. They divided on many issues, but Lecompton united them against a flagrantly proslavery perversion of popular sovereignty, which some Republicans now saw as a free-soil policy. Although only partial, this convergence disturbed Republican stalwarts and southern Democrats alike, for they both saw danger in Douglas's broad appeal.[162] Finally, that convergence promoted a parallel merger between southern Democrats and fire-eaters. As northern allies became unreliable, southern Democrats veered toward hardline proslavery policies to win support at home, thus moving closer to their extremist rivals.[163] This trend was foreshadowed in the 1840s when southern Democrats adopted Calhoun's position on slavery expansion, but the Lecompton battle accelerated the process.

Democrats thus entered the summer of 1858 more sectionally polarized than ever before. The competing claims of majority rule and property rights could not be reconciled with vague promises of "non-intervention," and party unity could not be ensured by shrill appeals to white supremacy. When forced to govern, northern and southern Democrats turned on each other, hailing Douglas and Davis as champions of hostile sectional factions. Soon, both faced constituents riled up by sectionalism and suspicious of Democratic duplicity. They weathered the storm, but winning at home further eroded the brittle bonds of party unity.

★ ★ ★

Lecompton demolished Davis's already fragile faith in Douglas Democrats, but not his determination to maintain a national party that would promote slaveholders' interests. So, when Congress adjourned in June 1858, Davis did not head south; instead, he embarked on a northern tour calculated to rebuild Democratic unity on his terms.[164]

Ostensibly seeking a healthier climate, Davis seized every opportunity to speak, from a shipboard Independence Day oration to speeches in New England and New York City. He promised that sectional agitators could not wreck the Union. He gloried in the Democracy's future, a fashionable theme at Maine's state Democratic convention, and quoted Thomas Jefferson's adage about northern Democrats being the South's natural allies. He dabbled in demagoguery, contrasting mongrelized Latin Americans with North America's spotless Anglo-Saxons who built their republic on the rock of white supremacy. He defended slavery as a positive good and accused abolitionists of assailing property rights.[165] It was familiar fare: a bid for cross-sectional unity grounded in nationalism, racism, and anti-abolitionism. The tour netted Davis an honorary degree from Bowdoin College and, as Varina recalled, nurtured his hopes for "a peaceful adjustment of the sectional dissonance."[166]

But the Democracy was in serious trouble. One deceptively minor incident illuminated the gap between Davis's values and those of his hosts. While in Maine, he and Varina attended commencement exercises at the Portland Free High School, where the daughter of what Varina deemed "a dissipated, ignorant washer-woman" exhibited her talent for calculus. The Davises wondered whether the young woman's state-sponsored education had made her dissatisfied—if a "cheery working woman" had been "spoiled" by book learning. They considered taking her back to Mississippi but decided that she had the "habits of her class" and could not be placed "on the social plane of our family."[167] Thus they spurned the ethos of upward mobility shared by Douglas, Lincoln, and northerners of all parties.[168]

Davis's audiences, moreover, consisted mainly of those northerners who were most likely to cheer him. New England Democrats like Caleb Cushing, who had served in Franklin Pierce's cabinet and introduced Davis at Faneuil Hall, were an embattled minority who depended on federal patronage. This left them sensitive to administration pressure and eager to toe the line on Lecompton.[169] Had Davis visited the Northwest, his reception would have been chilly.

Most alarming was the southern backlash against Davis's tour: even before the senator returned home, firebrands attacked him for courting Yankees and yielding on the territories. In Portland, Davis averred that territories were "the common property of the States" and that "whatever is property in any one of the States must be so considered in any of the territories." But then he observed that territorial legislatures could "refuse to enact such laws and police regulations" as were necessary to "give security" to slaveholders' property, thus practically nullifying their abstract right.[170] Davis was merely stating a fact, not advocating a policy.[171] But his comments provoked Deep South critics to call him a "Union-shrieking conservative" whose oratory was a "pitiable spectacle of human weakness."[172] Weeks before returning home, Davis began fighting to restore his reputation.[173] Sectionalism had shaken Mississippi's political landscape, and Davis staggered to regain his footing.

★ ★ ★

As Davis defended his northern overtures, Douglas struggled to prove that the Democracy was not a cat's-paw of the South. The stakes were enormous because he was running for reelection against a formidable challenger. "I shall have my hands full," Douglas mused upon learning that Abraham Lincoln sought his seat. He respected Lincoln's mastery of the politician's craft and praised the lanky lawyer as "the best stump-speaker, with his droll ways and dry jokes, in the West."[174] The 1858 Illinois senate race is a mainstay of Lincoln lore, but it also reveals much about Douglas and the Democracy.[175]

Lincoln and Douglas were neither polar opposites nor variations on a theme. Both had moved west and thrived in Illinois, where Lincoln settled after a hardscrabble boyhood in Kentucky and Indiana. They served together in the state legislature, clashing over tariffs and banking while cooperating on internal improvements. Since then, Douglas had soared to national prominence while Lincoln (save for one term in Congress) remained in Illinois, built a flourishing law practice, and helped organize the Republican Party. He narrowly missed a senate seat in 1855 but remained an incisive critic of Douglas and popular sovereignty. Some of Lincoln's views—support for enforcement of the Fugitive Slave Act, interest in colonization, and opposition to the Lecompton Constitution—resembled Douglas's, but on fundamental territorial policy they were starkly opposed. Douglas would defer to local majorities, while Lincoln would use a national majority to block slavery's expansion and steer it toward extinction. Lincoln's principled opposition to Douglas had fueled his personal and partisan advancement; now he hoped to topple the northern Democracy's leading senator.[176]

This comparison clarifies Lincoln and Douglas's hard-fought contest, which is sometimes misportrayed as a distillation of the sectional conflict. The debates, suggests one scholar, "held within themselves the essence of the whole tragic story of slavery, secession, and civil war," for Illinois "represented in microcosm the sectional forces that were tearing at the political fabric of America itself."[177] This reading dramatizes the campaign by distorting it. Lacking a cotton kingdom, Illinois was not a microcosm of antebellum America. Without a Calhounian contender, the Lincoln-Douglas canvass featured strictly northern political views, and without an abolitionist in the running, it did not even cover the range of northern opinion. Only by truncating the political spectrum and conscripting Douglas to represent a southern position, which he denounced throughout the Lecompton controversy, can the election encapsulate the sectional conflict. Its significance was subtler: for Lincoln, it was an opportunity to oust an opponent whom northern voters found all too appealing; for Douglas, it was a struggle to garner northern support without further alienating southern allies.

The Lincoln-Douglas race did, however, receive national attention. Many northern Democrats were up for reelection, but Douglas's race loomed largest because of his outsized political stature. "The eyes of the whole Nation are now directed to this State," wrote a Springfield resident in April 1858, "[and] the contest bids fair to be a most animated one."[178]

Complicating matters was a third candidate who, perhaps because he missed the renowned debates, is often overlooked. In late summer, Buchanan's Illinois supporters (called Danites) convinced ex-senator Sidney Breese to enter the field as the genuine Democratic candidate. Some Danites thought Breese could prevail; others accepted a probable Lincoln victory as the price of revenge against Douglas, whom they despised more than a Republican.[179] In hindsight, Breese's campaign seems quixotic, but it threatened to upend Douglas's strategy. Historians regularly identify southern Illinois—Egypt—as a Douglas stronghold, packed with southern sympathizers who loathed Lincoln's antislavery views. But Egypt was also where Breese expected to run best.[180] Thus, Douglas would have to parry Lincoln's attacks without driving Egyptians into Breese's camp. As Lincoln put it, Douglas was "lean[ing] Southward" to "keep the Buchanan party from growing in Illinois."[181] Eager to siphon votes away from Douglas, Republicans covertly cooperated with the Danite campaign.[182]

Breese's candidacy was part of a broader administration attack on Douglas. That a president would conspire against a leading senator of his own party underscores the severity of the Democratic rupture. Northeastern Buchananites like William Bigler and Daniel Dickinson advised Danites and aided their fund-raising efforts.[183] Pro-administration speakers crisscrossed Illinois, accusing Douglas of courting Republicans and urging Democrats to abandon him.[184] Southern Democrats pitched in, none more zealously than Louisiana senator John Slidell, who openly hoped for Lincoln's victory. Slidell encouraged prominent Democrats to disown Douglas and visited Chicago to coordinate with Danites, including postal employees who could suppress Douglas's campaign materials. There, he claimed that slaves on Douglas's Mississippi plantation were ill-clothed and malnourished, an accusation that soon appeared in Republican papers. After departing, Slidell advised Buchanan that Breese would probably lose but that patronage pressure could turn Illinois against Douglas by 1860.[185] So intense was the assault that some observers regarded the election as an extension of Douglas's battle against the administration.[186]

Still, Lincoln was Douglas's principal rival, and the resulting campaign was a key chapter in Lincoln's rise to the presidency. But the contest was also part of the history of the antebellum Democracy. This perspective foregrounds Republicans' ambivalence about the Lecompton controversy, their decisive influence on Democratic fragmentation, and the complex politics of race. By putting a wide swath of voters back into play, the Lecompton controversy shaped Lincoln's and Douglas's strategies. In their scores of speeches and seven famous debates, Lincoln and Douglas were not simply competing for Whig and Know-Nothing voters in central Illinois (although they were a key constituency) but were also seeking to influence Democrats throughout the state, including both Danites and wavering free-soilers who might return to the Democracy.[187] Douglas strove to rebuild Illinois's Democratic coalition, while Lincoln sought to turn both antislavery and proslavery Democrats against him.

Lincoln's alarm over Douglas's broadening appeal influenced his tactics. Appalled by some Republicans' readiness to embrace Douglas and popular sovereignty, Lincoln initially relied on a staple message: Douglas flouted northern interests and ideals. This meant downplaying the Lecompton rupture and running against the villain of 1854 rather than the hero of 1858, a key theme of the quotable "House Divided" speech with which Lincoln inaugurated his campaign in June. The Lecompton controversy was merely a "squabble," Lincoln insisted, and Douglas's "care not" attitude about slavery could not sustain real resistance to the Slave Power. Indeed, "Stephen" was plotting with "Franklin [Pierce], Roger [Taney], and James [Buchanan]" to legalize slavery nationwide; commencing with popular sovereignty and the *Dred Scott* decision, the four "workmen" had fashioned a monstrous edifice that needed one more Supreme Court ruling to elevate slavery beyond the reach of local, state, or federal law.[188] This was familiar ground: Lincoln had long condemned popular sovereignty as morally bankrupt and its leading spokesman as a proslavery Mephistopheles. Speaking to antislavery activists who now regarded Douglas as an ally, Lincoln dismissed Lecompton and leveled the conspiracy charge to prove that Douglas was still the same old doughface.[189]

But Lincoln sensed that this strategy was not foolproof. Privately, he acknowledged the severity of Democrats' sectional split, opining in late July that Douglas "care[d] nothing for the South—he knows he is already dead there," and he recognized that Douglas opposed the nationalization of slavery.[190] Especially damaging to the "four workmen" indictment was Douglas's readiness to embrace his image as a foe of the Slave Power. When Douglas launched his campaign in July, he cast the Lecompton quarrel in sectional terms, recalling how he "boldly and fearlessly" defended popular sovereignty against "the almost united South."[191] He also averred that popular sovereignty had advanced freedom by eliminating slavery in the Northeast and blocking it from the Old Northwest. During the final debate at Alton in mid-October, Douglas attributed the South's regional minority status to popular sovereignty's antislavery effects, an argument unlikely to gratify slaveholders.[192] These comments enabled sympathetic Republicans to regard Douglas as the free-soiler they wanted him to be.

Lincoln adapted by sapping the foundation of Douglas's ostensibly national party. During the fifth debate at Galesburg, Lincoln argued that Douglas was "becoming sectional too" and that the day was "rapidly approaching" when Douglas's popularity, like Republicans', would be restricted to the North.[193] More famously, at the second debate in Freeport, Lincoln confronted Douglas with the questions that divided him from the administration and its southern supporters, including whether a territorial government could outlaw slavery before statehood and whether he would endorse a Supreme Court ruling that states could not prohibit slavery.[194] This was a striking departure from the conspiracy charge: the more Lincoln isolated Douglas from the southern Democracy, the less Douglas resembled a proslavery artificer.[195] But rigid consistency is no prerequisite for political success, and Lincoln's aim was to inspire doubt about Douglas in as many minds as possible. Critiques of popular sovereignty would resonate with free-soilers, while the Freeport questions would rile the Danites.[196] Lincoln's layered strategy reflected the opportunities and pitfalls that the Lecompton battle presented to Republicans.

The Freeport exchange also spotlights how antislavery activism stoked Democratic infighting. This dynamic was already visible in the 1840s, when Free-Soilers blocked extension of the Missouri Compromise line and forced a showdown between popular sovereignty and the common-property doctrine. But it became especially clear when Lincoln propounded his questions and Douglas responded with his "Freeport Doctrine." To the question about the Supreme Court nixing state laws against slavery, Douglas lamely replied that the ruling was unthinkable.[197] He had to tread more carefully on the eminently practical question of whether a territory could prohibit slavery. Douglas's response was predictable: what mattered was local legislation, not Supreme Court rulings (or federal laws), since slavery "cannot exist a day or an hour anywhere, unless it is supported by local police regulations," which could be passed or rejected by local authorities. Territorial voters could elect representatives "who will by unfriendly legislation effectually prevent the introduction" of slavery.[198] Douglas rehashed this point in subsequent debates, insisting that unfriendly local legislation was constitutional and actually more effective than a federal ban.[199] In the final debate, Douglas quoted Davis's Portland speech, implying that southern Democrats concurred.[200]

Early Lincoln lore held Douglas's candor at Freeport derailed his presidential aspirations by ruining his reputation in the South. Scholars have shown, however, that Douglas had made similar statements before 1858, and some contend that the absence of backlash against previous iterations of the Freeport Doctrine proves that it had been acceptable to proslavery southerners until Douglas, reeking of Lecompton treachery, turned them against it.[201] That said, the Freeport statement did inhibit Democratic reunification. Northern admirers celebrated it as proof that Douglas was still resisting proslavery pressure.[202] And while the statement changed few southerners' minds about Douglas, opponents denounced his continued hostility toward the *Dred Scott* ruling and proslavery territorial policy.[203] Criticism of Davis's alleged flirtation with this heresy, moreover, forced him closer to the fire-eaters. Pressure from Republicans and fire-eaters prevented Democrats from veiling their territorial policy in artful ambiguity.

Douglas counterattacked by alluding to popular sovereignty's antislavery potential but also by unleashing some of the most maliciously racist demagoguery of his career.[204] He launched his campaign by affirming that the U.S. government was "made by the white man, for the benefit of the white man, to be administered by white men."[205] He echoed this preemptive perversion of the Gettysburg Address throughout the debates, insisting that American egalitarianism did not apply to black people, that Republicans would flood Illinois with emancipated slaves, and that abolitionists like Lincoln valued black equality more than white liberty.[206] With minutes left in the last debate, Douglas announced, "I care more for the great principle of self-government . . . than I do for all the negroes in Christendom." Warming to his theme, he added, "I would not endanger the perpetuity of this Union, I would not blot out the great inalienable rights of the white men for all the negroes that ever existed."[207] Lincoln made concessions to popular prejudice, but his expansive views of the Declaration of Independence and all workers' right to the fruits of their labor were, in contrast, remarkably enlightened.[208]

Why did Douglas harp on race? Historians have explored the strategic dimensions of Lincoln's sometimes racist rhetoric, but few have analyzed Douglas from this angle.[209] He was deeply prejudiced, but, like Lincoln, he was also a consummate politician whose words were intended to win votes, not bare his soul. In 1858, Douglas's vituperative remarks were sadly well suited to his aims. Appeals to white supremacy were standard Democratic fare, particularly amid intraparty conflicts, as seen when Davis sounded the horn of white supremacy in his New England tour. In resorting to race-baiting, Douglas was relying on a tested strategy.

Racism helped Douglas court two key constituencies: wavering free-soil Democrats and embittered Danites. Free-soil politics was compatible with racism, as demonstrated in Kansas's Topeka constitution, which barred black migration as well as slavery, and Douglas knew that racist second thoughts might tempt erstwhile Democrats to abandon the Republicans.[210] "There are scores of men," wrote friends in west-central Illinois, "who have voted with the Republicans who cannot swallow the doctrine of Negro Equality."[211] By denouncing Lincoln in explosively racist terms, Douglas sought to lure them back. Racist appeals could also convince Danites, and attentive southern Democrats, that Douglas was infinitely preferable to his opponent, thus soliciting their support without yielding anything substantive on territorial policy. Racism was the lowest common denominator among the diverse voters Douglas wanted to assemble into a rejuvenated Democratic coalition.

Ironically, however, Douglas's ugly campaign underscored differences between his views and those of proslavery crusaders. When Douglas criticized Lincoln's inclusive reading of the Declaration of Independence, for instance, he reaffirmed his belief in white men's equality; unlike proslavery radicals, he did not categorically dismiss Jefferson as a moonstruck idealist.[212] Douglas also qualified his claims about black inferiority in ways that defied proslavery doctrine. In his first debate with Lincoln, Douglas averred, "I do not hold that because a negro is our inferior that therefore he ought to be a slave." Rather, he believed that blacks should "have and enjoy every right, every privilege, and every immunity consistent with the safety" of American society. This, he concluded, "is a question which each State and each Territory must decide for itself." Conflating state and territorial self-government, Douglas extended popular sovereignty over every aspect of race relations and approved widely divergent local policies, including Maine's enfranchisement of African American men.[213] Douglas repeated these points in every debate where he spoke first, suggesting that he regarded it as a strategically advantageous position, and had made similar statements, including condoning black suffrage, in the Senate.[214] Proslavery southerners were not so flexible; secessionists later listed black enfranchisement among their grievances against the North.[215] Douglas's racism played better in Egypt than in Dixie.

After an exhausting campaign, Douglas prevailed. Republican candidates actually received a plurality of the votes, garnering 125,430 to the Douglas Democrats' 121,609 (Danites took around 5,000), but heavily Republican northern Illinois was underrepresented in the legislature, so Democrats retained a majority and in January 1859 elected Douglas over Lincoln, 54–46.[216] In response, Douglas proclaimed, "Let the voice of the people rule," a bit of majoritarian bravado that flouted the electoral arithmetic.[217] Nevertheless, his victory was a bright spot for northern Democrats, who lost a net total of eighteen seats in Congress and fared especially poorly in the Northeast, although they minimized their losses in the Northwest and actually drew more votes than in 1856. Northern Democrats were reeling, and recovery depended on steering toward Douglas and away from Buchanan and the South.[218]

★ ★ ★

Southern Democrats had mixed feelings about Douglas's success, but all their varied responses boded ill for party unity. Hardliners who opposed his reelection now contrived to depose him from party leadership. Pragmatists celebrated Lincoln's defeat but decreed that future cross-sectional cooperation must be on southern terms.

Mississippi Democrats exhibited the full range of reactions. Addressing the state legislature soon after the Illinois elections, Congressman Lucius Q. C. Lamar arraigned Douglas for having "shot a Parthian arrow into the ranks of his former allies" and "ranged himself under the banner of that hideous fanaticism which threatens to crush the constitution and the South." He scorned apologists who defended Douglas as the lesser evil. If Douglas was the "best issue which the Democracy of the North can present us, then perish the Democracy of the North! and, if need be, perish the Union! but preserve unblemished the honor, and unhurt the rights, of the South."[219] If planters could not command plain republicans, Lamar would secede.

A few weeks earlier, Senator Albert Gallatin Brown offered a contrary opinion but reached a similarly defiant conclusion. Brown first reviewed the Kansas controversy, vindicating the Lecompton Constitution and condemning popular sovereignty. This led him to Douglas. Brown chided southerners who "indulge[d] in wholesale denunciation" of the Illinoisan, and he hoped that Douglas would "thrash Abolition Lincoln out of his boots." He refused, however, to forfeit proslavery principle for partisan gain. He respected the "National Democratic party" as the "last bulwark of the Union," but "if it requires another compromise, and another sacrifice of southern rights, to save it, it may go." Which rights did he mean?

Brown offered a litany of proslavery initiatives: expansion into Central America ("because I want to plant slavery there"), conquests in Cuba and northern Mexico ("for the planting or spreading of slavery"), and, perhaps, reopening the African slave trade. His polestar was slavery—"a great moral, social, and political blessing"—and if the Union ever menaced "my property and my domestic peace, I will destroy it if I can."[220] Douglas derided extremists who threatened the Union by squabbling over slavery; Brown threatened to demolish the Union for slavery's sake. The Democracy could not serve two masters.

By late 1858, Mississippi Democrats had brought fringe ideas like reviving the African slave trade and enacting a federal slave code for the territories into the political mainstream. Some remained committed to preserving the national Democracy, but many wanted to realize Calhoun's dream of forging a southern party.[221] While Davis was off wooing New Englanders, one Mississippian declared that it was "useless to speak of the North and South uniting in one political party; oil and water will not mingle, and we will only learn too late, we pursue a mirage when we hope for a National party."[222] Thus, Davis returned to a Mississippi where he now appeared soft on slavery, a dramatic reversal from 1851, when his gubernatorial campaign foundered on charges of radicalism. Like Douglas, Davis faced rivals who questioned whether the national Democracy could advance sectional interests. Douglas had responded by insisting that Democrats could secure free soil in the West, while Davis delivered some of the most fire-eating oratory of his career.

Addressing the state legislature days after Lamar's scorching speech, Davis strove to restore his reputation. Insisting that he had visited New England only for medical purposes, Davis reported that proslavery southerners had "a large body of true friends" there. Douglas, of course, was not one of them. At considerable length, Davis refuted claims that he had endorsed "squatter sovereignty" in Maine. Newspapers had mangled the story, and Douglas had deliberately misrepresented him at Alton. Indeed, proclaimed Davis, he and Douglas had *never* agreed on territorial policy. Slaveholders' peculiar need for protection "does not confer a right to destroy" their property rights, as Douglas claimed, "but rather creates an obligation to protect." Rehashing an old argument, Davis condemned popular sovereignty and free soil as equally odious. "Between such positions, Mississippi cannot have a preference, because she cannot recognize anything tolerable in either of them." Looking to the future, Davis turned his guns on the Republicans and denounced their criticisms of slavery, an institution that promoted white equality by relegating menial labor to "the servile race." If a Republican were elected president, Mississippi must leave a union with those who would "deprive you of your birthright" and "reduce you to worse than the colonial dependence of your fathers." Rather than endure abolition rule, Davis would rally "Mississippi's best and bravest . . . to the harvest-home of death."[223]

Thus far it was all sound and fury, but Davis had tacked toward Lamar and Brown's extremism. He still cherished the Democracy, and perhaps he could temper radical words with moderate deeds.[224] But his constituents, like Douglas's, expected results. Douglas had failed to deliver a Pacific railroad, homestead legislation, or peace in Kansas, while Davis had neither made Kansas a slave state nor corralled wayward northern Democrats. With another session of Congress commencing in December and a presidential election less than two years away, the Democracy, battered by Lecompton and its bitter aftermath, was crumbling. Already planning for the 1860 convention, one of Davis's closest Mississippi allies predicted that "wholly unreliable" northern Democrats would "unite to force Douglas upon the south." In that event, southern Democrats should bolt and nominate their own candidate: Jefferson Davis.[225] The prophecy was only partially accurate, but it reflected serious damage already done to party unity.

6

Rule or Ruin

Stephen Douglas was the "pivot individual" of the Democratic Party's 1860 convention in Charleston, South Carolina. "Every delegate was for or against him," observed journalist Murat Halstead; every speech, scheme, and bargain sought to promote or prevent his nomination. Indeed, delegates began wrangling over Douglas long before they reached Charleston. On trains and at stations, in hotel rooms and at meals, they deliberated: Could Douglas win two-thirds of the delegates? Would southerners accept his nomination? Could he carry the general election?[1]

Halstead chronicled these conversations while mingling with delegates en route to Charleston. At dinner with an Indianan and a brace of Mississippians, he watched them toast the "health of the nominee." Did that include Douglas? No, for Douglas had "no chance" to prevail. Furious, the Indianan insisted that "Southern fanatics and fire-eaters" and "such men as Jeff. Davis" pledge to support the nominee, whoever he was. A Mississippian shot back that Jefferson Davis was a "patriot," while Douglas was "a traitor, d——d little better than [William] Seward," the New York Republican who spoke of an irrepressible conflict between slavery and freedom. The Indianan defensively cited northern Democrats' support for the Fugitive Slave Act, but the Mississippians swore that they could protect themselves "out of the Union, if not in it." The delegates averted a fistfight by wagering $1,000 on whether Douglas could win Mississippi's electoral votes. Onlookers were left "sh[aking] their heads and talk[ing] of stormy times ahead."[2]

The altercation was aggravated by fatigue and liquor, but, as what Halstead aptly deemed "the history of the Convention in miniature," it heralded a deeper struggle. It was the fruit of prolonged conflict, which had primed the Indianan to view southern rivals as embryonic traitors who would destroy a party they could not dominate. Sure enough, the Mississippians vowed to make the Democracy "serve the South." They loathed Douglas and his "janus-faced lying resolutions" about popular sovereignty, a doctrine "as bad as Sewardism." They brandished copies of his Freeport speech and planned to "bombard him in the Convention with ammunition drawn from it." They would place the Democracy squarely behind proslavery principles, or they would send the party and its dithering northern spoilsmen "to the devil."[3]

Within weeks, the anticipated split spawned competing candidacies. Personalities and tactics mattered, but the rupture was not merely the product of convention intrigues. Delegates arrived in Charleston with short tempers, long memories, and visceral animosities fueled by years of infighting. Democrats had always clashed along sectional lines, and the battle over the Lecompton Constitution had clarified the issues. "There is a Northern democratic party, and a Southern democratic party," mused the *New York Herald* in early 1859, "and the differences between them are as broad as the difference between 'popular sovereignty' and the Lecompton constitution—between niggers and no niggers, or between slave and free soil."[4] The party could stand for white men's democracy or white masters' property, but not both.

This contest over party leadership and principles raged until November 1860. Rival Democrats recognized its gravity: those on both sides warned that only *their* leaders and *their* ideals would bring victory and accused opponents of plotting to destroy the party, hand the presidency to the Republicans, and shatter the Union. Underlying Democrats' bickering about Douglas's electability or the propriety of popular sovereignty were long-submerged issues that threatened to disrupt the Union itself. Never had the tug-of-war between plain republicans and planters had such momentous consequences for all Americans.

★ ★ ★

The night before departing Chicago for Washington in November 1858, Douglas conferred with C. H. Ray, editor of the *Chicago Tribune*. Ray, a Republican, considered Douglas "an infernal rascal" but respected his opposition to proslavery intrigues. Worried that southern Democrats would demand resumption of the African slave trade and enactment of a federal slave code for the territories, Douglas promised Ray that he would "hit it between the eyes precisely as I did Lecompton."[5]

The slave trade and slave code had moved from the political fringe to the mainstream via the southern Democracy. For years, southern apologists had claimed, as a Mississippian did in 1846, that the Atlantic slave trade had bestowed "incalculable blessings" upon Africans by bringing them under the control of a superior civilization.[6] By 1853, South Carolina's Leonidas Spratt had launched a campaign to repeal laws barring American participation in overseas slave trading, and the idea soon caught fire among a significant minority of southern whites, particularly in the Mississippi Valley. Advocates exploited southern hopes and anxieties, arguing that an influx of cheap unfree labor would promote Caribbean expansion, secure western territories, and enhance slavery's mass appeal by elevating more whites into the master class. They also used loyalty politics, tarring critics as enemies of the South. And by spreading their message through southern commercial conventions, slave trade champions pressured mainstream politicians to endorse their cause; the effort culminated with a May 1859 gathering in Vicksburg, which proposed overturning all federal and state laws against international slave trading.[7]

Leading southern Democrats tracked the crusade nervously, recognizing that it could disrupt the national party.[8] Seeking a middle ground, many supported repealing laws that defined slave trading as piracy, but not bringing African captives into their communities.[9] Davis adopted this stance in a July 1859 speech to Mississippi's Democratic convention, in which he disparaged anti–slave trade laws and mocked those who "prate of the inhumanity and sinfulness of the trade." He would allow each state to regulate slave imports, arguing that Texas, the New Mexico Territory, and "future acquisitions" in northern Mexico could benefit from cut-rate African labor.[10] As on debt repudiation and resistance to the Compromise of 1850, Davis hoped to split the difference. But fire-eaters had pushed him toward an advanced proslavery position, and Davis sought to take the Democracy with him.

The slave trade controversy peaked in 1859, just as the campaign for a territorial slave code gained momentum. Davis framed the issue in his

November 1858 address to the Mississippi legislature: territorial governments could not "destroy" slaveholders' property rights through inaction or hostile legislation and indeed had an "obligation to protect" them.[11] But what if territories shirked their duty? By 1859, many proslavery southerners concluded that Congress must safeguard masters' property rights with federal legislation. This would nullify Douglas's Freeport heresy, give statutory teeth to Chief Justice Taney's ruling, and make explicit a responsibility long implied by the common-property doctrine. As the federal slave code became a test of sectional loyalty, southern Democrats recognized the need to embrace it, even to the detriment of national party unity. Meanwhile, fire-eaters like Albert Gallatin Brown and Alabama's William Lowndes Yancey, who scorned national parties while wearing the Democratic label, detected a new opportunity to split the party and hasten secession. Thus, party regulars pressed for the slave code to strengthen the Democracy's southern appeal, while extremists would use it to rule or ruin; similar in means if not ends, both stratagems jeopardized the party and the Union.[12]

Douglas spied both issues on the horizon as he departed Chicago, and he launched a preemptive counterattack while steaming down the Mississippi River. In speeches at Memphis and New Orleans, Douglas repeated a familiar litany: slavery was strictly local; there were no sectional rights to the territories; popular sovereignty was the only truly national policy on slavery expansion. Hoping to stifle the slave code movement, he urged southerners not to demand federal protection, lest they expose slavery to attack by a northern-dominated Congress. And, in response to popular interest, he endorsed peaceful acquisition of territory in Mexico, Central America, and Cuba.[13]

These tropical allusions represented a bid to rebuild party unity through additional expansion. Democrats of all sections had called for fresh conquests since the end of the war with Mexico, and land hunger was especially acute in the lower Mississippi Valley. Despite a series of private filibustering expeditions into northern Mexico, Nicaragua, and Cuba (including forays led by John A. Quitman, in which Davis politely declined to participate) and official efforts by Presidents Pierce and Buchanan, however, the U.S. snagged no new territory beyond the Gadsden Purchase. As slavery's prospects in Kansas waned, Douglas saw in Caribbean adventurism a means of deflecting southern discontent. It was a long-shot strategy: the Democracy had delivered little new territory in ten years, and southern radicals were not unanimously eager for Caribbean expansion, which some regarded as a distraction. Conversely, some expansionists hoped to append tropical provinces to a separate southern empire, not a reinvigorated United States. Expansionist bombast drew applause but was no panacea for Democratic infighting.[14]

Southern critics turned Douglas's riverboat journey into a running of the gauntlet. One Mississippi editor wrote that "duplicity is the chief element in [his] character . . . and he knows no country, no friendship, no party, no patriotism—nothing but Stephen A. Douglas."[15] Another likened him to David Wilmot, the renegade Democrat of proviso infamy.[16] But no one topped the widely reprinted diatribe unleashed by Davis's mouthpiece, the Jackson *Mississippian*: Douglas arrived "covered with the odium of such detestable heresies," "stained with the dishonor of a treachery without parallel," and "fresh from the warm embrace of Seward and [Horace] Greeley and [Joshua] Giddings." Southerners who resented Douglas's "outrageous injustice" would be justified in welcoming him "to the gibbet or the faggot"—that is, lynching him by rope or fire.[17]

More substantive was the attack on Douglas's leadership in Washington. He had chaired the Committee on Territories since entering the Senate and recently had won victories for the Greater Northwest, including passage of statehood bills for Minnesota and Oregon. (Oregon's admission was delayed because the House failed to consider the bill.)[18] Eager to strengthen their position by stripping Douglas of the chairmanship, a vital element of his power, southern Democrats and Buchananites caucused before Douglas reached Washington and replaced him with James S. Green of Missouri. A few dissenters warned against making Douglas a martyr, but Buchanan blessed the move and Davis, aided by John Slidell and Jesse Bright, led the charge in the caucus. One biographer ranks this among the "most disreputable acts" of Davis's career.[19]

The coup deepened northern Douglasites' antipathy toward Buchanan and southern Democrats. It was "a gross & unprecedented outrage"; a "disgracefull moove [sic]"; "the most contemptible of all acts on record"; the work of "cowardly poltroons."[20] An Illinois Democratic congressman was "outraged almost beyond endurance."[21] Some interpreted the maneuver in purely sectional terms. "This war on you," wrote one confidant, "all comes from the South."[22] An Illinoisan alliteratively denounced it as a "piece of petty proscription" designed to make a federal slave code the new party dogma.[23] Meanwhile, Mississippi Democrats rejoiced that Douglas was now "impotent" to betray them.[24]

In this toxic atmosphere, some admirers feared that Douglas's life was in danger. Southern Democrats had used violence against northern adversaries before—Charles Sumner's caning was a recent memory—and some observers believed Douglas was their next target. At the center of the alleged plot was Louisiana senator Slidell, an expert marksman who helped depose Douglas from his chairmanship after failing to foil his reelection. According to *Harper's Weekly*, the Louisianan was plotting to goad Douglas into a duel and thus hide a homicide behind the veil of honor. The possibilities were appalling: "If any noisy ranter can deprive the country of the services of such a man as Senator Douglas, by provoking him into an encounter in which he can gain nothing and may lose his life, this is not a civilized country."[25]

The likeliest trigger for a duel was Slidell's role in spreading rumors about the abuse of enslaved people on Douglas's Mississippi plantation. According to the *Chicago Tribune*, Slidell planted the story with Dr. Daniel Brainard, a Danite employed at Chicago's U.S. Marine Hospital. When the *Tribune* published the accusations, Democrats demanded the source and the *Tribune* revealed Slidell's name. James B. Sheridan, Douglas's secretary, called Slidell out as a liar, and Slidell blasted Douglas for authorizing the insult. The feud escalated, and pundits anticipated a bloody denouement; the question (and headline) was, "Will Douglas Fight?"[26]

Alarmed, Douglas hired crack-shot Kentucky duelist Tom Hawkins as his intermediary and bodyguard. Meanwhile, admirers begged him to master his emotions and avoid Slidell's snare. From Ohio came a plea to bear the "petty persecution" with "Christian resignation," a tall order for the hot-tempered Little Giant.[27] A Hoosier counseled Douglas to "take no offense at anything Slidell . . . or any other thief or murderer may say" and to "have the courage to decline any call to Combat."[28] Douglas curbed his anger and reconciled with Slidell by disavowing Sheridan's scathing rebuttal.[29] The danger abated by late February 1859, although its seriousness was retrospectively reaffirmed in September, when Senator David Broderick was slain on a California dueling ground by southern-born Democrat David S. Terry.[30] For anti-Lecompton Democrats, membership in the party of Andrew Jackson provided no immunity to violence inflicted by heirs of John C. Calhoun.

These rumors shadowed the second session of the Thirty-Fifth Congress, which extended into March 1859. Ever the western gadfly, Douglas scored a victory on Oregon when House Democrats, keen to add a friendly state before the 1860 election, united to pass the statehood bill over opposition from Republicans who, despite Oregon's free-state status, objected to its constitutional ban on black migration.[31] When Oregon was admitted in mid-February, Douglas hailed it as an exemplar of popular sovereignty.[32] The stalemate on a Pacific railroad, however, was nothing to crow about. As senators considered a bill to construct a line from the Missouri River to San Francisco, route selection remained the sticking point. Davis warned that the bill would fail if Congress attempted to fix the route and suggested allowing contractors hired to build the road to determine its course.[33] Douglas also cautioned against sectional squabbling but preferred to specify the route, suggesting that Congress authorize either one central road or three roads along northern, central, and southern lines.[34] The Senate bickered for six weeks before abandoning the bill.[35]

Still more explosive was the federal slave code, the issue that provoked the late February showdown between Davis and Douglas and prompted Alfred Iverson to complain that they could "go on . . . arguing against each other from this until doomsday."[36] After years of Democratic feuding, this encounter stood out for its intensity, the extreme position occupied by southern Democrats, and the implications for the 1860 election.

Democrats rejected free-soilism but agreed on little else. Building on Brown's call for proslavery legislation and his own "obligation to protect" theme, Davis cited the fugitive slave clause as proof that the Constitution elevated masters' property rights above state or federal interference. "What the Government owes to person and property is adequate protection," Davis argued, appointing himself the arbiter of adequacy, "and the amount of protection which must be given will necessarily vary with the character of the property and the place where it is held." Property owners deserved equal outcomes, not equal treatment. Territories lacked authority to determine how much assistance was due; this power belonged to Congress, which must give slaveholders more help than owners of less troublesome chattels. As for popular sovereignty, Davis denounced it as "a delusive gauze thrown over the public mind" that would deprive slaveholders of their rightful protection. Davis did not explicitly demand a territorial slave code, but he asserted that Congress must "compel" territorial legislatures to safeguard property or itself "enact the laws which are needed." A slave code might be a last resort, but it was available if a territory dared to follow the Freeport Doctrine.[37]

Speaking as a northerner, Douglas rebuffed Brown and Davis's demands for special treatment. Since territories could regulate, tax, or prohibit other property, why deny them this authority over slavery? He had made this argument for a decade, but now it took on a sharper edge. If there was "something peculiar in slave property" that made it uniquely fragile, "it is the misfortune of those who own that species of property." If lack of local protection "practically excludes slave property" from a territory, tough luck: that was the point of the Freeport speech. Boasting that he "never would vote for a slave code in the Territories by Congress," Douglas defended popular sovereignty on both strategic and principled grounds. Democrats must eschew proslavery and antislavery intervention alike or risk annihilating their northern wing. Recently condemned for apostasy, Douglas returned the charge: southerners who wanted a slave code must "step off the Democratic platform."[38]

In this bitter debate, Davis and Douglas entrenched themselves on lines they would hold for the next year and a half. Davis responded to fire-eaters' pressure by following the common-property principle to the conclusion that Congress must intervene to make slaveholders' abstract rights into practical realities. Negative liberty could not sustain slavery against apathetic or antagonistic local majorities, so he would tighten federal control over the West. Under pressure from Republicans, Douglas counterattacked along pragmatic and ideological lines. Davis's policy would either split the Democracy or slaughter its northern adherents, he warned, and it flouted ideals of decentralized white self-government. If localism thwarted slavery's expansion, so be it. Having expressed apathy over slavery's establishment in Kansas, he now signaled indifference to its exclusion. Douglas's "care not" slogan sounded no better to Davis than it did to Lincoln.

The February 1859 showdown was less a turning point than a moment of clarity that "opened all the waters of strife and bitterness" between rival Democratic factions battling over territorial policy.[39] A decade of infighting and calculated obfuscation had built up intolerable pressure, which now exploded into a brutal debate about what Democrats stood for. Both sides, moreover, girded for a protracted conflict. Admirers urged Douglas to drive his foes "to the wall," wondered why southern Democrats persisted in "cutting the throats" of their northern counterparts, and resolved to yield nothing to the South in the 1860 convention.[40] Meanwhile, southern Democrats divided over Brown and Davis's gambit. Some believed it was foolish to force northern friends to swallow a slave code.[41] But fire-eaters and their fellow travelers wielded considerable influence and the slave code gained popularity, particularly if popular sovereignty, which southern Democrats assailed as a "monstrous heresy" and a "swindle," was the only alternative. Democratic editors refused to retreat for the sake of "party obligations."[42] Without explicitly adopting fire-eaters' rule-or-ruin policy, many southern Democrats embraced the slave code as a test of party reliability.

Southern critics routinely compared popular sovereignty to the Wilmot Proviso—Davis had landed this jab in 1850—but the critique gained traction as some Republicans dabbled with the doctrine. The day after Davis and Douglas's senatorial slugfest, Bleeding Kansas veteran and Massachusetts congressman Eli Thayer embraced popular sovereignty as a free-soil policy that was "perfectly consistent" with Republican principles. Kansas, he said, proved it: despite being adjacent to slaveholding Missouri, Kansas would be free because northern migration had prevailed, as it always would. Erasing the Missouri Compromise line was a fatal mistake for the South, Thayer concluded in a stunning refutation of his party's founding credo, because it opened every territory to popular sovereignty and thus "secured . . . the freedom of every foot of the national domain."[43] According to a widely reprinted account, Douglas savored Thayer's speech and then grasped his hand and gloated, "We have just shoved Jeff. Davis off the Democratic platform—won't you get on in his place?"[44] Most Republicans still detested popular sovereignty, but even partial convergence between northern Democrats and Republicans stoked southern ire. The *Mississippian* decried popular sovereignty as "a more potent weapon of Abolitionism than the Wilmot Proviso itself" and denied that any southerner desired a place "on the Douglas-Thayer platform."[45] Following Lecompton, Freeport, and the great debate of February 1859, Thayer's speech and Douglas's reply confirmed southern Democrats' darkest suspicions about the Little Giant.

★ ★ ★

Congress adjourned shortly after the February 23 debate, but conflict continued. With the Democracy cracking along old fault lines and a presidential election looming, the intraparty fracas continued, and the breach between Davis and Douglas widened.

Whether the slave code movement was a disunionist ploy or a calculated gamble by southern Democrats, Douglas urged northern Democrats to repudiate it. His logic was simple: only a nationally united Democracy could preserve the Union, and only popular sovereignty could sustain party unity.[46] Douglas exuded confidence, but some northern Democrats were panicking. A New Yorker predicted that "unless there be a quick and permanent change in the policy of our Southern leaders, every northern or Free State . . . will decide for the Republicans in 1860."[47] From Cleveland came a tirade against the "apostasy, effrontery, dishonor, & insanity" of southerners who demanded "congressional intervention for the protection of Slavery in the Territories." They wanted to "make the democracy a pro-slavery party," and the Ohioan urged Douglas to oppose the effort at all costs. He preferred a "black republican administration and the blacker the better" over capitulation to southern radicalism.[48]

Douglas soon issued his own ultimatum. In June, he received a note from Joseph B. Dorr, a Democratic editor from Dubuque who later helped organize the 12th Iowa Infantry, suffered a serious wound near Atlanta, and survived a prisoner of war camp.[49] Dorr asked whether Douglas would accept a presidential nomination, and the senator seized the opportunity to declare his availability while renouncing proslavery extremism. If Democrats advocated the principles of the Compromise of 1850 as inscribed in the platforms of 1852 and 1856 and the Kansas-Nebraska Act—that is, if they endorsed popular sovereignty—he would run. But if they advocated "the revival of the African slave trade, or a Congressional slave code for the Territories, or the doctrine that the Constitution . . . establishes or prohibits slavery in the Territories beyond the power of the people legally to control it as other property," he would reject the nomination.[50] As a pretext for declaring his candidacy and dictating terms, the Dorr letter was presumptuous. As a northern battle cry, however, it was designed to restore Democratic spirits, prevent defections to the Republicans, and entice ex-Democrats away from Republicanism. And as a warning to southern Democrats, the Dorr letter, supplemented by published letters Douglas sent to southern contacts, was a plea for pragmatism: maintain party unity or risk a Republican triumph.[51]

Responses to the Dorr letter underscored the Democracy's polarization. A New Orleans editor correctly predicted that Douglas's statement "will raise him up hosts of friends in the North, and greatly embitter his enemies in the South."[52] Most northern Democrats relished Douglas's defiance, believing it would boost his presidential prospects, deflect antislavery attacks, and inspire more Republican conversions. Dorr thanked Douglas for his "bold and candid" statement, which would "prevent any farther [sic] disintegration of the Douglas forces in the North West."[53] Embattled southern Douglasites also praised the letter but admitted that Douglas stock was plummeting in their region.[54] Douglas's foes were predictably unconvinced by his reasoning. Buchanan fumed over the attempt to foist "squatter sovereignty" on the Democracy, arguing that masters' property rights were guaranteed by the Constitution and that Douglas's policy would enable "one set of squatters to confiscate the property of another set." He began to strategize Douglas's downfall at Charleston.[55] Privately, Davis excoriated the "low chicanery by which the Presidency is sought by certain ambitious demagogues."[56] Publicly, he defended slavery as a positive good, called for state control of the African slave trade, denounced Liberian colonization, and urged annexation of Cuba. Crucially, he reiterated that if territorial laws did not uphold property rights, he would support "the legislation needful to enable the General Government" to do so.[57] Mississippi Democrats echoed him in their state platform.[58]

Supporters advised Douglas to stand pat on the Dorr letter, but he yearned to defend popular sovereignty from an impregnable position. Accordingly, he spent much of the summer laboring on a deeply, if selectively, researched essay published in the September 1859 issue of *Harper's New Monthly Magazine* as "The Dividing Line between Federal and Local Authority: Popular Sovereignty in the Territories."[59] His thesis, which held that territories could establish or bar slavery just like states, directly refuted Calhoun's territorial doctrine and its slave-code corollary. Torturing logic and eliding inconvenient text, Douglas insisted that popular sovereignty embodied the *Dred Scott* decision. Although he concentrated his fire on proslavery southerners, Douglas also tried to outflank the Republicans by presenting popular sovereignty as the surest safeguard against slavery's nationalization. Equally striking was Douglas's claim that popular sovereignty was the key principle of the American Revolution. "Our fathers of the Revolution," he announced, fought not just for independence "but for the inestimable right of Local Self-Government . . . the right of every distinct political community—dependent Colonies, Territories, and Provinces, as well as sovereign States—to make their own local laws, form their own domestic institutions, and manage their own internal affairs in their own way."[60] Though hardly novel, the essay summarized Douglas's views for a wide audience and marked the culmination of his evolving thinking on popular sovereignty: for years, he had defended its pragmatism, and more recently its constitutionality. Now, he wove it into the nation's founding saga, arguing that it antedated the Constitution and the Union. Like antislavery activists who appealed to a higher law and southern authors who traced slavery to antiquity, Douglas sought to elevate his position to the loftiest possible plane.

The essay incited a furious backlash among Democratic critics. Using language typically reserved for abolitionist tracts, the *Richmond Enquirer* deemed it an "incendiary document" that marked "the most dangerous phase . . . which anti-slavery agitation has yet assumed."[61] The Jackson *Weekly Mississippian* rebuked Douglas's "extreme Squatter Sovereignty anti-State rights doctrines."[62] Northern doughfaces were equally harsh; a Philadelphian opined that slavery's influence made southerners superior statesmen and lamented that the northern rabble would "continue to hurrah for the little Giant."[63]

Opponents quickly counterattacked. Attorney General Jeremiah Black spoke for the administration in an article, reprinted as a pamphlet, defending the *Dred Scott* doctrines that informed southern demands for federal intervention.[64] This rejoinder triggered a series of thrusts and parries: Douglas responded in an Ohio stump speech; Black replied in an appendix to his pamphlet; Douglas answered in his own pamphlet.[65] Douglas attracted powerful allies, including Reverdy Johnson, a Marylander who had represented Dred Scott's owner before the Supreme Court.[66] But most southerners upheld the administration. A *DeBow's Review* contributor, concerned that Douglas's "ingenious unfairness" would "ambush" unwary readers, repudiated his constitutional and historical claims.[67] Davis penned a widely distributed response that restated his euphemistic demand for the "equality of the South in the right to enjoy the common unappropriated domain; and for adequate protection to all the constitutional rights of every citizen of the United States."[68]

The *Harper's* essay debate introduced few new ideas, but it did mark a milestone in the Democracy's disintegration. Douglas could not relent without losing northern support, while his foes could not concede without destroying the southern Democracy and emboldening the fire-eaters. The controversy confirmed southern antipathy for Douglas; one Mississippi editor accused him of soliciting "Abolition sympathy," while a resident of Holly Springs reported that the "assertion of *Territorial Sovereignty* has killed Douglas in the South."[69] Meanwhile, northern Douglasites grew more alienated from southern Democrats, including Davis, whom many now regarded as a fire-eater. One Oregonian used Davis as the yardstick of radicalism, describing a local proslavery man as being "as ultra a *southern fireeater* as Jeff Davis."[70] Davis was not contriving to splinter the Democracy and hasten secession, but he had been convicted in the court of northern public opinion, and indeed his views were converging with those of Yancey and other extremists.[71]

Fence-mending efforts only underscored the severity of the situation. After reading Douglas's essay, Albert Gallatin Brown damned it with faint praise in a letter to its author: "I think you have made the best of a bad cause." He conveyed his "cordial personal friendship" and "the highest regard for you politically in all things save *niggers*," but jovial racism was not going to save the Democracy. Brown warned that southerners meant to write a platform that recognized slavery in the territories and would bolt the 1860 convention if unsuccessful. Secession was on the table. "We have been faithful to the Demo[cratic] party and loyal to the government," he averred. "But we are prepared to abandon the one & sacrifice the other sooner than surrender our equal rights under the confederacy."[72]

★ ★ ★

Brown actually understated the tension between northern and southern Democrats, for slavery expansion was not the only source of strain. Other issues intensified the pressure on Democrats in both sections, disrupting their home fronts as they waged a bitter sectional war.

Davis faced two crises in 1859 that highlighted the fragility of planters' mastery. One was John Brown's October raid on Harpers Ferry, Virginia. Mississippi editors warned that the foray was not an isolated incident and that there was a broader movement afoot to provoke slave revolts; as rumors proliferated, white Mississippians mobilized to crush rebellion and repel invasion. In his inaugural address, delivered weeks after Brown's raid, fire-eating Democratic governor John J. Pettus advised that Harpers Ferry was "only the beginning of the end of this conflict." Thereafter, he worked with Senator Davis to secure arms for the state.[73] And while Democrats accused Republicans of conspiring with Brown, Harpers Ferry also exacerbated tensions within the party. Opportunistic Buchananites circulated a forged letter, allegedly found among Brown's papers, in which Douglas praised the abolitionist and donated $1,000 to his war chest.[74] In the South, the raid deepened Democrats' resolve to demand a southern presidential nominee. A Virginian informed Douglas that Brown "has done your cause in the South considerable damage."[75]

Mother Nature also wreaked havoc in Mississippi, where a devastating spring flood exposed the limits of planters' control over the environment. Rising waters called Jefferson Davis home to Brierfield shortly after Congress adjourned in March, while Varina, eight months pregnant, stayed in Washington to handle his correspondence and the family finances. By late April, levees had crumbled, and Davis evacuated his livestock as floodwaters inundated his cotton fields; he could row from his front steps straight to brother Joseph's home. Davis's wealth cushioned the blow, but the loss of an entire crop was demoralizing.[76] The next month, Douglas visited his own Mississippi estate. He feared the worst as he steamed upriver from New Orleans, seeing "nothing but destruction and desolation" along the way, but when he reached his sons' plantation, he found good prospects for replanting. Douglas's diversified portfolio also paid off: from Mississippi, he traveled to Chicago and marveled at the city's thriving real estate market, especially the hot neighborhood of Hyde

Park.[77] The flood gave Douglas headaches, but he had fewer Mississippi eggs in his basket than Davis did.

More disquieting was Douglas's failure to enact the legislative program demanded by his western constituents. From the late 1850s through the secession crisis, correspondents expressed keen interest in a Pacific railroad, homestead legislation, and internal improvements, and frustration with foot-dragging by southern and administration Democrats. Dismayed by congressional gridlock over the Pacific railroad, supporters from Washington, D.C., to California exhorted Douglas to rescue the project from strangulation by sectionalism.[78] From Illinois came familiar pleas for federal aid to infrastructure, including Illinois River improvements and upkeep of Chicago's perennially silty harbor.[79]

Most clamorous of all were supporters of a homestead bill, particularly after the Panic of 1857 triggered a sharp recession.[80] The Senate passed a bill in May 1860, but Buchanan vetoed it the following month.[81] The veto devastated northwestern Democrats and deepened their antipathy toward Buchanan and the southern Democracy. A Minnesotan begged Douglas to confirm his support for homestead legislation, complaining that the "present Administration . . . is so adverse to the interests of the North West that it is hard to make the less intelligent citizens here believe but that all Democrats hold the same *policy*."[82] Another warned that if homestead legislation did not pass soon, "the Democratic Party in Minnesota is gone up for the next four years," for many locals believed that all Democrats were "opposed to the homestead bill and . . . in favor of slavery."[83] Many elite southerners did oppose homestead legislation as a scheme to cover the West with nonslaveholding households and prevent formation of the large estates necessary for plantation agriculture.[84]

Vexed by repeated defeats, Douglas feared that Republicans might turn his western flank. As early as 1852, constituents had advised that if Democrats did not enact a homestead bill, rivals would co-opt the immensely popular measure.[85] As Republicans gained steam in the late 1850s, Douglas's friends worried that they might commandeer his western agenda.[86] Their concerns were well-founded: seeking support beyond their antislavery base, Republicans adopted much of Douglas's program and argued that Democrats could never carry it through. "The Pacific Railroad is in the same fix as the rivers and lakes," thundered Missouri Republican Francis P. Blair Jr. "The West will never have it till the Democratic party goes out of power."[87] The "Slave Labor Democracy," explained a New Yorker, obstructed homestead and railroad bills to "hinder the development . . . of the great West" by sabotaging those territories they could not control.[88] Republicans' 1860 platform backed homestead legislation, internal improvements, and a Pacific railroad; when enacted during the Civil War, this Douglas-inflected program became a signature Republican triumph.[89]

Pressures from home thus inflamed the struggle for party supremacy. Davis had to show that the Democracy could safeguard a beleaguered South, while Douglas labored to prove that it could serve an impatient North. Slavery expansion was the leading issue, but matters of internal security and economic development intensified conflicts over the party's future.

★ ★ ★

The Thirty-Sixth Congress opened under the shadow of Harpers Ferry, passed through the crucible of the 1860 election, and terminated amid secession. Conflict between majority rule and property rights shaped both sessions and hastened the Democracy's self-destruction. As leaders of rival factions, Douglas and Davis rallied their legions for a final confrontation, which ruptured the party and foreshadowed the dissolution of the Union.

Anticipations of Charleston left Democrats loath to compromise, lest concessions weaken them in the convention scheduled to begin on April 23. "Having laboured so earnestly and so long," wrote an Illinois Democrat, "I hate very much to give up our vantage ground to please a few Jack-asses of the Southern States."[90] Davis's disciples were equally adamant: slavery must be safeguarded in the territories, wrote one, "let the fanatics of the North snarl as much as they like about it."[91] Davis and Douglas shared this zeal, but both feared that a party split would mean defeat and disunion. Davis hoped Democrats would coalesce behind a sound platform and candidate, for "a division of the Democracy must be the forerunner of a division of the States."[92] Equally concerned, Douglas wondered why southerners wanted to replace the Cincinnati platform with a proslavery party test. If the old creed was no longer "satisfactory to some of our Southern friends we shall regret but cannot avoid it."[93] Torn between constituent pressure and party loyalty, between the need to win votes and the desire to defend principles, Davis and Douglas commenced a risky tug-of-war. Lose the contest and the Democracy would be assailed by critics back home; pull too hard, and a party breach would endanger the Union.

Some residual party unity remained. When Republican senator William Seward appealed to the "fundamental principle of American society"—all men are created equal—to demand free statehood for Kansas,

Democratic machinery whirred into motion.[94] Douglas counterattacked, praising popular sovereignty and denouncing Seward's egalitarianism. The Declaration of Independence "was referring only to the white man," he snarled; whites were and must remain "the governing race of this country."[95] Not missing a beat, Davis lauded slavery as the foundation of white freedom and equality. "With us and us alone," he concluded, "the white man attains to his true dignity in the Government."[96] In isolation, this episode suggested that racism sustained Martin Van Buren's battered coalition by shackling northern Democrats to the Slave Power. In fact, it was an increasingly rare moment of party harmony; racism provided neither a coherent platform nor a shared prescription for how the "governing race" should rule.

Indeed, even as they assailed Seward, Davis and Douglas were clashing over the slave code in a dispute as momentous as Douglas's debates with Lincoln. It was provoked by Albert Gallatin Brown, Davis's fiery colleague and a sharp critic of national parties. On January 18, Brown lobbed a senatorial bomb in the form of two resolutions. One asserted that owners of "every kind or description of property" had the right to hold their property in the territories and that Congress and territorial legislatures must pass laws "necessary for the adequate and sufficient protection of such property." The other instructed the Committee on Territories to add to all territorial bills a clause requiring the legislature to fulfill its duties to property owners and obliging Congress to "interfere and pass such laws" if it refused.[97] Debate on these resolutions wandered into tangential topics, from the prospects of a Republican presidency to the annexation of Texas, which muddied the issue while underscoring the precariousness of national unity.[98]

Davis soon introduced alternative resolutions, which threw down the gauntlet to Douglas and influenced Democratic infighting eleven weeks later and five hundred miles away in Charleston. Discussion of Brown's resolutions continued intermittently, but Davis's offerings, unveiled on February 2 and revised on March 1, provoked the stormiest debate. In final form, as approved by Buchanan and most of the Senate's Democratic caucus, Davis's seven resolutions affirmed proslavery doctrines worthy of Calhoun. The first argued that "intermeddling" across state lines—potentially anything from writing an abolitionist pamphlet to marching with John Brown—endangered the Union, while the second censured all "open or covert attacks" upon slavery. The third and fourth denounced discriminatory policies touching "persons or property in the Territories, which are the common possessions of the United States," and avowed that neither Congress nor territorial legislatures could infringe slaveholders' property rights, thus repudiating popular sovereignty as articulated by Douglas and Thayer. The sixth endorsed Davis's territorial dogma: only upon writing a state constitution could a nascent state prohibit slavery. The seventh censured as "revolutionary" northern state laws that hampered enforcement of the Fugitive Slave Act. But the fifth resolution was the most provocative: "If experience should at any time prove that the judiciary and executive authority do not possess means to insure adequate protection to constitutional rights in a Territory, and if the territorial government shall fail or refuse to provide the necessary remedies for that purpose, it will be the duty of Congress to supply such deficiency."[99]

Historians still debate whether Davis's fifth resolution sanctioned a territorial slave code. Those who argue the negative emphasize the differences between Davis's resolutions and Brown's, while those arguing the affirmative stress their similarity in content, if not tone.[100] These conflicting readings reflect the duality of Davis's aims. On one hand, he sought to outflank Brown by wrapping proslavery policy in temperate language that could win some northern approval and solidify Democratic unity before the convention. Thus, scholars who highlight discrepancies between the Mississippians' resolutions make a crucial point: Davis was wrestling with Brown over sectional leadership. Having tacked toward radicalism on the Atlantic slave trade issue, Davis now made a similar move on the territories, though he was not ready to abandon all northern allies. On the other hand, Davis also meant to smash popular sovereignty, torpedo Douglas's presidential hopes, and nail a plank into the party platform upon which Douglasites would not stand. Hardly conciliatory, his resolutions sought to commit the Democracy to a stridently proslavery position and cripple its most popular northern leader just before the national convention. Northern Democrats were not inclined to split hairs over the conditions in which a slave code was necessary, and they read the fifth resolution as a bid for proslavery intervention, which crossed the line drawn in the Dorr letter. Davis, like Brown, sought to dictate terms as the Charleston convention approached, and while his gambit was not intended to destroy the party, it certainly risked doing so.[101]

Douglasites excoriated Brown and Davis alike as fire-eaters, fearing that the resolutions would hobble the Democracy in local, state, and national elections. A New Hampshire Democrat marveled at the "madness" of calls for a "slave protection code" and hoped that northerners would rout the "incipient traitors" at Charleston.[102] A Chicagoan praised Douglas's opposition to "Southern hotspurs & fire eaters."[103] Davis and

Douglas's much-anticipated collision did not occur until May, however, and by then the long-feared party rupture had already begun.

★ ★ ★

If anyone could empathize with Douglas, it was Martin Van Buren, the northern Democrat who had been the odds-on favorite entering the 1844 convention, only to be thwarted by adversaries determined to shift party policy southward. A combination of public appeals, backroom deals, and the two-thirds rule had beaten Van Buren, and now northern Democrats worried that a similar fate awaited the Little Giant. Some encouraged him to consider an independent candidacy if enemies sabotaged his nomination, but Douglas had planted his flag within the party; this stubborn partisan loyalty fueled the relentless struggle that was tearing the Democracy apart.[104]

Another possible nominee was Davis, whose candidacy had been discussed for two years.[105] In December 1859, Mississippi's state Democratic convention endorsed Davis for president, and four months later, *Harper's Weekly* printed a two-page illustration that depicted Douglas and Davis among the eleven "Prominent Candidates for the Democratic Nomination."[106] Davis, however, discouraged friends from pressing his claims, arguing that, as a "radical advocate of southern rights," he had no chance. Hoping to see a northern conservative run on a proslavery platform, he favored Franklin Pierce.[107] Thus, while Davis would play a key role in the contest, it would not be as a major rival for the nomination.

Douglas was clearly the northern Democracy's leading candidate; a vocal minority of Buchananites loathed him, but most party adherents wanted no other standard-bearer. "We are for *Douglas or nobody*," averred an Iowan. "Douglas *first, last,* and *all the time*."[108] Admirers had hoisted his name in March 1857, and battles over Lecompton and the slave code deepened their determination to nominate him.[109] Victory over Lincoln in 1858 confirmed Douglas's availability and prompted grassroots organizing. Voters in Philadelphia's Thirteenth Ward, for instance, formed a Democratic Douglas Association in November 1858 and remained active for the next two years.[110] This zeal reflected admiration that shaded into hero worship, as well as an instinct for survival, for many northern Democrats saw Douglas as their only electable option. "All sensible men . . . agree, that unless you are our Candidate in '60, we should be beaten," wrote a Vermonter. "It is quite certain that *you* must be our next President, or some Black Rep[ublica]n will be."[111] Appalled by southern extremism, moreover, many preferred a Republican over a proslavery Democrat. As a Bostonian explained, if "Southern dictation"

"Prominent Candidates for the Democratic Nomination at Charleston, South Carolina," *Harper's Weekly*, April 21, 1860, 248–49.

produced "a candidate of radical Southern proclivities," then "thousands" of northern Democrats would "indignantly vote the Republican ticket, though the *Devil himself* 'W. H. Seward' be their candidate."[112] By 1860, Democratic infighting and partisan convergence had progressed far enough that some northern Democrats preferred losing to a Republican over surrendering to the South. This informed their convention strategy: spurred by necessity, principle, and pique, they would demand Douglas or split the party. Southern Democrats had their "rule or ruin" attitude; for northern Douglasites, it was "rule or Republican."

Some southern Democrats regarded Douglas's candidacy as a necessary evil, but most vehemently opposed him. Feelings of betrayal, coupled with aversion to popular sovereignty, steeled them to resist Douglas at all costs. In February 1860, Mississippi lawmakers resolved that a Republican victory would justify secession and portentously added that the election of "one who is opposed to the grant of protection" due to slave property in the territories, as defined in Davis's Senate resolutions, would warrant disunion as well.[113] Others equated a Douglas victory with a Republican triumph. An Alabamian reviled Douglas as the "champion of a theory of government" that was "destructive of equal rights." He hoped to save the Union but would "regard the nomination of Judge Douglas, or the election of a Black Republican as fatal to its perpetuity."[114] Other criticisms were more visceral. In a letter to Governor Pettus of Mississippi, one writer tarred Douglas as a "Benedict Arnold" of the "same New England rank Saxon Puritan blood descent" as William Seward.[115] Violent rhetoric remained widespread; days before the convention, an Alabama editor raged that Douglas deserved to "perish upon the gibbet of Democratic condemnation."[116] Hardened by years of internal conflict, Democrats in both sections embraced strategies of brinkmanship that could wreck the party and split the Union.

Convention delegates shared this outlook. Some northerners welcomed the prospect of a southern bolt: "Our only fear is that they will not go," announced an Ohio delegate. "They are a nuisance to the party and the country, and the sooner they get out the better."[117] Others stood ready to bolt themselves if the platform discarded popular sovereignty.[118] Most, however, expected to control the simple majority of votes needed to adopt a platform; the trouble would be securing the two-thirds vote necessary for Douglas's nomination. Affirming his commitment to white men's majoritarianism, a Minnesotan told Douglas that the "Majority have already Decided you are their choice, and it is not Right for one third to Rule a Party, or dictate a candidate to the whole People of the *union*," particularly not when that third represented only "one 6th of the *white* Population."[119] Thus, the battle for majority rule ranged from the territories to control of the Democracy itself, firing northerners with ire unappeased by bigotry. Homeward bound from Charleston, one northwesterner complained that the "Southerners had been ruling over niggers so long they thought they could rule white men just the same." Now he hoped they would "sweat under an Abolition President."[120]

Southern convention strategies varied. A faction led by William Lowndes Yancey, the "prince of the fire-eaters," would demand a platform consistent with Davis's resolutions and bolt the convention if northerners balked. Many welcomed this contingency, viewing northern Democrats as irredeemable free-soilers and national parties as obstacles to secession. Other southern Democrats preferred to fight Douglas within the Democracy and maintain southern influence over a national party that could vanquish the Republicans and safeguard slavery in the Union. The arms race of southern politics forced them to insist on a platform that met Davis's standards, but they hoped to secure northern support and keep the party afloat. Thus, fire-eaters and party loyalists allied against

Douglas and for a proslavery platform, but their mentalities were different. Yancey's disciples relished the rule-or-ruin strategy, while regular Democrats, hoping to repeat the victories of 1852 and 1856, embraced it reluctantly.[121]

Davis favored the latter approach, reiterating his belief that the South was safe if it controlled a triumphant Democratic Party. In early 1860, he urged southerners to preserve party unity while thwarting Douglas and securing a satisfactory platform.[122] Many of Mississippi's delegates preferred Yancey's approach, but the line between fire-eaters and party loyalists was blurry, not least because the delegation was led by Ethelbert Barksdale, a staunch Davis ally who edited the Jackson *Mississippian*.[123] Davis was more optimistic about the Democracy than his fire-eating rivals, but he, too, was more devoted to slavery than to the party or the Union. By presenting his resolutions as the price of southern allegiance, Davis issued an ultimatum that northerners could not accept, ensuring that the rule-or-ruin strategy led to the latter.[124]

★ ★ ★

The Democratic national convention that opened on April 23, 1860—Douglas's forty-seventh birthday—summoned a mélange of humanity unified only in name. The Democrats crowding Charleston's Institute Hall, wrote one pundit, included "the advocates of squatter sovereignty and of strict construction, the ultra pro-slavery men of the South, and those with free soil proclivities from the North, the tariff partisans and the freetraders, the southward extensionists, and those who think the area of freedom is extending itself as rapidly as is compatible with safety." He speculated that they were meeting "perhaps for the last time forevermore."[125]

Douglas and Davis remained in Washington, but their agents in Charleston kept them well informed. From the start, it seemed clear that Douglas commanded a majority of northern delegates and that the Deep South was intractably against him. Ominously, the Georgia, Mississippi, Louisiana, Florida, Arkansas, and Texas delegations had joined Yancey's Alabamians in pledging to bolt if Douglas were nominated or if the platform violated the "Alabama Platform," a January 1860 statement that anticipated Davis's resolutions. Mississippi's delegates were the first to join this fire-eating phalanx.[126]

The conventioneers opted to write a platform before choosing a candidate; Douglas's enemies hoped to checkmate him with a proslavery screed, while his friends wanted to bolster party unity before pressing his claims. But journalist Murat Halstead knew that compromise was impossible: southerners needed "unequivocal repudiation of the Douglas doctrine of squatter, or popular, sovereignty," while northerners, girding for battle against the Republicans, could not yield. This was the Democracy's "irrepressible conflict."[127] After several days of labor, the platform committee issued a proslavery majority report, which denied that territorial legislatures could "destroy or impair the right of property in slaves by any legislation whatever" and stipulated federal protection for property rights in the territories, and a Douglasite minority report, which reaffirmed the Cincinnati platform and referred any questions to the Supreme Court.[128] Douglasites, Halstead noted, embraced the Little Giant's neutrality on slavery expansion, while the southerners insisted that the Democracy stand for "exerting all powers of the Federal Government for the extension of slavery, and the increase of the political power of the master class of the Southern section." Anyone who disagreed was "hooted down as an Abolitionist."[129]

The dueling platforms inspired a spate of speechifying, including a fervid address from Barksdale, whom Halstead identified as a "disciple of Jefferson Davis."[130] The Democracy's problem, Barksdale insisted, was ambiguity. Henceforth, it must fight for the common-property doctrine as enshrined in Davis's resolutions and the majority platform.[131] But the star of the show was Yancey, whose fulminations thrilled the Carolinians packing the galleries. He warned that rejection of the majority platform would compel southerners to bolt. He contended that northerners had no complaints and that the South was the aggrieved party: "Ours is the property invaded; ours are the institutions which are at stake." Adding doses of demagoguery (slavery elevated poor whites into "the master race") and sectionalism (southerners must "yield nothing of principle for mere party success"), he demanded that the Democracy embrace an unequivocally proslavery position.[132] Impressed by Yancey's candor but repulsed by his creed, George Pugh, the anti-Lecompton Ohioan, replied for his section. "Gentlemen of the South," he cried, "you mistake us—you mistake us—we will not do it."[133]

It was all downhill from there. The Douglasite-dominated convention voted to accept the minority report minus the reference to the Supreme Court, effectively adopting the Cincinnati platform, and the Alabamians stormed out. Yancey had done this in 1848, but now he was joined by delegates from Mississippi, Louisiana, South Carolina, Florida, and Texas and shortly after by a sprinkling of delegates from Georgia, Arkansas, Virginia, Missouri, and Delaware. The bolt, as explained by departing Mississippians, paralleled the larger crisis of the Union: since the "controlling majority of northern representatives" had denied federal power to protect "a species of property recognized in fifteen sovereign States," they were compelled to withdraw.[134] Through an emissary, Davis urged them to remain and defeat Douglas, but the seceders resolved to reassemble in Richmond.[135] The rupture, long a calamity to be dreaded or a goal to be pursued, was now a reality. Strolling Charleston's streets that night, Halstead heard Lucius Q. C. Lamar denigrating Douglas and squatter sovereignty and then three cheers for an "Independent Southern Republic."[136]

These celebrations confirmed that there was more at stake than personal aversion to Douglas. The Illinoisan was the preeminent spokesman for popular sovereignty, a doctrine that southern Democrats had long despised, correctly or not, as a cloaked free-soil policy. He was also a northwesterner who, against southern opposition, had sought to yoke the Democracy to an ambitious program of regional development. The road to Institute Hall twisted and turned, but the party rupture stemmed from a larger conflict that was exacerbated by rivals—fire-eaters and Republicans—who pushed Democrats to take irreconcilable positions in Charleston.[137]

Less clear were the consequences for the election, since the convention adjourned without making a nomination. Douglasites who expected to prevail after the fire-eaters departed were crushed when convention chair Caleb Cushing, the Massachusetts doughface who had welcomed Davis to New England, ruled that two-thirds of the original number of delegates were still required for the nomination.[138] Thus Douglas, who commanded only an indecisive majority of the delegates, still could not prevail, and after fifty-seven ballots, the exhausted Democrats agreed to reconvene in Baltimore on June 18.[139] That inauspicious date marked the forty-fifth anniversary of the Battle of Waterloo.

★ ★ ★

Before the dust settled in Charleston, Douglasites were spoiling for another fight. "I hope that you will never withdraw your name," wrote a New Jerseyan. "I shall vote for you whether nominated or not . . . for we cannot see another Buchanan administration these southern fire eaters & Northern dough faces work to rule or ruin."[140] Fed up with proslavery extremism and the two-thirds rule, northern Democrats saw Douglas's nomination as the only way to beat the Republicans and punish the fire-eaters.[141] But before the next convention, the conflict shifted back to the Senate, where Douglas met Davis in a climactic showdown.

While scurrying between conventions, Murat Halstead paused in Washington to witness the battle. Both men impressed him, but fifteen years in national politics had taken a toll. Douglas's rotundity strained his vest, and his thinning hair was—as Halstead noted with a facetious "O! Little Giant!"—turning gray. Still, he exuded the energetic sociability that had propelled him to power; when he wasn't drumming his pudgy fingers on a chair, he was holding Senate colleagues by the knee. Davis evinced a grimmer determination. Eye ailments, malaria, and facial neuralgia gave him a tormented, skeletal appearance. He had "the face of a corpse," with "thin white wrinkled lips clasped close upon the teeth in anguish," and bore the look of "a brave but impatient sufferer."[142] Both men marshaled depleted reserves for another battle.

Four days after the Charleston debacle, Davis launched a new attack. He affirmed his lifelong dedication to the Democracy and his qualified faith that it would "reunite upon sound and acceptable principles. At least I hope so." But the rest of the speech indicated that acceptable principles were those expressed in his resolutions and in Taney's opinion on *Dred Scott*. Davis again repudiated "squatter sovereignty," deeming it a "fallacy fraught with mischief," and rejected the equation of territories with states. Following this train of thought, he recounted his 1850 battles with Douglas, which clearly remained fresh in his memory. In closing, he counseled against immediate action on a slave code but insisted that the Senate pass his resolutions and thus make "great declarations on which legislation may be founded." Pursuing a path between Brown and Douglas, Davis hugged the southern side of the road.[143]

Douglas replied in a long speech, titled "Property in Territories," on May 15 and 16. Countering Davis's historical arguments, Douglas insisted that he remained a true Democrat because popular sovereignty had been sound party doctrine ever since Lewis Cass's 1847 letter to Alfred O. P. Nicholson and had been reiterated in each subsequent presidential election, the Compromise of 1850, and the Kansas-Nebraska Act. By enumerating southern endorsements of popular sovereignty, Douglas challenged the loyalty politics that southern extremists used to press for a slave code, and encouraged southern moderates to help him at Baltimore. He granted that Davis had unwaveringly opposed popular sovereignty but pointed out—and here he touched a nerve—that Mississippi voters had "rebuked" him in 1851.

Pivoting from history to current events, Douglas claimed victory at Charleston, construing affirmation of the Cincinnati platform as personal vindication. "I am no longer a heretic," he announced. "I am no longer an outlaw from the Democratic party." Now the question was whether southerners would "desert the party because the party has not changed as suddenly as they have?" He reviled slave code champions as hypocrites who defended localism where locals loved slavery but wanted federal intervention everywhere else. Given northern power in Congress, moreover, this double standard was dangerous for the South. Ask the House for a slave code, Douglas taunted, and "you will get that sort of friendly hug that the grizzly bear gives to the infant." Only popular sovereignty would preserve the Democracy and the Union.[144]

Davis roared back with a two-day oration that again demanded party unity on southern terms. Democrats, he observed, bragged of their national orientation, particularly when disparaging Republicans as sectionalists. Now they must prove themselves by uniting behind the principles etched into his resolutions. Both men wanted to use party fealty and fear of disunion as levers to move the party toward their pet doctrines, but neither got many critics to budge. Reviewing the convention, Davis defended the bolting delegations and pledged loyalty to the Democracy so long as it affirmed federal power to protect slave property in the territories. His party and national fidelity were avowedly conditional.[145]

Douglas had no truck with provisional loyalties and piously proclaimed that old-time popular sovereignty was "good enough for me." Then he accused the bolters of plotting to destroy the party and the country. Led by Yancey, they would "disrupt the party, and plunge the cotton States into revolution," all to forge a "separate southern confederacy." Not everyone who bolted was a disunionist, but "disunion was the prompting motive" behind it, and the slave code was "a disunion platform." Locked in a spiraling rhetorical battle, Douglas now arraigned his proslavery critics as incipient traitors: whether by design or by chance, they were jeopardizing the Union.[146] Like Davis, Douglas sent a clear message to his friends at Baltimore: yield nothing.

The Senate passed Davis's resolutions while Douglas was out sick in late May, but public attention fixated on the rhetorical slugfest, which escalated intraparty conflict by summoning the specter of disunion.[147] Douglas, seeking the patriotic high ground, repudiated southern conspirators, while Davis delivered a final ultimatum and avowed his willingness to secede. Pundits leaped to predictable conclusions. A Georgian accused Douglas of making a "declaration of war against the South."[148] Barksdale charged him with "falsehood and vituperation" and praised southern Democrats for resisting popular sovereignty, "that abomination of all the abominations which the enemies of the South have ever devised to accomplish her ruin."[149] To northern Democrats, however, Douglas had "proved himself the victor as usual," while treacherous southerners had forsaken popular sovereignty upon realizing it would spread free labor.[150] Republicans savored the spectacle. The "irrepressible conflict," quipped a Vermonter, "has already commenced in the United States Senate between Senators Davis and Douglas."[151] An Ohioan likened them to the Kilkenny cats of limerick fame, fighting tooth and claw until nothing remained of either one.[152] Memories of this "Davis-Douglas Debate" lingered into the twentieth century.[153]

The Senate struggle also inspired another torrent of verbiage from Douglas's northern admirers, who revisited familiar themes: Davis got the drubbing he deserved; Douglas was unrivaled in the north and west; many Democrats would vote Republican before swallowing a slave code. Yearning to reunite the Democracy on a sustainable platform, northerners urged Douglas to walk a razor-thin line between castigating the fire-eaters and garnering southern approval.[154] Soon, however, their attention turned to Baltimore.

★ ★ ★

Even before it began, the Baltimore convention spawned another bitter intraparty struggle. The key issues going into the meeting were whether the bolters would seek admission and whether other delegates would welcome them. Preconvention deliberations reflected desire for unity and inflexibility on doctrine. In early May, Davis and other prominent southern Democrats, including John Slidell and Lucius Q. C. Lamar, issued a statement urging the bolters, scheduled to meet at Richmond, to seek a rapprochement at Baltimore. Yet they insisted that the Democracy must meet southern demands, accused northerners of perverting the Cincinnati platform, and encouraged their delegations to stand firm on the territories, even if forced to bolt again. This was less an olive branch than a call for united southern action within the Democratic Party.[155] Douglas authorized supporters to withdraw his name for harmony's sake, provided the platform sanctioned popular sovereignty and rejected proslavery intervention.[156] With both sides posing as the country's last, best hope, prospects for compromise dimmed.

The convention inflamed Democrats' irrepressible conflict into political war. It opened with a blistering dispute over the claims of rival southern delegations: all the bolting states save South Carolina and Florida sought to participate at Baltimore, but several had chosen new delegates (more amenable to Douglas) who jockeyed with the bolters for places in the convention. Douglasites knew that seating the bolters would doom their candidate, while many southerners demanded that Douglas abandon the nomination. Douglas was willing to yield to a southern moderate, particularly Alexander H. Stephens of Georgia, but his disciples would concede nothing to the South. With northwesterners tarring southerners as "disorganizers, bolters, traitors, and disunionists" and being scorned in turn as "a sneaking species of Abolitionists," a second split was imminent.[157] When Douglas-friendly delegates from Alabama and Louisiana were seated, Virginians withdrew, followed by southern and Pacific Coast delegations and some northeastern Buchananites, including Cushing. Douglas was nominated soon after; his platform lamely referred Democrats' "difference of opinion" over territorial matters to the Supreme Court.[158] Styling themselves National Democrats, seceding delegates nominated John C. Breckinridge of Kentucky, wrote a platform that endorsed the protection of property three times in its first three sentences, and listened to Yancey proclaim that Douglas had been "buried . . . beneath the grave of squatter sovereignty."[159]

★ ★ ★

The 1860 presidential election signaled the political maturation of the West. All four major candidates hailed from west of the Appalachians: the dueling Democrats from Illinois and Kentucky, Republican Abraham Lincoln from Illinois, and John Bell, heading the emphatically moderate Constitutional Union Party, from Tennessee. With Joseph Lane, an Oregon Buchananite, serving as Breckinridge's running mate, and Isaac Stevens (former governor of the Washington Territory) managing his campaign, the Pacific Northwest loomed larger than ever before.[160] Douglas might have celebrated this power shift, except that the candidates were seeking to lead a grievously divided country. The election mocked his sunny predictions that western ascendancy would safeguard the Union.

Davis promptly enlisted with the National Democrats, whose support came mainly from southerners and the Buchananites, who were especially influential in the Northeast and Far West. In early July, Davis endorsed Breckinridge and defined the territorial question as the key campaign issue, demanding full federal support for masters' property rights in the territories and declaring that to accept anything less was to be "degraded"; this was a matter of regional pride as well as constitutional theory.[161] He also helped convince Breckinridge to accept the nomination. Davis invited the Kentuckian to dinner at his Washington home, where he, Cushing, and Robert Toombs persuaded Breckinridge to heed the National Democratic call and then yield to a new fusion candidate. The plan was for Breckinridge, Bell, and Douglas to bow out and permit one fresh nominee, perhaps Franklin Pierce or New York's Horatio Seymour, to face Lincoln.[162] Davis still hoped that the fragmented anti-Republican forces could coalesce behind a northern Democrat with impeccable pro-slavery principles.

Davis reportedly floated his fusion plan with all three candidates, receiving positive responses from Bell and Breckinridge and curt refusal from Douglas, who recognized that merging with National Democrats would legitimize their bolt. Douglas also believed he was the only candidate who could beat Lincoln and predicted, with good reason, that many northern Democrats would stay home or vote Republican if he dropped out. Personal pique surely influenced him as well, since Davis, one historian aptly observes, "had been a harpoon in the back of Douglas for years" and was hardly the ideal messenger to ask Douglas for a major sacrifice.[163] Thus, while fusion gained some traction in the mid-Atlantic states, the election generally remained a four-sided contest.

Breckinridge's campaign strategy was hostile to majority rule. Some National Democrats saw their effort as quixotic, but many envisioned a path to victory: win enough states in the South, Northeast, and Pacific West to deny any candidate an electoral majority, and throw the election into the House of Representatives. There, the one-state, one-vote procedure for choosing a president would enable the slave states, plus California and Oregon, to select Breckinridge.[164] This was a massive departure from the party's roots in Andrew Jackson's diatribes against the corrupt bargain he blamed for thwarting the popular will in 1824.

National Democrats' campaign rhetoric was equally antimajoritarian. From the White House portico, Buchanan lauded Breckinridge as a champion of the common-property doctrine. "Squatter sovereignty," by contrast, would empower territorial legislatures to "confiscate" property at will. "When," asked the incredulous president, "was property ever submitted to the will of a majority?"[165] A Breckinridge Democrat in Richmond deplored *"slavish submission* to a mere numerical majority" and rejected fusion with "that desperate political gambler Stephen Arnold Douglass [*sic*]."[166] These sentiments ran so deep that some Breckinridge partisans saw little difference between Lincoln and Douglas, Republicans and northern Democrats, or free soil and popular sovereignty. "Now what difference is it to the people," asked an Alabamian, "whether Lincoln or Douglas shall be elected? The same ends are sought by each."[167] A Mississippian agreed, claiming that popular sovereignty was designed to stymie southern expansion. Douglas "proposes popular sovereignty, with the positive certainty that the scum of Europe and the mudsills of Yankeedom can be shipped in" to make free states, as in California, Minnesota, and Oregon.[168] One pamphleteer deemed Douglas worse than

Lincoln because he pretended to be friendly. In fact, his "Squatter Sovereignty doctrines" were "more dangerous and injurious to the Slave-holding States than the election of a Black Republican."[169]

In late summer, Davis plunged into the campaign, praising Breckinridge as the only reliably proslavery candidate; Douglas was a lying demagogue, and Bell would bargain away southern rights for the sake of national peace.[170] But Davis spent more time discussing the election's consequences than the candidates, and with good reason: talk of secession crackled like lightning in the humid air. "The papers are beginning to hint at 'dark possibilities' 'threatening contingencies' which may arise" if Lincoln should win, a northern-born Mississippi resident noted in June.[171] Amid the uncertainty, voters wanted Davis's counsel, but while he affirmed the abstract right of secession, he did not specify when it should be exercised. Just before Election Day, Davis spoke of resisting "the rule of an arrogant and sectional North," pledged to support Mississippi if it seceded, and vowed to welcome federal invaders with a "harvest of death."[172] This was less a stump speech than a call to arms, but, like Davis's other efforts, it was short on details, including whether Lincoln's election alone would justify secession.[173] This elusiveness was strategic: Davis had outrun public opinion in 1851 and did not want to repeat that disaster. As fire-eaters fulminated and Bell supporters tarred Breckinridge Democrats as secessionists, Davis balanced militancy with caution.

Meanwhile, Douglas launched one of the most brazen campaigns contemporaries had ever seen: eschewing the traditional passivity of the presidential candidate, he pitched into a grueling nationwide canvass. It reflected his feisty passion for politics but also the desperation of his uphill battle for the presidency. Douglas needed 152 electoral votes, but even if he won all five free states carried by Buchanan in 1856 and added Minnesota and Oregon, he would still need 83 electoral votes from slave states. The five relatively moderate border states could provide 47, but that would leave him seeking 36 more in hostile territory farther south, where most Democratic personnel, including party leaders and newspaper editors, opposed him. In a typical report from Mississippi, a sympathizer warned that the Breckinridge organization, "sustained by Jeff Davis, has a large majority in the democratic organization in this state," including the "wealth & newspaper influences" that allowed them to manipulate the flow of information.[174] August Belmont, the chairman of the Democratic National Committee, toiled to raise funds, but Douglas lacked the cash needed to circulate campaign materials, sponsor public speakers, and sustain friendly presses.[175] Ironically, it was want of the most modern of political necessities that spurred Douglas to commence his innovative campaign.

Admirers encouraged Douglas's break with tradition. A Bay Area supporter stressed that his campaign's style should match its democratic substance. "Why not disregard aristocratic prejudices & speak to the people . . . why not take the stump," he wrote. "I believe the public welfare demands that you should canvass the South," for "if you do not Politicians will obtain the ear of the Southern people" and give "a triumph to principles that are alike dangerous & anti American."[176] Southern friends concurred, stressing that only a personal visit would give southern voters an honest account of Douglas's principles.[177]

Douglas began with a summer tour of New England in which he reiterated that only popular sovereignty could preserve the Union. Republicans were likely to dominate that region, but Douglas sought to keep northeastern Democrats out of Breckinridge's camp.[178] It was his southern tours, however, that provoked the most commentary and controversy. In August, he visited Virginia and North Carolina to rally upper South moderates, including Democrats repulsed by Breckinridge's extremism, and voters who had backed the American Party in 1856. Douglas's oratory covered familiar ground. In Petersburg, he proclaimed that local majorities must rule in states and territories alike and that popular sovereignty did not violate property rights. He also used self-deprecating humor to deflect accusations of duping southerners into supporting popular sovereignty: did critics really believe that "a man from the backwoods of the Northwest" had swindled every southerner in Congress?[179]

But the most prominent theme was secession, and the more it came up, the more obvious it was that Douglas was also campaigning for the Union. While he spoke at Norfolk, someone handed him a slip of paper bearing two questions: Would Lincoln's election warrant secession, and would Douglas support using force against seceded states? Douglas answered the first query with an emphatic no and, to much consternation, answered the second in the affirmative: presidents must treat secessionists as Andrew Jackson had handled the nullifiers, with a willingness to use military might.[180] At Petersburg, Douglas warned that northwesterners would never allow the lower Mississippi Valley, their outlet to global markets, to fall under foreign control. Losing an election did not justify secession anyway, and southerners were bound by law and honor to accept the outcome.[181] On the Union and secession, Douglas anticipated the position taken by Lincoln.[182]

Responses to Douglas's "Norfolk Doctrine" highlighted the sectional polarization that mocked his pleas for peace. Northern editors praised his firmness, with Republicans thanking him for giving the "chivalry" some "wholesome truths" about secession.[183] Northern allies predicted that the speech would win him thousands of votes.[184] But white southerners, particularly Breckinridge Democrats, erupted against Douglas's latest treachery. One southern editor accused him of speaking with the "forked tongue of the Abolition adder."[185] Another revived the lynching theme, opining that Douglas was wise to return north, for his sentiments would have would have gotten him killed in "some portions of the South."[186] Delighted Breckinridge partisans reckoned that the tour had obliterated Douglas's southern support.[187] Davis joined the chorus of criticism: Douglas was an "itinerate advocate of his own claims," he declared, and "this of itself disqualified him for the Presidency."[188] If President Lincoln and Lieutenant-General Douglas attempted to "coerce" Mississippi, Davis would hang them both: "as one was six feet four, and the other five feet four, the yard-arms of the gallows which our people would erect for them would have to be elevated accordingly."[189] This was more than gallows humor. The speech escalated Davis and Douglas's ongoing debate, which now transcended presidential politics and encompassed a violent quarrel over the Union itself.

Douglas departed for friendlier latitudes, speaking in Ohio and Indiana before reaching Chicago in early October. Observers noted his haggard appearance, weak voice, and heavy drinking. Trekking westward, Douglas was in Cedar Rapids, Iowa, when he learned that Republicans had triumphed in Pennsylvania and Indiana's state elections, almost ensuring Lincoln's victory in November. "Mr. Lincoln is the next President," Douglas told his secretary. "We must try to save the Union. I will go South."[190] Douglas's first southern tour reflected concern; the second, which took him through Missouri, Tennessee, Georgia, and Alabama, reflected panic fueled by messages from southern moderates who shrieked that "we are in the midst of a Revolution."[191] Abandoning his own presidential hopes, Douglas launched a final campaign to forestall secession once Lincoln captured the prize.[192]

As fire-eaters heated their rhetoric, Douglas urged coolness. He blasted the Charleston bolters as disunionists, exhorted southerners to resist secessionist conspiracies, and averred that secession was treason.[193] Bell partisans and Douglas's beleaguered southern supporters cheered him, but Breckinridge Democrats retaliated ruthlessly. Douglas was a "desperate and already defeated candidate" whose electioneering would disgrace "a grog-shop loafer"; his southern friends were "truculent toadies."[194] In Montgomery, locals pelted him and his companions with eggs, one of which splattered across Adele Douglas's face.[195] Douglas reached the end of his road in Mobile, where he spent a mercifully quiet Election Day on November 6. By nightfall he knew the result.

★ ★ ★

Following months of speculation about fusion, new candidates, and a decision in the House of Representatives, the election returns seemed simple: Lincoln won just under 40 percent of the popular ballots but nearly swept the free states to amass 180 electoral votes, a decisive majority. Douglas ran second in the popular vote but trailed Lincoln across the North and secured only a dozen electoral votes, including 9 from Missouri (which he carried by a tiny plurality) and 3 of New Jersey's 7. Breckinridge placed second in the Electoral College thanks to a dominant performance in the Cotton Kingdom, while Bell finished third with a strong showing in the border states, where his peaceful message resonated with anxious moderates. Everything had followed constitutional procedure, and Lincoln would become the sixteenth president on March 4, 1861.

The voters had spoken, but what exactly had they said? Several messages emerged from the cacophony. First, Republicans cemented their place as the leading party in the North, where Lincoln won 54 percent of the popular vote, a remarkable achievement for an organization no more than six years old. This triumph, of course, set secession's wheels in motion; seven weeks later, South Carolina radicals warned that the free states "have united in the election of a man to the high office of President of the United States whose opinions and purposes are hostile to slavery."[196] Still, Lincoln received a smaller portion of the national popular vote than *losing* candidates typically receive; three in five American voters had opposed the Republicans, leaving Lincoln with a rather ambiguous mandate.[197]

The election was especially messy in the South, where the returns underlined serious divisions, including between the border states and the Cotton Kingdom. A vote for Breckinridge was a vote for Davis's program of using federal power to safeguard slavery, but this policy won approval from only 44 percent of southern voters. Breckinridge carried every state of the future Confederacy except Tennessee and Virginia (where the divided Democratic vote enabled Bell to eke out a victory) and won a commanding 56 percent of the popular vote in the Deep South. Stridency on slavery in the territories had played well in the cotton states, but moderation had prevailed along much of the South's northern border.[198]

The election was a disaster for the Democrats: their dueling candidates together received less than 48 percent of the popular vote, an improvement over Buchanan's showing in 1856 but worse than Pierce's in 1852 or Polk's in 1844. Most alarming, of course, was the party split. It is true that if every anti-Republican vote had gone to a single competitor, Lincoln still would have prevailed, and some scholars have argued that the Democratic rupture actually helped Douglas in the North by distancing him from southern extremism.[199] Northern Douglasites' resolve to elect Douglas or throw the race to the Republicans strengthens this argument. But it imagines a simple transference of the Bell, Breckinridge, and Douglas votes to another candidate and assumes that an unbroken Democratic Party would not have drawn any additional support. In practice, however, the breach deprived Democrats of a crucial selling point: national unity. Douglas's boasts about popular sovereignty's unifying appeal rang hollow after the bolts at Charleston and Baltimore, and Democratic defeatism may have been decisive. If 5 percent of Republican voters in California, Oregon, Illinois, and Indiana had shifted to Douglas, the House would have chosen a president. This analysis is inherently counterfactual, but the Democratic split had wide-ranging consequences that should be considered even if they defy precise quantification.[200]

The party rupture had an especially ominous effect in the South, where it signaled the collapse of Davis's strategy of controlling the Democracy to preserve slavery within the Union. This plan had presumed infinite northern flexibility, but northern delegates' intransigence in convention, along with Breckinridge's dismal showing in the free states (where he won 8 percent of the popular vote), demonstrated that northern Democrats would not always swallow southern-approved tickets or platforms.[201] Southern Democrats had been converging with fire-eaters on policy issues well before 1860, and now the party's disarray removed a crucial obstacle to separatism. Southerners' loss of power over the Democracy may or may not have been "as important in their decision to secede as Republican victory," but secessionists had prayed for the party rupture and gained momentum when it occurred.[202]

Meanwhile, the party split furthered the northern sectionalization of Stephen Douglas. Backed by an increasingly defiant northern Democracy, Douglas had grasped the nomination only by alienating much of the South. He continued to pose as a national figure, but the election returns suggested otherwise: 88 percent of Douglas's popular votes came from the free states, and he won under 13 percent of the total southern vote, most of it from the border states.[203] His 4.7 percent of the vote in Mississippi (where he actually ran better than in North Carolina, Florida, or Texas) highlighted his weakness in the Cotton Kingdom, while Breckinridge's inability to win even 1 percent of the Illinois vote dramatized the destruction of partisan bonds in the Mississippi Valley. Douglas's dreams of a solid Democratic West were shattered.

Two other trends merit consideration. One was Douglas's relatively strong showing among working-class urban southerners, especially immigrants, and hill country farmers in places like northwestern Virginia and northern Alabama.[204] In the South, therefore, he ran best among white nonslaveholders whose politics had long troubled regional leaders, who feared Douglas's subversive appeals to white men's majoritarianism.[205] Douglas's lingering appeal among marginalized southern whites revealed the limits of sectional solidarity, fueling elite anxieties already intensified by the potential growth of the Republican Party in the South. Proslavery critics saw Douglas as a uniquely plausible, and therefore dangerous, enemy, so his southern support, limited as it was, actually stoked secessionist fervor.[206]

Douglas's supporters, meanwhile, joined a mammoth national majority opposed to Breckinridge, the Davis resolutions, and southern Democratic extremism. A neglected feature of the returns is that over 69 percent of voters nationwide, and nearly 90 percent of northerners, supported either Lincoln or Douglas. Despite their major differences and iconic rivalry, they were not poles apart in 1860, particularly not in the eyes of southern Democrats who regularly equated popular sovereignty and free soil and who sometimes insisted that a victory by either one would justify disunion. To comprehend the danger, wrote a Tuscaloosa secessionist, one must combine "the Northern votes given to both Lincoln *and* Douglas," for "*Northern Douglas men are unquestionably Republican*" in principle.[207] Lincolnites and Douglasites formed a vast majority that rejected the platform upon which southern Democrats had taken their stand.

In January 1861, a southern essayist blamed this northern majority for myriad evils, including free-soilism, river and harbor improvements, public education, and homestead legislation. "Black Republicanism" was but a symptom of a disease that was degenerating "all Northern politics . . . into the most licentious and destructive agrarianism" and was poised to unleash a radical assault on property rights. To shelter its peculiar property from the onslaught of "King Numbers," the South must secede.[208] In this view, the Union was fragmenting over issues entwined with those that had split the Democracy. These disputes about property, majority rule, and the Union would continue to shape national politics as Douglas and Davis returned to Washington for their final months in the Senate. Their party in shambles, the two Democratic stalwarts would subordinate partisan considerations to broader concerns about nations: one being ripped apart and another being born.

Epilogue

COUNTRIES OVER PARTY

In the blood-drenched summer of 1864, northern journalist James R. Gilmore met unofficially with Jefferson Davis to explore the possibility of compromise, but the Confederate president was thoroughly uncompromising. When Gilmore suggested a joint referendum to choose between permanent separation and reunion with emancipation, Davis adamantly refused. That would mean "the *majority* shall decide it," he protested. "We seceded to rid ourselves of the rule of the majority."[1] This was not just bitter talk from the leader of a dying country; Davis had made similar statements throughout the war. In early 1862, he exhorted Confederates to resist the "tyranny of an unbridled majority, the most odious and least responsible form of despotism."[2]

Davis readily deployed antimajoritarian rhetoric in wartime because it had suffused southern politics in peacetime, including during the secession crisis. Debate over the power of majorities, and their threat to slaveholders' property rights, inflamed the brutal political battles fought between Lincoln's election and the outbreak of war. During their final months together in the Senate, Davis and Douglas wrangled over issues that had divided them for years.

There was, however, one major difference: in 1861, Davis and Douglas put competing national loyalties ahead of their deeply held partisan ties. When Davis followed Mississippi into the Confederacy, he pledged allegiance to a nation from which political parties were ostensibly banished. Douglas, meanwhile, made a last-ditch effort for peace before rallying northern Democrats behind his great Republican rival. As political conflict escalated into armed strife, Davis and Douglas, whose intraparty duel had done so much to divide the Union, strove for patriotic statesmanship. Ironies abounded as Douglas exhorted northerners to fight a war he had long deemed preventable and Davis assumed leadership of a southern republic he had long considered unnecessary. Both had pinned their hopes on the Democratic Party, only to shatter it and unleash the bloodletting they feared. Douglas did not live to see the results, but Davis confronted another shocking irony: his new nation could not evade the conflicts over property and democracy that he had hoped to transcend.

★ ★ ★

White Mississippians erupted over news of Lincoln's victory. Individually and in mass meetings, many denounced the president-elect and endorsed Governor John J. Pettus's call for the state legislature to commence the process of secession; simultaneously, they stockpiled weapons and organized military units to repel invasion and suppress slave revolt.[3] Public rhetoric reflected antimajoritarian feelings nourished by determination to defend slaveholders' property. Pettus set the tone in his mid-November message to the legislature, proclaiming that the "existence or abolition of African slavery" was at stake and urging immediate secession. The "lives, liberty and property of the people of Mississippi" could not be "safely entrusted to the keeping of that sectional majority which must hereafter administer the Federal Government."[4] Secessionists, including most pro-Breckinridge newspaper editors, followed suit, provokingly exhorting white men never to "submit" to a hostile majority.[5] When reminded that Lincoln faced an unfriendly Congress, Mississippi secessionists expressed little faith in the Douglas Democrats, who were "nearly identical with the Lincolnites in their views on the slavery question."[6] Far from a check on Black Republican rule, the northern Democracy was part of an odious sectional majority. Mustering these formidable arguments amid the pageantry of militia rallies and fluttering flags, Deep South secessionists gained momentum in the weeks after Lincoln's victory.[7]

Keen to strike while fervor glowed white-hot, Pettus convened state legislators on November 26 and urged them to authorize a convention that would take Mississippi out of the Union. Five days later the lawmakers, 85 percent of them slave owners, unanimously approved a special election to choose 100 delegates for a convention to begin January 7.[8] Pettus also bolstered Mississippi's defenses, appointing Senator Davis to command state military forces and working with him to purchase arms and ammunition.[9] Despite Pettus's decisiveness, however, divisions emerged between proponents of immediate secession and those who preferred coordinating with other southern states to maintain a united front. Although focused on means rather than ends, the debate threatened to split Mississippi's leaders at a perilous moment. Predictably, Davis and Albert Gallatin Brown took opposite sides: Brown backed separate secession, while Davis favored cooperation. Just before the legislature met, Pettus huddled with most of the state's congressional delegation, and Davis, the lone dissenter, pledged to abide by their endorsement of separate secession.[10]

In light of his fiery campaign rhetoric, Davis's hesitation demands explanation. Some scholars attribute it to continued interest in compromise and reluctance to break up the Union.[11] This argument corrects the distortion, long promoted by indignant Unionists, that Davis was among the arch-conspirators who had plotted disunion for years. But in explaining his position to South Carolina fire-eater Robert Barnwell Rhett Jr., Davis's reasoning was strategic, not sentimental: the southern states had a powerful common interest—slavery—which necessitated concerted action, and since precipitate secession might alienate friends in Georgia or Louisiana, it was best to bolster sectional unity before plunging ahead. Davis's thinking was likely shaped by painful memories of 1850–51, when he had outpaced public opinion. Acknowledging his ignorance of the popular mood in Mississippi, Davis wanted to gauge voter sentiment before taking a gamble far greater than the one that burned him badly in 1851.[12] Davis had already avowed that his first loyalty was to Mississippi and its peculiar social order, and aversion to risk explained his temporary diffidence. When Pettus recommended independent action, Davis acceded immediately and never mentioned cooperative secession again.[13]

Secession gained steam after the election for convention delegates. Held on December 20, the same day South Carolina seceded, the contest drew surprisingly few voters—only 60 percent of the turnout for November's general election—in part because many assumed that secessionists were unbeatable. The delegates, predominantly young and ambitious slaveholders, soon gathered in Jackson, where Lucius Q. C. Lamar read a secession ordinance and called for its immediate ratification. The "safety of the South" was at stake, he proclaimed, along with "the integrity of society, the inviolability [sic] of our hearth-stones, and the purity of our Anglo-Saxon race." Cooperationists' delay tactics failed, and the ordinance passed 84–15 on January 9.[14] Within a month, five Deep South states had followed Mississippi and South Carolina out of the Union.

As secession thundered ahead, senators and representatives gathered for what some hoped, and others feared, would be another Union-saving session of Congress. Debate centered on federal protection for slaveholders' property rights, and while the Democratic conventions and general election foreshadowed the elusiveness of compromise, Douglas was as eager to repeat the events of 1850 as Davis was to avoid them. Given the speed with which secessionists were moving, compromisers would have to work swiftly.

Douglas arrived in Washington fortified by encouragement from beleaguered southern Unionists who begged him to save the country. A few invited Douglas to speak at Union rallies, including one in Vicksburg in late November and others in Virginia and Maryland the following spring.[15] Some forwarded compromise proposals that they wanted him to share with the Senate.[16] Most confided their mounting fears, often aggravated by secessionists' threats or acts of violence.[17] One Mississippian derided Davis as "the great Leader of the secession movement," a bloodthirsty opportunist determined to be "Emperor or King or President for Life" of a "cotton state empire." Three days before Mississippi seceded, this outraged southerner, still proud of having named his son for Douglas, turned to the Illinoisan as his last hope.[18]

Northern Democrats, meanwhile, were dazed and divided. Some blamed the Republicans, echoing campaign rhetoric that a Lincoln victory would destroy the Union.[19] Others, still bitter over the Charleston bolt, longed to punish the "chivalry."[20] They continued to support majority rule against proslavery dictation and urged Douglas to rebuff southern demands that would foist slavery upon unwilling majorities. As a New Englander put it, northerners must *"crush out the treason first"* and then discuss compromise.[21] With some constituents shuddering at the prospect of war and others itching to hang all the traitors, northern Douglas Democrats were united only in name.[22] Particularly alarming were reports of secessionist sympathies in southern Illinois, where Douglas's racism was more widely shared than his Unionism.[23] Thus, as whites in the Deep South closed ranks and suppressed dissenters, northerners split over how to respond. While battling to save the Union, Douglas would also have to unite his party and section: any compromise must reconcile disparate northern factions as well as disaffected southerners.

Davis received similarly mixed messages. Fire-eaters wrote to plot strategy, asking whether Mississippi would spearhead secession and urging swift action if South Carolina went first.[24] Mississippi confidants updated him on secession's progress and lamented lingering pockets of Unionism, especially among Douglas voters.[25] More disturbing were rumors of abolition plots in counties along the Mississippi River, which now represented a potential avenue for invasion.[26] One scheme in particular stood out: according to an anonymous letter written from Illinois in late February, a so-called Mississippi Society was preparing to send two hundred agents downriver to break levees and unleash a "certain and terable [sic]" flood that would devastate plantations, facilitate slave escapes, and topple the Cotton Kingdom. Davis took the warning seriously enough to forward it to Governor John J. Pettus.[27] Secessionists raced to mobilize against lurking enemies, even as they promised that disunion would promote safety.

Representing their agitated constituencies, Douglas and Davis were both present when the second session of the Thirty-Sixth Congress opened on December 3, and both soon clarified their positions. On the day South Carolina seceded, Douglas proclaimed that "there must be conciliation and concession, or civil war."[28] Six days earlier, however, Davis had signed a statement that rejected compromise and called for immediate secession. "The argument is exhausted," he announced with twenty other southern senators and representatives. "All hope of relief in the Union through the agency of committees, congressional legislation or constitutional amendments, is extinguished." Thus, "the honor, safety, and independence of the Southern people require the organization of a Southern confederacy," achievable only through "separate State secession."[29]

Davis revealed his rapid conversion from cooperative to immediate secession through this endorsement of a document crafted for maximum impact.[30] Rhetorically, it opened with a slogan that had peppered southern politics since 1825, when Georgia governor George M. Troup, an early champion of states' rights and Indian removal, had exhorted his legislature "to step forward, and having exhausted the argument, to stand by your arms."[31] Thereafter, southern firebrands regularly invoked Troup to argue that the argument *was* exhausted and an appeal to arms imminent: William Lowndes Yancey in 1850, Preston Brooks in 1855, and Georgia governor Joseph E. Brown in a November 1860 call for a secession convention, among others, had turned Troup's conditional command into a sectional battle cry.[32] The communiqué was timed to reach southern voters at a critical moment. Carried across the South at telegraphic speed, it hit newspapers shortly before an enfranchised minority of southerners chose delegates to state secession conventions: Mississippi's special election was on December 20, Florida's two days later, Alabama's on the twenty-fourth, Georgia's on January 2, and Louisiana's on the seventh.[33]

Historian William Freehling aptly deems the document a "death certificate for the Union."[34]

Davis's signature on this secessionist appeal must be remembered when assessing his subsequent actions. Significantly, the statement repudiated the recently commenced work of a special House committee, the Committee of Thirty-Three, tasked with forging a compromise. Davis's endorsement of a secessionist critique of the committee's aims, coupled with his brusque treatment of Mississippi congressman Reuben Davis upon learning of the latter's service on the committee, indicates an aversion to compromise.[35] Why, then, did he agree to serve on the Senate's comparable Committee of Thirteen, created a few days later? Davis participated reluctantly, first refusing to join before changing his mind the next day.[36] The abrupt reversal might be attributed to vacillation shaped by bitter memories of 1850, although some scholars accuse Davis of aiming to sabotage the committee from within.[37] A clue regarding Davis's motives is his proposed rule, adopted by the committee, that any compromise reported to the Senate must be approved by majorities of the committee's Republican and non-Republican members. Variously interpreted as a sensible response to political polarization and a device to torpedo compromise, the proposal reflected Davis's strategic impatience. It would allow the committee to gauge the prospects for compromise while avoiding delays that might raise false hopes for reconciliation, derail secession, and expose the South to danger. Davis wanted to ensure that the Committee of Thirteen would either make a workable recommendation or demonstrate that the argument was indeed exhausted.[38] Having watched Mississippi voters' zeal sputter out during the year preceding his calamitous gubernatorial campaign in 1851, Davis appreciated the value of speed.

Davis's service on the Committee of Thirteen brought him into contact with Douglas for the last time. Along with Georgia's Robert Toombs, three upper South senators, five Republicans, and two other northern Democrats, they spent late December reviewing compromise formulas meant to extinguish the fuse lit by South Carolina. Davis and Douglas contributed their own proposals, first presented to the Senate as constitutional amendments on December 24 and immediately referred to the committee.[39] Davis's proposal would have nationalized slavery by embedding in the Constitution the principle that masters' property could not be impaired by Congress or any state or territory; thus he set repudiation of both free soil and popular sovereignty as the price of Union and would force an overwhelming majority of northern voters to abandon the positions they took in the recent election. Toombs offered his own pro-slavery amendments, which would have repudiated popular sovereignty, denied accused fugitive slaves the right to jury trials and writs of habeas corpus, required that a majority of slave-state senators and representatives approve federal laws affecting slavery, and mandated that slavery-related constitutional amendments receive unanimous support from the slave states. Anathema to most northerners, Davis's and Toombs's proposals would have sheltered slavery from territorial, state, or national majorities of any size.[40]

Meanwhile, Douglas's amendments revealed a desperate disposition to jettison long-cherished ideals to preserve the Union.[41] One would enshrine an altered form of popular sovereignty in the Constitution by freezing the status of slavery in all territories until their respective populations reached 50,000, when they could exercise full self-government; it would also prohibit future acquisition of territory without two-thirds majority support in Congress. The second outlawed voting and office holding by African Americans nationwide, offered federal funds for colonizing free blacks abroad, and barred Congress from interfering with the domestic slave trade or abolishing slavery in the District of Columbia. These amendments mixed racism and restrictions on expansion with marginal protection for slavery in order to calm the crisis and prevent its recurrence. Offering no sweeping safeguards, they fell short of Davis's demands, but they also flouted several of Douglas's core ideals, including the sanctity of local white self-government.[42] Douglas had championed decentralized governance to cement the Union and now would abandon it for the same purpose. It was a panicky effort at statesmanship.

The compromise package that received the most attention, however, was authored by Kentucky senator John J. Crittenden, a longtime Whig who had supported Douglas's reelection in 1858. Personally friendly and politically aligned against the Lecompton Constitution, Douglas and Crittenden now collaborated in an effort that resembled Douglas's partnership with Henry Clay ten years earlier.[43] Crittenden's eponymous compromise included unamendable amendments that guaranteed slavery in the states against federal interference; prohibited slavery in all current and future territories north of the Missouri Compromise line and protected it to the south; barred Congress from meddling with the interstate slave trade or abolishing slavery on federal property within slave states or in Washington, D.C., without local consent and only if Virginia and Maryland had abolished it first; and authorized federal compensation for masters who were prevented from recovering fugitives in free states.

Additional resolutions repudiated personal liberty laws, urged alterations to the Fugitive Slave Act to appease northerners, and called for suppression of the African slave trade.[44]

Many northern Democrats and southern moderates embraced the Crittenden Compromise as the best way to prevent secession of the upper and border South states. Douglas preferred his own amendments because they preserved some form of popular sovereignty, but he applauded Crittenden's proposal, which embraced both proslavery and antislavery intervention, because it would remove the territorial issue from Congress.[45] The compromise offered less than the ironclad guarantees Davis wanted, but he knew that if Republicans swallowed Crittenden's amendments, there was perhaps a chance to forestall secession by proving that southern Democrats could still extract concessions from the North.[46] Their spines stiffened by communications from President-elect Lincoln, who would yield on fugitive slaves but not slavery expansion, and who criticized Crittenden's guarantee of slavery in future territories as an invitation to tropical imperialism, Republicans refused to budge.[47] On December 22, Republicans on the Committee of Thirteen voted against Crittenden's proposal, with Davis and Toombs joining them against the upper southerners and northern Democrats. Six days later, the committee gave up. Thus, Davis recalled, "the last reasonable hope of a pacific settlement of difficulties within the Union was extinguished."[48] Crittenden's conciliatory efforts had unwittingly confirmed that the argument *was* exhausted; with the wind at their backs, secessionists pushed seven cotton states out of the Union by February 1.[49]

Who was responsible for the failure of compromise? Davis, predictably, blamed Republicans.[50] Douglas, predictably, blamed extremists in both sections.[51] Historians have echoed both of these positions, but others properly attribute the crisis to secessionists who demanded that Republicans abandon a core principle and etch its antithesis into the Constitution. Republican stalwarts knew blackmail when they saw it and sensed that escalating proslavery ultimatums, born of the rivalry between Democratic loyalists and fire-eaters, meant that no settlement could be final. Tellingly, Lincoln worried that Republicans of Eli Thayer's stamp might accept a compromise based on popular sovereignty. This had troubled him for years, and now as president-elect he quietly but firmly ordered congressional Republicans to stand fast. Lincoln was not choosing war, but he was refusing to capitulate.[52]

Davis had given up on compromise, but Douglas had not. In a speech on January 3, he denounced Republican talk of slavery's ultimate extinction and blasted fire-eaters for rushing toward disunion.[53] He continued experimenting with legislative solutions, including a bill to fine-tune the Fugitive Slave Act by providing jury trials for defendants and compensation for masters who lost property. He later pondered a North American customs union, modeled on the German Zollverein, which might preserve the benefits of economic integration even if secession proved irreversible. By session's end, he was backing a Thirteenth Amendment, which forever barred Congress from interfering with slavery in the states. Lincoln and many Republicans approved it, but it joined other compromise schemes in the dustbin of history.[54]

Davis lingered for a different purpose. Most of Mississippi's congressional delegation had resigned on January 12 after receiving official confirmation of the state's secession, but Davis remained behind, citing poor health.[55] Yet neuralgia did not prevent him from funneling intelligence on federal activities to the governor of South Carolina, whom he warned of war, or from seeking to block objectionable appointments and defeat legislation to mobilize federal might.[56] As Davis told fellow southerners, he dallied in Washington to oppose "hostile legislation."[57] Ultimately, he stayed twelve days past Mississippi's secession, representing constituents ostensibly unconnected to the U.S. government. On January 21, Davis bade the Senate farewell in a brief address later freighted with rather mawkish memories. True, he denied feeling "hostility" toward the North. But he also defended disunion, acknowledged his role in encouraging Mississippi to secede, and rebuked antislavery activists for spouting "the theory that all men are created free and equal."[58] Nineteen days later, he was relaxing at Brierfield when he learned of his selection as president of the Confederate States of America. Davis felt the burden of this duty, but he never looked back, proclaiming in his inaugural address that reunion was "neither practicable nor desirable."[59] Davis had transferred his allegiance to a new country, which he hoped would avoid the conflicts and heresies that had plagued the old.

★ ★ ★

In his Senate valedictory, inaugural address, and private correspondence, Davis openly anticipated that secession meant war.[60] And when the war came, Davis authorized firing its first shot, a bold gambit to unite the slave states, eight of which still had not seceded, in the nascent Confederacy.[61] Meanwhile, Douglas entered the most statesmanlike phase of his career, in which he abandoned partisanship to serve the United States.

Douglas abhorred war, but throughout the presidential election and subsequent crisis he had repudiated secession and was therefore predisposed to welcome Lincoln's tactfully tough inaugural pledge to enforce the law. Douglas may not have held Lincoln's hat during the speech, but he did defend Lincoln against upper South and northern critics who read his words as a declaration of war.[62] During a special Senate session held after Lincoln took office, Douglas insisted that the inaugural was a "peace-offering rather than a war message" and seconded Lincoln's view that the Union was unbroken. He promised to support the administration in executing its constitutional duties and, in a powerful statement from a pugnacious partisan, promised to "do justice to those who, by their devotion to the Constitution and the Union, show that they love their country more than their party."[63] The speech heartened northerners who hoped that other Democrats would follow suit, and Lincoln was reportedly "elated" by it.[64] Douglas sent other signals of support for the new administration as well. He met with Lincoln privately several times before and after the inauguration, updating the Washington outsider on congressional doings and suggesting a cautious course that would keep the border states in the Union. These gestures were not entirely altruistic, for Douglas knew that he could wield more influence as a loyal critic than as a mindless obstructionist.[65]

There was no doubt where Douglas stood after war commenced. Days after Davis shattered the fragile peace by bombarding Fort Sumter, Douglas encountered longtime friend John Forney on Pennsylvania Avenue. When the despondent Philadelphian asked what could be done, Douglas thrilled him with his answer: "We must fight for our country and forget all differences. There can be but two parties—the party of patriots and the party of traitors. We belong to the first."[66] Douglas huddled with Lincoln soon after, advising him to increase his request for volunteers.[67] Their political differences remained significant but did not prevent united action against a common foe, as Douglas explained in an April 14 press release that pledged loyalty to the president and urged "prompt action" to defend the country "at all hazards."[68] Some northern Democrats gagged this bipartisanship, but it was consistent with Douglas's position throughout the secession winter. Early in December, he had vowed to cooperate with "any individual of any party" who would work for "the preservation of the Constitution and the Union."[69] At that point, he still hoped for peace and rebuked Republicans and secessionists alike. But now Republicans stood for a Union under assault by southern rebels, and cooperation was essential to saving the country.

Douglas's leadership was crucial because some northern Democrats remained sullenly reluctant to sustain a Republican administration. As they wrestled with mixed emotions, many solicited Douglas's advice. "It is evident that we are on the verge of Civil War," wrote an Illinoisan. "We are now in view of the awful crisis . . . [and] exceedingly anxious to know what we ought to do?"[70] An Ohioan who sought Douglas's counsel loved the Union but did not want to "engage in a Black Republican, Abolition, Negro fight." Confused, he asked about the proper course for an anti-abolition Unionist.[71] Other northwesterners reported that Democrats were loath to enlist and perhaps even sympathetic to the Confederacy, and they urged Douglas to rally them to the cause.[72]

To unite northwesterners under a bipartisan Union banner, Douglas launched a final campaign as tireless as any of his career, and far more statesmanlike. He traveled west to Illinois, determined to bring wavering Democrats into a mighty Unionist coalition.[73] Upon arriving on April 25, Douglas expressed his zeal to "produce harmony and concert of action" between Republicans and Democrats and to "put down treason and rebellion in the South." Orville H. Browning, a longtime Whig who helped build the Illinois Republican Party, was impressed.[74] Douglas delivered several speeches, including one to the state legislature in which he emphasized the magnitude of the crisis by denouncing the "widespread conspiracy . . . to destroy the best government the sun of heaven ever shed its rays upon." Excoriating the southern "minority" for "raising the traitorous hand of rebellion," he urged Unionists of all parties to "turn back the tide of revolution and usurpation." To loud applause, Douglas proclaimed, "You all know that I am a very good partisan fighter in partisan times. [Laughter and cheers.] And I trust you will find me equally as good a patriot when the country is in danger. [Cheers.]"[75]

Douglas appealed primarily to patriotism, but a key subtheme was secession's impact on the northwestern economy. Generations of northwesterners had feared that foreign control of the Mississippi River would isolate them from global markets. Aware of this insecurity, some secessionists hoped that Confederate leverage over northwesterners would compel them to accept peaceful separation or even to join the new republic.[76] During the 1850s, railroads had siphoned much of the region's commerce away from the river and toward the Northeast.[77] But Douglas relied on the persistence of river traffic to turn secessionists' economic weapon against them, warning that rebels manning a "battery of cannon upon the banks of the Mississippi" would fleece northwesterners for customs duties. "Can we submit to taxation without representation?" Douglas asked, drawing a chorus of noes. "Can we permit nations foreign to us to collect revenues off our products—the fruits of our industry?" Would residents of the great valley consent to become "dependent provinces upon powers that thus choose to surround and hem us in?"[78] This was a less inspiring battle cry than "Union" or "emancipation," but it was tuned for northwestern Democrats who needed a casus belli untainted by Black Republicanism. Striving to muster Unionists under the broadest of tents, Douglas revisited an old theme for a new purpose. Once convinced that the mighty Mississippi was an unbreakable bond of Union, he now exhorted northwesterners to fight and reunite the Father of Waters under one flag.

Unionists of all parties respected these efforts. An Alton resident who was recruiting volunteers thanked Douglas for his "prudent, *Statesman-like & patriotic* course" in convincing Democrats that sustaining the Union did not mean bowing to the Republicans. "Your late speeches," he enthused, "have opened the eyes of many good, but *timid* Democrats."[79] From Douglas's old hometown of Jacksonville came praise that channeled his bipartisan spirit. "In yourself & Mr Lincoln," wrote J. B. Tanner, "Illinois has everything to be proud of."[80]

Five weeks after arriving in Illinois, Douglas died in Chicago. Years of campaigning, speaking, and drinking had wrecked his health, and rheumatism, liver problems, and throat ulcers left the Little Giant bedridden for much of May. On the morning of June 3, he passed away at age forty-eight.[81] He was buried near Lake Michigan under a statue that overlooks the silty harbor.

Douglas left northern Democrats bereft of his leadership and saddled with a legacy that grew more contradictory as the Civil War progressed. War Democrats used his name to rally Unionists, including members of the "Douglas Brigade" raised by Cook County lawyer David Stuart, which commenced training at Camp Douglas in early summer 1861.[82] But Copperheads also deployed Douglas against an increasingly radical war effort. The notorious John Van Evrie enshrined one of Douglas's most demagogic lines from the 1858 debates on the masthead of the *New York Day-Book*: "I hold that this Government was made on the WHITE BASIS, by WHITE MEN, for the benefit of WHITE MEN and THEIR POSTERITY FOREVER."[83] As emancipation drove a wedge between the late senator's patriotism and racism, northern Democrats responded in a variety of ways. Many served nobly, others shouted crudely, and some dabbled in treason.

★ ★ ★

Douglas died before war shattered his illusion that the Union could endure half-slave and half-free, but Davis lived to face his own reckoning. A longtime champion of white southern solidarity, Davis commenced his star-crossed presidency insisting that the Confederacy's power came from the absence of conflict between classes, factions, or ideologies. The central theme of his oratory was uniformity. If war came, President-elect Davis announced upon reaching the Confederate capital of Montgomery, Alabama, "we have nothing to fear at home, because at home we have homogeneity." Confederate citizens were "men of one flesh and one bone, one interest, one purpose and of identity of domestic institutions."[84] Days later, in his inaugural address, Davis rejected reunion with the free states, arguing that without "homogeneity," sectional "antagonisms" would inevitably drive them apart.[85] After being elected to a full term the following February, he exulted that Confederates had escaped "the despotism of numbers" and made "a new association, composed of States homogeneous in interest, in policy, and in feeling."[86] For Davis, history's lessons were clear: slavery was insecure when free people were divided, but in the Confederacy, it was a source of unity and therefore would be safe.

Soon, however, Davis's slaveholding republic would crash back into the realm of conflict in which all nations reside. Beset by a powerful foe and riven by disputes over property, government authority, and wartime mobilization, neither the Confederacy nor its labor system would survive. Wartime strain exposed the heterogeneity of interests among southern whites, and conflicts over property and power, which had called the Confederacy into existence, helped to undermine it from within.[87]

The most obvious of these conflicts pitted slaveholders, and a Confederate government that seemed beholden to them, against nonslaveholding whites. Hungry yeomen noticed when planters refused to shift from cotton to food production, or when they surreptitiously sold cotton to U.S. agents. Conscription provoked still more class resentment, especially after the Confederate Congress exempted masters or overseers of twenty or more slaves. This policy ignited protests that revealed the limits of proslavery propaganda: bitter nonslaveholders did not believe that black slavery made all white men equal or that they had more to lose from emancipation than planters did. One Georgian condemned planters for growing as much cotton as they pleased while demanding rigid enforcement of conscription. "Their negroes must make cotton," he seethed, "and whilst doing it the poor men must be taken from their families and put in the Army to protect their negroes."[88] Soldiers who told Davis that they were "tired of fighting for this negro aristockracy" belied his exuberant claims about Confederate solidarity.[89] Indeed, some resentful plain folk questioned the sanctity of masters' property rights. A Georgian incensed by the Twenty Negro Law proclaimed that "owners of twenty hands . . .

ought to be made to fight for their property or ought to be deprived of it."[90] Some scholars see this internal disaffection as decisive. Unable to inspire unflinching loyalty from the nonslaveholding white majority, perhaps the Confederacy's epitaph should be "Died of Class Conflict."[91]

Yet Confederate politics involved more than a clash between haves and have-nots, as conflicts over government power and personal property fractured citizens along multiple axes. This was bad news for Davis, who faced resistance and resentment from whites of all classes. Thus, even though the Confederate government addressed yeomen's grievances with some success, varied and vexing disputes over property continued to disrupt the war effort.[92]

Nonslaveholding whites, for instance, jealously guarded their own property even as they excoriated selfish planters. Military impressment and a 10 percent tax-in-kind on livestock and food crops left larders bare and small property holders hungry. Certainly, this demoralized yeomen who hated being squeezed to support a rich man's war.[93] But it also raised deeper questions about balancing public necessity and private subsistence, and in this context, white nonslaveholders, particularly women, made striking new claims for government support, even as they resisted encroachment on their own humble property.[94] Other Confederates felt the heavy hand of central power fall upon property they held jointly with citizens of the United States. Under the Sequestration Act, Confederate courts seized property owned by U.S. citizens, but cases in which this property was physically held by a Confederate citizen—often a relative or business partner of the legal owner—made enforcement more complex and less popular.[95] Seeking to raise revenues and punish Yankees, the Confederacy moved aggressively against private property, but Confederates sometimes were caught in the net.

Even planters felt the pinch. Astute observers urged them to contribute to a war being fought "in great part for the defence of the slaveholder in his property rights," but when military necessity demanded infringement of those rights, many slaveholders balked.[96] The impressment of enslaved people to build fortifications, for example, alienated many slaveholders from their government. One master who watched Confederate officers take four of his slaves denounced impressment as "villainous" and grumbled that he had enjoyed more liberty and security before secession.[97] Efforts to assuage slaveholders by compensating those whose slaves died or escaped while working on public projects aggravated nonslaveholders, who wondered why survivors of soldiers killed in action received no restitution. Confederate authorities did impress tens of thousands of enslaved laborers into government service but at the cost of sowing disaffection.[98] By 1863, Davis's assistant secretary of war opined that the "sacrosanctity of slave property" had "operated most injuriously to the Confederacy," a supreme irony unforeseen during the secession crisis.[99] Even when the Confederate Congress made a last, desperate move to attempt to recruit black soldiers, the sanctity of masters' property rights remained intact; the law, based on a bill introduced by Davis's antebellum spokesman Ethelbert Barksdale, simply authorized masters to volunteer their slaves to fight.[100] Full mobilization of its human and material resources clashed with foundational Confederate principles.

Interpreting these multidimensional conflicts over property and power is largely a question of whether the glass was half full or half empty. Many yeomen fought to the end; others became disillusioned, and some became Unionists. Many slaveholders contributed unselfishly to the war effort; others stubbornly resisted inroads on their property. Whether these conflicts can explain Confederate defeat remains a debated question. Clearly, however, the Confederacy fell short of the ironclad solidarity that Davis hailed in 1861. After fifteen years of conflict with Stephen Douglas over public power and private property, majority rule and slaveholders' prerogatives, Davis hoped that a republic unshackled from free states could achieve a more perfect unity. Any internal friction was, therefore, a bitter disappointment. Before the Civil War, Davis had wanted a government empowered to protect, but powerless to harm, slaveholders' property rights. Whites of all classes wanted something similar in the Confederacy—a government that would vigorously protect them while leaving their persons and property untouched—but divided over the details. The Confederacy's internal conflicts were hardly unique, but Davis's peculiarly high hopes set him up for disappointment.

Much like the antebellum Democratic Party, Davis's Confederacy promised to safeguard property rights while ensuring equality among white men. If the antebellum era was any guide, Davis might have recognized the difficulty of achieving this balance. The wages of whiteness had not kept northern Democrats in line, nor were they enough to keep every hungry and cynical southern yeoman in the ranks. Much like northern Democrats, the Confederacy's plain folk generally respected masters' property rights but would not sacrifice everything to maintain them.

★ ★ ★

Jefferson Davis and Stephen Douglas were profoundly antidemocratic by modern standards, but history need not be inspiring to be instructive. The story of their rivalry is not simply one of good versus evil but of two warped visions of self-government colliding and ultimately succumbing, in dramatically different ways, to a common rival. Although Davis and Douglas aligned against the abolitionists with whom most modern interpreters identify, the differences between them were vastly important, and their rivalry reflected and fueled a wider clash that shattered the Democracy and hastened secession. It is tempting to lump Davis and Douglas together as racist anti-abolitionists, but ignoring their bitter feud risks distorting our view of antebellum politics and overlooking important cracks in the wall standing between slavery's opponents and a new birth of freedom. Exploring Democrats' internal conflicts underscores the enduring significance of the tension between property and democracy, illuminates a shadowy corner of the sectional conflict, and shows that no political coalition is ever monolithic.

Abraham Lincoln understood the Democracy's fragility. After his 1858 defeat, he predicted that Douglas, who had campaigned "both as the best means to *break down*, and to *uphold* the Slave interest," could not "keep those antagonistic elements in harmony long." Encouraged by this nuanced understanding of his opponents, Lincoln's keenness to exploit their disagreements steeled his resolve. "The fight must go on," he vowed. "The cause of civil liberty must not be surrendered at the end of *one*, or even, one *hundred* defeats."[101]

Acknowledgments

In academia, as in antebellum politics, networks are everything. As I wrote this book, I benefited from an extraordinary network of mentors, colleagues, friends, and family, whose generosity is humbling. All of them have my admiration and my gratitude.

For expert assistance with archival research, many thanks go to the archivists and staff at Special Collections Research Center, University of Chicago; the Papers of Jefferson Davis, Woodson Research Center, Rice University; Special Collections and Archives, Transylvania University; the Mississippi Department of Archives and History; the Abraham Lincoln Presidential Library; the Oregon Historical Society; the Alabama Department of Archives and History; William L. Clements Library, University of Michigan; the Historical Society of Pennsylvania; Houghton Library, Harvard University; the Massachusetts Historical Society; the Missouri History Museum Archives; the Ohio Historical Society; the David M. Rubenstein Rare Book and Manuscript Library, Duke University; and Special Collections, Virginia Tech. Thanks are also due the Library of Congress and the Indiana State Library for making available materials that I accessed remotely.

Closer to home, the librarians and staff at Marshall University's Drinko Library and Morrow Library have provided immense help in tracking down research materials and making Marshall a wonderful place to work. Special thanks go to Lori Thompson, Jack Dickinson, and Seth Nichols for assistance in preparing some of the images for this book.

Given the costs of research travel, this project would not have been possible without financial support. For much-appreciated funding, even in lean budgetary times, I am profoundly grateful to the West Virginia Humanities Council (Fellowship Grant #14014); the Special Collections Research Center at the University of Chicago (Robert L. Platzman Memorial Fellowship); Marshall University (Summer Research Award); Virginia Tech Special Collections and the Virginia Center for Civil War Studies (Research Grant); and the National Endowment for the Humanities (Summer Stipend, Federal Award ID Number FT-248750-16).

I completed most of the research, and all of the writing, at Marshall University, where a remarkable group of faculty, students, and staff have made it a joy to teach and write. Special thanks go to my department chairs, Dan Holbrook and Greta Rensenbrink, and my dean, Robert Bookwalter, for making research and conference travel a priority. Thanks also go to my colleagues for making the history department a vibrant place to work and to my students for asking so many good questions about the past—and for inspiring hope for the future.

I presented portions of this project at several conferences, including the James K. Polk and His Time Conference (2019); the Society of Civil War Historians (2018); the Western History Association (2017); the Organization of American Historians (2017); and the Maple Leaf and Eagle Conference on North American Studies (2016). My sincere thanks go to fellow panelists, chairs, commentators, and audiences for thoughtful feedback and insightful questions.

Numerous colleagues and friends have helped me in myriad ways, and I am thankful to all of them. For sharing research materials with me, I am grateful to Mark Summers and Andrew Wiley. For hospitality on research trips, many thanks are due Monica Felix, Patrick Kelly, Stephen Parkin, Jill Parkin, and Paul Quigley. For reading part or all of the manuscript, I am grateful to Jason Phillips, Christian Pinnen, Paul Quigley, Rachel Shelden, and John Suval. Conversations with these readers, as well as with Erik Alexander, Aaron Astor, Corey Brooks, Daniel Crofts, James Huston, Joshua Lynn, Megan Kate Nelson, Brian Schoen, Tara Strauch, and Frank Towers, have been invaluable.

My sincere thanks go to everyone at the University of North Carolina Press who made this book possible. Mark Simpson-Vos and Aaron Sheehan-Dean have encouraged me throughout the project, and I am honored to be published in the Civil War America series. Many thanks go to Jessica Newman, Cate Hodorowicz, Jay Mazzocchi, Dino Battista, and everyone who guided me through the production process, and to Julie Bush for outstanding copyediting. Special thanks are due my readers Matthew Mason and Adam I. P. Smith for constructive criticism and enthusiastic feedback on the manuscript.

While reading in the archives or hunching over a keyboard, it is easy to feel like a lone wolf, but I'm thankful that I run with such a supportive pack. My extended family and in-laws, scattered across the Pacific Rim, have provided love and support, which is always appreciated wherever I roam. Special thanks go to my parents, Rick and Jennifer Woods, for their encouragement of my love of history from a very early age. To Jack, Nino, and my wife, Beth, thank you for everything.

Notes

ABBREVIATIONS

ALPL   Abraham Lincoln Presidential Library, Springfield, Ill.

CG   *Congressional Globe*

Cooper, *JDA*   William J. Cooper Jr., *Jefferson Davis, American* (New York: Alfred A. Knopf, 2000)

CWAL   *The Collected Works of Abraham Lincoln*, ed. Roy P. Basler, 8 vols. (New Brunswick, N.J.: Rutgers University Press, 1953–55)

HSP   Historical Society of Pennsylvania, Philadelphia

JD   Jefferson Davis

JDC   *Jefferson Davis, Constitutionalist: His Letters, Papers, and Speeches*, ed. Dunbar Rowland, 10 vols. (Jackson, Miss.: printed for the Mississippi Department of Archives and History, 1923)

JDM   [Varina Howell Davis], *Jefferson Davis, Ex-President of the Confederate States of America, a Memoir*, 2 vols. (New York: Belford, 1890)

JDPDU   Jefferson Davis Papers, David M. Rubenstein Rare Book and Manuscript Library, Duke University, Durham, N.C.

JDPTU   Jefferson Davis Papers, Special Collections and Archives, Transylvania University, Lexington, Ky.

Johannsen, *SAD*   Robert W. Johannsen, *Stephen A. Douglas* ([1973] Urbana: University of Illinois Press, 1997)

LC   Manuscript Division, Library of Congress

LSAD   *The Letters of Stephen A. Douglas*, ed. Robert W. Johannsen (Urbana: University of Illinois Press, 1961)

MDAH   Mississippi Department of Archives and History, Jackson

ORHS   Oregon Historical Society, Portland

PJD   *The Papers of Jefferson Davis*, ed. Lynda Lasswell Crist et al., 14 vols. (Baton Rouge: Louisiana State University Press, 1971–2015)

PJDRU   Papers of Jefferson Davis, Woodson Research Center, Fondren Library,
        Rice University, Houston, Tex.
SAD   Stephen A. Douglas
SADP   Stephen A. Douglas Papers, Special Collections Research Center,
        University of Chicago

INTRODUCTION

1. *CG*, 35th Cong., 2nd Sess., 1259–60 (February 23, 1859).

2. *CG*, 35th Cong., 2nd Sess., 1203–25 (February 22, 1859).

3. *CG*, 35th Cong., 2nd Sess., 1241–44 (February 23, 1859).

4. *CG*, 35th Cong., 2nd Sess., 1244–45, 1246–47 (February 23, 1859).

5. *CG*, 35th Cong., 2nd Sess., 1247–48 (February 23, 1859).

6. Pollard, *Life of Jefferson Davis*, 40; Freeman, *Field of Blood*, 208–64.

7. *CG*, 35th Cong., 2nd Sess., 1255–60 (February 23, 1859).

8. *CG*, 35th Cong., 2nd Sess., 1249 (February 23, 1859).

9. *Yazoo Democrat* (Yazoo City, Miss.), April 23, 1859.

10. "Congressional Intervention," *Marshall County Democrat* (Plymouth, Ind.), March 3, 1859.

11. Douglas, *Non-intervention*.

12. Ferdinand Kennett to SAD, February 25, 1859, box 24, folder 13, SADP.

13. The standard Douglas biography remains Johannsen, *SAD*. See also Quitt, *Stephen A. Douglas*; Huston, *Stephen A. Douglas*; Johannsen, *Frontier, the Union, and Stephen A. Douglas*; Wells, *Stephen Douglas*; and Capers, *Stephen A. Douglas*. Despite its faulty assumptions about slavery, abolitionism, and Civil War causation, Milton, *Eve of Conflict*, contains useful information. The best Davis biographies are Cooper, *JDA*; and W. Davis, *Jefferson Davis*. Cooper provides deeper coverage of the antebellum and postwar years, while Davis offers superb psychological insights. I have also profited from Sanders, "Jefferson Davis"; Eaton, *Jefferson Davis*; McElroy, *Jefferson Davis*; and Dodd, *Jefferson Davis*. Allen, *Jefferson Davis*, is impressively researched but highly partisan and sometimes hagiographic. Strode, *Jefferson Davis*, is engaging but interpretively suspect.

14. Dirck, *Lincoln and Davis*, and Catton and Catton, *Two Roads to Sumter*, cover both men's pre–Civil War lives; a shorter account is Crist, "Jefferson Davis and Abraham Lincoln." For comparisons of their executive leadership, see Chadwick, *Two American Presidents*; Mark E. Neely Jr., "Abraham Lincoln vs. Jefferson Davis: Comparing Presidential Leadership in the Civil War," in McPherson and Cooper, *Writing the Civil War*, 96–111; L. Johnson, "Jefferson Davis and Abraham Lincoln"; and Werstein, *Abraham Lincoln versus Jefferson Davis*.

15. Cooper, "Jefferson Davis and the Sudden Disappearance of Southern Politics," in *Jefferson Davis and the Civil War Era*, 3–10.

16. James L. Huston, "The Continuing Debate about the 'Great Debates' of 1858: A Critical Review of Recent Literature," in Johannsen, *Lincoln-Douglas Debates*, iv–xxxvi; Johannsen, *Lincoln, the South, and Slavery*; Burt, *Lincoln's Tragic Pragmatism*; May, *Slavery, Race, and Conquest*; Guelzo, *Lincoln and Douglas*; Zarefsky, *Lincoln, Douglas, and Slavery*; Jaffa, *Crisis of the House Divided*.

17. The Douglas-Davis rivalry has not received intensive analysis in previous scholarship. For allusions to its importance, see Johannsen, "Introduction," *LSAD*, xxiii; Jones, *Davis Memorial Volume*, 146; Fehrenbacher, *South and Three Sectional Crises*, 59; and Dirck, *Lincoln and Davis*, 127. Similarly, although historians regard the breakup of the Democratic Party as a precursor to disunion and war, they have given the process of party fragmentation little sustained attention since Roy F. Nichols's Pulitzer Prize–winning *Disruption of American Democracy*. Despite its solid research and engaging prose, Nichols's book shows its age. It was written when most historians saw slavery as a dying relic rather than a ruthlessly expanding sector of the modern global economy; when many scholars regarded sectionalism as the product of demagoguery rather than of substantive differences; and when political historians confined their attention to set speeches, editorials, and elite correspondence. Built upon scholarship unavailable to Nichols, *Arguing until Doomsday* offers new perspectives on the Democratic Party's rupture. For recent studies of the Old South's flourishing slave society, see Karp, *This Vast Southern Empire*; Baptist, *Half Has Never Been Told*; W. Johnson, *River of Dark Dreams*; and Schoen, *Fragile Fabric of Union*. On antebellum political historiography, see Woods, "What Twenty-First-Century Historians Have Said"; and Towers, "Partisans, New History, and Modernization." Some excellent models of what William Freehling termed the "reintegration of American history"—the incorporation of social, economic, and cultural history into political analysis—include Link, *Roots of Secession*; Dusinberre, *Slavemaster President*; and Olsen, *Political Culture and Secession*; as well as W. Freehling, "Toward a Newer Political History—and a Reintegrated Multicultural History," in *Reintegration of American History*, 253–74. *Arguing until Doomsday* also studies the democracy's self-destruction within a broader temporal and geographical context. Nichols focused strictly on the late 1850s, but this book traces the roots of the split back to the party's birth in the 1820s. Nichols emphasized clashing personalities; this book uses a biographical lens to explore more fundamental sectional conflicts. Most of the action in Nichols's book unfolded in Washington, D.C.; I situate Davis and Douglas in their starkly contrasting portions of the booming Mississippi River valley.

18. "Col. Jeff Davis—Hail to the Chief!," *Mississippi Free Trader* (Natchez), October 8, 1860; JD to Franklin Pierce, June 13, 1860, *JDC*, 4:496.

19. Varina Howell Davis to My dear Father and Mother, September 15, 1856, in Strode, *Jefferson Davis: Private Letters*, 80–81.

20. James H. Smith to SAD, September 21, 1859, box 26, folder 16, SADP.

21. R. J. Jackson to JD, January 2, 185[8], JDPTU.

22. "Autobiography of Jefferson Davis," *JDC*, 1:xxv, xxvii. Written in November 1889, a month before Davis's death, this sketch was published posthumously in *Belford's Magazine*. Davis made a similar argument in *Short History*, 25–26, 32.

23. Scholars know that debates *about* the North American West shaped antebellum politics, but in most studies, western peoples are objects of debate rather than participants; Bleeding Kansas is a notable exception. This book joins the effort to incorporate them more fully into studies of the Civil War era. For a historiographical overview, see S. Smith, "Beyond North and South." Much of this scholarship focuses on the war years or on Reconstruction, but there is much to be gained by integrating diverse western places and peoples into analyses of Civil War causation. Insightful examples include S. Smith, *Freedom's Frontier*; and L. Richards, *California Gold Rush*.

24. Cooper, *JDA*, is excellent on Davis's postbellum life. Key works on Davis as Confederate president include Atchison, *War of Words*; McPherson, *Embattled Rebel*; Cooper, *Jefferson Davis and the Civil War Era*; Hattaway and Beringer, *Jefferson Davis*; Woodworth, *Davis and Lee at War*; Woodworth, *Jefferson Davis and His Generals*; and Escott, *After Secession*.

25. Steven Hahn argues that the key nineteenth-century U.S. struggle was between the Northeast and the Mississippi valley and that the disruption of the northwestern-southwestern alliance, reflected in the rupture of the Democratic Party, made secession and war possible. Hahn, *Nation without Borders*, 3. By tracing that rupture's roots back to the 1830s, this book integrates Hahn's geopolitical insights into a narrative of intraparty conflict.

26. See especially the work of Holt, including *Political Crisis of the 1850s* and *Rise and Fall of the American Whig Party*.

27. D. Brown, "Slavery and the Market Revolution"; R. Brown, "Missouri Crisis"; Ashworth, *Slavery, Capitalism, and Politics*; Landis, *Northern Men*.

28. Earle, *Jacksonian Antislavery*; Feller, "Brother in Arms"; Wilentz, "Jeffersonian Democracy."

29. Neely, *Lincoln and the Democrats*; A. Smith, *Stormy Present*; Baker, *Affairs of Party*; Collins, "Ideology of the Ante-bellum Northern Democrats."

30. On the founding era, see Beard, *Economic Interpretation*; Nedelsky, *Private Property*; Bouton, *Taming Democracy*; and Holton, *Unruly Americans*. On the Jacksonian era, see Schlesinger, *Age of Jackson*; Sellers, *Market Revolution*; and Wilentz, *Rise of American Democracy*. On the Gilded Age, see Brands, *American Colossus*; Beatty, *Age of Betrayal*; and Cohen, *Reconstruction of American Liberalism*. On the New Deal, see Leuchtenburg, *Supreme Court Reborn*. For an overview, see Ely, *Guardian of Every Other Right*.

31. See especially Huston, *Calculating the Value*. Scholars of slavery's legal history have also explored issues of property rights in human beings. See T. Morris, *Southern Slavery and the Law*; Finkelman, *Slavery and the Law*; and Gross, *Double Character*.

32. Mason, *Apostle of Union*, esp. p. 9.

33. Fehrenbacher, *Slaveholding Republic*; Bonner, *Mastering America*; Van Cleve, *Slaveholders' Union*; Ericson, *Slavery in the American Republic*; Karp, *This Vast Southern Empire*.

CHAPTER 1

1. *CG*, 31st Cong., 1st Sess., appendix, 365 (March 13, 1850).

2. *CG*, 31st Cong., 2nd Sess., appendix, 348 (March 1, 1851).

3. "Stephen A. Douglas, 'The Giant of the West,'" *New York Sunday Atlas*, January 5, 1860; "Stephen A. Douglas—The Giant Intellect of the West!!!," *Republican Times* (La Porte, Ind.), February 24, 1857; Gordon, *Reminiscences of the Civil War*, 22.

4. Claiborne, *Life and Correspondence of John A. Quitman*, 1:38–40.

5. *CG*, 31st Cong., 1st Sess., appendix, 1615 (August 21, 1850); *CG*, 31st Cong., 1st Sess., appendix, 365 (March 13, 1850). On the riverine West's nineteenth-century significance, see Arenson, *Great Heart of the Republic*; C. Phillips, *Rivers Ran Backward*; and Hahn, *Nation without Borders*, 3.

6. [Baird], *View of the Valley*, 25, 28, iii.

7. [Baird], 215–34.

8. [Baird], 262–70.

9. [Baird], 54–67.

10. [Baird,] 100–101.

11. For 1808, see Cooper, *JDA*, 711n1; for 1807, see W. Davis, *Jefferson Davis*, 709n8.

12. "Autobiographical Sketch," *PJD*, 1:lxviii.

13. Gideon Gibson to JD, April 27, 1859, PJDRU.

14. JD to William H. Sparke, February 19, 1858, *PJD*, 4:170.

15. Baptist, *Half Has Never Been Told*; W. Johnson, *River of Dark Dreams*; J. H. Moore, *Emergence of the Cotton Kingdom*; C. Morris, *Becoming Southern*; A. Rothman, *Slave Country*.

16. C. Morris, *Becoming Southern*, xiv, xviii–xix, 3–28.

17. J. H. Moore, *Emergence of the Cotton Kingdom*, 16.

18. John Edmund Gonzales, "Flush Times, Depression, War, and Compromise," in McLemore, *History of Mississippi*, 1:284.

19. Quitman to his father, January 16, 1822, in Claiborne, *Life and Correspondence of John A. Quitman*, 1:71–72.

20. R. Davis, *Recollections of Mississippi*, 78.

21. Haynes, *Mississippi Territory*, 133.

22. William K. Scarborough, "Heartland of the Cotton Kingdom," in McLemore, *History of Mississippi*, 1:314; J. H. Moore, *Emergence of the Cotton Kingdom*, 286.

23. C. Morris, *Becoming Southern*, 29.

24. [Ingraham], *South-West*, 2:95.

25. Scarborough, "Heartland of the Cotton Kingdom," 1:311.

26. J. H. Moore, *Emergence of the Cotton Kingdom*, 6–7.

27. A. Rothman, *Slave Country*, 13–14, 17.

28. A. Rothman, 180; J. H. Moore, *Emergence of the Cotton Kingdom*, 158; Fulkerson, *Random Recollections*, 17; Gudmestad, *Steamboats*.

29. Cooper, *JDA*, 16–17, 19.

30. R. Davis, *Recollections of Mississippi*, 78.

31. Porter L. Fortune Jr., "The Formative Period," in McLemore, *History of Mississippi*, 1:259–66; Sydnor, *Development of Southern Sectionalism*, 184–85.

32. A. Rothman, *Slave Country*, 45.

33. Montgomery, *Reminiscences of a Mississippian*, 33.

34. Worster, *Under Western Skies*, 53–63.

35. Quoted in MacLeod, *Slavery, Race and the American Revolution*, 64.

36. [Ingraham], *South-West*, 1:79–80.

37. Everett, *Brierfield*, 7–8; C. Morris, *Becoming Southern*, 141; C. Morris, *Big Muddy*, 116; Hermann, *Pursuit of a Dream*, 6, 11. Humbler neighbors called for public levees so that they, too, might grow cotton in riparian soil. Unwilling to help finance the project and fearful that new levees might elevate the annual floodwaters and inundate their private levees, Joseph and Jefferson Davis defeated the proposal. C. Morris, *Becoming Southern*, 141–42.

38. Quoted in A. Rothman, *Slave Country*, 49.

39. Rothman, 51.

40. Scarborough, "Heartland of the Cotton Kingdom," 1:310.

41. Miles, *Jacksonian Democracy in Mississippi*, 123; Deyle, *Carry Me Back*; W. Johnson, *Soul by Soul*; Tadman, *Speculators and Slaves*.

42. By 1840, half of Mississippians were enslaved, and the free black population was negligible. If roughly half of the whites were female and a significant number of the white males were under twenty-one, then the voting population—referred to as "the people" by politicians then and many historians today—made up a very small minority. In 1840, the number of votes cast in the presidential election was 9.7 percent of the state's population; given the high voter turnout in that age, the enfranchised portion of Mississippi's population was minuscule. Voting was similarly restricted by age, race, and gender in Illinois, but voters still made up a larger portion of the population: in 1840, the number of presidential ballots cast represented 19.5 percent of the total, twice the Mississippi proportion.

43. Sanders, "Jefferson Davis," 36.

44. C. Morris, *Becoming Southern*, xviii.

45. Tate, *Jefferson Davis*, 34; S. Foote, *Civil War*, 1:6; Cooper, *JDA*, 14.

46. Sanders, "Jefferson Davis," 32, 34. Before resolving to judge Davis solely by the values of his time, it is worth remembering that no single set of values on race and slavery prevailed during Davis's life (or today). If one had, the Civil War would not have occurred. Obviously, historians should not simply disparage Davis, but we need not defer to his worldview in order to understand it. Measured by his own yardstick, Davis was a noble statesman and an upright master. As W. E. B. Du Bois pointed out, this tells us less about Davis than about the dubious standards by which admirers measured him. "Judged by the whole standard of Teutonic civilization," wrote Du Bois, "there is something noble in the figure of Jefferson Davis; and judged by every canon of human justice, there is something fundamentally incomplete about that standard." Du Bois, "Jefferson Davis as a Representative of Civilization," W. E. B. Du Bois Papers, Special Collections and University Archives, University of Massachusetts Amherst.

47. "Autobiographical Sketch," *PJD*, 1:lxxiii–lxxiv.

48. C. Morris, *Big Muddy*, 106–7; William Ziegler to JD, February 25, 1849, *PJD*, 4:12–13.

49. [Ingraham], *South-West*, 2:86–87.

50. Beckert, *Empire of Cotton*, 103; Olmsted, *Journey in the Back Country*, 19–20.

51. W. Freehling, *Road to Disunion*, 1:77–97; Paulus, *Slaveholding Crisis*.

52. Olmsted, *Journey in the Back Country*, 444 (quotation); Scarborough, "Heartland of the Cotton Kingdom," 1:329–30; Crane, "Controlling the Night."

53. Quoted in A. Rothman, *Slave Country*, 123–24.

54. "Autobiographical Sketch," *PJD*, 1:lxix (quotation); Sanders, "Jefferson Davis," 45–60.

55. [Ingraham], *South-West*, 2:84–85, 91.

56. [Jennings], *Nine Years of Democratic Rule*, 300.

57. Silver, *Mississippi*, 6 (quotation); Bond, *Political Culture*, 89, 95; Cooper, *South and the Politics of Slavery*.

58. This tension is brilliantly examined in W. Freehling, *Road to Disunion*.

59. Sydnor, *Gentleman of the Old Natchez Region*, 70–72; Fortune, "Formative Period," 1:252, 280–81; Sydnor, *Development of Southern Sectionalism*, 283–84; W. Jordan, *Tumult and Silence*, 61; Gonzales, "Flush Times," 1:284–85.

60. C. Morris, *Becoming Southern*, 143–49; Olsen, *Political Culture and Secession*, 121–22.

61. Olsen, *Political Culture and Secession*, 132–33.

62. D. Jordan, "Mississippi's Antebellum Congressmen," 158–60, 169–70.

63. Hahn, *Nation without Borders*, 106.

64. W. Davis, *Jefferson Davis*, 80.

65. Sanders, "Jefferson Davis," 96, 213–17.

66. W. Davis, *Jefferson Davis*, 19–25; Cooper, *JDA*, 23–28; Sanders, "Jefferson Davis," 90, 114–15.

67. JD to Amanda Davis Bradford, August 2, 1824, in Cooper, *Jefferson Davis: The Essential Writings*, 3.

68. "Autobiographical Sketch," *PJD*, 1:lxxix.

69. JD to Amanda Davis Bradford, August 2, 1824, in Cooper, *Jefferson Davis: The Essential Writings*, 3.

70. Hattaway and Beringer, *Jefferson Davis*, 4.

71. W. Davis, *Jefferson Davis*, 27, 37; Sanders, "Jefferson Davis," 114–25; Catton and Catton, *Two Roads to Sumter*, 37. For a more positive account, see Cooper, *JDA*, 28–40.

72. JD to Joseph Emory Davis, January 12, 1825, *PJD*, 1:18. Emphasis original.

73. W. Davis, *Jefferson Davis*, 30–31; "Proceedings of a Court Martial—Fifth Day Trial of Jefferson Davis," *PJD*, 1:39–41.

74. Cooper, *JDA*, 41–64; W. Davis, *Jefferson Davis*, 39–60.

75. *JDM*, 1:83–92.

76. *JDM*, 1:142–43; Black Hawk, *Life of Ma-Ka-Tai-Me-She-Kia-Kiak*, 137.

77. Shelton, "Young Jefferson Davis," 88–93; W. Davis, *Jefferson Davis*, 58–60.

78. JD to Lucinda Davis Stamps, June 3, 1829, in Cooper, *Jefferson Davis: The Essential Writings*, 9–11.

79. W. Davis, *Jefferson Davis*, 64–69.

80. Cooper, *JDA*, 65–68. Cooper denies that Davis wanted to duel Taylor over his refusal to consent to the marriage. Other scholars, including Sanders ("Jefferson Davis," 193–94), credit the story and point out how extraordinary it would be for Davis to assume that killing his fiancée's father would ensure matrimonial bliss. William C. Davis concludes that Davis did intend to challenge Taylor but was provoked by a professional quarrel (*Jefferson Davis*, 52–53).

81. JD to Sarah Knox Taylor, December 16, 1834, *PJD*, 1:345–47.

82. Cooper, *JDA*, 68–70.

83. J. Rothman, *Flush Times*; Miles, "Mississippi Slave Insurrection Scare"; H. Foote, *Casket of Reminiscences*, 251–62.

84. Cooper, *JDA*, 70–72; Eaton, *Jefferson Davis*, 22.

85. W. Davis, *Jefferson Davis*, 83–85.

86. Bleser, "Marriage of Varina Howell," 6.

87. Cooper, *JDA*, 76–80; Sanders, "Jefferson Davis," 219–20, 228–80; Eaton, *Jefferson Davis*, 37; Everett, *Brierfield*, 22–50; McPherson, *Embattled Rebel*, 29.

88. For clearheaded analysis, see Hermann, *Pursuit of a Dream*, 3–34; and Sanders, "Jefferson Davis," 228–80. Many early biographers readily accepted Varina Davis's postbellum portrait of Brierfield, but she was not recording unvarnished memories; rather, she was making a presentist argument for white supremacy. Writing on the eve

of Mississippi's push to construct the Jim Crow system, Davis used racist nostalgia for the Old South to defend an emerging racist regime in the New. To argue that love and kindness prevailed on plantations in the past was to insist that southern whites should manage race relations in the present. She wrote, "As I look now upon the change in the *personnel* of some of the free negroes, their often declared hostility and armed neutrality toward the whites, I revert with regret to the days when 'love was law' with them; when we nursed their children and they ours, and there was entire mutual confidence." *JDM*, 1:180. On the politics of nostalgia in the New South, see Litwack, *Trouble in Mind*, 184–97; and David Anderson, "Telling Stories, Making Selves: Nostalgia, the Lost Cause, and Postbellum Plantation Memoirs and Reminiscences," in Deslandes, Mourlon, and Tribout, *Civil War and Narrative*, 21–38. On Davis's memoir, see Cashin, *First Lady*, 266–68.

89. Sanders, "Jefferson Davis," 228–30.

90. E. Marsh, *Stephen A. Douglas*, 39–40; Quitt, *Stephen A. Douglas*, 13.

91. James Monaghan to William Bigler, December 31, 1857, box 8, folder 19, William Bigler Papers, HSP.

92. *CG*, 37th Cong., 1st Sess., 35 (July 9, 1861).

93. Douglas's relatives spelled their surname "Douglass," but he switched to "Douglas" in 1846. Johannsen, *SAD*, 876n7. To avoid confusion, I use the more familiar spelling throughout this book.

94. SAD, autobiography, September 1, 1838, box 52, folder 2, SADP; Johannsen, *SAD*, 5–14; Quitt, *Stephen A. Douglas*, 1–36. Douglas's autobiographical sketch is also available in *LSAD*, 56–68.

95. Jefferson G. Thurber to SAD, January 31, 1845, box 1, folder 5, SADP.

96. SAD, autobiography.

97. SAD, autobiography.

98. SAD to Julius N. Granger, December 15, 1833, *LSAD*, 2–3.

99. SAD to Julius N. Granger, November 14, 1834, *LSAD*, 10.

100. Pooley, *Settlement of Illinois*, 313–21, 362–69; Pease, *Frontier State*, 2–11; Doyle, *Social Order*, 19–20; Faragher, *Sugar Creek*, 5–6, 13–14, 21–24, 27–35, 62–67; Capers, *Stephen A. Douglas*, 8–9; "Illinois in 1840," Hezekiah M. Wead Diary (SC 2458), ALPL; Peck, *Making an Antislavery Nation*, 20–22, 40.

101. Huston, *British Gentry*, 72, 82–83, 195–96; Faragher, *Sugar Creek*, 181–87.

102. Doyle, *Social Order*, esp. p. ix.

103. Doyle, 18–38.

104. Peck, *Making an Antislavery Nation*, 44.

105. SAD to Julius N. Granger, July 13, 1834, *LSAD*, 7–8.

106. Pease, *Frontier State*, 150–72; Bowes, *Land Too Good for Indians*, 149–81; Jung, *Black Hawk War*.

107. Pease, *Frontier State*, 31–43.

108. SAD to Julius N. Granger, April 25, 1835, *LSAD*, 13–14.

109. Johannsen, *SAD*, 37–38; Pease, *Frontier State*, 303–4; Buley, *Old Northwest*, 1:626–30.

110. Pease, *Frontier State*, 92, 114–36, 140–43.

111. Tutorow, *Texas Annexation*, 8; Johannsen, *SAD*, 38–39.

112. Quoted in Hammond, *Slavery, Freedom, and Expansion*, 9.

113. Heerman, *Alchemy of Slavery*; Guasco, "'Deadly Influence,'" 10–13; Peck, *Making an Antislavery Nation*, 13–15; Pease, *Frontier State*, 49; Leichtle and Carveth, *Crusade against Slavery*, 74–75; Guasco, *Confronting Slavery*, 89.

114. Hezekiah M. Wead Diary, ALPL (quotation); Pease, *Frontier State*, 47–49; Guasco, *Confronting Slavery*, 86–87; Weiner, *Race and Rights*, 43–45, 209.

115. Pease, *Frontier State*, 70.

116. Pease, *Frontier State*, 73–89; Leichtle and Carveth, *Crusade against Slavery*; Guasco, *Confronting Slavery*; Heerman, *Alchemy of Slavery*, 101–2. For a different interpretation, see Simeone, *Democracy and Slavery*.

117. Guasco, "Deadly Influence," 10.

118. Pease, *Frontier State*, 89; Peck, *Making an Antislavery Nation*, 31–33.

119. Weiner, *Race and Rights*.

120. L. Richards, *"Gentlemen of Property and Standing,"* 100–111; Weiner, *Race and Rights*, 102–8.

121. Allen Persinger to Lyman Trumbull, December 24, 1857, reel 3, Papers of Lyman Trumbull, LC.

122. Pooley, *Settlement of Illinois*, 347; Ankrom, *Stephen A. Douglas*, 14; Huston, *British Gentry*, 74, 159; Guasco, "Deadly Influence," 26–27; Faragher, *Sugar Creek*, 45–49; Berwanger, *Frontier against Slavery*.

123. Doyle, *Social Order*, 6; Buley, *Old Northwest*, 1:47–48.

124. Etcheson, *Emerging Midwest*; Guasco, "Deadly Influence," 9, 26–27.

125. Fehrenbacher, *Prelude to Greatness*, 6; Fehrenbacher, "Illinois Political Attitudes," 197–98. On divisions between the upper and lower South, see W. Freehling, *Road to Disunion*.

126. Finkelman, "Slavery and the Northwest Ordinance"; Zarefsky, *Lincoln, Douglas, and Slavery*, 148–49. On the Southwest, see Hammond, *Slavery, Freedom, and Expansion*.

127. Johannsen, *SAD*, 18–22.

128. D. Roberts, "Reminiscence of Stephen A. Douglas," 958.

129. "Reminiscences of Stephen A. Douglas," 208.

130. Hezekiah M. Wead Diary, ALPL. On the politics of Douglas's sociability, see Quitt, *Stephen A. Douglas*, 6, 65–86. Douglas was not unique; for a similar case of arm-draping and lap-sitting, see Faragher, *Sugar Creek*, 153.

131. SAD to Julius N. Granger, November 14, 1834, *LSAD*, 11.

132. Johannsen, *SAD*, 37; Milton, *Eve of Conflict*, 7.

133. Forney, *Anecdotes of Public Men*, 1:18–20.

134. Ranck, *Albert Gallatin Brown*, 5, 22; Miles, *Jacksonian Democracy in Mississippi*, 5; Oakes, *Ruling Race*; Latner, "New Look at Jacksonian Politics."

135. Hearon, "Nullification in Mississippi," 50–51. The Illinois legislature adopted similar resolutions and ordered 3,000 copies of Jackson's anti-nullification proclamation for distribution. Pease, *Frontier State*, 142.

136. Miles, *Jacksonian Democracy in Mississippi*, 63–69, 155–59, 170–71.

137. John A. Quitman to his brother, October 17, 1835, in Claiborne, *Life and Correspondence of John A. Quitman*, 1:138–39; *JDM*, 1:190; Sydnor, *Development of Southern Sectionalism*, 263; Winston, "Mississippi and the Independence of Texas"; Winston, "Texas Annexation Sentiment"; Winston, "Annexation of Texas."

138. Fletcher, "Oregon or the Grave"; Pletcher, *Diplomacy of Annexation*, 106; Pease, *Frontier State*, 328.

139. Wilentz, *Rise of American Democracy*, 196–99.

140. "The Northwestern Democracy," *Feliciana Democrat* (Clinton, La.), May 23, 1857.

141. Committee of the Regiment, *Story of the Fifty-Fifth Regiment*, 36–37, 230–31.

142. McMahon, "Stephen A. Douglas" (April 1908), 211; Merk, *Manifest Destiny*, 213; Capers, *Stephen A. Douglas*, 87; Hahn, *Nation without Borders*, 3.

CHAPTER 2

1. W. A. Parker to SAD, February 13, 1859, box 24, folder 4, SADP.

2. R. Nichols, *Disruption of American Democracy*.

3. On this literature, see Sellers, "Andrew Jackson versus the Historians"; Formisano, "Toward a Reorientation of Jacksonian Politics"; and Sean Patrick Adams, "Introduction: The President and His Era," in Adams, *Companion to the Era of Andrew Jackson*, 1–11.

4. Historians disagree over using the lenses of section, class, or culture to interpret the party, though scholars of the late antebellum period often use a sectional approach. On the Democracy as a southern-oriented, proslavery force, see D. Brown, "Slavery and the Market Revolution"; R. Brown, "Missouri Crisis"; Ashworth, *Slavery, Capitalism, and Politics*; and Landis, *Northern Men*. For the labor emphasis, see Schlesinger, *Age of Jackson*; and Wilentz, *Rise of American Democracy*. For the western focus, see Latner, "New Look at Jacksonian Politics." Other scholars have emphasized ethnocultural factors; see Benson, *Concept of Jacksonian Democracy*. The relationship between the Democracy and capitalism is also contested: some scholars view the party as a guardian of precapitalist values (Sellers, *Market Revolution*), others as a champion of rising capitalists (Hofstadter, *American Political Tradition*).

5. Martin Van Buren to Thomas Ritchie, January 13, 1827, in Remini, *Age of Jackson*, 3–7 (quotation p. 6).

6. Remini, *Martin Van Buren*; Niven, *Martin Van Buren*; D. Cole, *Martin Van Buren*; Silbey, *Martin Van Buren*.

7. Quoted in Peterson, *Jefferson Image*, 48.

8. Peterson, 3–209; J. Miller, *Wolf by the Ears*.

9. Riley, *Slavery and the Democratic Conscience* (quotation p. 3); Padraig Riley, "Slavery and the Problem of Democracy in Jeffersonian America," in Hammond and Mason, *Contesting Slavery*, 227–46; Wilentz, "Jeffersonian Democracy"; L. Richards, *Slave Power*, 52–82.

10. Remini, *Martin Van Buren*, 28–29, 62, 120–29; Niven, *Martin Van Buren*, 178.

11. Remini, *Age of Jackson*, 6.

12. D. Brown, "Slavery and the Market Revolution"; R. Brown, "Missouri Crisis"; L. Richards, *Slave Power*; Ashworth, *Slavery, Capitalism, and Politics*; Landis, *Northern Men*.

13. Wilentz, *Rise of American Democracy*, 295–96, 860n31; Remini, *Martin Van Buren*, 132; Silbey, *Partisan Imperative*, 87–115; McFaul, "Expediency vs. Morality."

14. T. J. Wharton, "Address to the Senate and House of Representatives of Tennessee," in *Journal of the State Convention*, 160 (quotation); Fehrenbacher, *Slaveholding Republic*; Ericson, *Slavery in the American Republic*; Karp, *This Vast Southern Empire*; Bestor, "State Sovereignty and Slavery."

15. Silbey, *Martin Van Buren*, 41–42, 68–71; Goldman, *Search for Consensus*, 36.

16. Ashworth, *"Agrarians" and "Aristocrats,"* 2–4.

17. Wilentz, *Rise of American Democracy*, 430–31, 509; Miles, *Jacksonian Democracy in Mississippi*, 83–86.

18. Ellis, *Union at Risk*; W. Freehling, *Prelude to Civil War*.

19. Quoted in Sinha, *Counterrevolution of Slavery*, 35.

20. Quoted in Hearon, "Nullification in Mississippi," 60.

21. Ford, *Deliver Us from Evil*, 481–99 (quotations p. 499).

22. Quoted in Ashworth, *"Agrarians" and "Aristocrats,"* 49.

23. Wilentz, *Rise of American Democracy*, 320–21, 429–33, 535–37; Ashworth, *"Agrarians" and "Aristocrats,"* 240–44; Leonard, *Invention of Party Politics*, 252–59; Bean, "Anti-Jeffersonianism in the Antebellum South"; Sydnor, *Development of Southern Sectionalism*, 334; Schlesinger, *Age of Jackson*, 242–49; Peterson, *Jefferson Image*, 164–71.

24. Cooper, *South and the Politics of Slavery*, 104–8.

25. Rugemer, *Problem of Emancipation*; Karp, *This Vast Southern Empire*; Paulus, *Slaveholding Crisis*.

26. Stewart, *Holy Warriors*; Walters, *Antislavery Appeal*; Harrold, *Abolitionists and the South*; Sinha, *Slave's Cause*.

27. Wilentz, "Jeffersonian Democracy."

28. *Register of Debates*, 24th Cong., 1st Sess., 2678 (March 2, 1836).

29. *Register of Debates*, 24th Cong., 1st Sess., 3429 (April 28, 1836).

30. Earle, *Jacksonian Antislavery*; Feller, "Brother in Arms."

31. R. Brown, "Missouri Crisis," 70–71.

32. Cooper, *South and the Politics of Slavery*, 52–53, 74–83, 94–95.

33. D. Cole, *Martin Van Buren*, 266–72; Wilentz, *Rise of American Democracy*, 446–53.

34. [Tucker], *Partisan Leader*, 23.

35. Shade, "'Most Delicate and Exciting Topics.'"

36. W. Freehling, *Road to Disunion*, 1:339–40.

37. M. Wilson, *Presidency of Martin Van Buren*; D. Cole, *Martin Van Buren*, 285–380; Rediker, Amistad *Rebellion*.

38. Quoted in D. Cole, *Martin Van Buren*, 261.

39. Cooper, *South and the Politics of Slavery*, 132–48; W. Freehling, *Road to Disunion*, 1:361–63; Monroe, *Republican Vision of John Tyler*, 50–76.

40. *Madison (Miss.) Whig Advocate*, August 15, 1840.

41. W. Freehling, *Road to Disunion*, 1:363.

42. Ashworth, *"Agrarians" and "Aristocrats,"* 243–44.

43. Walker, *Letter of Mr. Walker*.

44. Paul, *Rift in the Democracy*, 33–123; Silbey, *Storm over Texas*, 52–79.

45. Martin Van Buren to W[illiam] H[enry] Hammet[t], April 20, 1844, Papers of Martin Van Buren, Cumberland University.

46. Paul, *Rift in the Democracy*, 122–80; Silbey, *Storm over Texas*, 80–90.

47. Rayback, *Free Soil*; Blue, *Free Soilers*; Mayfield, *Rehearsal for Republicanism*; Earle, *Jacksonian Antislavery*, 144–80; C. Brooks, *Liberty Power*, 105–54.

48. D. Cole, *Martin Van Buren*, 419, 424–25.

49. For this tension in southern politics, see W. Freehling, *Road to Disunion*, 2:xii–xiii. A similar tension emerged as northerners debated whether slavery or antislavery activism posed the greater threat to union and liberty.

50. SAD to Adele Cutts, September 8, 10, 19, 21, 24, 28, October 1, 6, 10, 12, 14, 15, 19, 23, 27, November 2, 1856, box 52, folder 10, SADP.

51. *Biographical Sketch of Stephen A. Douglas*, 7.

52. Milton, *Eve of Conflict*, 16.

53. Ankrom, *Stephen A. Douglas*, 7; *Biographical Sketch of Stephen A. Douglas*, 2; Quitt, *Stephen A. Douglas*, 65.

54. *CG*, 28th Cong., 1st Sess., appendix, 43–46 (January 7, 1844).

55. *Biographical Sketch of Stephen A. Douglas*, 5. Critics dismissed the meeting, first described in 1844 and widely recounted in 1852, as apocryphal; see, for instance, Pease and Randall, *Diary of Orville Hickman Browning*, 390–91. Robert Johannsen, citing sources written closer to the alleged event, argues that it was real; see Johannsen, *SAD*, 889n1.

56. Invitation to Andrew Jackson's Funeral, June 9, 1845, box 55, folder 11, SADP.

57. SAD to Gehazi Granger, November 9, 1835, *LSAD*, 20–21.

58. "To the Democratic Republicans of Illinois," [November 1837], *LSAD*, 42.

59. "To the Democratic Republicans of Illinois," [December 31, 1835], *LSAD*, 24–31.

60. Johannsen, *SAD*, 44–45.

61. Buley, *Old Northwest*, 2:222; Ankrom, *Stephen A. Douglas*, 68–69; Johannsen, *SAD*, 46–47.

62. "Autobiographical Sketch," *LSAD*, 67.

63. Pratt, "Stephen A. Douglas," pt. 1, 157; Ankrom, *Stephen A. Douglas*, 55; Johannsen, *SAD*, 31–35.

64. SAD to Julius N. Granger, April 8, 1836, *LSAD*, 36.

65. Quitt, *Stephen A. Douglas*, 66–68, 85.

66. Pratt, "Stephen A. Douglas," pt. 1, 160; Johannsen, *SAD*, 47–48.

67. "Autobiographical Sketch," *LSAD*, 68.

68. Johannsen, *SAD*, 48–51.

69. "Autobiographical Sketch," *LSAD*, 68; Johannsen, *SAD*, 50–51.

70. Pease, *Frontier State*, 216–35; Peck, *Making an Antislavery Nation*, 46; A. Roberts, *America's First Great Depression*, 59–60.

71. Ankrom, *Stephen A. Douglas*, 123; *History of Sangamon County*, 564.

72. SAD to Julius N. Granger, December 18, 1837, *LSAD*, 51.

73. McConnell, "Recollections of Stephen A. Douglas," 42.

74. SAD to Lewis W. Ross, August 12, 1837, *LSAD*, 39 (quotation); Johannsen, *SAD*, 64–65.

75. Sheahan, *Life of Stephen A. Douglas*, 36–37; Pierce, *History of Chicago*, 1:377; Johannsen, *SAD*, 64–67.

76. SAD to John T. Stuart, March 4, 1839, *LSAD*, 70–72 (quotation p. 70); SAD to Francis Preston Blair, November 2, 1838, *LSAD*, 69; Thomas H. Benton to SAD, Octo-

ber 27, 1838, box 1, folder 1, SADP; Johannsen, *SAD*, 67–72; Huston, *Stephen A. Douglas*, 18–19; Pierce, *History of Chicago*, 1:423; Faragher, *Sugar Creek*, 149.

77. *Quincy Whig*, September 22, 1838, quoted in R. Morris, *Long Pursuit*, 20; Johannsen, *SAD*, 69.

78. SAD to L. W. Ross, June 27, 1840, box 1, folder 1, Stephen A. Douglas Papers, ALPL.

79. Herndon and Weik, *Herndon's Lincoln*, 127; Donald, *Lincoln*, 79.

80. Abraham Lincoln to John T. Stuart, March 1, 1840, *CWAL*, 1:206.

81. Johannsen, *SAD*, 73–82; Wilentz, *Rise of American Democracy*, 482–507.

82. Hezekiah M. Wead Diary, ALPL.

83. Johannsen, *SAD*, 104–10; Pratt, "Stephen A. Douglas," pt. 2, 236–37; Brigham Young to SAD, December 17, 1845, box 1, folder 5, and Brigham Young to SAD, April 29, 1852, box 42, folder 5, SADP.

84. The tome is in box 63, folder 1, SADP. Douglas also cosigned a message "To the Anti-Mormon Citizens of Hancock County" [October 4, 1845], which vindicated Mormons' rights; see *LSAD*, 122–24.

85. SAD to Adele Cutts, November 2, 1856, box 52, folder 10, SADP.

86. Johannsen, *SAD*, 101–3; Huston, *Stephen A. Douglas*, 31–32.

87. Johannsen, *SAD*, 116–23; "Election Returns for Congress," *Illinois Free Trader and LaSalle County Commercial Advertiser* (Ottawa), September 8, 1843.

88. Silbey, *Storm over Texas*, 28–79; Paul, *Rift in the Democracy*, 1–30.

89. Johansen and Gates, *Empire of the Columbia*, 227–29; Woodworth, *Manifest Destinies*, 57–72; Fletcher, "Oregon or the Grave"; Pease, *Frontier State*, 328; "Oregon—the New El Dorado," *Illinois Free Trader and LaSalle County Commercial Advertiser*, March 10, 1843; "Oregon Territory," *Illinois State Journal* (Springfield), February 23, 1843; "Missionaries to Oregon," *Illinois State Journal*, October 25, 1839.

90. *Alton (Ill.) Telegraph*, November 9, 1839, quoted in Pletcher, *Diplomacy of Annexation*, 66; "What Is Oregon Worth?," *Illinois State Journal*, February 5, 1846; "The Oregon Trade—a Peep into the Pacific," *Illinois State Journal*, October 30, 1845; "The Oregon Meeting," *Illinois State Journal*, June 26, 1845; Graebner, *Empire on the Pacific*, 127–28, 223.

91. Pletcher, *Diplomacy of Annexation*, 106; Schwantes, *Pacific Northwest*, 108; Hietala, *Manifest Design*, 55–94.

92. Unruh, *Plains Across*, 3.

93. Edward Smith to SAD, November 25, 1844, box 1, folder 2; Mark Skinner to SAD, December 11, 1844, box 1, folder 4; James Shields to SAD, January 12, 1845, box 1, folder 5; Jefferson G. Thurber to SAD, January 31, 1845, box 1, folder 5; Benjamin Douglass to SAD, December 8, 1845, box 1, folder 5, SADP.

94. Robert W. Johannsen, "Meaning of Manifest Destiny," in Johannsen et al., *Manifest Destiny and Empire*, 16–17.

95. *CG*, 28th Cong., 1st Sess., appendix, 23 (December 19, 1843).

96. *CG*, 28th Cong., 1st Sess., 527–28 (April 17, 1844).

97. *CG*, 28th Cong., 1st Sess., 527–28 (April 17, 1844).

98. *CG*, 28th Cong., 1st Sess., 541–42 (April 20, 1844).

99. Mark Skinner to SAD, December 11, 1844, box 1, folder 4, SADP.

100. James K. Scott to SAD, December 18, 1844, box 1, folder 4, SADP.

101. *CG*, 28th Cong., 2nd Sess., 384–85 (March 1, 1845).

102. *CG*, 28th Cong., 2nd Sess., 224–27 (January 31, 1845).

103. *CG*, 28th Cong., 2nd Sess., 197–98 (January 27, 1845); Greenhow, *History of Oregon and California*.

104. *CG*, 28th Cong., 2nd Sess., 173 (January 22, 1845).

105. *CG*, 28th Cong., 2nd Sess., 41 (December 17, 1844).

106. *JDM*, 2:12.

107. Pollard, *Lost Cause*, 90–91.

108. Crist, "Jefferson Davis and Abraham Lincoln"; Escott, *After Secession*; David M. Potter, "Jefferson Davis and the Political Factors in Confederate Defeat," in Donald, *Why the North Won the Civil War*, 57–69. For a contrasting view, see L. Johnson, "Jefferson Davis and Abraham Lincoln."

109. *JDM*, 1:206, 225, 470.

110. William J. Cooper Jr., "Jefferson Davis and the Sudden Disappearance of Southern Politics," in *Jefferson Davis and the Civil War Era*, 3–10. On Davis's restless ambition, see Dirck, *Lincoln and Davis*, 22–23, 75.

111. McElroy, *Jefferson Davis*, 61; Werstein, *Abraham Lincoln versus Jefferson Davis*, 2; H. Hamilton, *Three Kentucky Presidents*, 13–14.

112. "Manuscript Material for *Rise and Fall* or for Proposed Autobiography [1877–80]," *PJD*, 13:587.

113. Cooper, *JDA*, 83–85.

114. JD to William Allen, July 24, 1840, *JDC*, 1:5.

115. *JDM*, 1:188.

116. Watson Van Benthuysen to JD, February 12, 1838, PJDRU.

117. Joseph Emory Davis to JD, July 23, 1840, *PJD*, 1:464–65.

118. JD to George W. Jones, February 9, 1839, *JDC*, 1:2–4.

119. W. Davis, *Jefferson Davis*, 92; Allen, *Jefferson Davis*, 100.

120. Cooper, *JDA*, 81–83; Sanders, "Jefferson Davis," 252–53; Shelton, "Young Jefferson Davis," 111–14.

121. *CG*, 25th Cong., 2nd Sess., 55 (December 27, 1837).

122. Cooper, *South and the Politics of Slavery*, 112; Wilentz, *Rise of American Democracy*, 476.

123. Cooper, *JDA*, 86.

124. *Vicksburg Sentinel*, November 1, 1843, quoted in McElroy, *Jefferson Davis*, 46; Cooper, *JDA*, 86–87.

125. Hansen, "Jefferson Davis"; "Notice of the Warren County Election Returns," *PJD*, 2:49; Cooper, *JDA*, 88–89; W. Davis, *Jefferson Davis*, 93–95.

126. Varina Banks Howell to Margaret K. Howell, [December 19, 1843], *PJD*, 2:52–53.

127. "Speech of Jefferson Davis before the State Democratic Convention Held in Jackson, Mississippi, January 3, 1844," *JDC*, 1:6–9 (quotation p. 7).

128. JD to Martin Van Buren, March 25, 1844, and enclosure, *JDC*, 1:11–12.

129. Winston, "Mississippi and the Independence of Texas."

130. Siegel, *Political History of the Texas Republic*, 5–6.

131. *JDM*, 1:190.

132. Winston, "Texas Annexation Sentiment," 5 (quotation); Sydnor, *Development of Southern Sectionalism*, 322.

133. C. A. Bradford to C. D. Fontaine, April 19, 1844, box 1, folder 3, Fontaine (Charles D.) and Family Papers, MDAH (quotation); Cooper, *South and the Politics of Slavery*, 208–18.

134. Dusinberre, *Slavemaster President*.

135. Winston, "Texas Annexation Sentiment," 15; Cooper, *JDA*, 100–104.

136. See the speeches reprinted in *PJD*, 2:165–216; Cooper, *JDA*, 101–2; and W. Davis, *Jefferson Davis*, 102–5.

137. Johannsen, *SAD*, 143–44.

138. *CG*, 28th Cong., 1st Sess., appendix, 598–602 (June 3, 1844).

139. Johannsen, *SAD*, 149–51.

140. Wilentz, *Rise of American Democracy*, 373–75; W. Freehling, *Road to Disunion*, 1:437–39.

141. JD to Varina Banks Howell, November 22, 1844, *PJD*, 2:224–25.

142. Cooper, *JDA*, 90–98.

143. *JDM*, 1:206.

144. Cooper, *JDA*, 105–10; W. Davis, *Jefferson Davis*, 108–14.

145. "The Election," *Yazoo Democrat*, November 12, 1845.

146. For Douglas's resolutions, see *CG*, 28th Cong., 2nd Sess., 65–66 (December 23, 1844). For debates, see pp. 84–89 (January 3, 1845), and appendix, 65–68 (January 6, 1845). For the final vote, see pp. 193–94 (January 25, 1845). See also Silbey, *Storm over Texas*, 80–90; and Johannsen, *SAD*, 153–57. One of Davis's first acts in Congress was to vote with Douglas and a large majority to admit the state of Texas, the final step of annexation. *CG*, 29th Cong., 1st Sess., 65 (December 16, 1845).

147. *CG*, 28th Cong., 2nd Sess., appendix, 68 (January 6, 1845). Emphasis original.

148. *CG*, 28th Cong., 2nd Sess., 201–2 (January 27, 1845).

149. Varina Banks Howell Davis to Margaret K. Howell, January 30, 1846, *PJD*, 2:421.

150. *CG*, 29th Cong., 1st Sess., 25 (December 8, 1845). For Douglas's efforts to manage Oregon legislation, see p. 172 (January 9, 1846).

151. "Notice of a Political Meeting—Speech by Jefferson Davis [September 2, 1845]"; "Notice of a Political Meeting—Speech by Jefferson Davis [September 5, 1845]"; and "Notice of a Political Meeting—Speech by Jefferson Davis [September 15, 1845]," in *PJD*, 2:324–25, 326–37, 337–38.

152. George D. Phillips to Howell Cobb, February 25, 1845, in U. Phillips, "Correspondence of Robert Toombs," 67.

153. Robert Toombs to George W. Crawford, February 6, 1846, in U. Phillips, "Correspondence of Robert Toombs," 74.

154. Benjamin Douglass to SAD, December 8, 1845, box 1, folder 5, SADP. Emphasis original.

155. Pletcher, *Diplomacy of Annexation*, 272n115.

156. *CG*, 29th Cong., 1st Sess., 86 (December 19, 1845).

157. *CG*, 29th Cong., 1st Sess., 125–27 (January 2, 1846) (quotation p. 126); 131–32, 137 (January 3, 1846).

158. *CG*, 29th Cong., 1st Sess., 126 (January 2, 1846).

159. "Oregon," *Ottawa (Ill.) Free Trader*, January 23, 1846.

160. *CG*, 29th Cong., 1st Sess., appendix, 212–17 (February 6, 1846).

161. For the former, Cooper, *JDA*, 117; for the latter, see Sanders, "Jefferson Davis," 335–36.

162. *CG*, 29th Cong., 1st Sess., 526 (March 19, 1846).

163. Taylor, *Internal Enemy*; G. Smith, *Slaves' Gamble*; Karp, *This Vast Southern Empire*, 32–49, 51–57.

164. *CG*, 29th Cong., 1st Sess., 685–87 (April 17, 1846).

165. Pletcher, *Diplomacy of Annexation*, 217–20, 402–17.

166. "1844 Democratic Party Platform," American Presidency Project; James K. Polk, "Inaugural Address," American Presidency Project.

167. *CG*, 29th Cong., 1st Sess., 1224 (June 18, 1846).

168. Persinger, "'Bargain of 1844.'"

169. Graebner, *Empire on the Pacific*, 36; Foner, "Wilmot Proviso Revisited"; Earle, *Jacksonian Antislavery*, 235–36n37.

170. *Cleveland Plain Dealer* quoted in M. Morrison, *Slavery and the American West*, 43.

171. Quoted in Pletcher, *Diplomacy of Annexation*, 335.

172. Charles Fletcher to SAD, August 3, 1846, box 1, folder 7, SADP.

173. John H. Lumpkin to Howell Cobb, November 13, 1846, in U. Phillips, "Correspondence of Robert Toombs," 86.

174. John H. Lumpkin to Howell Cobb, November 13, 1846, in Phillips, "Correspondence of Robert Toombs," 86.

175. Merk, *Manifest Destiny*, 70–71; Johannsen, *SAD*, 170–71; *Journal of the Proceedings of the South-Western Convention*.

176. *CG*, 29th Cong., 1st Sess., 530–31 (March 20, 1846).

177. *CG*, 29th Cong., 1st Sess., 497 (March 13, 1846).

178. *CG*, 29th Cong., 1st Sess., appendix, 434–37 (March 16, 1846). On his support for Mississippi improvements, see p. 119 (December 30, 1845).

179. *CG*, 29th Cong., 1st Sess., 530 (March 20, 1846).

180. *CG*, 29th Cong., 1st Sess., 1183–84 (August 3, 1846).

181. *CG*, 29th Cong., 1st Sess., 559 (March 26, 1846).

182. Greeley, *Recollections of a Busy Life*, 288.

183. Quaife, *Diary of James K. Polk*, 1:280.

184. "Annexation," *United States Magazine and Democratic Review* 17 (July and August 1845): 5.

185. *Boston Daily Atlas*, December 23, 1845, quoted in May, *Slavery, Race, and Conquest*, 36.

CHAPTER 3

1. Thomas C. Charles to Emma C. Crutcher, January 13, 1853, Charles-Crutcher-McRaven Papers, MDAH.

2. Thomas C. Charles to My Dear Father, December 28, 1854, Charles-Crutcher-McRaven Papers, MDAH.

3. *CG*, 29th Cong., 1st Sess., appendix, 212 (January 10, 1846).

4. Ellen Charles to Malvina Charles, April 2, 1853, Charles-Crutcher-McRaven Papers, MDAH.

5. Mary Jane Lanier to Ellen Charles, May 9, June 21, 1853, Charles-Crutcher-McRaven Papers, MDAH.

6. John W. McRaven to Ellen Charles, July 10, 1855, Charles-Crutcher-McRaven Papers, MDAH.

7. Laura DeFrance to Thomas C. Charles, August 20, 1865, Charles-Crutcher-McRaven Papers, MDAH. Emphasis original.

8. John J. Hardin to SAD, June 13, 1846, box 1, folder 6, SAD papers.

9. *Illinois State Register* (Springfield), July 17, 1846, quoted in Greenberg, *Wicked War*, 113; Tutorow, *Texas Annexation*, 128, 137, 196.

10. W. Alexander Hacker to John A. McClernand, January 22, 1848, box 1, folder 6, John A. McClernand Papers, ALPL.

11. Quaife, *Diary of James K. Polk*, 1:482–85.

12. *CG*, 29th Cong., 1st Sess., appendix, 903–8 (May 13, 1846); Johannsen, *SAD*, 195–200.

13. Quaife, *Diary of James K. Polk*, 2:275–76, 284–85; 3:236–37.

14. Quaife, 4:193.

15. SAD to Sidney Breese, October 20, 1846; SAD to Harry Wilton, November 14, 1846; SAD to Hall Simms, November 16, 1846; SAD to William Martin, November 16, 1846; SAD to Sidney Breese, November 19, 1846; SAD to John D. Caton, November 24, 1846, *LSAD*, 144, 146–47, 147, 147–48, 148–49, 149–50; Johannsen, *SAD*, 187–89.

16. John A. Quitman to Jacob Thompson et al., May 22, 1846, *Vicksburg Sentinel and Expositor*, June 2, 1846.

17. Winders, *Panting for Glory*, 5.

18. Winders, 11.

19. Varina Banks Howell Davis to Margaret K. Howell, June 6, 1846, *PJD*, 2:641–42; *JDM*, 1:246.

20. Jefferson Davis to the People of Mississippi, July 13, 1846, *JDC*, 1:52–58. Polk asked Davis to stay until the tariff bill passed; see McElroy, *Jefferson Davis*, 74.

21. Joseph E. Davis to JD, [October] 7, 1846, *PJD*, 3:55–56; see also 56n5.

22. JD to Robert J. Walker, July 22, November 30, 1846; Joseph E. Davis to JD, April 16, 23, May 13, 1847, *PJD*, 3:11–12, 89–91, 164–65, 167–68, 172–73.

23. W. Davis, *Jefferson Davis*, 175.

24. The sketch of Davis's wartime exploits draws on Winders, *Panting for Glory*; Cooper, *JDA*, 129–56; and W. Davis, *Jefferson Davis*, 129–60.

25. *JDM*, 1:332, 359.

26. Winders, *Panting for Glory*, 81.

27. *Vicksburg Sentinel* quoted in *True Democrat* (Paulding, Miss.), October 14, 1846.

28. Robert W. Johannsen, "Young America and the War with Mexico," in Francaviglia and Richmond, *Dueling Eagles*, 167.

29. Winders, *Panting for Glory*, 47–48; Cooper, *JDA*, 144–46.

30. John A. Quitman to Frederick Henry Quitman, January 11, 1847, Quitman (John A.) Papers, MDAH.

31. Tingley, "Jefferson Davis–William H. Bissell Duel."

32. William H. Bissell to Joseph Gillespie, March 11, 1850, box 1, folder 1, Joseph Gillespie Papers, ALPL.

33. Joseph Davis to JD, May 13, 1847, *PJD*, 3:172.

34. Albert Gallatin Brown to JD, August 10, 1847, *JDC*, 1:92–93.

35. JD to Albert Gallatin Brown, August 15, 1847, *JDC*, 1:93–94.

36. JD to [Simon Cameron], July 26, 1847, *PJD*, 3:196–97.

37. JD to C. J. Searles, September 19, 1847, *JDC*, 1:94–96.

38. Clinton, "Stephen Arnold Douglas"; Johannsen, *SAD*, 206–9, 299–300, 337–38, 689–90; Quitt, *Stephen A. Douglas*, 186–94. Douglas's absentee management can be traced through his correspondence with Strickland and his New Orleans agents, Brander Williams and Ward, Hunt, and Company. See SADP and Stephen A. Douglas Incoming Correspondence and Papers, ALPL.

39. *Weekly Chicago Democrat*, October 27, 1847, quoted in Pierce, *History of Chicago*, 1:122–23; Pierce, *History of Chicago*, 1:44n4, 47–48, 57–58, 67–68, 77, 91–95, 119–22, 127, 128, 2:35, 40, 50–53, 76, 77; Johannsen, *SAD*, 209.

40. Pierce, *History of Chicago*, 1:91–95, 394; Johannsen, *SAD*, 209–211; Salzmann, *Liquid Capital*, 1–7, 14–42; Egnal, *Clash of Extremes*, 101–2.

41. Jentz and Schneirov, *Chicago in the Age of Capital*, 13–17, 24.

42. Pierce, *History of Chicago*, 2:144; Milton, *Eve of Conflict*, 7.

43. Cronon, *Nature's Metropolis*.

44. SAD to Asa Whitney, October 15, 1845, *LSAD*, 127–33.

45. Johannsen, *Frontier, the Union, and Stephen A. Douglas*, 103–19.

46. R. J. Ryan to SAD, January 27, 1858, box 14, folder 9, SADP.

47. Gardner, *Life of Stephen A. Douglas*; Milton, *Eve of Conflict*; Capers, *Stephen A. Douglas*.

48. *CG*, 30th Cong., 1st Sess., 526 (March 22, 1848).

49. *CG*, 30th Cong., 1st Sess., 467 (March 15, 1848).

50. *CG*, 30th Cong., 1st Sess., 765 (May 13, 1848), 772 (May 16, 1848).

51. *CG*, 30th Cong., 1st Sess., 1009 (July 28, 1848) (quotation); Addis, "Whitman Massacre."

52. Pacheco, *The* Pearl; Sewell, *John P. Hale*, 114–18.

53. *CG*, 30th Cong., 1st Sess., appendix, 501 (April 20, 1848).

54. *CG*, 30th Cong., 1st Sess., appendix, 506 (April 20, 1848).

55. H. Foote, *Casket of Reminiscences*, 75.

56. *CG*, 30th Cong., 1st Sess., appendix, 506 (April 20, 1848).

57. Estes, *Defence of Negro Slavery*. On "positive good" proslavery, see Tise, *Proslavery*; McCardell, *Idea of a Southern Nation*, 49–91; Ford, *Deliver Us from Evil*, 505–34; and Fox-Genovese and Genovese, *Slavery in White and Black*.

58. *CG*, 30th Cong., 1st Sess., appendix, 506–7 (April 20, 1848).

59. *JDM*, 1:377.

60. Varina Davis remembered Oregon as "the most important issue" of the Thirtieth Congress. *JDM*, 1:379.

61. Lee, "Slavery and the Oregon Territorial Issue"; Ranck, *Albert Gallatin Brown*, 54; Bergeron, *Presidency of James K. Polk*, 200–206; Johannsen, *Frontier Politics*, 16–17.

62. Harmon, "Douglas and the Compromise of 1850," 454.

63. W. Davis, *Jefferson Davis*, 178–83; McElroy, *Jefferson Davis*, 103; Cooper, *JDA*, 169–75.

64. *CG*, 30th Cong., 1st Sess., appendix, 907–14 (July 12, 1848).

65. Johannsen, *SAD*, 224–25.

66. *CG*, 30th Cong., 1st Sess., 1078 (August 12, 1848).

67. Johannsen, *SAD*, 225.

68. Potter, *Impending Crisis*, 54–61.

69. C. Morrison, *Democratic Politics and Sectionalism*; Foner, "Wilmot Proviso Revisited."

70. Blue, *Free Soilers*, 16–103; Mayfield, *Rehearsal for Republicanism*, 8–125; C. Brooks, *Liberty Power*, 105–54.

71. JD to Malcom D. Haynes, August 18, 1849, *PJD*, 4:26–44 (quotations); "Speech at Jackson" [September 23, 1848], *PJD*, 3:379.

72. "Protest against the California Bill" [August 13, 1850], *JDC*, 1:504; "Speech at Raymond" [October 26, 1850], *PJD*, 4:135–36.

73. Tutorow, *Texas Annexation*, 145–48.

74. Quoted in Tutorow, 180.

75. "Politics," *National Era* (Washington, D.C.), May 4, 1848.

76. Johannsen, *SAD*, 252–54.

77. "Senator Douglas's Speech, Delivered at the Representatives' Hall, at Springfield, on the Evening of the 23d October, 1849," *Washington (D.C.) Daily Union*, November 29, 1849 (quotations); *CG*, 30th Cong., 2d Sess., 314–15 (January 22, 1849); Huston, *Stephen A. Douglas*, 72; Collins, "Ideology of the Ante-bellum Northern Democrats," 105–6.

78. *CG*, 31st Cong., 1st Sess., 343 (February 12, 1850) (quotation); *CG*, 31st Cong., 1st Sess., appendix, 152 (February 13, 1850).

79. *CG*, 29th Cong., 2nd Sess., 455 (February 19, 1847); Lee, "Slavery and the Oregon Territorial Issue," 112–13; Bestor, "State Sovereignty and Slavery."

80. *CG*, 31st Cong., 1st Sess., 343 (February 12, 1850).

81. Cooper, *South and the Politics of Slavery*, 236.

82. JD to C. J. Searles, September 19, 1847, *JDC*, 1:95 (quotation); "Speech at Jackson" [September 23, 1848], *PJD*, 3:379; JD to Malcom D. Haynes, August 18, 1849, *PJD*, 4:32, 43–44; Escott, "Jefferson Davis and Slavery in the Territories."

83. Brown, "Last Annual Message as Governor of Mississippi" [January 3, 1848], in Cluskey, *Speeches, Messages, and Other Writings*, 103–4.

84. "Public Meeting," *Mississippi Creole* (Canton), February 23, 1849.

85. Johannsen, *SAD*, 200–205; Cooper, *JDA*, 172–73.

86. Quaife, *Diary of James K. Polk*, 3:502–3.

87. *CG*, 30th Cong., 1st Sess., 1061 (August 10, 1848).

88. Childers, *Failure of Popular Sovereignty*, 9–101; Dennison, "Empire of Liberty."

89. Childers, *Failure of Popular Sovereignty*, 102–65; Lewis Cass to Henry Horn, January 6, 1848, box 3, Lewis Cass Papers, William L. Clements Library, University of Michigan.

90. Lewis Cass to A. O. P. Nicholson, December 24, 1847, in *Washington Daily Union*, December 30, 1847.

91. Dennison, "Empire of Liberty"; Willard Carl Klunder, "Lewis Cass, Stephen Douglas, and Popular Sovereignty: The Demise of Democratic Party Unity," in McDonough

and Noe, *Politics and Culture of the Civil War Era*, 129–53; Childers, "Interpreting Popular Sovereignty." On Douglas's role, see McMahon, "Stephen A. Douglas" (April 1908 and July 1908); Hubbart, "Revisionist Interpretations"; Nevins, "Stephen A. Douglas"; Jeffrey, "Stephen Arnold Douglas"; E. Dean, "Stephen A. Douglas"; Huston, "Democracy by Scripture"; and Peck, "Was Stephen A. Douglas Antislavery?"

92. Johannsen, "Stephen A. Douglas and the South," 34; Bestor, "State Sovereignty and Slavery."

93. Etcheson, "'Living, Creeping Lie'"; Huston, "Democracy by Scripture"; Burt, *Lincoln's Tragic Pragmatism*, 62–88, 84–177; A. Smith, *Stormy Present*, 100–133.

94. JD to Howell Hinds, September 30, 1856, *PJD*, 4:50–52 (quotation); W. Davis, *Jefferson Davis*, 171–72.

95. JD to Woodville Citizens, October 23, 1848, *PJD*, 3:390 (quotations); "Speech at Aberdeen [October 18, 1849]," *Southron* (Jackson, Miss.), October 26, 1849; Cooper, *JDA*, 178; Escott, "Jefferson Davis and Slavery in the Territories," 100–104.

96. *CG*, 31st Cong., 1st Sess., 1004 (May 15, 1850).

97. James C. Dobbin to Howell Cobb, June 14, 1848, in U. Phillips, "Correspondence of Robert Toombs," 108.

98. Johannsen, *SAD*, 225–34; Capers, *Stephen A. Douglas*, 55.

99. "Speech of the Hon. S. A. Douglas, U.S. Senator," *Washington Daily Union*, June 24, 1848.

100. On expected free-soil outcomes, see May, "'Southern Strategy'"; Hubbart, "Revisionist Interpretations," 104; Collins, "Ideology of the Ante-bellum Northern Democrats," 105–7; Huston, *Stephen A. Douglas*, 72; Burt, *Lincoln's Tragic Pragmatism*, 46–47; Hyman and Wiecek, *Equal Justice under Law*, 134; and M. Morrison, *Slavery and the American West*, 123.

101. *CG*, 31st Cong., 1st Sess., appendix, 371 (March 13, 1850).

102. James L. Huston, "The Continuing Debate about the 'Great Debates' of 1858: A Critical Review of Recent Literature," in Johannsen, *Lincoln-Douglas Debates*, xxvi–xxviii.

103. "Speech of the Hon. S. A. Douglas, U.S. Senator," *Washington Daily Union*, June 24, 1848.

104. *CG*, 31st Cong., 1st Sess., appendix, 369–70 (March 13, 1850) (quotations); *CG*, 33rd Cong., 1st Sess., 278–79 (January 30, 1854); SAD to Edward Coles, February 18, 1854, *LSAD*, 290–98; "Speech of Stephen A. Douglas at Columbus, Ohio, September 7, 1859," in Jaffa and Johannsen, *In the Name of the People*, 137. See also James M. Lucas to SAD, December 9, 1857, box 10, folder 5, SADP.

105. Hammond, *Slavery, Freedom, and Expansion*; Saler, *Settlers' Empire*; St. John, "State Power in the West." On the strength of Douglas's argument, see Zarefsky, *Lincoln, Douglas, and Slavery*, 148–49; and Quitt, *Stephen A. Douglas*, 115n36.

106. Quitt, *Stephen A. Douglas*.

107. Jesse Applegate to Joseph Lane, October 5, 1851, box 1, folder 4; D. R. Bigelow to Joseph Lane, December 21, 1851, box 1, folder 7; Anson G. Henry to Joseph Lane, March 4, 1852, box 1, folder 12, Joseph Lane Papers, ORHS; Joseph Lane to Asahel Bush, January 24, December 17, 1856, box 1, folder 19, Asahel Bush Letters, ORHS; Samuel R. Thurston to Elizabeth Thurston, June 9, 1850, in Perry, Chused, and DeLano, "Spousal Letters of Samuel R. Thurston," 33–34.

108. Austin Phelps to Joseph Lane, February 15, 1852, box 3, folder 15, Joseph Lane Papers, ORHS.

109. "A Memorial to the Congress of the United States" [ca. 1849], box 41, folder 5; "Protection of Intercourse between the Atlantic and Pacific States, by an Overland Route," Joint Resolutions of the General Assembly of the State of Iowa, January 25, 1855, box 44, folder 1; "To the Senate and House of Representatives in Congress Assembled," n.d., box 41, folder 6; W. A. Gorman to SAD, February 9, 1857, box 6, folder 2; Horace Saxton and Thomas Clark to SAD, December [?], 1857, box 9, folder 14; Anonymous to SAD [ca. 1859], box 41, folder 13; William M. Morrow to SAD, January 5, 1859, box 23, folder 1; M. Tucker to SAD, January 25 [1859], box 41, folder 11; John Pope to SAD, March 9, 1860, box 31, folder 6, SADP.

110. Isaac I. Stevens to SAD, April 21, 1856, box 5, folder 3, SADP.

111. Johannsen, *Frontier, the Union, and Stephen A. Douglas*, 3–18; Johansen and Gates, *Empire of the Columbia*, 254, 289–94; K. Richards, *Isaac I. Stevens*, 158; Mahoney, *Salem Clique*, 87–89; Lamar, *Far Southwest*, 7–12; Rogers, *Unpopular Sovereignty*, 61–62.

112. A. B. Johnson to Sidney Breese, June 23, 1848, box 1, folder 8, Sidney Breese Papers, ALPL. See also *Kaskaskia Western Intelligencer*, August 21, 1816, quoted in Buley, *Old Northwest*, 1:79; and B. Driscoll to SAD, February 16, 1857, box 6, folder 5, and Delazon Smith to SAD, January 4, 1858, box 12, folder 18, SADP.

113. Jesse Applegate to Asahel Bush, November 8, 1851, box 1, folder 6, Asahel Bush Letters, ORHS (quotations). Emphasis original. See also An Old Oregonian to Asahel Bush, November 16, 185[1], box 1, folder 6, Asahel Bush Letters, ORHS; John Orvis Waterman to Joseph Lane, May 18, 1852, box 4, folder 19, Joseph Lane Papers, ORHS; and Jesse Applegate to Matthew P. Deady, January 26, 1852, box 2, folder A73–86; Joseph Lane to Matthew P. Deady, February 19, 1854, box 6, folder L27–56; and J. C. Avery to Matthew P. Deady, March 7, 1854, box 2, folder A42–72, Matthew Paul Deady Papers, ORHS.

114. Matthew P. Deady to Joseph Lane, September 27, 1852, box 1, folder 21, (quotation); Joseph W. Drew to Joseph Lane, May 1, 1852, box 1, folder 24, Joseph Lane Papers, ORHS.

115. *CG*, 36th Cong., 2nd Sess., 640 (January 30, 1861).

116. *CG*, 33rd Cong., 1st Sess., 280 (January 30, 1854).

117. Blaine, *Twenty Years of Congress*, 1:128–29.

118. SAD to Samuel Treat, February 19, 1848, box 1, Samuel Treat Papers, Missouri History Museum Archives, St. Louis.

119. E. S. Kimberly to SAD, April 10, 1848, box 1, folder 13; N. T. Rosseter to SAD, January 2, 1848, box 1, folder 11, SADP; Johannsen, *SAD*, 228.

120. Walther, *William Lowndes Yancey*, 109–10.

121. Johannsen, *SAD*, 231–34.

122. SAD to Lewis Cass, June 13, 1848, *LSAD*, 160–61.

123. *Raleigh Register* quoted in "The Register—Judge Douglas," *North Carolina Standard* (Raleigh), May 2, 1848.

124. Cooper, *South and the Politics of Slavery*, 244–53, 257–68.

125. Zachary Taylor to JD, July 27, 1847, *PJD*, 3:198–204; Zachary Taylor to JD, December [?], 1847, PJDRU; Zachary Taylor to JD, July 10, 1848, *JDC*, 1:208–10.

126. JD to Hugh R. Davis, June 4, 1848, *PJD*, 3:325–26.

127. "Speech at Raymond" [September 22, 1848], *PJD*, 3:374–76.

128. "Speech at Jackson" [September 23, 1848], *PJD*, 3:376–87 (quotation p. 379); JD to H. R. Davis and Others, October 6, 1848, *JDC*, 1:213–17.

129. JD to Woodville Citizens, October 23, 1848, *PJD*, 3:389–91.

130. Blue, *Free Soilers*, 141–51.

131. William H. Sparke to JD, November 17, 1848, *PJD*, 3:391–92; Lewis L. Taylor to John Duncan, September 7, 1849, box 1, folder 4, McRaven (W. H.) Papers, MDAH.

132. Francis G. Baldwin to JD, November 19, 1848, *PJD*, 3:392–93.

133. J. McRoberts to Charles H. Lanphier, February 16, 1849, box 1, folder 2, Charles H. Lanphier Papers, ALPL.

134. Merk, *Manifest Destiny*, 214.

135. James K. Polk to Lewis Cass, December 15, 1848, box 3, Lewis Cass Papers, William L. Clements Library, University of Michigan.

136. *CG*, 30th Cong., 2nd Sess., 21 (December 11, 1848); Quaife, *Diary of James K. Polk*, 4:232–33.

137. Quaife, *Diary of James K. Polk*, 4:236–37, 257–58, 302–3, 312–13.

138. *CG*, 30th Cong., 2nd Sess., 551 (February 17, 1849).

139. Hopkins Holsey to Howell Cobb, February 13, 1849, in U. Phillips, "Correspondence of Robert Toombs," 149–50; Childers, *Failure of Popular Sovereignty*, 171–76; Johannsen, *SAD*, 244–45; Harmon, "Douglas and the Compromise of 1850," 457.

140. Crallé, *Works of John C. Calhoun*, 6:290–313.

141. Howell Cobb to [Mary Ann Cobb], February 8, 1849, in R. Brooks, "Howell Cobb Papers" (June 1921), 38.

142. W. Freehling, *Road to Disunion*, 1:479–80; Holt, *Rise and Fall of the American Whig Party*, 387; Perman, *Pursuit of Unity*, 88.

143. Cooper, *South and the Politics of Slavery*, 287–89; Cooper, *JDA*, 179–80.

144. *Vicksburg Sentinel* quoted in Hattaway and Beringer, *Jefferson Davis*, 9 (quotation); Lawrence Johnson to JD, May 31, [1855], JDPTU; Alfriend, *Life of Jefferson Davis*, 32; Rhodes, *History of the United States*, 1:380; Merk, *Manifest Destiny*, 211–12; Escott, "Jefferson Davis and Slavery in the Territories," 97; Eaton, *Jefferson Davis*, 68, 71.

145. Joseph D. Howell to Margaret K. Howell, November 21, 1845, *PJD*, 2:374–76. Calhoun was en route to the Memphis convention on internal improvements.

146. *JDM*, 1:462.

147. *CG*, 31st Cong., 2nd Sess., appendix, 325 (February 24, 1851); "Speech at Jackson" [June 9, 1852], *PJD*, 4:266–67.

148. E. Lander, *Reluctant Imperialists*, 58–79, 150–70; W. Davis, *Jefferson Davis*, 176.

149. Cooper, *South and the Politics of Slavery*, 258; Perman, *Pursuit of Unity*, 52–59; I. Bartlett, *John C. Calhoun*, 361.

150. Escott, *After Secession*, 4.

151. *CG*, 30th Cong., 2nd Sess., 1 (December 4, 1848).

152. "Mr. Douglass' California Bill," *Illinois State Journal*, December 27, 1848.

153. Johannsen, *SAD*, 249–50; Wingerd, *North Country*, 179.

154. John Peniman to SAD, July 25, 1859, box 25, folder 23 (quotation); Alex Ramsey to SAD, July 11, 1850, box 2, folder 2; Daniel F. Browley to SAD, December 16, 1851, box

2, folder 8; William B. Dodd to SAD, March 1, 1852, box 3, folder 2; Henry M. Rice to SAD, December 8, 1853, box 4, folder 2; W. A. Gorman to SAD, February 9, 1857, box 6, folder 2; John B. Brisbin to SAD, August 15, 1857, box 8, folder 13, SADP; Wills, *Boosters, Hustlers, and Speculators*, 3–95.

155. H. Smith, "Historic Washington Homes," 263.

156. Hearon, "Mississippi and the Compromise of 1850," 45–50.

157. John C. Calhoun to Collin S. Tarpley, July 9, 1849, in "Calhoun and Secession," 415–16.

158. Hearon, "Mississippi and the Compromise of 1850," 62–71; May, *John A. Quitman*, 225; Jennings, *Nashville Convention*, 25–27, 35–40.

159. Claiborne, *Life and Correspondence of John A. Quitman*, 2:22–23.

160. "Speech at Jackson" [May 7, 1849], *PJD*, 4:19–20.

161. *Southron*, October 26, 1849.

162. JD to Samuel A. Cartwright, June 10, 1849, *PJD*, 4:21–23. See also JD to Stephen Cocke, August 2, 1849, *JDC*, 1:243–45; JD to Malcom D. Haynes, August 18, 1849, *PJD*, 4:26–44; "Speech of Jefferson Davis in the Democratic State Convention," *JDC*, 1:236–43; and "Speech at Holly Springs" [October 25, 1849], *PJD*, 4:47–50.

163. *CG*, 31st Cong., 1st Sess., 75 (December 24, 1849), 87 (December 27, 1849), 263, 266 (January 30, 1850).

164. *CG*, 31st Cong., 1st Sess., 99 (January 3, 1850) and passim. For the final Senate vote, in which Douglas and Davis joined in the affirmative, see *CG*, 31st Cong., 1st Sess., 904 (May 2, 1850). Johannsen, *SAD*, 306–17; Gates, *Illinois Central Railroad*, 31–34, 41–42, 64; Peck, *Making an Antislavery Nation*, 104–5.

165. John Pearson et al. to SAD, July 10, 1858, box 21, folder 3, SADP (quotations; emphasis original); "Central Rail Road," *Ottawa Free Trader*, September 28, 1850. For constituent pressure, see Resolution of Citizens of Franklin County [Ill.], March 4, 1848, box 1, folder 12; S. P. Lacey to SAD, January 28, 1849, box 1, folder 15; and James K. Scott to SAD, February 12, 1850, box 2, folder 1, SADP.

166. H. Hamilton, *Prologue to Conflict*; Russel, "What Was the Compromise of 1850?"

167. Harmon, "Douglas and the Compromise of 1850"; H. Hamilton, "Democratic Senate Leadership"; Johannsen, *SAD*, 262–98; Thomas L. Harris to Charles H. Lanphier, September 25, 1850, box 1, folder 3, Charles H. Lanphier Papers, ALPL; SAD to Charles H. Lanphier, October 2, 1850, *LSAD*, 196–97.

168. *CG*, 31st Cong., 1st Sess., 1830 (September 16, 1850).

169. Bremer, *Homes of the New World*, 1:467.

170. Crist, "'Duty Man,'" 283.

171. *CG*, 31st Cong., 1st Sess., appendix, 149–54 (February 13, 1850).

172. *CG*, 31st Cong., 1st Sess., appendix, 154–55 (February 14, 1850).

173. Green, *Democracy in the Old South*, 3–49; Worster, *Under Western Skies*, 53–63; Howard Lamar, "From Bondage to Contract: Ethnic Labor in the American West, 1600–1890," in Hahn and Prude, *Countryside in the Age of Capitalist Transformation*, 293–324.

174. *CG*, 31st Cong., 1st Sess., appendix, 156–57 (February 14, 1850).

175. Craven, *Growth of Southern Nationalism*, 73–74; Sanders, "Jefferson Davis," 398.

176. *CG*, 31st Cong., 1st Sess., appendix, 364–75 (March 13, 14, 1850).

177. W. Freehling, *Road to Disunion*, 2:xii.

178. "Speech at Raymond" [September 22, 1848], *PJD*, 3:375.

179. JD to William R. Cannon, January 8, 1850, *PJD*, 4:56. See also Hopkins Holsey to Howell Cobb, February 13, 1849, in U. Phillips, "Correspondence of Robert Toombs," 149–50; and Mayes, *Lucius Q. C. Lamar*, 46, 48–49.

180. *CG*, 31st Cong., 1st Sess., appendix, 151 (February 13, 1850).

181. *CG*, 31st Cong., 1st Sess., 402 (February 20, 1850).

182. *CG*, 31st Cong., 1st Sess., 917 (June 18, 1850).

183. *CG*, 31st Cong., 1st Sess., 919 (June 18, 1850).

184. *CG*, 31st Cong., 1st Sess., appendix, 1384 (July 18, 1850).

185. *CG*, 31st Cong., 1st Sess., 1003–6 (May 15, 1850), 1074, 1084 (May 28, 1850).

186. *CG*, 31st Cong., 1st Sess., 1074 (May 28, 1850).

187. *CG*, 31st Cong., 1st Sess., 1114–15 (June 3, 1850).

188. *CG*, 31st Cong., 1st Sess., 1115–16 (June 3, 1850).

189. *CG*, 31st Cong., 1st Sess., 182 (January 17, 1850).

190. Timothy Roberts Young to Augustus C. French, January 13, 1850, box 2, folder 3, Augustus C. French Papers, ALPL.

191. Thomas L. Harris to Friends L. & W., January 12, 1850, box 1, folder 3, Charles H. Lanphier Papers, ALPL.

192. James A. Shields to Augustus C. French, February 1, 1850, box 2, folder 3, Augustus C. French Papers, ALPL.

193. William H. Bissell to Joseph Gillespie, February 12, 1850, box 1, folder 1, Joseph Gillespie Papers, ALPL.

194. Thomas L. Harris to Augustus C. French, February 16, 1850, box 2, folder 3, Augustus C. French Papers, ALPL.

195. Milton, *Eve of Conflict*, 57; John A. McClernand to Augustus C. French, July 4, 1850, box 2, folder 5, Augustus C. French Papers, ALPL.

196. William H. Bissell to Joseph Gillespie, April 19, 1850, box 1, folder 1, Joseph Gillespie Papers, ALPL.

197. H. Hamilton, *Prologue to Conflict*, 143–44, 163–64; Harmon, "Douglas and the Compromise of 1850"; W. Freehling, *Road to Disunion*, 1:508–9.

198. See appendixes A and C in H. Hamilton, *Prologue to Conflict*, 191–92, 195–200.

199. Johannsen, *SAD*, 296.

200. H. Hamilton, *Prologue to Conflict*, appendix A (pp. 191–92).

201. Hamilton, appendix C (pp. 195–200).

202. Hamilton, appendix A (pp. 191–92); Gonzales, "Henry Stuart Foote," 129–31.

203. "Protest against the California Bill," *JDC*, 1:502–4.

204. "Autobiography of Jefferson Davis," *JDC*, 1:xxv–xxvi.

205. *JDM*, 1:463.

206. Landis, *Northern Men*, 10–37; Paul Finkelman, "The Appeasement of 1850," in Finkelman and Kennon, *Congress and the Crisis of the 1850s*, 36–79.

207. "Speech at Lexington [Va.], October 18, 1850," *Southern Press* (Washington, D.C.), November 23, 1850.

208. "Speech at Raymond" [October 26, 1850], *PJD*, 4:135–36 (first, second, and

third quotations; emphasis original); JD to B. Pendleton et al., November 10, 1850, *JDC*, 1:582 (fourth quotation).

209. JD to B. Pendleton et al., November 10, 1850, *JDC*, 1:587–88; "Hon. Jefferson Davis's Speech, Delivered in Jackson, May 6th, 1851," *Vicksburg Weekly Whig*, May 14, 1851; "Speech of Jefferson Davis at Aberdeen, Mississippi, May 26, 1851," *Monroe (Miss.) Democrat*, June 4, 1851.

210. W. Davis, *Jefferson Davis*, 206.

211. "The Fugitive Slave Bill in Chicago," *Ottawa Free Trader*, October 26, 1850.

212. Douglas, *Speech of Hon. Stephen A. Douglas, on the "Measures of Adjustment"* (quotations p. 6); A. Cole, *Era of the Civil War*, 69–74; Johannsen, *SAD*, 298–303; Mann, *Chicago Common Council*.

213. Pierce, *History of Chicago*, 2:195–97.

214. Peck, *Making an Antislavery Nation*, 102.

215. "A Compliment to Senator Douglas," *Washington (D.C.) Union*, March 28, 1851.

216. "Proclamation," in Claiborne, *Life and Correspondence of John A. Quitman*, 2:43.

217. John A. Quitman to J. J. McRae, September 28, 1850, in Claiborne, *Life and Correspondence of John A. Quitman*, 2:48–49.

218. "Senator Davis before His Constituents," *Vicksburg Weekly Whig*, November 6, 1850; *Flag of the Union* (Jackson, Miss.), December 6, 1850; "Speech at Raymond" [October 26, 1850], *PJD*, 4:135–36; "Speech at Benton" [November 2, 1850], *PJD*, 4:136–37; JD to S. Cobun and others, November 7, 1850, *JDC*, 1:592–96; JD to B. Pendleton et al., November 10, 1850, *JDC*, 1:579–89; JD to B. D. Nabors and others, November 19, 1850, *JDC*, 1:597–600; JD to Lowndes County Citizens, November 22, 1850, *PJD*, 4:138–45.

219. Hearon, "Mississippi and the Compromise of 1850," 150, 154–55, 159–60.

220. Mayes, *Lucius Q. C. Lamar*, 46, 48–49; Montgomery, *Reminiscences of a Mississippian*, 8–9; W. Jordan, *Tumult and Silence*, 62–63.

221. Hearon, "Mississippi and the Compromise of 1850," 165–71, 183–87, 202.

222. James Brewer to John A. Quitman, January 18, 1851, box 3A, folder 7B; Thomas Jones Pope to John A. Quitman, May 5, 1851, box 3a, folder 9, Quitman (John A.) and Family Papers, MDAH; John A. Quitman to John S. Preston, March 29, 1851, in Claiborne, *Life and Correspondence of John A. Quitman*, 2:127; Andrew P. Butler to JD, June 15, 1851, PJDRU; Whitemarsh B. Seabrook to John A. Quitman, July 15, 1851, in Claiborne, *Life and Correspondence of John A. Quitman*, 2:143; F.[?] Richards, H. H. Raymond, and W. H. Perouneau to JD, August 19, 1851, box 1, folder 2, JDPDU.

223. JD to Varina Howell Davis, May 8, 1851, box 1, folder 1, Jefferson Davis and Family Papers, MDAH; Cooper, *JDA*, 216–18.

224. Hearon, "Mississippi and the Compromise of 1850," 206–7; "Speech at Fayette" [July 11, 1851], *PJD*, 4:183–214.

225. "Speech of Jefferson Davis at Aberdeen, Mississippi, May 26, 1851," *JDC*, 2:70–82. Emphasis original.

226. Cooper, *JDA*, 218–19.

227. Ethelbert Barksdale to JD, September 19, 1851, *JDC*, 2:83–84; May, *John A. Quitman*, 258–63.

228. JD to E. C. Wilkerson, September 17, 1851, *JDC*, 2:86.

229. "Speech at Athens" [October 27, 1851], *PJD*, 4:231–32; *JDM*, 1:469–70.

230. Robert W. Barnwell to JD, October 20, 1851, *PJD*, 4:227–28.

231. "Autobiography of Jefferson Davis," *JDC*, 1:xxvi.

232. Sanders, "Jefferson Davis," 431.

233. John Edmund Gonzales, "Flush Times, Depression, War, and Compromise," in McLemore, *History of Mississippi*, 1:306–7.

234. Catton and Catton, *Two Roads to Sumter*, 86.

235. Reuben Davis to JD, [November 1851], *PJD*, 4:232–33.

236. Leonard, *Invention of Party Politics*, 258–60.

237. Dirck, *Lincoln and Davis*, 141.

238. Craven, *Growth of Southern Nationalism*, 132–33, 140–41.

CHAPTER 4

1. Samuel Ashton to SAD, March 18, 1854, box 4, folder 5, SADP.

2. Samuel Ashton to SAD, March 5, 1856, box 4, folder 21, SADP.

3. J. W. Sheahan to SAD, February 8, 1855, box 4, folder 12, SADP.

4. SAD to JD, March 30, 1855, *LSAD*, 336 (quotations); James Shields and SAD to JD, March 23, 1854, and JD to SAD, March 15, 1854, box 42, folder 5, SADP.

5. JD to SAD, April 5, 1855, *JDC*, 2:448–50.

6. JD to SAD, February 10, 16, 1857, box 42, folder 6, SADP.

7. Malavasic, *F Street Mess*, 181.

8. H. A. Cooke to James E. Cooke, January 21, 1852, Cooke (H. A.) Letters, MDAH.

9. E. Wilcox to Augustus C. French, January 27, 1851, box 2, folder 7, Augustus C. French Papers, ALPL.

10. Rawson, "Democratic Resurgence," 2–3, 8–10.

11. "Resolutions of the Committee of Thirteen," *Woodville (Miss.) Republican*, November 25, 1851.

12. "Speech of Jefferson Davis at the Democratic State Convention at Jackson, Mississippi, January 8, 1852," *JDC*, 2:117–25.

13. Rawson, "Democratic Resurgence," 13; Cooper, *JDA*, 243.

14. JD to J. J. McRae, September 17, 1853, *JDC*, 2:264–65.

15. James Phelan to JD, July 18, 1853, JDPTU; JD to B. Tucker, October 8, 1853, *JDC*, 2:271–72; JD to ——, October 6, 1853, *JDC*, 2:272–73; Rawson, "Democratic Resurgence," 14–15.

16. Seraiah the Scribe, *Chronicles of the Fire-Eaters*, 3 (first quotation), 4 (second quotation).

17. Rawson, "Democratic Resurgence," 23–26; McKee, "William Barksdale"; Carter, "Henry Stuart Foote," 224.

18. Wynne, "Politics and Pragmatism," 222–23; Ranck, *Albert Gallatin Brown*, 117–22.

19. R. Nichols, *Democratic Machine*, 22; Eyal, *Young America Movement*, 188–89.

20. Edward West to SAD, November 15, 1853, box 4, folder 1 (quotation); Andrew Harvie to SAD, November 14, 1853, box 4, folder 1; Charles H. Lanphier to SAD, November 21, 1853, box 4, folder 4, SADP.

21. Johannsen, *SAD*, 339–41, 343–44; Peck, *Making an Antislavery Nation*, 103.

22. SAD to William J. Brown, June 21, 1851, *LSAD*, 226–27.

23. "Stephen A. Douglas," *Ottawa Free Trader*, June 21, 1851; "The Presidency," *Baltimore Argus* reprinted in *Grand River Times* (Grand Haven, Mich.), November 19, 1851; A. H. Buckner to SAD, September 16, 1851, box 2, folder 4; Winslow S. Pierce to SAD, November 4, 1851, box 2, folder 5; H. V. Wilson to SAD, November 8, 1851, box 2, folder 5; John Law to SAD, December 6, 1851, box 2, folder 6; D. P. Rhodes to SAD, January 9, 1852, box 2, folder 10; John P. Heiss to SAD, February 20, 1852, box 3, folder 1; Wilford D. Wyatt to SAD, February 26, 1852, box 3, folder 2; Samuel F. Rand to SAD, March 2, 1852, box 3, folder 3; John D. McConnell to SAD, March 8, 1852, box 3, folder 3; H. S. Van Eaton to SAD, March 15, 1852, box 3, folder 5; Floyd Silly to SAD, March 28, 1852, box 3, folder 8, SADP; Johannsen, *SAD*, 344–46.

24. Horatio J. Harris to SAD, February 4, 1852, box 2, folder 13, and April 1, 1852, box 3, folder 9, SADP.

25. Douglas, *Speeches of Mr. Douglas, of Illinois, at the Democratic Festival at Jackson Hall.*

26. Curti, "Young America"; Danbom, "Young America Movement"; R. Nichols, *Democratic Machine*, 107–18; Hahn, *Nation without Borders*, 154–56; Eyal, *Young America Movement*; James O'Donnell to SAD, November 29, 1852, box 3, folder 16, SADP.

27. "Eighteen-Fifty-Two and the Presidency," *United States Magazine and Democratic Review* 30 (January 1852): 9.

28. SAD to George Nicholas Sanders, February 10, 1852, *LSAD*, 239–40 (first quotation); SAD to William A. Seaver, February 10, 1852, *LSAD*, 240 (second quotation); SAD to Caleb Cushing, February 4, 1852, *LSAD*, 237–38; SAD to George Nicholas Sanders, April 15, 1852, *LSAD*, 246–47; Johannsen, *SAD*, 360–63.

29. Orlando B. Ficklin to Augustus C. French, April 23, 1852, box 2, folder 15, Augustus C. French Papers, ALPL; William H. Bissell to Sidney Breese, June 10, 1852, box 1, folder 9, Sidney Breese Papers, ALPL.

30. *Proceedings of the Democratic National Convention, Held at Baltimore*, 21–36.

31. R. Nichols, *Democratic Machine*, 144; Wilentz, *Rise of American Democracy*, 662.

32. R. F. Stockton to John A. Whestone et al., March 11, 1852, *JDC*, 2:172–73; Sanders, "Jefferson Davis," 443.

33. "1852 Democratic Party Platform," American Presidency Project.

34. Quoted in Cooper, *South and the Politics of Slavery*, 334 (first and second quotations); Benjamin F. Dill to Charles D. Fontaine, July 6, 1852, box 1, folder 7, Fontaine (Charles D.) and Family Papers, MDAH (third quotation).

35. Edmund Burke to Franklin Pierce, June 10, 1852, "Some Papers of Franklin Pierce," 117.

36. G. C. Hebbé to Edmund Burke, July 15, 1852, "Some Papers of Franklin Pierce," 123.

37. R. G. Murphy to SAD, June 17, 1852, box 3, folder 14, SADP.

38. Johannsen, *SAD*, 370–73.

39. *Mississippian* (Jackson), July 30, 1852 (quotations); *Vicksburg Weekly Whig*, June 16, 1852; "Speech at Jackson" [June 9, 1852], *PJD*, 4:258–71; "Speech of Jefferson Davis at Memphis, Tenn.," *JDC*, 2:174–76.

40. Wilentz, *Rise of American Democracy*, 666; Cooper, *South and the Politics of Slavery*, 340–41; W. Freehling, *Road to Disunion*, 1:554.

41. Horatio J. Harris to Joseph Lane, December 14, 1852, box 2, folder 11, Joseph Lane Papers, ORHS.

42. Holt, *Franklin Pierce*, 66–71; R. Nichols, *Democratic Machine*, 171, 189–99.

43. Franklin Pierce to JD, December 7, 1852, *JDC*, 2:177–78.

44. "Col. Jefferson Davis," *Mississippi Free Trader*, February 2, 1853 (quotation); W. Scott Haynes to John A. Quitman, February 27, 1853, box 3A, folder 13, Quitman (John A.) and Family Papers, MDAH.

45. Cooper, *JDA*, 243–44; *JDM*, 1:476.

46. Ezell, "Jefferson Davis Seeks Political Vindication," 312–13; Cooper, *JDA*, 272–74; W. Davis, *Jefferson Davis*, 244–45; Sanders, "Jefferson Davis," 469–70; Eli Abbott to JD, April 1, 1853, JDPTU; JD to Eli Abbott, April 17, 1853, *PJD*, 5:9; Madison McAfee to JD, April 20, 1853, *JDC*, 2:208–9; James Phelan to JD, July 19, 1853, *PJD*, 5:34–37; JD to William R. Cannon, December 13, 1853, *PJD*, 5:52–53; JD to Stephen Cocke, December 19, 1853, *JDC*, 2:334–37; Yazoo County Democrats to JD, n.d., *JDC*, 2:337–38; Reuben Davis to JD, January 10, 1854, *PJD*, 5:55; John J. McRae to JD, January 13, 1855, *JDC*, 2:437–41; William E. Starke to JD, October 4, 1855, JDPTU; JD to Thomas J. Hudson, November 25, [1855], *PJD*, 5:137–39; Thomas J. Johnston to JD, December 7, 1855, JDPTU; Joseph M. Jayne to JD, December 9, 1855, JDPTU; William R. Cannon to JD, December 12, 1855, *PJD*, 5:144–45; Stephen Cocke to JD, December 13, 1855, JDPTU; JD to Collin S. Tarpley, December 19, 1855, *PJD*, 5:147–49; JD to Stephen Cocke, January 6, 1856, *JDC*, 2:584–86.

47. James Gadsden to JD, April 13, 1853, PJDRU.

48. James Gadsden to JD, April 25, 1853, PJDRU.

49. "Col. Jefferson Davis—the Secretary of War," *Mississippian*, reprinted in *Mississippi Free Trader*, April 5, 1853; "Democratic Meeting in Holmes," *Yazoo Democrat*, April 20, 1853. Davis, too, saw his role as a boon for the South. He refused to leave the cabinet unless he could move into the Senate, because his "services here" were "more beneficial to the South than those I could render elsewhere." JD to Joseph Davis, September 22, 1855, box 1, folder 2, JDPDU.

50. *New York Express* quoted in "Affairs at Washington," *Athens (Tenn.) Post*, June 17, 1853.

51. "Appointments under the Pierce Administration," *Flag of the Union*, April 15, 1853 (quotation); George W. Jones to Howell Cobb, February 11, 1853, in U. Phillips, "Correspondence of Robert Toombs," 323; Craven, *Growth of Southern Nationalism*, 145.

52. Philip Clayton to Howell Cobb, March 7, 1853, in R. Brooks, "Howell Cobb Papers" (March 1922), 35–36.

53. Rable, *Confederate Republic*, 6–19; Silbey, "Southern National Democrats"; Craven, *Growth of Southern Nationalism*, 173–74; Escott, *After Secession*, 4.

54. JD to [?], [August–October 1852], *PJD*, 4:293–97.

55. Utley, *Frontiersmen in Blue*, 2–3, 11–12; Cooper, *JDA*, 245–47.

56. Karp, *This Vast Southern Empire*, 223; W. Davis, *Jefferson Davis*, 223–39; Cooper, *JDA*, 249–60.

57. Waite, "Jefferson Davis and Proslavery Visions of Empire"; Karp, *This Vast Southern Empire*, 208–16; Lamar, *Far Southwest*, 110–11.

58. S. Smith, "Remaking Slavery"; S. Smith, *Freedom's Frontier*, 7–79; Broussard, "Slavery in California Revisited"; Albin, "Perkins Case"; Parish, "Project for a Califor-

nia Slave Colony." Some southerners still dreamed of slicing a slave state out of southern California. See Olmsted, *Journey through Texas*, 112–13; McAfee, "California's House Divided"; and Lynch, "Southern California Chivalry."

59. Ganaway, *New Mexico and the Sectional Controversy*, 35–76; Kiser, *Borderlands of Slavery*, 31–33, 112–41; Stegmaier, "Law That Would Make Caligula Blush?"

60. James J. Deavenport to JD, December 31, 1856, PJDRU. See also Philip A. Roach to JD, February 15, 1855, *JDC*, 2:442–43; Roach to JD, July 5, 1858, May 27, 1859, JDPTU; and Roach to JD, May 17, June 27, July 19, 25, 1859, *JDC*, 4:52–53, 59–61, 91–92, 92.

61. Torget, *Seeds of Empire*, 264.

62. Campbell, *Empire for Slavery*, 56; Barr, *Black Texans*, 17.

63. *Texas State Gazette* (Austin), July 17, 1858, quoted in Campbell, *Empire for Slavery*, 65–66.

64. Liles, "Slavery and Cattle."

65. Olmsted, *Journey in the Back Country*, 21–22.

66. Olmsted, *Journey through Texas*, 105–6, 257, 440, 453–57; *Gonzales (Tex.) Inquirer*, August 13, 1853; *Texas Planter* (Brazoria), September 20, 1854; *Dallas Herald*, November 24, 1858.

67. S. Kelley, *Los Brazos de Dios*, 99–100; Olmsted, *Journey through Texas*, 323–27; J. Nichols, "Line of Liberty"; S. Kelley, "'Mexico in His Head'"; Tyler, "Fugitive Slaves in Mexico."

68. Olmsted, *Journey through Texas*, 331–34; Persifor F. Smith to JD, December 22, 1853, *JDC*, 2:338–40; Campbell, *Empire for Slavery*, 62–63; Carrigan, *Making of a Lynching Culture*, 72–73; J. Nichols, "Line of Liberty," 418–19, 423, 427–32; Tyler, "Fugitive Slaves in Mexico," 4, 7–10.

69. Olmsted, *Journey through Texas*, 245 (quotations); Anderson, *Conquest of Texas*; Kennedy, *Cotton and Conquest*; Carrigan, *Making of a Lynching Culture*, 1–74; Lack, "Slavery and Vigilantism."

70. Campbell, *Empire for Slavery*, 218–19.

71. JD to P. H. Bell, September 19, 1853, *JDC*, 2:265–66; Anderson, *Conquest of Texas*, 9, 251–72, 360.

72. JD to William R. Cannon, December 7, 1855, *PJD*, 5:141–42. Cannon liked the plan; see William R. Cannon to JD, December 18, 1855, box 1, folder 4, Jefferson Davis and Family Papers, MDAH.

73. Modern writers often use the term "transcontinental railroad," but antebellum Americans usually spoke of a "Pacific railroad," since the projected line would run from the Mississippi River (already linked by rail to the Atlantic Ocean) to the Pacific coast.

74. John R. Bartlett to JD, December 29, 1850, *PJD*, 4:145–49; JD to Millard Fillmore, February 21, 1851, *PJD*, 4:164–67.

75. "Speech of Jefferson Davis at Philadelphia," "Speech of Jefferson Davis at the Crystal Palace Banquet in New York," and "Jefferson Davis and the Pacific Railway," *JDC*, 2:242–45, 246–51, 256–61.

76. Russel, *Improvement of Communication*, 24–25; Roberson, "South and the Pacific Railroad."

77. JD to John Pope, January 5, 1855, *JDC*, 2:434–37.

78. JD, "Report of the Secretary of War on the Several Railroad Explorations," in

Reports of Explorations and Surveys, 1:1–30; Cooper, *JDA*, 258; Russel, *Improvement of Communication*, 168–85. Davis's 1855 War Department report echoed this argument; see "Report of the Secretary of War" [December 3, 1855], *JDC*, 2:567–69.

79. Parish, "Project for a California Slave Colony"; J. Nichols, "Line of Liberty," 418–19; Waite, "Jefferson Davis and Proslavery Visions of Empire," 540–46.

80. Russel, *Improvement of Communication*, 130–49; Gara, *Presidency of Franklin Pierce*, 129–33; L. Richards, *California Gold Rush*, 144–68.

81. J. D. Baldwin to Charles Sumner, February 2, 1854, reel 10, Charles Sumner Papers, Houghton Library, Harvard University (quotations); Jenkins, "Gadsden Treaty."

82. *JDM*, 1:526, 558.

83. Fabens, *Camel Hunt*; Heap, *Central Route to the Pacific*, 128–31; J. Bartlett, *Personal Narrative*, 2:576–84; G. Marsh, *Camel*; G. H. Heap to Joseph Lane, December 10, 1852, box 1, folder 12, Joseph Lane Papers, ORHS; Faulk, *U.S. Camel Corps*, 18–34.

84. *CG*, 31st Cong., 2nd Sess., 826–27 (March 3, 1851). Southerners supported Davis's proposal 12–9, while northerners opposed it 15–7.

85. Faulk, *U.S. Camel Corps*; Carroll, *Government's Importation of Camels*; Fleming, "Jefferson Davis's Camel Experiment"; Lesley, "Purchase and Importation of Camels"; Lammons, "Operation Camel." Key documents include JD to Henry C. Wayne, May 10, 1855, *JDC*, 2:461–62; JD to D. D. Porter, May 16, 1855, *JDC*, 2:464–66; and "Report of the Secretary of War" [December 1, 1856], *JDC*, 3:93–95. On other uses of camels in the West, see Gray, Farquhar, and Lewis, *Camels in Western America*.

86. "Frosts and Famine in Texas," *Weekly North Carolina Standard* (Raleigh), April 29, 1857; "Camels and Dromedaries," *Richmond (Va.) Daily Dispatch*, May 19, 1857.

87. Henry C. Wayne to the Editors of the *National Intelligencer*, reprinted as "The Camel—His Nature, Habits, and Uses," *Southern Cultivator* 17 (January 1859): 29; G. W. T., "Who's Got a Camel for Sale?," *Southern Cultivator* 17 (March 1859): 81.

88. *Okolona (Miss.) Prairie News*, May 12, 1859; *Ripley (Miss.) Advertiser*, January 18, 1860; Derry, "Camels in Cahawba."

89. "Camels in Alabama," *Ohio Cultivator* 15 (1859): 215; *Yazoo Democrat*, May 28, 1859.

90. R. G. J., "The Camel and 'Cuffy,'" *Southern Cultivator* 17 (March 1859): 81.

91. Takaki, *Pro-slavery Crusade*.

92. Du Bois, *Suppression of the African Slave-Trade*, 179; Marques, *United States and the Transatlantic Slave Trade*, 11.

93. Du Bois, *Suppression of the African Slave-Trade*, 112–13, 165–66; Obadele-Starks, *Freebooters and Smugglers*, 115–19; Barker, "African Slave Trade in Texas"; S. Kelley, "Blackbirders and *Bozales*"; McGhee, "Black Crop."

94. Fornell, *Galveston Era*, viii–ix.

95. Obadele-Starks, *Freebooters and Smugglers*, 168.

96. Manning, *Six Months on a Slaver*, 21–24, 40, 125–26; Howard, *American Slavers*, 2–3; Marques, *United States and the Transatlantic Slave Trade*, 196–97; Diouf, *Dreams of Africa in Alabama*, 31, 42, 51.

97. Fornell, *Galveston Era*, 251–63 (quotation p. 254); McGhee, "Black Crop," 223–31; Derry, "Camels in Cahawba."

98. "The Slave-Trade in New York; Rearrest of John A. Machado," *New York Times*, September 21, 1862; Howard, *American Slavers*, 50–51, 178, 252, 261; Obadele-Starks,

Freebooters and Smugglers, 168; Marques, *United States and the Transatlantic Slave Trade*, 194, 196–97, 215, 222–23, 243–53, 298n17.

99. Emmett, *Texas Camel Tales*, 129–30.

100. *New York Herald*, November 18, 1859; "Curious Enterprise of a Pretty Widow," *Yazoo Democrat*, November 19, 1858; "The Slave-Trade in New York; Rearrest of John A. Machado," *New York Times*, September 21, 1862; Howard, *American Slavers*, 252; Obadele-Starks, *Freebooters and Smugglers*, 137, 180.

101. "'Old Douglas'—the Camel Burden Bearer," *Times Dispatch* (Richmond, Va.), November 29, 1903; Bell, *Camel Regiment*.

102. L. Richards, *Slave Power*; Gara, "Slavery and the Slave Power."

103. Johannsen, *SAD*, 381–86.

104. SAD to J. H. Crane, D. M. Johnson, and L. J. Eastin, December 17, 1853, *LSAD*, 268–72; Peck, *Making an Antislavery Nation*, 113; Hahn, *Nation without Borders*, 154–56; Eyal, *Young America Movement*, 36–37, 55, 66, 70; Holt, *Franklin Pierce*, 70–71.

105. Timothy B. Dwyer to SAD, February 10, 1853, box 3, folder 21; To the Senate and House of Representatives of the United States in Congress assembled, undated petition, box 44, folder 6; Memorial of the St. Louis Chamber of Commerce[,] To the Senate and House of Representatives of the United States, in Congress assembled, undated petition, box 44, folder 6; Brigham Young to SAD, April 29, 1854, box 42, folder 5; F. J. Carter to SAD, March 25, 1856, box 4, folder 24; Charles B. Fletcher to SAD, July 4, 1857, box 8, folder 4; "Pacific Rail Road" [undated handwritten manuscript], box 41, folder 13; Thomas Jefferson Sutherland to SAD, January 14, 1852, box 2, folder 11, and May 24, 1852, box 3, folder 12, SADP. In 1852, Douglas presented a memorial to Congress from constituents in Upper Alton, Illinois, asking for the organization of Nebraska. *CG*, 32nd Cong., 1st Sess., 967 (April 5, 1852).

106. D. L. Gregg to Charles H. Lanphier, September 20, 1853, box 1, folder 4, Charles H. Lanphier Papers, ALPL.

107. Johannsen, *SAD*, 372–73.

108. "What the Democrats Have Done for Illinois!," *Galena (Ill.) Jeffersonian*, n.d., reprinted in *Ottawa Free Trader*, August 28, 1852; Fehrenbacher, "Illinois Political Attitudes," 6–8, 11, 185–95; Harris, *Lincoln's Rise to the Presidency*, 84–85.

109. Johannsen, *SAD*, 304–38.

110. *CG*, 32nd Cong., 2nd Sess., 1117 (March 3, 1853).

111. *CG*, 32nd Cong., 1st Sess., 1952 (July 28, 1852).

112. "Our Washington Correspondence," *New York Herald*, March 2, 1851.

113. *CG*, 31st Cong., 2nd Sess., appendix, 338–41 (quotation p. 339) (March 1, 1851).

114. "Affairs at the National Capital," *New York Herald*, March 20, 1851.

115. Pierce, *History of Chicago*, 2:204.

116. *CG*, 31st Cong., 2nd Sess., appendix, 340 (March 1, 1851).

117. Quitt, *Stephen A. Douglas*, 99–106; Johannsen, *SAD*, 341–43.

118. *CG*, 32nd Cong., 1st Sess., appendix, 951 (August 16, 1852), 1127–31, 1137–38 (August 23, 1852).

119. SAD to Joel A. Matteson, January 2, 1854, *LSAD*, 272–82; SAD to [Charles H. Lanphier], November 11, 1853, *LSAD*, 267–68. The Matteson letter was distributed as a pamphlet: Douglas, *River and Harbor Improvements*.

120. "Judge Douglas's Plan of Tonnage Duties," *St. Louis Daily Democrat*, quoted in *Washington (D.C.) Republic*, November 23, 1852 (quotation); "Tonnage Duties—the New Dodge," *Milwaukie Sentinel*, reprinted in *Illinois State Journal*, October 18, 1852; "River and Harbor Improvements," *Illinois State Journal*, February 2, 1854.

121. "Harbor Appropriations," *Chicago Press and Tribune*, May 16, 1860.

122. Douglas, *Atlantic & Pacific Railroad*. Whitney's initial proposal is in *CG*, 28th Cong., 2nd Sess., 218–19 (January 28, 1845).

123. Brigham Young to SAD, April 29, 1854, box 42, folder 5; Charles B. Fletcher to SAD, July 4, 1857, box 8, folder 4; Charles B. Fletcher to SAD, July 31, 1857, box 8, folder 10; "Pacific Rail Road" [undated handwritten manuscript], box 41, folder 13; Horace Saxton and Thomas Clark to SAD, December [no date] 1857, box 9, folder 14; J. W. McCorkel to SAD, December 13, 1857, box 10, folder 10; A. Watson to SAD, April 17, 1858, box 18, folder 15; James S. Drew to SAD, November 12, 1858, box 22, folder 3; D. Pat. Henderson to SAD, December 8, 1858, box 22, folder 16; "Memorial for a Pacific Railroad. Presented by W. A. Gwyer, G. C. Monell and A. D. Jones, and Adopted by the Convention at Omaha City [Nebraska Territory], January 29th, 1859," box 23, folder 19; Albert L. Collins to SAD, February 8, 1859, box 24, folder 8; D. J. Connely to SAD, February 14, 1859, box 24, folder 5; James Ritchie to SAD, June 4, 1859, box 25, folder 13; A. M. Gibson to SAD, October 19, 1859, box 27, folder 1; D. P. Henderson to SAD, January 30, 1860, box 29, folder 6; David Smoke to SAD, [February 1860], box 29, folder 10; James T. Swants to SAD, February 20, 1860, box 30, folder 7; B. B. Meeker to SAD, February 25, 1860, box 30, folder 13; Thomas H. Merry to SAD, February 29, 1860, box 30, folder 18; W. R. Hurley to SAD, December 10, 1860, box 36, folder 17; James M. Martin to SAD, January 4, 1861, box 37, folder 7; Henry Farnam to SAD, January 16, 1861, box 37, folder 20, SADP.

124. Charles B. Fletcher to SAD, July 31, 1857, box 8, folder 10, SADP.

125. Isaac Stevens to SAD, September 18, 1853, box 4, folder 1, and December 5, 1853, box 4, folder 2, SADP; K. Richards, *Isaac I. Stevens*, 95–98, 139–42; Johannsen, *SAD*, 394–95. Douglas helped Stevens secure his subsequent position as Washington Territory's governor; SAD to Franklin Pierce, March 7, 1853, *LSAD*, 262.

126. *CG*, 35th Cong., 1st Sess., 1645 (April 17, 1858).

127. Capers, *Stephen A. Douglas*, 91; Johannsen, *SAD*, 305; Larson, *Internal Improvement*, 245.

128. "Important Railroad Intelligence," *Caddo Gazette*, reprinted in *Flag of the Union*, April 15, 1853; "Southern Route to the Pacific," *New Orleans Bee*, reprinted in *Opelousas (La.) Courier*, May 21, 1853; "Pacific Railroad," *New Orleans Picayune*, reprinted in *Franklin (La.) Planters' Banner*, November 10, 1853; "The 'Moonshine' Pacific Railroad," *New Orleans Bulletin*, reprinted in *Flag of the Union*, November 25, 1853; "Regular Washington Correspondence," *Nashville Union and American*, December 7, 1853.

129. L. Richards, *California Gold Rush*, 155–60; Sansing, "Happy Interlude," 308–9.

130. "Douglas bill" was widely used; for examples of the others, see Stephen Higginson to Charles Sumner, February 23, 1854, and Calvin E. Stowe to Charles Sumner, February 20, 1854, reel 10, Charles Sumner Papers, Houghton Library, Harvard University.

131. Quoted in Cutts, *Brief Treatise*, 122.

132. For historiographical analysis, see R. Nichols, "Kansas-Nebraska Act"; Malava-

sic, *F Street Mess*, 10–14; and Peck, *Making an Antislavery Nation*, 236–37n33. For a critique of the focus on Douglas, see Fehrenbacher, *Dred Scott Case*, 179–80.

133. Von Holst, *Constitutional and Political History*, 4:317; Schouler, *History of the United States*, 5:285–86; Rhodes, *History of the United States*, 1:424–30; H. Wilson, *History of the Rise and Fall*, 2:378–405.

134. Hodder, "Railroad Background"; Hodder, "Genesis of the Kansas-Nebraska Act"; Potter, *Impending Crisis*, 145–63. Impatient with scholars' fixation on sectionalism, Hodder wanted to showcase the explanatory power of a railroad-centered interpretation of U.S. history. Thus, he replaced one monocausal explanation with another; in private correspondence with Douglas's grandson, he insisted that Douglas's stance "was determined wholly by railroad considerations." F. H. Hodder to Martin F. Douglas, March 24, 1917, box 1, folder 16, Douglas Family Collection, Special Collections Research Center, University of Chicago Library.

135. Malin, "Motives of Stephen A. Douglas"; Clyde A. Milner II, "National Initiatives," in Milner, O'Connor, and Sandweiss, *Oxford History of the American West*, 171; White, *"It's Your Misfortune and None of My Own,"* 160; Fiege, *Republic of Nature*, 174; Hine and Faragher, *Frontiers*, 89.

136. Johannsen, *Frontier, the Union, and Stephen A. Douglas*, 19–32; Billington, *Westward Expansion*, 512; Quitt, *Stephen A. Douglas*; Burt, *Lincoln's Tragic Pragmatism*, 49.

137. Holt, *Rise and Fall of the American Whig Party*, 806–7; M. Morrison, *Slavery and the American West*, 142; Leonard, *Invention of Party Politics*, 262–64; Peck, *Making an Antislavery Nation*, 97–122.

138. Ray, *Repeal of the Missouri Compromise*; Parrish, *David Rice Atchison*, 124–31, 150–51; Lampton, "Kansas-Nebraska Act Reconsidered."

139. Malavasic, *F Street Mess*.

140. Eyal, "With His Eyes Open."

141. *CG*, 32nd Cong., 2nd Sess., 1010 (March 2, 1853).

142. *CG*, 32nd Cong., 2nd Sess., 1116 (March 3, 1853).

143. Johannsen, *SAD*, 390–400.

144. Quoted in Etcheson, *Bleeding Kansas*, 11. Emphasis in the quoted source.

145. *CG*, 32nd Cong., 1st Sess., 1762 (July 13, 1852).

146. Malavasic, *F Street Mess*, 1–80; R. Nichols, "Kansas-Nebraska Act," 201–3.

147. *CG*, 32nd Cong., 2nd Sess., 1020 (March 2, 1853); Fehrenbacher, *Dred Scott Case*, 639–40n76; K. Richards, *Isaac I. Stevens*, 155.

148. "Senator Atchison—Nebraska," *Glasgow (Mo.) Weekly Times*, November 10, 1853; Ray, *Repeal of the Missouri Compromise*, 142–94; Johannsen, *SAD*, 395–400.

149. Russel, "Issues in the Struggle," 210.

150. *CG*, 33rd Cong., 1st Sess., 44 (December 14, 1853).

151. Quoted in Ray, *Repeal of the Missouri Compromise*, 197–98.

152. Johannsen, *SAD*, 404; A. Dean, *Agrarian Republic*, 37–38, 93–94.

153. Malavasic, *F Street Mess*, 87–88.

154. *CG*, 33rd Cong., 1st Sess., 115 (January 4, 1854); Senate Report No. 15, 33rd Cong., 1st Sess. (January 4, 1854), in *Reports of the Committees of the Senate*, 1–3.

155. "A Bill to Organize the Territory of Nebraska," *Washington (D.C.) Sentinel*, January 10, 1854; Malavasic, *F Street Mess*, 89–91; Johannsen, *SAD*, 408.

156. "Nebraska Territory," *Wilmington (N.C.) Journal*, February 3, 1854.

157. Learned, "Relation of Philip Phillips," 310.

158. *CG*, 33rd Cong., 1st Sess., 175 (January 16, 1854) (quotation); Dixon, *True History*, 432–44.

159. Hyman and Wiecek, *Equal Justice under Law*, 164; Malavasic, *F Street Mess*, 91–93.

160. *CG*, 33rd Cong., 1st Sess., 239–40 (January 24, 1854).

161. Dixon, *True History*, 446–47.

162. *CG*, 33rd Cong., 1st Sess., 240 (January 24, 1854).

163. Hyman and Wiecek, *Equal Justice under Law*, 164–65.

164. Dixon, *True History*, 444–45 (quotation); Malavasic, *F Street Mess*, 94–95.

165. Malavasic, *F Street Mess*, 95–96; Johannsen, *SAD*, 414

166. Johannsen, *SAD*, 414–15; Cooper, *JDA*, 266–70; W. Davis, *Jefferson Davis*, 246–49; SAD to Charles H. Lanphier, February 13, 1854, *LSAD*, 283–84. On Davis's involvement in legislative maneuvers, see JD to John C. Breckinridge, May 15, 1854, *PJD*, 5:67.

167. *CG*, 33rd Cong., 1st Sess., 221–22 (January 23, 1854); Johannsen, *SAD*, 415–17.

168. *CG*, 33rd Cong., 1st Sess., 352–53 (February 7, 1854) (quotation), 520 (March 2, 1854).

169. *CG*, 33rd Cong., 1st Sess., 281–82 (January 30, 1854) (quotations p. 281), 617–23 (March 14, 1854); SAD to Twenty-five Chicago Clergymen, April 6, 1854, *LSAD*, 300–322.

170. For praise, see Edmund Burke to SAD, January 9, 1854, box 4, folder 4; Howell Cobb to SAD, February 5, 1854, box 4, folder 5; Green C. Bronson to SAD, February 8, 1854, box 4, folder 5; Hayden to SAD, March 16, 1854, box 4, folder 5; and D. P. Rhodes to SAD, March 27, 1854, box 4, folder 6, SADP. For friendly warnings, see M. McConnel to SAD, January 28, 1854, box 4, folder 4; W. B. Laurence to SAD, February 1, 1854, box 4, folder 5; Isaac Cook to SAD, February 9, 1854, box 4, folder 5; Samuel Ashton to SAD, March 18, 1854, box 4, folder 5; H. Hoyne to SAD, March 18, 1854, box 4, folder 5; and Horatio Seymour Jr. to SAD, April 14, 1854, box 4, folder 6, SADP. For criticism, see William Penn to SAD, March 25, 1854, box 4, folder 6, SADP.

171. *CG*, 33rd Cong., 1st Sess., 239 (January 24, 1854).

172. *CG*, 33rd Cong., appendix, 788 (May 25, 1854).

173. *CG*, 33rd Cong., 1st Sess., 278–79 (January 30, 1854); Edward Coles to SAD, February 13, 1854, in *National Intelligencer* (Washington, D.C.), February 18, 1854; SAD to Edward Coles, February 18, 1854, *LSAD*, 290–99.

174. *CG*, 33rd Cong., 1st Sess., 279 (January 30, 1854).

175. *CG*, 33rd Cong., 1st Sess., 278 (January 30, 1854); *CG*, 33rd Cong., 1st Sess., appendix, 661 (May 8, 1854).

176. Gara, *Presidency of Franklin Pierce*, 86–88; Johannsen, *SAD*, 436–39.

177. Holt, *Franklin Pierce*, 80–81.

178. *CG*, 33rd Cong., 1st Sess., 532 (March 3, 1854).

179. *CG*, 33rd Cong., 1st Sess., 1254 (May 22, 1854).

180. Quoted in Johannsen, *SAD*, 451.

181. "Senator Douglas in Chicago," *Ottawa Free Trader*, September 9, 1854 (first and second quotations); G. Davis, "Douglas and the Chicago Mob"; Cutts, *Brief Treatise*, 97–101 (third quotation p. 100). Davis argued that Cutts invented the apocryphal "Go to

hell!" comment, but an 1860 campaign biography was the first to misplace the speech on a Saturday night, claiming that Douglas had told the crowd to "go to the devil." [Flint], *Life of Stephen A. Douglas*, 74.

182. "Emigration to Nebraska," *New York Evangelist*, June 15, 1854 (first quotation); "The Nebraska Swindle," *New York Tribune*, May 12, 1854 (second quotation); "The Pennsylvania Black List," *Harrisburg (Pa.) Morning Herald*, May 22, 1854 (third quotation); *Albany Evening Journal*, May 23, 1854 (fourth quotation).

183. Quoted in Pierce, *History of Chicago*, 2:207 (first and third quotations), 206 (second quotation).

184. Pease and Randall, *Diary of Orville Hickman Browning*, 132–33.

185. A. Cole, *Era of the Civil War*, 139–43; Krug, *Lyman Trumbull*, 76–96; Lyman Trumbull to John [Trumbull], December 4, 1854, box 1, folder 3, Lyman Trumbull Family Papers, ALPL.

186. Paul Selley to Richard Yates, April 8, 1854, box 1, folder 5, Yates Family Papers, ALPL.

187. Burlingame, *Abraham Lincoln*, 1:363–406; Donald, *Lincoln*, 173–78.

188. Swan and Swan, "James W. Sheahan"; SAD to Dear Sir [circular letter], September 4, 1854, box 43, folder 3, SADP.

189. "Nebraska," *Grand River Times*, February 22, 1854 (quotations); "New Territories," *Detroit Free Press*, January 6, 1854; "Glorious News from Washington—Passage of the Nebraska Bill," *Cincinnati Daily Enquirer*, May 24, 1854; "The Nebraska Bill," *New Hampshire Patriot* (Concord), May 31, 1854; "The Principle," *Ottawa Free Trader*, July 15, 1854; "Will Kansas Become a Slave State," *Clearfield (Pa.) Republican*, August 25, 1854; "The Election," *Ottawa Free Trader*, October 28, 1854.

190. Mahoney, *Salem Clique*, 94; Johannsen, *Frontier, the Union, and Stephen A. Douglas*, 19–32.

191. "Judge Douglas in Ottawa," *Ottawa Free Trader*, September 16, 1854; Peck, "New Records of the Lincoln-Douglas Debate," 48–55; Sheahan, *Life of Stephen A. Douglas*, 274–75; Johannsen, *SAD*, 455–61.

192. Holt, *Franklin Pierce*, 83; Huston, *Stephen A. Douglas*, 112; A. Smith, *Stormy Present*, 73.

193. *Joliet Signal*, November 14, 1854, quoted in Burlingame, *Abraham Lincoln*, 1:390.

194. *New York Tribune*, November 10, 1854.

195. Krug, *Lyman Trumbull*, 94–103.

196. John J. McRae to L. Q. C. Lamar, February 20, 1855, Lamar (L. Q. C.) and Edward Mayes Papers, MDAH. Emphasis original.

197. David S. Reid to SAD, June 17, 1854, box 4, folder 7, SADP.

198. James W. Williams to JD, May 30, 1854, *JDC*, 2:359–60.

199. Craven, *Growth of Southern Nationalism*, 192–203; Childers, *Failure of Popular Sovereignty*, 221.

200. "An Act to Organize the Territories of Nebraska and Kansas," *Public Acts of the Thirty-Third Congress*, 283, 289.

201. Fehrenbacher, *Dred Scott Case*, 184–85, 640–41n77; Russel, "Issues in the Struggle," 188–89.

202. *CG*, 33rd Cong., 1st Sess., appendix, 466–67 (March 30, 1854).

203. *CG*, 33rd Cong., 1st Sess., appendix, 229–30 (February 24, 1854).

204. *CG*, 33rd Cong., 1st Sess., appendix, 549 (April 24, 1854) (quotation), 618 (April 27, 1854).

205. For the former, see "The Territorial Question," *Mississippi Free Trader*, March 14, 1854; and "The Importance of the Early Passage of the Nebraska Bill," *Mississippian*, April 21, 1854. For the latter, see "Squatter Sovereignty," *Yazoo Democrat*, April 12, 1854.

206. Burt, *Lincoln's Tragic Pragmatism*, 94–117; Pfau, *Political Style of Conspiracy*.

207. "The Great Southern Convention in Charleston," *DeBow's Review* 17 (August 1854): 209.

208. *Prattville (Ala.) Statesman*, June 18, 1855, quoted in Craven, *Growth of Southern Nationalism*, 221.

209. Quoted in Johannsen, "Stephen A. Douglas, 'Harper's Magazine,' and Popular Sovereignty," 611n12. Emphasis original.

210. "As We Expected," *Thibodaux (La.) Minerva*, September 30, 1854.

211. Pollard, *Lost Cause*, 68–70; Tate, *Jefferson Davis*, 8–9, 80; Strode, *Jefferson Davis*, 1:267; Sanders, "Jefferson Davis," 458.

212. David R. Atchison to JD, September 24, 1854, box 1, folder 2, JDPDU.

213. *Semi-Weekly Mississippian* (Jackson), December 28, 1855.

214. Childers, *Failure of Popular Sovereignty*, 166–99.

215. Russel, "Issues in the Struggle," 204–5.

216. Utley, *Frontiersmen in Blue*, 12; Anderson, *Conquest of Texas*, 9; Faulk, *U.S. Camel Corps*, 34–35; Russel, *Improvement of Communication*, 178–85.

217. Cooper, *JDA*, 273–74.

218. C. S. Tarpley to SAD, November 15, 1855, box 4, folder 14, SADP.

219. *CG*, 33rd Cong., 2nd Sess., 210 (January 9, 1855), 991 (February 28, 1855), 1149–50 (March 3, 1855).

220. *CG*, 33rd Cong., 2nd Sess., appendix, 215, 216 (February 23, 1855).

221. Etcheson, *Bleeding Kansas*, 56–66, 69–88; Ponce, *To Govern the Devil*, 59–64; A. H. Reeder to SAD, February 12, 1855, box 4, folder 12, SADP.

222. Samuel J. Mills to SAD, February 22, 1856, box 4, folder 18 (quotation); James N. Shine to SAD, February 11, 1856, box 4, folder 16; James Shields to SAD, March 6, 1856, box 4, folder 21, SADP.

223. SAD to Howell Cobb, October 6, 1855, *LSAD*, 342.

224. W. D. Latham to Charles H. Lanphier, November 9, 1855, box 1, folder 5; Robert Smith to Charles H. Lanphier, November 23, 1855, box 1, folder 5, Charles H. Lanphier Papers, ALPL; SAD to Howell Cobb, January 8, 1856, *LSAD*, 346–47; SAD to David S. Reid, January 11, 1856, *LSAD*, 347; Johannsen, *SAD*, 476–85.

225. W. D. Latham to Charles H. Lanphier, November 9, 1855, box 1, folder 5, Charles H. Lanphier Papers, ALPL.

226. Joseph M. Jayne to JD, December 9, 1855, PJDRU.

227. M. Skinner to Lyman Trumbull, January 28, 1856, box 1, folder 5, Lyman Trumbull Family Papers, ALPL.

CHAPTER 5

1. G. W. Armstrong to SAD, December 30, 1857, box 12, folder 5, SADP.

2. See Pierce's special message to Congress in *CG*, 34th Cong., 1st Sess., 296–98 (January 24, 1856), and his February 11 proclamation in *Washington Daily Union*, February 12, 1856.

3. *CG*, 34th Cong., 1st Sess., 663 (March 17, 1856).

4. *CG*, 34th Cong., 1st Sess., appendix, 280–89 (March 20, 1856).

5. *Report of the Committee on Territories*; Johannsen, *SAD*, 492–93; Fehrenbacher, *Dred Scott Case*, 196.

6. Etcheson, *Bleeding Kansas*, 97–100, 126–28; Ponce, *To Govern the Devil*, 99–129.

7. *CG*, 34th Cong., 1st Sess., 1958 (August 6, 1856), 1723 (July 23, 1856).

8. Etcheson, *Bleeding Kansas*, 100–126, 131–38; Ponce, *To Govern the Devil*, 76–98.

9. H. V. Wilson to SAD, May 29, 1856, box 5, folder 7, SADP.

10. *CG*, 34th Cong., 1st Sess., appendix, 529–47 (quotation p. 531) (May 19–20, 1856).

11. Quoted in Johannsen, *SAD*, 503.

12. Woods, *Emotional and Sectional Conflict*, 155; "Freedom in Debate," *Indianapolis Locomotive*, May 23, 1856; "An Atrocious Speech and a Disgraceful Assault," *Detroit Free Press*, May 23, 1856; "Assault in the United States Senate Chamber," *Illinois State Register*, May 26, 1856; Henry A. Morrow to Charles Sumner, May 25, 1856, reel 13, Charles Sumner Papers, Houghton Library, Harvard University.

13. JD to South Carolina Citizens, September 22, 1856, *PJD*, 6:44 (quotation); "Capt. Brooks' Castigation of Senator Sumner," *Edgefield (S.C.) Advertiser*, May 28, 1856; "The Assault on W. T. Butler," *Texas State Gazette*, June 14, 1856.

14. Johannsen, *SAD*, 505–7.

15. C. S. Tarpley to SAD, November 15, 1855, box 4, folder 14; Samuel Ashton to SAD, March 5, 1856, box 4, folder 21; D. Hayden to SAD, March 20, 1856, box 4, folder 23; William B. Hood to SAD, April 19, 1856, box 5, folder 3; Ellis B. Schnabel to SAD, April 22, 1856, box 5, folder 3; B. H. Cheever to SAD, April 29, 1856, box 5, folder 4; J. A. Matteson to SAD, May 3, 1856, box 5, folder 5, SADP.

16. C. S. Tarpley to JD, May 6, 1853, *JDC*, 2:211–14; Martin W. Philips to JD, August 27, 1853; Peter J. Sullivan to JD, September 16, 1853, PJDRU; Joseph M. Jayne to JD, December 9, 1855, JDPTU; S. W. C., "The Next President," *United States Magazine and Democratic Review* 37 (April 1856): 323, 325.

17. R. Nichols, *Disruption of American Democracy*, 25–28; Holt, *Franklin Pierce*, 96; JD to William L. Ellsworth, June 5, 1856, *PJD*, 6:25–26; R. C. Hancock to John A. Quitman, April 5, 1856, box 5A, folder 7, and B. Maron to John A. Quitman, April 28, 1856, box 5A, folder 8, Quitman (John A.) and Family Papers, MDAH; May, *John A. Quitman*, 318–19.

18. *Official Proceedings of the National Democratic Convention, Held in Cincinnati*, 39–59.

19. "1856 Democratic Party Platform," American Presidency Project.

20. Wells, *Stephen Douglas*, 71; Johannsen, *Frontier, the Union, and Stephen A. Douglas*, 147; Fehrenbacher, *Dred Scott Case*, 201.

21. Horatio J. Harris to JD, June 30, 1856, PJDRU.

22. John S. Cunningham to SAD, June 6, 1856, box 5, folder 8, SADP (quotation); R. Nichols, *Disruption of American Democracy*, 29–30.

23. SAD to William A. Richardson, June 5, 1856, *LSAD*, 362; Johannsen, *SAD*, 533–37; Milton, *Eve of Conflict*, 243.

24. "Republican Party Platform of 1856," American Presidency Project.

25. *Port Gibson (Miss.) Daily Southern Reveille*, October 30, 1856, quoted in Craven, *Growth of Southern Nationalism*, 244; "Great Speech of Gov. Wise," *North Carolina Standard*, October 8, 1856; Potter, *Impending Crisis*, 263; Varon, *Disunion*, 274; Bicknell, *Lincoln's Pathfinder*, 254.

26. JD to Herschel V. Johnson, [October 1856], *PJD*, 6:54–55; Cooper, *JDA*, 276.

27. Catton and Catton, *Two Roads to Sumter*, 129.

28. R. Nichols, *Disruption of American Democracy*, 57–59; Varon, *Disunion*, 274–77.

29. Gienapp, *Origins of the Republican Party*, 414–15; Holt, *Franklin Pierce*, 109.

30. Michael A. Morrison, "President James Buchanan: Executive Leadership and the Crisis of the Democracy," in Quist and Birkner, *James Buchanan*, 147; Johannsen, *SAD*, 538; Wilentz, *Rise of American Democracy*, 701.

31. Horatio J. Harris to JD, December 3, 1856, *JDC*, 3:99.

32. W. Freehling, *Road to Disunion*, 2:104; Collins, "Democrats' Electoral Fortunes," 316; Varon, *Disunion*, 291; Cooper, *South and the Politics of Slavery*, 373–74.

33. "Marriage of Senator Douglas," *Marshall County Democrat*, December 4, 1856.

34. Varina Howell Davis to My dear Father and Mother, September 15, 1856, in Strode, *Jefferson Davis: Private Letters*, 80–81 (quotations); Johannsen, *SAD*, 542.

35. Baker, *James Buchanan*, 80; E. Smith, *Presidency of James Buchanan*, 19–21; Klein, *President James Buchanan*, 263.

36. James Buchanan to John Y. Mason, December 29, 1856, in J. B. Moore, *Works of James Buchanan*, 10:100.

37. Buchanan, "Inaugural Address," American Presidency Project.

38. Fehrenbacher, *Dred Scott Case*, 239–321.

39. Chief Justice Taney, "Opinion of the Court," *Scott v. Sandford*, Legal Information Institute; Fehrenbacher, *Dred Scott Case*, 322–414.

40. R. J. Walker to SAD, January 9, 1857, box 5, folder 13, SADP.

41. M. McConnel to SAD, July 2, 1857, box 8, folder 8, SADP.

42. Douglas, *Remarks of the Hon. Stephen A. Douglas, on Kansas, Utah, and the Dred Scott Decision*, 5.

43. "Speech at Jackson" [May 29, 1857], *PJD*, 6:122–23; "Speech at Mississippi City" [October 2, 1857], *PJD*, 6:140–41.

44. Peterson, *Jefferson Image*, 168.

45. *CG*, 31st Cong., 1st Sess., appendix, 917 (June 18, 1850).

46. Wilson, *History of the Rise and Fall*, 2:291; W. Freehling, *South vs. the South*, 28–29; Ely, *Guardian of Every Other Right*, 61–62.

47. Breen, *Land Shall Be Deluged in Blood*, 9–10, 138, 168; A. Freehling, *Drift toward Dissolution*.

48. Helper, *Impending Crisis*; D. Brown, *Southern Outcast*; Merritt, *Masterless Men*, 1–2, 273–74.

49. Burt, *Lincoln's Tragic Pragmatism*, xii–xiv, 48.

50. McCardell, *Idea of a Southern Nation*, 71–84; Fredrickson, *White Supremacy*, 151–62.

51. "Speech at Mississippi City" [October 2, 1857], *PJD*, 6:147–48.

52. *CG*, 30th Cong., 2nd Sess., appendix, 298 (February 28, 1849).

53. Ashworth, *Slavery, Capitalism, and Politics*, 2:367–69, 375–76, 425; Alexander Saxton, "Blackface Minstrelsy, Vernacular Comics, and the Politics of Slavery in the North," in Roediger and Blatt, *Meaning of Slavery*, 157–76; Robert D. Sampson, "John L. O'Sullivan and the Tragedy of Radical Jacksonian Thought," in McDonough and Noe, *Politics and Culture of the Civil War Era*, 53–71; Gerring, *Party Ideologies in America*, 163–66. For critiques, see Stephen E. Maizlish, "Race and Politics in the Northern Democracy: 1854–1860," in Abzug and Maizlish, *New Perspectives*, 79–90; Baker, *Affairs of Party*, 177–258; and Riley, *Slavery and the Democratic Conscience*, 2–3.

54. Rawley, *Race and Politics*, viii; Frymer, *Building an American Empire*; Takaki, *Pro-slavery Crusade*; Berwanger, *Frontier against Slavery*; Ford, *Deliver Us from Evil*; Burin, *Slavery and the Peculiar Solution*.

55. Burlingame, *Abraham Lincoln*, 1:xii; and Striner, *Lincoln and Race*, 21–30. For thoughtful critiques, see Quitt, *Stephen A. Douglas*, 129n30; and Burt, *Lincoln's Tragic Pragmatism*, 382.

56. James Oakes, "Commentary: Conflict vs. Racial Consensus in the History of Antislavery Politics," in Hammond and Mason, *Contesting Slavery*, 291–303.

57. "Speech of Jefferson Davis before the Democratic State Convention at Jackson, Miss., July 6, 1859," *JDC*, 4:64–65, 71–73.

58. *Ottawa Free Trader*, April 24, 1846; American Colonization Society, *Forty-Second Annual Report*, 3, *Forty-Third Annual Report*, 3, and *Forty-Fourth Annual Report*, 3; Egerton, "Averting a Crisis"; "Speech of Jefferson Davis before the Democratic State Convention at Jackson, Miss., July 6, 1859," *JDC*, 4:72–73; Burt, *Lincoln's Tragic Pragmatism*, 367–82.

59. R. S. Lankins to SAD, January 15, 1858, box 13, folder 14; LeRoy Shattuck to SAD, June 8, 1860, box 35, folder 1, SADP. On dominative versus aversive racism, see Kovel, *White Racism*.

60. "The Northern Press—'The Day-Book,'" *DeBow's Review* 29 (December 1860): 793.

61. *Dred Scott Decision*.

62. Van Evrie, *Negroes and Negro "Slavery,"* 3 (quotation); Fredrickson, *Black Image*, 62–64, 91–96.

63. JD to John Van Evrie, June 3, 1853, in Van Evrie, *Negroes and Negro "Slavery,"* inside front cover.

64. JD to Robert McClelland, October 6, 1854, *PJD*, 5:85–86; John Cowden to JD, December 17, 1860, PJDRU; Jacob W. Elseffer to John A. Quitman, February 20, 1856, box 5A, folder 4A; F. R. Witter to John A. Quitman, March 5, 1856, box 5A, folder 5; Thomas S. Harney to John A. Quitman, March 7, 1856, box 5A, folder 5; Isaac R. Wade to John A. Quitman, March 9, 1856, box 5A, folder 5, Quitman (John A.) and Family Papers, MDAH.

65. H. R. Campbell to JD, July 27, 1860, JDPTU.

66. J. H. Van Evrie to JD, November 2, 1855, *JDC*, 2:546–47.

67. Sinha, *Counterrevolution of Slavery*; McCurry, *Confederate Reckoning*; Genovese, *Slaveholders' Dilemma*; Read, *Majority Rule versus Consensus*; Hettle, *Peculiar Democracy*; Huston, *Calculating the Value*, 24–66; Sydnor, *Gentleman of the Old Natchez Region*, 119, 293.

68. *CG*, 35th Cong., 1st Sess., 1138 (March 16, 1858) (first two quotations); *CG*, 35th Cong., 1st Sess., appendix, 145 (March 19, 1858) (third and fourth quotations); Linton Stephens to Alexander H. Stephens, February 8, 1858, in Waddell, *Biographical Sketch of Linton Stephens*, 138 (fifth and sixth quotations).

69. Dew, *Review of the Debate*, 20 (quotation); "Professor Dew's Essays on Slavery," *DeBow's Review* 11 (July 1851): 25; *Pro-slavery Argument*, 312.

70. JD to Malcolm D. Haynes, August 18, 1849, *PJD*, 4:39.

71. William S. Rockwell to Howell Cobb, January 20, 1856, in R. Brooks, "Howell Cobb Papers" (June 1922), 165. Emphasis original.

72. L. Richards, *Slave Power*, 114–15; "Hon. Jefferson Davis's Speech, Delivered in Jackson, May 6th, 1851," *Vicksburg Weekly Whig*, May 14, 1851.

73. W. Miller, *Arguing about Slavery*; W. Freehling, *Road to Disunion*, 1:287–352.

74. "Mississippi Constitution of 1832," Mississippi History Now.

75. *Register of the Debates and Proceedings of the Va. Reform Convention*, 284 (quotation); Zucconi, "'Preserve Us from Such Democracy.'"

76. "The Constitution of Virginia. 1851," *Southern Quarterly Review* 12 (October 1855): 363–84 (quotation p. 372).

77. "Inaugural Address of Robert J. Walker, Governor of Kansas Territory," in Gihon, *Geary and Kansas*, 328–48; Etcheson, *Bleeding Kansas*, 143–47; Ponce, *To Govern the Devil*, 150–61; Johannsen, *SAD*, 563–65.

78. *Laws of the State of Mississippi*, 136–37 (quotation p. 137); Horatio J. Harris to John Duncan, July 30, 1857, box 1, folder 4, McRaven (W. H.) Papers, MDAH; Lucius Q. C. Lamar to Howell Cobb, July 17, 1857, in U. Phillips, "Correspondence of Robert Toombs," 406; "Position of the Southern Democracy," *Columbus (Ga.) Times and Sentinel*, reprinted in *Feliciana Democrat*, August 15, 1857.

79. Etcheson, *Bleeding Kansas*, 139–47, 152–55; R. Nichols, *Disruption of American Democracy*, 125–33.

80. "The Lecompton Constitution," Kansas Memory (quotations); Nicole Etcheson, "General Jackson Is Dead: James Buchanan, Stephen A. Douglas, and Kansas Policy," in Quist and Birkner, *James Buchanan*, 98–99.

81. James H. Forsyth to SAD, September 7, 1857, box 9, folder 1; J. Calhoun to SAD, September 28, 1857, box 9, folder 3; William Weer to SAD, November 8, 1857, box 9, folder 8; Joel Fisk to SAD, November 13, 1857, box 9, folder 9, SADP.

82. Charles E. Stuart to SAD, March 29, 1857, box 6, folder 16 (quotation); James D. Eads to SAD, November 19, 1857, box 9, folder 9; John W. Detrich to SAD, November 28, 1857, box 9, folder 12; E. M. Huntington to SAD, November 29, 1857, box 9, folder 12, SADP.

83. Thomas W. Thomas to Alexander H. Stephens, June 15, 1857, January 21, 1858, in U. Phillips, "Correspondence of Robert Toombs," 401, 428.

84. James P. France to William Bigler, December 9, 1857, box 8, folder 13, William Bigler Papers, HSP; Zimmerman, "Origin and Rise," 354; C. Zarley to James Buchanan, July 15, 1858, reel 35, James Buchanan Papers, HSP; McMaster, *History of the People of the United States*, 8:308.

85. SAD to John A. McClernand, November 23, 1857, *LSAD*, 403.

86. SAD to Charles H. Lanphier and George Walker, December 6, 1857, *LSAD*, 405. For the claim that Douglas fought Buchanan over personal and patronage matters, see Auchampaugh, "Buchanan-Douglas Feud"; and Luthin, "Democratic Split." For rebuttals that emphasize principle as well as self-preservation, see Stenberg, "Unnoted Factor"; Meerse, "Origins of the Buchanan-Douglas Feud Reconsidered"; Wells, *Stephen Douglas*, 32–33; and Johannsen, *SAD*, 582–84.

87. Thomas L. Harris to Charles H. Lanphier, December 3, 1857, box 1, folder 6, Charles H. Lanphier Papers, ALPL.

88. *New Orleans Daily Delta*, September 15, 1857; "Speech at Mississippi City" [October 2, 1857], *PJD*, 6:138–55; *New Orleans Daily Delta*, October 13, 1857; "Speech at Jackson" [November 4, 1857], *PJD*, 6:157–62.

89. Cooper, *JDA*, 283–85; Collins, "Democrats' Electoral Fortunes," 316–18.

90. "Coming to a Head," *Feliciana Democrat*, December 12, 1857; Etcheson, "General Jackson Is Dead," in Quist and Birkner, *James Buchanan*, 88.

91. Robert J. Walker to James Buchanan, June 28, 1857, box 1, folder 1, Walker (Robert J.) Papers, MDAH.

92. George Bancroft to James Buchanan, December 5, 1857, reel 34, James Buchanan Papers, HSP.

93. Buchanan, "First Annual Message to Congress," American Presidency Project (quotations); Baker, *James Buchanan*, 93; E. Smith, *Presidency of James Buchanan*, 16, 42–43; W. Freehling, *Road to Disunion*, 2:135–37.

94. *CG*, 35th Cong., 1st Sess., 5 (December 8, 1857).

95. *CG*, 35th Cong., 1st Sess., 15–18 (quotations p. 18) (December 9, 1857).

96. Nevins and Thomas, *Diary of George Templeton Strong*, 2:376.

97. *Marshall County Democrat*, December 24, 1857.

98. S. B. Benson to SAD, December 12, 1857, box 10, folder 8, SADP.

99. G. A. Smith to SAD, December 16, 1857, box 10, folder 8, SADP.

100. R. H. Stevens to SAD, December 28, 1857, box 12, folder 2, SADP. See also P. R. George to SAD, December 11, 1857, box 10, folder 7; Harley Green to SAD, December 13, 1857, box 10, folder 10; V. Dalrymple to SAD, December 14, 1857, box 10, folder 11; James Anderson to SAD, December 25, 1857, box 11, folder 18; Cornelius Dorrough to SAD, December 26, 1857, box 11, folder 19, SADP.

101. Martin Ryerson to SAD, December 18, 1857, box 11, folder 2, SADP.

102. George W. Lumbard to SAD, December 19, 1857, box 11, folder 4, SADP.

103. William W. Langer to SAD, December 14, 1857, box 10, folder 12 (quotation); John Haddock Smith to SAD, December 9, 1857, box 10, folder 5; N. P. Tallmadge to SAD, December 14, 1857, box 10, folder 14, SADP; A. Smith, *Stormy Present*, 117–18.

104. William Barrett to SAD, December 14, 1857, box 10, folder 11, SADP.

105. Charles E. Clarke to SAD, December 15, 1857, box 10, folder 15, SADP.

106. Enoch Moore to SAD, December 21, 1857, box 11, folder 9 (quotation); W. L.

Deneen to SAD, December 21, 1857, box 11, folder 8, SADP; Jesse Spangler to D. W. Spangler, March 10, 1858, Jesse Spangler Correspondence, Ohio Historical Society, Columbus.

107. William J. Allen to SAD, December 19, 1857, box 11, folder 3, SADP (quotation); *New York Evening Post*, December 14, 1857.

108. Lyman Trumbull to Abraham Lincoln, December 5, 1857, box 1, folder 8, Lyman Trumbull Family Papers, ALPL.

109. Lyman Trumbull to Abraham Lincoln, December 25, 1857, box 1, folder 8, Lyman Trumbull Family Papers, ALPL (quotation); Samuel Galloway to Lyman Trumbull, December 12, 1857; Charles S. Wilson to Lyman Trumbull, December 14, 1857; C. H. Ray to Lyman Trumbull, December 18, 1857, reel 3, Papers of Lyman Trumbull, LC.

110. W. H. Herndon to Lyman Trumbull, December 25, 1857, reel 3, Papers of Lyman Trumbull, LC.

111. William H. Herndon to Theodore Parker, December 26, 1857, Theodore Parker Papers, Massachusetts Historical Society, Boston (quotation); Samuel C. Parks to Lyman Trumbull, December 26, 1857, reel 3, Papers of Lyman Trumbull, LC; William Dennison to Joshua R. Giddings, February 23, 1858, Joshua R. Giddings Papers, Ohio Historical Society, Columbus.

112. Henry Wilson to Theodore Parker, February 28, 1858, Theodore Parker Papers, Massachusetts Historical Society, Boston. Emphasis original.

113. Lyman Trumbull to Abraham Lincoln, January 3, 1858, Abraham Lincoln Papers, LC; Lyman Trumbull to W. C. Flagg, January 8, 1858, box 1, folder 8, Lyman Trumbull Family Papers, ALPL; Burlingame, *Abraham Lincoln*, 1:445–56.

114. Abraham Lincoln to Lyman Trumbull, December 28, 1857, *CWAL*, 2:430 (quotation); B. C. Cook to Ozias M. Hatch, May 19, 1858, box 1, folder 2, O. M. Hatch Papers, ALPL.

115. Charles Adams to SAD, December 12, 1857, box 10, folder 8 (quotation); James A. Briggs to SAD, December 10, 1857, box 10, folder 6; George M. Davis to SAD, December 10, 1857, box 10, folder 6; A[mos] Nourse to SAD, December 13, 1857, box 10, folder 10; M. W. Barnett to SAD, December 17, 1857, box 10, folder 19; William K. Gibbs to SAD, December 22, 1857, box 11, folder 11; W. Perkins to SAD, December 23, 1857, box 11, folder 15; Samuel Harper to SAD, December 28, 1857, box 12, folder 3, SADP.

116. William R. Smith to SAD, December 18, 1857, box 11, folder 2, SADP; see also Joseph Fell to SAD, December 21, 1857, box 11, folder 8, SADP.

117. W. H. Settle to SAD, December 21, 1857, box 11, folder 10, SADP.

118. J. F. Shafer to SAD, December 16, 1857, box 10, folder 18 (quotation); J. K. Morehead to SAD, December 15, 1857, box 10, folder 16; O. F. Moore to SAD, December 20, 1857, box 11, folder 6, SADP.

119. J. F. White to SAD, December 16, 1857, box 10, folder 18, SADP.

120. Norman Eastman to SAD, December 18, 1857, box 10, folder 22; J. J. Browne to SAD, December 28, 1857, box 11, folder 22; F. S. Goble to SAD, December 28, 1857, box 11, folder 22, SADP.

121. Henry Langston to SAD, December 29, 1857, box 12, folder 3, SADP. For similar analysis from a Buchananite who worried about Douglas's appeal among Free-Soilers, see Adam Slemmer to James Buchanan, December 29, 1857, reel 34, James Buchanan Papers, HSP.

122. H. W. Moulton to SAD, December 16, 1857, box 10, folder 18 (quotations); A. E. Rogers to SAD, December 14, 1857, box 10, folder 13; Charles P. Denison to SAD, December 16, 1857, box 10, folder 17, SADP.

123. Samuel C. Frey to SAD, December 18, 1857, box 11, folder 3 (quotations); R. B. Warden to SAD, December 21, 1857, box 11, folder 10, SADP.

124. Earle, *Jacksonian Antislavery*; Wilentz, "Jeffersonian Democracy."

125. John Wyatt to SAD, December 8, 1857, box 10, folder 4 (quotation); W. B. Farrell to SAD, December 17, 1857, box 10, folder 20; J. B. Taylor to SAD, December 21, 1857, box 11, folder 10; C. B. Waite to SAD, December 29, 1857, box 12, folder 4, SADP.

126. James W. Davidson to SAD, December 12, 1857, box 10, folder 8 (quotation); A. G. Porter to SAD, December 28, 1857, box 12, folder 2, SADP.

127. Seth Paine to SAD, December 14, 1857, box 10, folder 13; Isaac G. Wilson to SAD, December 16, 1857, box 10, folder 18; C. Goudy to SAD, December 20, 1857, box 11, folder 6; A. J. Anderson to SAD, December 24, 1857, box 11, folder 16, SADP.

128. [Nathan] Knapp to O. M. Hatch, March 31, 1858, box 1, folder 2, O. M. Hatch Papers, ALPL; H. Prather to SAD, March 1, 1858, box 16, folder 6; P. W. Randle to SAD, July 4, 1858, box 21, folder 1, SADP.

129. David B. Malone, "Jonathan Blanchard," in Rodriguez, *Slavery in the United States*, 1:196–97.

130. J. Blanchard to SAD, May 1, 1858, box 19, folder 4, SADP.

131. [Schuyler Colfax], "Memorandum of Interview, Burlingame & Colfax with Douglas, at his residence, Dec 14 1857, 8½ to 11½ P.M.," box 1, folder 3, Schuyler Colfax Papers, Indiana State Library, Indianapolis. Thanks go to Andrew Wiley for sharing a copy of this document with me.

132. *New Orleans Daily Picayune*, December 17, 1857.

133. R. H. Jackson to JD, January 2, [1858], JDPTU.

134. J. C. Van Dyke to William Bigler, December 10, 1857, box 8, folder 14, William Bigler Papers, HSP; Adam Slemmer to James Buchanan, December 29, 1857, reel 34; Madison Kelley to James Buchanan, July 10, 1858, reel 35, James Buchanan Papers, HSP; James B. Miller to SAD, December 30, 1857, box 12, folder 6, SADP.

135. "The Apostacy of Stephen A. Douglas," *Charleston (S.C.) Herald*, reprinted in *The Liberator*, January 29, 1858.

136. *JDM*, 1:651.

137. John A. Quitman to John Marshall, February 1, 1858, in Claiborne, *Life and Correspondence of John A. Quitman*, 2:251–53; Leonard H. Mangum to Martha P. Mangum, January 15, 1858, in Shanks, *Papers of Willie Person Mangum*, 5:343–44; Craven, *Growth of Southern Nationalism*, 288.

138. *CG*, 35th Cong., 1st Sess., 858 (February 24, 1858) (quotations); Fehrenbacher, *Dred Scott Case*, 480–81; Etcheson, *Bleeding Kansas*, 171; Rawson, "Party Politics in Mississippi," 237–38.

139. L. Q. C. Lamar to B. S. Rozell, March 8, 1858, in Mayes, *Lucius Q. C. Lamar*, 73.

140. *JDM*, 1:574–77; *CG*, 35th Cong., 1st Sess., 390 (January 25, 1858).

141. Etcheson, *Bleeding Kansas*, 157–58, 163–67.

142. Fehrenbacher, *Dred Scott Case*, 470–71.

143. *CG*, 35th Cong., 1st Sess., 521, 524 (February 2, 1858).

144. *CG*, 35th Cong., 1st Sess., 618–19 (February 8, 1858).

145. *CG*, 35th Cong., 1st Sess., appendix, 194–201 (quotations p. 200) (March 22, 1858). Douglas specifically objected to two articles: "Free-Soilism," *Washington Daily Union*, November 17, 1857; and "Kansas and Her Constitution," *Washington Daily Union*, November 18, 1857.

146. Joseph Adolphus to SAD, January 30, 1858, box 14, folder 12; William Creighton to SAD, February 14, 1858, box 15, folder 11; Edward Barrington to SAD, February 22, 1858, box 15, folder 21; W. P. Bartlett to SAD, March 1, 1858, box 16, folder 5; Benjamin H. Moore to SAD, March 6, 1858, box 16, folder 15; Samuel Swasey to SAD, March 10, 1858, box 16, folder 21, SADP.

147. Jacob Brinkerhoff to SAD, March 29, 1858, box 17, folder 18; A. M. Bowker to SAD, January 8, 1858, box 13, folder 1; Andrew J. Ashton to SAD, January 11, 1858, box 13, folder 6; Franklin Fairchild to SAD, February 25, 1858, box 15, folder 26; [?] Cooley to SAD, March 12, 1858, box 16, folder 23; William H. Adams to SAD, March 15, 1858, box 16, folder 26; John Young to SAD, April [?], 1858, box 18, folder 25, SADP.

148. R. B. Hayes to SAD, January 1, 1858, box 12, folder 12; J. S. Roberts to SAD, January 7, 1858, box 12, folder 24; O. E. Hannum to SAD, January 16, 1858, box 13, folder 16; C. L. Barrett to SAD, January 18, 1858, box 13, folder 22; G. N. F. Muller to SAD, February 4, 1858, box 14, folder 21; Lew Hubbell to SAD, February 18, 1858, box 15, folder 15; L. Francis to SAD, February 23, 1858, box 15, folder 23; H. Bingham to SAD, February 26, 1858, box 15, folder 27; "Anti-Lecompton" to SAD, March 16, 1858, box 16, folder 27; S. Francis to SAD, May 3, 1858, box 19, folder 6, SADP.

149. M[ansfield] French to SAD, March 27, 1858, box 17, folder 14, SADP.

150. Hiram Martz to SAD, January 20, 1858, box 13, folder 24; John J. Quarles to SAD, January 30, 1858, box 14, folder 12; H. H. Wadlington to SAD, February [?], 1858, box 14, folder 14, SADP.

151. Baker, *James Buchanan*, 93–106; Summers, *Plundering Generation*, 251–54; *Covode Investigation Report*, esp. pp. 6–9; Holt, *Election of 1860*; Fry, *Republican "Campaign" Text-Book*, 94–96.

152. SAD to Samuel Treat, February 28, 1858, box 2, Samuel Treat Papers, Missouri History Museum Archives, St. Louis.

153. R. Nichols, *Disruption of American Democracy*, 170; Meerse, "Buchanan, the Patronage, and the Lecompton Constitution"; Etcheson, *Bleeding Kansas*, 169–70; Morrison, "President James Buchanan," in Quist and Birkner, *James Buchanan*, 153–56.

154. *CG*, 35th Cong., 1st Sess., 1264–65 (March 23, 1858).

155. *CG*, 35th Cong., 1st Sess., 1437–38 (April 1, 1858).

156. Etcheson, *Bleeding Kansas*, 179–80; Ponce, *To Govern the Devil*, 187.

157. See Davis's public letter in the *Mississippi Free Trader*: JD to F. Bostick, May 14, 1858, *JDC*, 3:228–31.

158. Quoted in Nevins, *Emergence of Lincoln*, 1:300.

159. *CG*, 35th Cong., 1st Sess., 1868–71 (quotation p. 1869) (April 29, 1858).

160. *CG*, 35th Cong., 1st Sess., 1899 (April 30, 1858).

161. *CG*, 35th Cong., 1st Sess., 1905–6 (April 30, 1858); Etcheson, *Bleeding Kansas*, 180–84; Ponce, *To Govern the Devil*, 187–92; Johannsen, *SAD*, 610–13.

162. Woods, *Emotional and Sectional Conflict*, 170–78; A. Smith, *Stormy Present*, 17, 121, 100–133; Foner, *Free Soil*, 305–8; Maizlish, *Strife of Tongues*, 7–8, 49–59.

163. Wilentz, *Rise of American Democracy*, 731–32; Rainwater, *Mississippi*, 59–62.

164. *JDM*, 1:584–643; Ralph Richardson, "Jefferson Davis, Sectional Diplomat, 1858," in Auer, *Antislavery and Disunion*, 51–70; W. Davis, *Jefferson Davis*, 265–68; Cooper, *JDA*, 290–93.

165. "Speech of Jefferson Davis on Fourth of July, 1858, at Sea"; "Speech of Jefferson Davis at the Portland Serenade, July 9th, 1858"; "Speech of Jefferson Davis at the Portland Convention" [August 24, 1858]; "Speech of Jefferson Davis at the Portland Meeting"; "Speech of Jefferson Davis at State Fair at Augusta, Me." [September 23, 1858]; "Speech of Jefferson Davis at the Grand Ratification Meeting, Faneuil Hall, Monday Evening, Oct. 11th, 1858"; "Speech of Jefferson Davis in the City of New York, Palace Garden Meeting, Oct. 19, 1858," all in *JDC*, 3:271–73, 274–81, 284–88, 295–305, 305–315, 315–32, 332–39. The speeches were compiled and published as J. Davis, *Speeches of the Hon. Jefferson Davis, of Mississippi, Delivered during the Summer of 1858*.

166. *JDM*, 1:641 (quotation); Crafts J. Wright to JD, July 19, [1858], *JDC*, 3:281–82; Anonymous to JD, November 25, 1858, *JDC*, 3:360–62; Escott, *After Secession*, 7–10.

167. *JDM*, 1:588–89.

168. Eaton, *Jefferson Davis*, 109; William E. Gienapp, "The Republican Party and the Slave Power," in Abzug and Maizlish, *New Perspectives*, 52; A. Smith, *Stormy Present*, 17; Collins, "Ideology of the Ante-bellum Northern Democrats," 104–5.

169. Catton and Catton, *Two Roads to Sumter*, 171.

170. "Speech of Jefferson Davis at the Portland Meeting," *JDC*, 3:299.

171. Burt, *Lincoln's Tragic Pragmatism*, 525; W. Davis, *Jefferson Davis*, 269; Escott, "Jefferson Davis and Slavery in the Territories," 106.

172. *Okolona Prairie News* quoted in Crist, "'Duty Man,'" 291 (first quotation); *Charleston (S.C.) Mercury*, quoted in W. Davis, *Jefferson Davis*, 266 (second quotation).

173. JD to Arthur C. Halbert, August 22, 1858, *PJD*, 4:204–7; Escott, "Jefferson Davis and Slavery in the Territories," 108–9.

174. Forney, *Anecdotes of Public Men*, 2:179.

175. For superb historiographical analysis, see James L. Huston, "The Continuing Debate about the 'Great Debates' of 1858: A Critical Review of Recent Literature," in Johannsen, *Lincoln-Douglas Debates*, iv–xxxvi.

176. Burlingame, *Abraham Lincoln*, 1:1–442; Johannsen, *Lincoln, the South, and Slavery*; Fehrenbacher, *Prelude to Greatness*; Etcheson, "'Living, Creeping Lie.'"

177. Wells, *Stephen Douglas*, 81 (first quotation), 89 (second quotation).

178. C. F. Rock to SAD, April 6, 1858, box 18, folder 3, SADP. On the national attention, see Zarefsky, *Lincoln, Douglas, and Slavery*, x–xi.

179. Henry S. Fitch to James Buchanan, August 17, 1858, reel 35; Isaac Cook to James Buchanan, October 27, 1858, reel 36, James Buchanan Papers, HSP; I. Cook to Sidney Breese, August 27, 1858; James J. Clarkson to Sidney Breese, August 30, 1858; Isaac H. Sturgeon to Sidney Breese, September 11, 14, 1858; George W. Jones to Sidney Breese, September 17, October 17, 1858, Sidney Breese Papers re: Election of 1858, ALPL.

180. Letter, R. B. Carpenter to James Buchanan, June 23, 1858, ALPL; Collins, "Lincoln-Douglas Contest," 401–3; Zarefsky, *Lincoln, Douglas, and Slavery*, 58; Guelzo, *Lincoln and Douglas*, 170–71.

181. Abraham Lincoln to Henry Asbury, July 31, 1858, *CWAL*, 2:530.

182. Donald, *Lincoln*, 212–13.

183. Charles Leib to William Bigler, June 16, 19, 1858, box 9, folder 23; Henry S. Fitch to William Bigler, September 22, 1858, box 9, folder 27, William Bigler Papers, HSP; Daniel S. Dickinson to James Buchanan, August 27, 1858, reel 35, James Buchanan Papers, HSP.

184. W. N. Coler to SAD, August 30, 1858, box 21, folder 14, SADP; Henry S. Fitch to James Buchanan, August 17, 1858, reel 35, James Buchanan Papers, HSP; George W. Jones to Sidney Breese, October 17, 1858, Sidney Breese Papers re: Election of 1858, ALPL; Isaac H. Sturgeon to Howell Cobb, May 17, 1858, in R. Brooks, "Howell Cobb Papers" (September 1922), 237.

185. H. Foote, *Casket of Reminiscences*, 135; James S. Green to Samuel Treat, September 29, 1858, box 2, Samuel Treat Papers, Missouri History Museum Archives, St. Louis; John Slidell to James Buchanan, August 8, 1858, reel 35, James Buchanan Papers, HSP; Herndon and Weik, *Herndon's Lincoln*, 410; Sheahan, *Life of Stephen A. Douglas*, 439–42.

186. Thomas Foster to SAD, September 16, 1858, box 21, folder 16; B. B. Weeks to SAD, October 5, 1858, box 21, folder 18, SADP.

187. Douglas received detailed advice on how to win them back; see Luther Dearborn to SAD, June 11, 1858, box 20, folder 16; A. H. Terrell to SAD, July 27, 1858, box 21, folder 9, SADP.

188. Johannsen, *Lincoln-Douglas Debates*, 16 (first quotation), 17 (second quotation), 18 (third, fourth, and fifth quotations).

189. Wells, *Stephen Douglas*, 96; Burt, *Lincoln's Tragic Pragmatism*, 94–177; Jaffa, *Crisis of the House Divided*, vi; Etcheson, "'Living, Creeping Lie.'"

190. Abraham Lincoln to Henry Asbury, July 31, 1858, *CWAL*, 2:339.

191. Johannsen, *Lincoln-Douglas Debates*, 26 (quotations), 24.

192. Johannsen, 289–90.

193. Johannsen, 223.

194. Johannsen, 79. Some Douglasites anticipated this question; for advice written one day too late, see S. W. Randall to SAD, August 28, 1858, box 21, folder 14, SADP.

195. Zarefsky, *Lincoln, Douglas, and Slavery*, 96; Donald, *Lincoln*, 219.

196. Jaffa, *Crisis of the House Divided*, vi, 2.

197. Johannsen, *Lincoln-Douglas Debates*, 90–91.

198. Johannsen, 88.

199. Johannsen, 145–49, 159–61, 217, 269–71.

200. Johannsen, 298.

201. Fehrenbacher, *Dred Scott Case*, 455–56, 496, 501; Wells, *Stephen Douglas*, 124; Harris, *Lincoln's Rise to the Presidency*, 112, 123.

202. M. H. Maginnis to SAD, September 20, 1858, box 21, folder 16, SADP.

203. "Judge Douglas Repudiates the Dred Scott Decision," *Washington Daily Union*, September 4, 1858; "The Cause of Douglas in the South," *Alexandria Gazette* (Washington, D.C.), September 4, 1858; "The Nullification of Rights by the Denial of Remedies," *Washington Daily Union*, September 11, 1858; "Douglas," *Mississippian*, reprinted in *Yazoo Democrat*, September 18, 1858; "Judge Douglas and the Dred Scott Decision," *Abbeville (S.C.) Independent Press*, October 15, 1858; *Port Gibson Daily Southern Reveille*, February 25, 1859.

204. For an enumeration of Douglas's racist rhetoric, see Burlingame, *Abraham Lincoln*, 1:468, 473–74, 489–90, 494–95, 506–7, 511, 512–13, 515–16, 517–18, 520–21.

205. Johannsen, *Lincoln-Douglas Debates*, 33.

206. Johannsen, 45–46, 127–28, 196, 212–16, 237–38, 263–64, 299–300.

207. Johannsen, 326.

208. Dirck, *Abraham Lincoln and White America*, 63–84; Fredrickson, *Big Enough to Be Inconsistent*, 43–84; Striner, *Lincoln and Race*, 21–30.

209. On Lincoln, see especially Oakes, *Radical and the Republican*, 117–31. For a superb point about the strategic elements of Douglas's racism, which pulls back from its conclusions, see Burt, *Lincoln's Tragic Pragmatism*, 382.

210. Berwanger, *Frontier against Slavery*; Bilotta, *Race and the Rise of the Republican Party*.

211. John C. Pepper et al. to SAD, August 12, 1858, box 21, folder 12, SADP.

212. Burt, *Lincoln's Tragic Pragmatism*, 519; Bean, "Anti-Jeffersonianism in the Ante-bellum South."

213. Johannsen, *Lincoln-Douglas Debates*, 46–48 (quotations p. 46).

214. Johannsen, 128–29, 216, 299–300; *CG*, 35th Cong., 1st Sess., 1965 (May 5, 1858).

215. *Journal of the Convention of the People of South Carolina*, 465; Levine, *Fall of the House of Dixie*, 46.

216. Johannsen, *SAD*, 677–79.

217. SAD to C. H. Lanphier, January 6, 185[9], box 1, folder 7, Charles H. Lanphier Papers, ALPL. The telegraph operator mistakenly dated it 1858.

218. A. Smith, *Stormy Present*, 117; R. Nichols, *Disruption of American Democracy*, 223–24; Collins, "Lincoln-Douglas Contest," 397–98; Meerse, "Northern Democratic Party."

219. Mayes, *Lucius Q. C. Lamar*, 619.

220. "Speech Delivered at Hazlehurst, Mississippi, on the 11th of September, 1858," in Cluskey, *Speeches, Messages, and Other Writings*, 588–99.

221. Rainwater, *Mississippi*, 59–62, 67; Rawson, "Party Politics in Mississippi," 244–45.

222. "The Southern League," *Okolona Prairie News*, August 12, 1858.

223. "Speech of Jefferson Davis before the Mississippi Legislature, November 16, 1858," *JDC*, 3:339–60. See also "Speech at Vicksburg" [November 27, 1858], *PJD*, 4:228–29; and JD to Mississippi Citizens, December 18, 1858, *PJD*, 6:229–31.

224. Escott, *After Secession*, 11.

225. Collin S. Tarpley to JD, December 1, 1858, PJDRU.

CHAPTER 6

1. Halstead, *Caucuses of 1860*, 1.

2. Halstead, 2.

3. Halstead, 3–4.

4. "The Re-election of Senator Douglas," *New York Herald*, January 9, 1859.

5. C. H. Ray to Ozias M. Hatch, [November 1858], box 1, folder 3, O. M. Hatch Papers, ALPL.

6. Estes, *Defence of Negro Slavery*, 92 (quotations), 95.

7. Takaki, *Pro-slavery Crusade*; Sinha, *Counterrevolution of Slavery*, 125–52; L. W. Spratt to John A. Quitman, September 7, 1857, box 5B, folder 16, Quitman (John A.) and Family Papers, MDAH; "Southern Commercial Convention," *Yazoo Democrat*, May 14, 1859.

8. R. Davis, *Recollections of Mississippi*, 375–76; JD to Clement C. Clay, May 17, 1859, *PJD*, 6:251–52; JD to J. L. M. Curry, June 4, 1859, *PJD*, 6:253–54; Joseph R. Davis to JD, June 6, 1859, *JDC*, 4:54–55; Horatio J. Harris to JD, June 7, 1859, *JDC*, 4:55–56; William F. Mason to JD, June 21, 1859, JDPTU.

9. McCardell, *Idea of a Southern Nation*, 136–37.

10. "Speech of Jefferson Davis before the Democratic State Convention at Jackson, Miss., July 6, 1859," *JDC*, 4:65–70 (first quotation p. 69, second quotation p. 70). In 1851, Davis and Douglas divided over Henry Clay's resolution calling for research into suppression of American participation in the African slave trade. It passed 45–9, with Douglas in favor and Davis voting with the predominantly southern Democratic minority. *CG*, 31st Cong., 2nd Sess., 307–8 (January 20, 1851).

11. "Speech of Jefferson Davis before the Mississippi Legislature, November 16, 1858," *JDC*, 3:345.

12. Burt, *Lincoln's Tragic Pragmatism*, 557; Wilentz, *Rise of American Democracy*, 754–56; McCardell, *Idea of a Southern Nation*, 315–19; Ranck, *Albert Gallatin Brown*, 162–64.

13. "Mr. Douglas on His Southern Pilgrimage," *New York Herald*, December 6, 1858; Douglas, *Speeches of Senator S. A. Douglas*, 3–10.

14. May, "'Southern Strategy'"; May, *Southern Dream*; May, *Manifest Destiny's Underworld*; May, *Slavery, Race, and Conquest*. On Davis's multifaceted interaction with filibusters and southward expansion, see Quaife, *Diary of James K. Polk*, 3:499–500; *JDM*, 1:412–13; James Gadsden to JD, July 19, 1854, *PJD*, 5:78–81; "Speech at Vicksburg" [May 18, 1857], *PJD*, 4:118–19; "Speech at Jackson" [May 29, 1857], *PJD*, 4:120–25; and "Speech at Vicksburg" [November 27, 1858], *PJD*, 4:228–29. Following the Lecompton battle, some southerners urged Douglas to promote tropical expansion in order to boost his popularity; see Edward Deloney to SAD, November 8, 1858, box 21, folder 25; James S. Drew to SAD, November 12, 1858, box 22, folder 3; and James Barton S. Pringle to SAD, February 22, 1859, box 24, folder 10, SADP.

15. "Senator Douglas Once More—Read!," *Port Gibson Daily Southern Reveille*, December 4, 1858.

16. "Douglas and Wilmot," *Brandon (Miss.) Republican*, reprinted in *Port Gibson Daily Southern Reveille*, December 25, 1858.

17. See the comments and quoted text in "Awful!—Won't Somebody Hold Him?," *Clarksville (Tenn.) Chronicle*, January 7, 1859. Similar blurbs appeared in the *Wheeling (Va.) Daily Intelligencer*, January 10, 1859; *Middlebury (Vt.) Register*, January 12, 1859; *The Liberator*, January 14, 1859; *New York Herald*, January 18, 1859; *Buchanan County Guardian* (Iowa), February 3, 1859; and *Highland Weekly News* (Hillsborough, Ohio), February 3, 1859.

18. For the final Senate vote on the Minnesota bill, see *CG*, 35th Cong., 1st Sess., 1516 (April 7, 1858). Davis did not vote. For the vote on the Oregon bill, which Davis opposed, see *CG*, 35th Cong., 1st Sess., 2209 (May 18, 1858).

19. Eaton, *Jefferson Davis*, 110–11 (quotation); Johannsen, *SAD*, 685–88; R. Nich-

ols, *Disruption of American Democracy*, 228–29; James S. Green to Samuel Treat, December 14, 1858, box 2, Samuel Treat Papers, Missouri History Museum Archives, St. Louis; "Interesting from Washington," *New York Herald*, December 10, 1858; "Washington News and Gossip," *Washington (D.C.) Evening Star*, December 10, 1858; "The Case of Mr. Douglas among the Democracy of the Senate," *New York Herald*, December 11, 1858; "Mr. Douglas, Degraded, but Not Excommunicated," *National Era*, December 16, 1858.

20. Allen Smith to SAD, December 11, 1858, box 22, folder 18 (first quotation); James D. Eads to SAD, December 22, 1858, box 22, folder 21 (second quotation); W. G. Cogar to SAD, January 27, 1859, box 23, folder 18 (third quotation), SADP; J. C. Allen to Charles H. Lanphier, December 12, 1858, box 1, folder 7, Charles H. Lanphier Papers, ALPL (fourth quotation).

21. S. S. Marshall to Charles H. Lanphier, December 9, 1858, box 1, folder 7, Charles H. Lanphier Papers, ALPL.

22. M. McConnell to SAD, December 10, 1858, box 22, folder 17, SADP.

23. "A Lick at Judge Douglas," *Ottawa Free Trader*, December 18, 1858.

24. *Yazoo Democrat*, January 1, 1859 (quotation); *Port Gibson Daily Southern Reveille*, December 21, 1858; "The Committee on Territories," *Port Gibson Daily Southern Reveille*, January 14, 1859.

25. "The Duello," *Harper's Weekly*, January 8, 1859, 18. On the long history of proslavery violence in Congress, see Freeman, *Field of Blood*.

26. "'Will Douglas Fight?'—That's the Question," *Wabash Express* (Terre Haute, Ind.), January 5, 1859; Herndon and Weik, *Herndon's Lincoln*, 410; Sheahan, *Life of Stephen A. Douglas*, 439–42; Johannsen, *SAD*, 689.

27. James B. Steadman to SAD, January 5, 1859, box 23, folder 1, SADP.

28. W. W. Wick to SAD, December 30, 1858, box 22, folder 24, SADP.

29. Johannsen, *SAD*, 689–90; Wells, *Stephen Douglas*, 168.

30. Quinn, *Rivals*, 260–76; Wells, *Stephen Douglas*, 170–71; M. D. Leggett to SAD, February 14, 1860, box 29, folder 29; John D. Bromer to SAD, March 20, 1860, box 31, folder 18; A. D. Ferren to SAD, December 10, 1860, box 36, folder 17, SADP.

31. *CG*, 35th Cong., 2nd Sess., 1004–11 (February 12, 1859); Matthew Glassman, "Beyond the Balance Rule: Congress, Statehood, and Slavery, 1850–1859," in Finkelman and Kennon, *Congress and the Crisis of the 1850s*, 80–96.

32. "Oregon Admitted into the Union," *Philadelphia Press*, February 14, 1859.

33. *CG*, 35th Cong., 2nd Sess., 73 (December 14, 1858).

34. *CG*, 35th Cong., 2nd Sess., 333–34 (January 12, 1859), 358 (January 13, 1859), 416 (January 18, 1859).

35. Russel, *Improvement of Communication*, 229–32.

36. *CG*, 35th Cong., 2nd Sess., 1260 (February 23, 1859).

37. *CG*, 35th Cong., 2nd Sess., 1247–48, 1256–57, 1259 (February 23, 1859).

38. *CG*, 35th Cong., 2nd Sess., 1244–47, 1258–59 (February 23, 1859).

39. *Alexandria Gazette*, February 25, 1859 (quotation); Dickerson, "Stephen A. Douglas," 205–10; Ranck, *Albert Gallatin Brown*, 166–68; R. Nichols, *Disruption of American Democracy*, 233–35; Fehrenbacher, *Dred Scott Case*, 506–13; Johannsen, *SAD*, 693–97.

40. Ferd. Kennett to SAD, February 25, 1859, box 24, folder 13 (first quotation); Benjamin Patten to SAD, March 3, 1859, box 24, folder 18 (second quotation); Sam F.

Tappan to SAD, February 24, 1859, box 24, folder 12; James D. Eads to SAD, March 4, 1859, box 24, folder 19; Solomon Parsons to SAD, March 18, 1859, box 24, folder 24, SADP.

41. Clement C. Clay to JD, May 23, 1859, JDPTU; B. F. Jones to SAD, February 28, 1859, box 24, folder 15, SADP; Fehrenbacher, *Dred Scott Case*, 512–13.

42. *Columbus (Ga.) Times* reprinted in *Richmond (Va.) Enquirer*, March 15, 1859.

43. *CG*, 35th Cong., 2nd Sess., 236–39 (February 24, 1859).

44. "Eli Thayer, of Massachusetts," *M'Arthur (Ohio) Democrat*, March 31, 1859 (quotation); *The Liberator*, March 25, 1859; "Douglas and Davis," *Sacramento Daily Union*, April 7, 1859.

45. "Worthy of Note," *Mississippian*, reprinted in *Nashville Patriot*, April 2, 1859.

46. SAD to [James W. Singleton], March 31, 1859, *LSAD*, 439; SAD to [James M. Scofield], [March 1859], *LSAD*, 440.

47. J. H. Clay Mudd to SAD, April 9, 1859, box 25, folder 3 (quotation); Otis Bullard to SAD, April 11, 1859, box 25, folder 3; A. E. Harmon to SAD, July 12, 1859, box 25, folder 20, SADP.

48. H. B. Payne to SAD, April 13, 1859, box 25, folder 4, SADP.

49. Stuart, *Iowa Colonels and Regiments*, 639–50; Evans, *Sherman's Horsemen*, 234–36, 270–71; Joseph B. Dorr, "Journal of My Imprisonment in the Rebellion," in Genoways and Genoways, *Perfect Picture of Hell*, 92–109.

50. SAD to J. B. Dorr, June 22, 1859, *LSAD*, 446–47.

51. SAD to John L. Peyton, August 2, 1859, *LSAD*, 452; SAD to Henry K. McCoy, September 27, 1859, *LSAD*, 468–69; Douglas, *Removal of Judge Douglas*; Wells, *Stephen Douglas*, 174–79.

52. "Senator Douglas's Letter," *New Orleans Bee*, reprinted in *West Baton Rouge (La.) Sugar Planter*, July 2, 1859.

53. J. B. Dorr to SAD, June 30, 1859, box 25, folder 17 (quotation); W. C. Rice to SAD, June 24, 1859, box 25, folder 15; Cyrus Powers to SAD, June 30, 1859, box 25, folder 17; W. W. Wick to SAD, July 7, 1859, box 25, folder 19, SADP. For Republican concern over the letter's impact, see J. M. Lucas to [Ozias M. Hatch], June 24, 1859, box 1, folder 5, O. M. Hatch Papers, ALPL. Publicly, however, most Republicans wrote it off as a shallow ploy for the presidency; see "The 'True Intent and Meaning' of Mr. Douglas' Letter," *Chicago Press and Tribune*, July 11, 1859.

54. James A. Nisbet to SAD, June 25, 1859, box 25, folder 16; L. V. B. Martin to SAD, June 28, 1859, box 25, folder 17, SADP.

55. James Buchanan to Robert Tyler, June 27, 1859, in J. B. Moore, *Works of James Buchanan*, 10:325–26.

56. JD to Franklin Pierce, September 2, 1859, *JDC*, 4:93–94. See also "The Best Yet," *North-Carolinian* (Fayetteville), July 2, 1859; "The Charleston Convention—Gov. Wise," *Jeffersonville (Va.) Advocate*, reprinted in *Richmond Enquirer*, July 4, 1859; "The Issue," *Richmond Enquirer*, July 12, 1859; "Green on Douglas," *Glasgow Weekly Times*, July 21, 1859; and "The Douglas Ultimatum," *Weekly Mississippian* (Jackson), April 11, 1860.

57. "Speech of Jefferson Davis before the Democratic State Convention at Jackson, Miss., July 6, 1859," *JDC*, 4:61–88 (quotation p. 77).

58. "Platform of the Democracy of Mississippi," *Weekly Mississippian*, July 20, 1859; "Democratic Platform," *Okolona Prairie News*, July 21, 1859.

59. On the essay's origins, see Johannsen, *SAD*, 705–8; SAD to George Bancroft, April 11, 1859, *LSAD*, 442–43; and SAD to William A. Seaver, July 17, 1859, *LSAD*, 449. On its contents, see Johannsen, "Stephen A. Douglas, 'Harper's Magazine,' and Popular Sovereignty"; Burt, *Lincoln's Tragic Pragmatism*, 560–73; and Fehrenbacher, *Dred Scott Case*, 514–23.

60. Stephen Douglas, "The Dividing Line between Federal and Local Authority: Popular Sovereignty in the Territories," *Harper's New Monthly Magazine*, September 1859, 519–37 (quotations p. 521).

61. "Senator Douglas' Last Essay on Territorial Government," *Richmond Enquirer*, September 9, 1859. The *Enquirer's* attack was widely reprinted and approved in the southern press; see "The Richmond Enquirer on the Douglas Magazine Essay," *Weekly Mississippian*, September 21, 1859.

62. "The Downward Road," *Weekly Mississippian*, October 5, 1859.

63. George W. Woodward to Jeremiah S. Black, September 19, 1859, reel 12, Jeremiah Sullivan Black Papers, LC.

64. [Black], *Observations on Senator Douglas's Views.*

65. Johannsen, *SAD*, 711–14, 948n60.

66. Southern Citizen [Reverdy Johnson], *Remarks on Popular Sovereignty.*

67. [Percy Roberts], "Popular Sovereignty. A Review of Mr. Douglas's Article on Popular Sovereignty," *DeBow's Review* 27 (December 1859): 625–47 (quotations p. 625).

68. JD to John P. Heiss, September 8, 1859, *PJD*, 6:261–62. The letter appeared in the *Washington (D.C.) Statesman*, September 14, 1859, and was widely reprinted, including as "Letter from Hon. Jefferson Davis," *Weekly Mississippian*, September 21, 1859. See also Davis's November 17, 1859, speech at Jackson in *Vicksburg Weekly Whig*, November 23, 1859.

69. "Another Manifesto," *Mississippian*, reprinted in *Yazoo Democrat*, November 12, 1859 (first quotation); C. H. Mott to James Willis Nesmith, September 29, 1859, box 2, folder 18, James Willis Nesmith Papers, ORHS (second quotation). Emphasis original.

70. A. W. Sweet to SAD, November 27, 1859, box 27, folder 18, SADP (quotation), emphasis original; N. J. Eaton to [Ferdinand Kennett], September 11, 1859, Kennett Family Papers, Missouri History Museum Archives, St. Louis.

71. Cooper, *JDA*, 300–304; Sanders, "Jefferson Davis," 487; Wilentz, *Rise of American Democracy*, 731–32.

72. Albert G. Brown to SAD, September 10, 1859, box 26, folder 13, SADP. Emphasis original.

73. D. Kelley, "Harper's Ferry" (quotation p. 352); "An Abolitionist" to John J. Pettus, November 30, 1859, and Charles C. Thornton to John J. Pettus, December 13, 1859, roll 1769, Mississippi Governor (1859–1863: Pettus) Correspondence and Papers, MDAH; John J. Pettus to JD, December 20, 1859, and JD to John J. Pettus, December 29, 1859, PJDRU.

74. Milton, *Eve of Conflict*, 396. See also M. Gross to SAD, November 6, 1859, box 27, folder 9, SADP.

75. James D. Eads to SAD, November 17, 1859, box 27, folder 15, SADP.

76. W. Davis, *Jefferson Davis*, 271–72; Everett, *Brierfield*, 60–63; Bleser, "Marriage of Varina Howell," 15; Varina Howell Davis to JD, April 3, 10, 1859, PJDRU.

77. SAD to Adele Cutts Douglas, May 27, 1859, box 52, folder 11 (quotation), May 28, June 8, September 11, 1859, box 52, folder 12, SADP.

78. George S. Park to SAD, January 8, 1858, box 13, folder 4; A. Watson to SAD, April 17, 1858, box 18, folder 15; D. Pat. Henderson to SAD, December 8, 1858, box 22, folder 16; J. J. Worley to SAD, December 12, 1858, box 22, folder 18; Memorial for a Pacific Railroad, Presented by W. A. Gwyer, G. C. Monell and A. D. Jones, and Adopted by the Convention at Omaha City, January 29, 1859, box 23, folder 19; Albert L. Collins to SAD, February 8, 1859, box 24, folder 8; D. Connely to SAD, February 14, 1859, box 24, folder 5; James Ritchie to SAD, June 4, 1859, box 25, folder 13; D. P. Henderson to SAD, January 30, 1860, box 29, folder 6; David Smoke to SAD, [February 1860], box 29, folder 10; B. B. Meeker to SAD, February 25, 1860, box 30, folder 13; W. R. Hurley to SAD, December 10, 1860, box 36, folder 17; James M. Martin to SAD, January 4, 1861, box 37, folder 7; Henry Farnam to SAD, January 16, 1861, box 37, folder 20; J. F. Soutter to SAD, January 23, 1861, box 38, folder 1, SADP.

79. George B. Loring to SAD, February 7, 1857, box 6, folder 1; Tarleton Jones to SAD, February 12, 1857, box 6, folder 4; Samuel W. Fuller to SAD, February 24, 1857, box 44, folder 2; Charles Ellet Jr. to SAD, April 4, 1857, box 7, folder 1; William Gooding to SAD, September 25, 1857, box 9, folder 3, SADP.

80. William S. Wait to SAD, February 13, 1858, box 15, folder 10; Benjamin Price to SAD, May 28, 1858, box 20, folder 5; S. F. Clark to SAD, [February ?, 1859], box 23, folder 22; Charles H. Strong to SAD, March 7, 1859, box 24, folder 21; G. W. Stokes to SAD, February 6, 1860, box 29, folder 19; William Quartermass to SAD, March 20, 1860, box 31, folder 18; Ralph Leete to SAD, April 4, 1860, box 32, folder 8; Benjamin Price to SAD, June 5, 1860, box 34, folder 25; Jonathan Kidd Sutton et al. to SAD, June 28, 1860, box 35, folder 13; Reuben Searls et al. to SAD, August 24, 1860, box 36, folder 6; George Berry to SAD, December 10, 1860, box 36, folder 17, SADP; Huston, *Panic of 1857*.

81. For Senate passage, see *CG*, 36th Cong., 1st Sess., 2043 (May 10, 1860). Davis and Douglas voted together with the majority, though most of the negative votes came from the South. For Buchanan's veto message, see *CG*, 36th Cong., 1st Sess., 3263 (June 23, 1860). Davis opposed the Senate's failed attempt to override the veto; Douglas was absent but had paired off with Clement Clay of Alabama. See *CG*, 36th Cong., 1st Sess., 3272 (June 23, 1860).

82. W. S. Beatty to SAD, July 15, 1860, box 35, folder 20, SADP. Emphasis original.

83. R. Jones to SAD, December 18, 1859, box 28, folder 4, SADP (quotation); Klein, *President James Buchanan*, 346–47; Rutland, *Democrats*, 104; Catton and Catton, *Two Roads to Sumter*, 204.

84. Gates, "Struggle for Land"; A. Dean, *Agrarian Republic*, 37, 93–97; Huston, *British Gentry*; Frymer, *Building an American Empire*, 142–43; "Passage of the Homestead Bill," *Richmond Whig and Public Advertiser*, March 19, 1860, in Dumond, *Southern Editorials on Secession*, 59–62.

85. R. G. Murphy to SAD, June 17, 1852, box 3, folder 14, SADP.

86. Ellis Smalley to SAD, January 20, 1858, box 13, folder 25; S. Baker to SAD, June 2, 1858, box 20, folder 10; C. Basting to SAD, April 17, 1860, box 32, folder 20, SADP.

87. "Speech of F. P. Blair Jr., of Missouri," *Wabash Express*, August 3, 1859.

88. W. J. Fowler, "Opposition of Sham Democracy to Western Development," *National Era*, October 20, 1859 (quotations); "Homes to the Actual Settlers," *Wabash Express*, March 21, 1860; "To Candid Democrats—a Few Plain Suggestions," *Hartford Evening Press*, October 25, 1860, in Perkins, *Northern Editorials on Secession*, 1:63–64.

89. "Republican Party Platform of 1860," American Presidency Project; Fehrenbacher, "Illinois Political Attitudes," 310; Richardson, *Greatest Nation of the Earth*. Interestingly, supporters urged Douglas to endorse a precursor to the Morrill Act, which supported higher education by providing for land-grant colleges. See W. A. Pemill to SAD, February 14, 1858, box 15, folder 11; Charles D. Bragdon to SAD, April 28, 1858, box 19, folder 1; and Amos Brown to SAD, December 20, 1859, box 28, folder 5, SADP. When a land-grant college bill came up in 1859, Davis voted against it, while Douglas, who missed the vote but favored the bill, paired off with Robert Toombs of Georgia. *CG*, 35th Cong., 2nd Sess., 857 (February 7, 1859).

90. B. F. Bristow to SAD, December 26, 1859, box 28, folder 7, SADP.

91. Amos B. Corwine to JD, February 2, 1860, JDPTU.

92. JD to Sidney Webster, January 9, 1860, PJDRU (quotation); JD to Edwin De Leon, January 21, 1860, *PJD*, 6:270–71; JD to John R. Pease, February 10, 1860, *PJD*, 6:276–77.

93. SAD to Henry K. McCoy, September 27, 1859, *LSAD*, 468–69.

94. *CG*, 36th Cong., 1st Sess., 910–14 (quotation p. 910) (February 29, 1860).

95. *CG*, 36th Cong., 1st Sess., 916 (February 29, 1860).

96. *CG*, 36th Cong., 1st Sess., 916–17 (February 29, 1860).

97. *CG*, 36th Cong., 1st Sess., 494 (January 18, 1860).

98. *CG*, 36th Cong., 1st Sess., 568–78 (January 25, 1860), 592–602 (January 26, 1860).

99. *CG*, 36th Cong., 1st Sess., 935 (March 1, 1860) (quotations). Davis's earlier resolutions are in *CG*, 36th Cong., 1st Sess., 658 (February 2, 1860).

100. For the former, see Cooper, *JDA*, 304–7; Holt, *Election of 1860*, 44–45; and W. Freehling, *Road to Disunion*, 2:277–78. For the latter, see Hyman and Wiecek, *Equal Justice under Law*, 207; Durden, *Self-Inflicted Wound*, 79; and Johannsen, *SAD*, 729.

101. Escott, "Jefferson Davis and Slavery in the Territories," 110–13; Sanders, "Jefferson Davis," 498; Catton and Catton, *Two Roads to Sumter*, 182, 191.

102. John H. Steele to Strider, January 15, 1860, box 28, folder 17 (quotation); George W. Houk to SAD, January 16, 1860, box 28, folder 18; D. Gilchrist to SAD, January 17, 1860, box 28, folder 20; J. A. Cravens to SAD, January 20, 1860, box 28, folder 23; A. McKay to SAD, January 20, 1860, box 28, folder 23; H. V. Willson to SAD, January 21, 1860, box 28, folder 24; J. N. McClanahan to SAD, February 8, 1860, box 29, folder 22; S. G. Danby to SAD, February 13, 1860, box 29, folder 27; Sidney Lawrence to SAD, February 14, 1860, box 29, folder 29; J. Bayard Thomas to SAD, March 2, 1860, box 30, folder 21; Clement Webster to SAD, March 7, 1860, box 31, folder 3; Philo Wilson to SAD, March 16, 1860, box 31, folder 15, SADP.

103. W. B. Scates to SAD, January 20, 1860, box 28, folder 23, SADP.

104. Asa B. Merrill to SAD, May 28, 1860, box 34, folder 13, SADP.

105. W. W. Wick to SAD, November 22, 1858, box 22, folder 9, SADP; Gideon Gibson to JD, April 27, 1859, PJDRU; Isaac E. Morse to SAD, September 29, 1859, box 26, folder 19, SADP; Franklin Pierce to JD, January 6, 1860, *JDC*, 4:118–19; John R. Pease to JD, February 6, 1860, JDPTU; Howell Cobb to John B. Lamar, April 8, 1860,

in R. Brooks, "Howell Cobb Papers" (September 1922), 247; Alexander Hamilton to JD, April 16, 1860, published in *New York Herald*, April 22, 1860; H. M. Solomon to JD, April 27, 1860, *JDC*, 4:247–48; William H. Winder to JD, May 18, 1860, JDPTU.

106. "Mississippi Democratic State Convention," *Memphis Daily Appeal*, December 17, 1859; Joseph R. Davis to JD, December 13, 1859, *PJD*, 6:264.

107. JD to Edwin De Leon, January 21, 1860, *PJD*, 6:270–71.

108. J. C. Bennett to SAD, January 10, 1860, box 28, folder 15, SADP. Emphasis original.

109. "Hon S. A. Douglas," *Jersey City (N.J.) Daily Telegraph*, March 10, 1857; John Pearson to SAD, May 25, 1857, box 7, folder 14, SADP.

110. Democratic Douglas Arthur Association Minute Book (1858–1860), HSP.

111. D. A. Smalley to SAD, February 1, 1859, box 23, folder 22 (emphasis original) (quotation); George Clinton Bates to SAD, February 24, 1860, box 30, folder 12, SADP; R. S. Murphy to John A. McClernand, January 14, 1860, box 1, folder 13, John A. McClernand Papers, ALPL; Anthony Ten Eyck to Andrew Johnson, February 20, 1860, in Graf, Haskins, and Bergeron, *Papers of Andrew Johnson*, 3:437–39.

112. Thomas Farmer to SAD, March 8, 1860, box 31, folder 4, SADP. Emphasis original.

113. Legislature of the State of Mississippi, Resolutions, February 10, 1860, roll 1879, Mississippi Governor (1859–1863: Pettus) Correspondence and Papers, MDAH.

114. Levi W. Lawler to Lewis E. Parsons, December 28, 1859, Lewis E. Parsons Papers, Alabama Department of Archives and History, Montgomery.

115. W. B. Davis to John J. Pettus, November 23, 1859, roll 1769, Mississippi Governor (1859–1863: Pettus) Correspondence and Papers, MDAH.

116. *Opelika Weekly Southern Era*, April 18, 1860, quoted in R. Morris, *Long Pursuit*, 139.

117. *Cleveland Plain Dealer*, May 4, 1860, quoted in R. Morris, *Long Pursuit*, 149.

118. H. B. Payne to SAD, March 17, 1860, box 31, folder 16, SADP.

119. R. G. Murphy to SAD, March 26, 1860, box 31, folder 23 (quotations) (emphasis original); H. W. Harrington to SAD, March 31, 1860, box 32, folder 4, SADP.

120. Halstead, *Caucuses of 1860*, 230.

121. Halstead, 5 (quotation); Python, "The Secession of the South," *DeBow's Review* 28 (October 1860): 357–92; R. Nichols, *Disruption of American Democracy*, 256, 289–90; Wells, *Stephen Douglas*, 208–9, 218–19; Venable, "Conflict between the Douglas and Yancey Forces."

122. JD to Sidney Webster, January 8, 1860, PJDRU; JD to Edwin De Leon, January 21, 1860, *PJD*, 6:270–71; JD to Franklin Pierce, January 30, 1860, *JDC*, 4:184–85; JD to John R. Pease, February 10, 1860, *PJD*, 6:276–77; Cooper, *JDA*, 310–11.

123. Dubay, *John Jones Pettus*, 57–58.

124. Sanders, "Jefferson Davis," 495–96; Eaton, *Jefferson Davis*, 109, 115.

125. "The Charleston Convention—Importance of Its Bearings and Its Results," *New York Herald*, April 10, 1860.

126. Halstead, *Caucuses of 1860*, 8; Milton, *Eve of Conflict*, 428.

127. Halstead, *Caucuses of 1860*, 34–35.

128. *Proceedings of the Conventions at Charleston and Baltimore*, 45–46 (quotations

p. 45). Massachusetts delegate Benjamin Butler wrote a second minority report, which restated the Cincinnati Platform.

129. Halstead, *Caucuses of 1860*, 44 (first quotation), 42 (second quotation).

130. Halstead, 47.

131. *Proceedings of the Conventions at Charleston and Baltimore*, 60–62. On Barksdale's role in the convention, see Peterson, "Ethelbert Barksdale."

132. *Proceedings of the Conventions at Charleston and Baltimore*, 66–79 (first quotation p. 69; second quotation p. 77; third quotation p. 79).

133. Halstead, *Caucuses of 1860*, 49–50.

134. *Proceedings of the Conventions at Charleston and Baltimore*, 122.

135. Cooper, *JDA*, 311–12.

136. Halstead, *Caucuses of 1860*, 75.

137. Robert W. Johannsen, "Comment on 'Why the Democratic Party Divided,'" in Knoles, *Crisis of the Union*, 51–59; Hyman and Wiecek, *Equal Justice under Law*, 207; R. Nichols, *Disruption of American Democracy*, 320; Blaine, *Twenty Years of Congress*, 1:152.

138. *Proceedings of the Conventions at Charleston and Baltimore*, 138–40.

139. *Proceedings of the Conventions at Charleston and Baltimore*, 141–55.

140. L. Schuerman to SAD, May 2, 1860, box 33, folder 1, SADP.

141. J. Haddock Smith to SAD, May 5, 1860, box 33, folder 3; J. L. Foster to SAD, May 7, 1860, box 33, folder 4; James O'Donnell to SAD, May 8, 1860, box 33, folder 5; Asa B. Merrill to SAD, May 28, 1860, box 34, folder 13; Charles Raymond to SAD, June 5, 1860, box 34, folder 25, SADP; John M. Cook to SAD, June 12, 1860, box 1, folder 3, Stephen A. Douglas Incoming Correspondence and Papers, ALPL.

142. Halstead, *Caucuses of 1860*, 101–3.

143. *CG*, 36th Cong., 1st Sess., 1937–42 (May 7, 1860) (first quotation p. 1939; second and third quotations p. 1940; fourth quotation p. 1941).

144. *CG*, 36th Cong., 1st Sess., appendix, 301–16 (May 15–16, 1860) (first quotation p. 306; second, third, and fourth quotations p. 312; fifth quotation p. 314).

145. *CG*, 36th Cong., 1st Sess., appendix, 452–61 (May 16–17, 1860).

146. *CG*, 36th Cong., 1st Sess., 2151–55 (May 17, 1860) (first quotation p. 2151; subsequent quotations p. 2154).

147. *CG*, 36th Cong., 1st Sess., 2321–22 (May 24, 1860), 2350–52 (May 25, 1860).

148. "The Washington Abortion," *Augusta Daily Chronicle and Sentinel*, May 24, 1860, in Dumond, *Southern Editorials on Secession*, 110.

149. "The Consistency of the Democracy of Mississippi on the Question of Protection in the Territories" and "Speech of Hon. Jefferson Davis," *Weekly Mississippian*, May 30, 1860.

150. "News and Items," *Weekly North Iowa Times* (McGregor), May 23, 1860 (quotation); "The Speech of Mr. Douglas, and His Doctrine," *Penn-Yan (N.Y.) Democrat*, May 23, 1860.

151. *Vermont Phoenix* (Brattleboro), May 26, 1860.

152. "Douglas and Davis," *Ashtabula (Ohio) Weekly Telegraph*, May 26, 1860.

153. C. S. Wooten, "The Davis-Douglas Debate," *Charlotte Observer*, reprinted in *LaGrange (N.C.) Sentinel*, November 2, 1906.

154. William S. Everett to SAD, May 17, 1860, box 33, folder 14; Calvin Record to SAD, May 17, 1860, box 33, folder 15; Finlay W. King to SAD, May 18, 1860, box 33, folder 17; Charles Cole to SAD, May 21, 1860, box 33, folder 22; Daniel Phillips to SAD, May 23, 1860, box 34, folder 3; P. H. Tompkins to SAD, May 28, 1860, box 34, folder 13; Henry Mettle to SAD, June 5, 1860, box 34, folder 25, SADP. Shrewd Republicans recognized that many northern Democrats would defect if Douglas were defeated; Thurlow Weed advised Lincoln that if Douglas failed to win the nomination, "we shall have many of his Friends with us." Thurlow Weed to Abraham Lincoln, June 10, 1860, Abraham Lincoln Papers, LC.

155. "Address to the National Democracy," May [7], 1860, *PJD*, 6:289–93. See also L. Q. C. Lamar to C. H. Mott, May 29, 1860, in Mayes, *Lucius Q. C. Lamar*, 83; and JD to Franklin Pierce, June 13, 1860, *JDC*, 4:495–96.

156. SAD to William A. Richardson, June 20, 1860, *LSAD*, 492.

157. Halstead, *Caucuses of 1860*, 186.

158. "1860 Democratic Party Platform," American Presidency Project (quotation); *Proceedings of the Conventions at Charleston and Baltimore*, 155–241; Johannsen, *SAD*, 767–73.

159. *Proceedings of the Conventions at Charleston and Baltimore*, 241–55 (quotation p. 253).

160. K. Richards, *Isaac I. Stevens*, 347–57.

161. JD to William B. Sloan, July 8, 1860, *PJD*, 6:356–57.

162. Holt, *Election of 1860*, 129–30; W. Davis, *Jefferson Davis*, 282–84.

163. E. Smith, *Presidency of James Buchanan*, 125 (quotation); J. Davis, *Rise and Fall*, 1:52; Johannsen, *SAD*, 792, 793; Cooper, *JDA*, 313–14. Damon Wells doubts Davis's claims about this fusion strategy and Douglas's refusal to participate. Davis's account is short on details, and there is no evidence in Douglas's papers that he received such a proposal or discussed it with anyone. See Wells, *Stephen Douglas*, 246. I am inclined to accept that the offer was made and rejected for the aforementioned reasons, but Davis's postwar commentary should be read critically.

164. Halstead, *Caucuses of 1860*, 36; R. Nichols, *Disruption of American Democracy*, 338–39; K. Richards, *Isaac I. Stevens*, 349–51; Holt, *Election of 1860*, 137, 146. A. James Fuller downplays the House strategy but notes that some National Democrats pondered it. See Fuller, "A Forlorn Hope: Interpreting the Breckinridge Campaign as a Matter of Honor," in *Election of 1860 Reconsidered*, 69–102.

165. "Speech, July 9, 1860," in J. B. Moore, *Works of James Buchanan*, 10:457–64 (quotations p. 460).

166. John H. Cochran to Dear Mother, October 8, 1860, Cochran Family Letters, Special Collections, Virginia Polytechnic Institute and State University, Blacksburg. Emphasis original.

167. *Montgomery Daily Mail*, July 6, 1860, quoted in Craven, *Growth of Southern Nationalism*, 342 (quotation); "The Democratic Party," *Charleston Mercury*, in Dumond, *Southern Editorials on Secession*, 67–69; Zimmerman, "Origin and Rise," 402–3.

168. Aughey, *Tupelo*, 22–23.

169. *R. R. B's Southern Platform*, pamphlet in William Harrison Hamman Papers, box 2, folder 5, Woodson Research Center, Fondren Library, Rice University.

170. "Speech at Corinth" [September 21, 1860], *PJD*, 6:364–66; "Speech at Memphis" [September 22, 1860], *PJD*, 6:366–67; "Davis vs. Bell," *Mississippi Free Trader*, October 8, 1860; "Col. Jeff Davis—Hail to the Chief!," *Mississippi Free Trader*, October 8, 1860; "A Tribute to Jefferson Davis by a Lady," *Mississippian*, November 6, 1860; "Arrogance," *Daily Vicksburg Whig*, November 7, 1860. Davis also stumped for Breckinridge in Washington, D.C.; see "Speech at Washington" [July 9, 1860], *PJD*, 6:358–60.

171. Bunkers, *Diary of Caroline Seabury*, 59.

172. "Arrogance," *Daily Vicksburg Whig*, November 7, 1860.

173. Rainwater, *Mississippi*, 152–56; Cooper, *JDA*, 314–15.

174. James W. Williams to SAD, September 22, 1860, box 36, folder 9, SADP.

175. R. Nichols, *Disruption of American Democracy*, 333–34; Milton, *Eve of Conflict*, 488–90; Johannsen, *SAD*, 781–82; H. H. Sibley to SAD, July 16, 1860, box 35, folder 21; Miles Taylor to SAD, August 13, 1860, box 36, folder 4; V. Hickox to SAD, September 16, 1860, box 36, folder 9, SADP.

176. M. A. Sarles to SAD, August 10, 1860, box 36, folder 3, SADP.

177. H. B. Tebbetts to SAD, August 19, 1860, box 36, folder 6; E. J. Sullivan to SAD, September 10, 1860, box 36, folder 8, SADP.

178. Johannsen, "Stephen A. Douglas' New England Campaign."

179. Douglas, *Speech of Hon. S. A. Douglas, of Illinois, Delivered in the City of Petersburg* (quotation p. 8); James L. Huston, "The 1860 Southern Sojourns of Stephen A. Douglas and the Irrepressible Separation," in Fuller, *Election of 1860 Reconsidered*, 29–67; Lionel Crocker, "The Campaign of Stephen A. Douglas in the South, 1860," in Auer, *Antislavery and Disunion*, 262–78.

180. "Movements of Senator Douglas," *New York Herald*, August 27, 1860.

181. Douglas, *Speech of Hon. S. A. Douglas, of Illinois, Delivered in the City of Petersburg*, 6–7, 14–15.

182. Huston, "1860 Southern Sojourns," 40. Northern Douglasite editors agreed: see "The Right to Secede," *Davenport Democrat and News*, November 17, 1860; "The People, the States and the Union," *Providence Daily Post*, November 19, 1860; and "Secession," *Burlington (Vt.) Weekly Sentinel*, December 14, 1860, all in Perkins, *Northern Editorials on Secession*, 1:176–77, 181–84, 195–96.

183. "Douglas in Virginia," *Cleveland Morning Leader*, August 28, 1860 (quotation); "Douglas in Virginia," *Anti-Slavery Bugle* (New Lisbon, Ohio), September 1, 1860.

184. R. E. Goodell to SAD, September 3, 1860, box 36, folder 7, SADP.

185. "An Infamous Speech," *Weekly Mississippian*, September 5, 1860.

186. *Weekly Advertiser* (Montgomery), September 19, 1860, quoted in R. Morris, *Long Pursuit*, 186–87.

187. Isaac I. Stevens to Matthew P. Deady, September 18, 1860, box 9, folder S230–253, Matthew Paul Deady Papers, ORHS; Bolling Hall Jr. to Bolling Hall, October 6, 1860, Hall Family Papers, Alabama Department of Archives and History, Montgomery.

188. "Behaved Himself Like a Gentleman," *Natchez (Miss.) Daily Courier*, October 12, 1860.

189. "Col. Jeff. Davis—Hail to the Chief!," *Mississippi Free Trader*, October 8, 1860.

190. H. Wilson, *History of the Rise and Fall*, 2:700 (quotations); Johannsen, *SAD*, 794–98.

191. D. C. Humphrey to SAD, October 28, 1860, box 36, folder 11 (quotation); James W. Williams to SAD, September 22, 1860, box 36, folder 9; Benjamin Ellis to SAD, [November 1860?], box 36, folder 11, SADP.

192. Egerton, *Year of Meteors*, 203.

193. "Douglas among the Cotton Lords," *Nashville Patriot*, reprinted in unidentified newspaper clipping, box 62, folder 3, SADP; "Great Douglas Demonstration in Atlanta," *Daily Southern Confederacy* (Atlanta), November 1, 1860; Johannsen, *SAD*, 798–801.

194. "Disgraceful," *Oxford (Miss.) Intelligencer*, October 31, 1860 (first two quotations); *Memphis Avalanche*, quoted in "Douglas in the South," *Cleveland Morning Leader*, October 30, 1860 (third quotation).

195. "That Egging Case," *Cass County Republican* (Dowagiac, Mich.), November 22, 1860.

196. *Declaration of the Immediate Causes*, 9.

197. Potter, *Lincoln and His Party*, xxii, 189–90.

198. W. Freehling, *Road to Disunion*, 2:339; Link, *Roots of Secession*, 208.

199. Fehrenbacher, *Prelude to Greatness*, 160; Fehrenbacher, *Dred Scott Case*, 563.

200. W. Freehling, *Road to Disunion*, 2:338; Holt, *Election of 1860*, 177–78.

201. W. Freehling, *Road to Disunion*, 2:338.

202. Michael F. Holt, "The Democratic Party, 1828–1860," in Schlesinger, *History of U.S. Political Parties*, 1:535.

203. Johannsen, *SAD*, 803. Michael F. Holt estimates that 16 percent of Douglas's popular votes came from slave states, but he agrees on the significance of Douglas's poor showing in the South. Holt, *Election of 1860*, 173.

204. Link, *Roots of Secession*, 199–200, 208; Carey, *Parties, Slavery, and the Union*, 229; A. Smith, *Stormy Present*, 146; Gleeson, *Green and the Gray*, 30–34; Holt, *Election of 1860*, 173–75.

205. Towers, *Urban South*; W. Freehling, *Road to Disunion*; M. Johnson, *Toward a Patriarchal Republic*.

206. W. Freehling, *Road to Disunion*, 2:102–4, 394; Bolton, *Poor Whites*, 139–49; Merritt, *Masterless Men*, 266–73, 293.

207. "The Final Result," *Tuscaloosa Observer*, reprinted in *Weekly Mississippian*, December 19, 1860. Emphasis original. See also "The Presidential Election and Union Savers," *Charleston Mercury*, August 4, 1860, in Dumond, *Southern Editorials on Secession*, 158; "Address of Durant da Ponte before the Breckinridge and Lane Club of New Orleans," *Weekly Mississippian*, November 7, 1860; Egerton, *Year of Meteors*, 306; and Nevins, *Emergence of Lincoln*, 2:316–17.

208. "The Union: Its Benefits and Dangers," *Southern Literary Messenger* 32 (January 1861): 1–4.

EPILOGUE

1. Kirke, *Down in Tennessee*, 274. Emphasis original. Gilmore wrote under the pseudonym Edmund Kirke.

2. "Jefferson Davis's Second Inaugural Address," Papers of Jefferson Davis (digital), Woodson Research Center, Fondren Library, Rice University.

3. "Minutes of Town Meeting in Shieldsboro, Mississippi," November 8, 1860, and Rufus R. Rhodes to John J. Pettus, November 10, 1860, roll 1769, Mississippi Governor (1859–1863: Pettus) Correspondence and Papers, MDAH; Resolutions, Bethesda Baptist Church, Oktibbeha County, December [1], 1860; W. C. Falkner to John J. Pettus, December 28, 1860, roll 1812, Mississippi Governor (1859–1863: Pettus) Correspondence and Papers, MDAH; Bunkers, *Diary of Caroline Seabury*, 60; "Meeting in Lauderdale County," "Meeting in Tippah County," "Meeting in Yazoo," "Meeting in Holmes," "Clarke County," "Panola County," "Pike County," "Copiah County," "Meeting in Vicksburg," all in *Weekly Mississippian*, November 21, 1860.

4. "Governor's Message," *Oxford Intelligencer*, December 12, 1860.

5. Holt, *Election of 1860*, 184; Rainwater, *Mississippi*, 162–63; "1775 and 1860" and "The Real Danger," *Oxford Intelligencer*, November 28, 1860; "Meeting in Carroll," *Weekly Mississippian*, December 5, 1860.

6. "A Broken Staff," *Weekly Mississippian*, November 28, 1860.

7. Rainwater, *Mississippi*, 172–73.

8. Dubay, *John Jones Pettus*, 67, 69–71; T. Smith, *Mississippi Secession Convention*, 12, 15–18.

9. Dubay, *John Jones Pettus*, 83–84; John J. Pettus to JD, December 16, 31, 1860, box 1, folder 2, JDPDU; JD to J. J. Pettus, December 26, 31, 1860, January 4, 1861, *JDC*, 4:559–60, 560–61, 564–65.

10. O. R. Singleton to [?], July 14, 1877, in Jones, *Davis Memorial Volume*, 210–12; R. Davis, *Recollections of Mississippi*, 390–92; Ranck, *Albert Gallatin Brown*, 201–2.

11. Cooper, "Jefferson Davis and the Politics of Secession," in *Jefferson Davis and the Civil War Era*, 19–32.

12. JD to R. B. Rhett Jr., November 10, 1860, *JDC*, 4:541–43.

13. Sanders, "Jefferson Davis," 514.

14. T. Smith, *Mississippi Secession Convention*, 27–79.

15. A. Burwell to SAD, November 16, 1860, box 36, folder 12; John S. Carlile to SAD, March 11, 1861, box 39, folder 20; H. S. Hunt to SAD, April 4, 1861, box 40, folder 18; William P. Maulsby to SAD, April 5, 1861, box 40, folder 18, SADP.

16. C. L. Dubuisson to SAD, November 22, 1860, box 36, folder 13; Herschel V. Johnson to SAD, November 25, 1860, box 36, folder 13; William C. Smedes to SAD, December 10, 1860, box 36, folder 17; A Citizen of Mississippi to SAD, January 13, 1861, box 37, folder 16; Philip Poindexter to SAD, January 15, 1861, box 37, folder 19; B. N. Kinyon to SAD, February 5, 1861, box 38, folder 16; William A. Stone to SAD, March 27, 1861, box 40, folder 13, SADP.

17. Thomas J. Wiggin to SAD, November 25, 1860, box 36, folder 13; J. W. Williams to SAD, December 1, 1860, box 36, folder 14; J. S. Johnson to SAD, December 11, 1860, box 36, folder 18; B. N. Kinyon to SAD, December 17, 1860, box 36, folder 21; J. A. Stewart to SAD, December 26, 1860, box 37, folder 1; J. G. Green to SAD, January 8, 1861, box 37, folder 11; J. M. Marshall to SAD, January 10, 1861, box 37, folder 13; Thomas M. Peters to SAD, January 16, 1861, box 37, folder 20; J. W. Williams to SAD, January 18, 1861, box 37, folder 22; Robert M. Barton to SAD, January 31, 1861, box 38, folder 9; W. D. Jones to SAD, March 15, 1861, box 40, folder 2, SADP

18. C. A. Dunham to SAD, January 6, 1861, box 37, folder 8, SADP.

19. John Moore to SAD, February 5, 1861, box 38, folder 16, SADP.

20. D. P. Rhodes to SAD, February 5, 1861, box 38, folder 16, SADP (quotation); John A. McClernand to Charles H. Lanphier, February 4, 1861, box 1, folder 10, Charles H. Lanphier Papers, ALPL; John McCook to Andrew Johnson, February 12, 1861, in Graf, Haskins, and Bergeron, *Papers of Andrew Johnson*, 4:284; and J. W. Bend Letter to William G. Bend, June 9, 1861 (Mss 1500), ORHS.

21. Amicus to SAD, December 17, 1860, box 36, folder 21 (quotation; emphasis original); Joseph Longaker to SAD, December 16, 1860, box 36, folder 20; Theodore Williams to SAD, April 1, 1861, box 40, folder 17, SADP.

22. For opposition to coercion, see J. W. Sheahan to SAD, December 17, 1860, box 36, folder 21; Thomas Gibson to SAD, January [?], 1861, box 37, folder 5; and A. Bainbridge to SAD, January 18, 1861, box 37, folder 22, SADP. For militant rhetoric, see John J. McKinnon to SAD, February 12, 1861, box 38, folder 23; and An American Citizen to SAD, February 28, 1861, box 39, folder 10, SADP.

23. R. J. Smith to SAD, February 12, 1861, box 38, folder 23, SADP; W. R. Wilkinson to Richard Yates, June 6, 1861, box 2, folder 8, Yates Family Papers, ALPL.

24. Wade Hampton to JD, November 13, 1860, PJDRU.

25. Simeon Oliver to JD, December 3, 1860; Price Williams to JD, December 14, 1860; John Cowden to JD, December 17, 1860; L. Q. C. Lamar to JD, December 24, 1860, PJDRU; Joseph E. Davis to JD, January 2, 1861, *JDC*, 4:561–62.

26. C. G. Mitchell to JD, April 27, 1861, box 1, folder 3), JDPDU; W. Jordan, *Tumult and Silence*.

27. Anonymous to JD, February 22, 1861, roll 1812, Mississippi Governor (1859–1863: Pettus) Correspondence and Papers, MDAH.

28. *CG*, 36th Cong., 2nd Sess., 158 (December 20, 1860).

29. "To Our Constituents," December 14, 1860, *PJD*, 6:377.

30. W. Davis, *Jefferson Davis*, 289–90.

31. Harden, *Life of George M. Troup*, 299.

32. Walther, *William Lowndes Yancey*, 126; "California Bill," *Southern Press*, August 12, 1850; "Gov. Bell's Message to the Texas Legislature," *Woodville Republican*, September 10, 1850; "Address of Hon. P. S. Brooks to the People of the Fourth Congressional District," *Edgefield Advertiser*, August 15, 1855; "Message of Gov. Brown of Georgia," *Richmond Enquirer*, November 20, 1860.

33. R. Nichols, *Disruption of American Democracy*, 399; Dumond, *Secession Movement*, 148n3; Baptist, *Creating an Old South*, 270.

34. W. Freehling, *Road to Disunion*, 2:469–70.

35. R. Davis, *Recollections of Mississippi*, 396–99; R. Nichols, *Disruption of American Democracy*, 398–99; Cooper, *We Have the War upon Us*, 52–54.

36. *CG*, 36th Cong., 2nd Sess., 182 (December 21, 1860); Cooper, *JDA*, 319.

37. Compare W. Davis, *Jefferson Davis*, 290, with Sanders, "Jefferson Davis," 517.

38. Potter, *Lincoln and His Party*, 171.

39. *CG*, 32nd Cong., 2nd Sess., 183, 190 (December 24, 1860).

40. William E. Gienapp, "The Republican Party and the Slave Power," in Abzug and Maizlish, *New Perspectives*, 69; Hyman and Wiecek, *Equal Justice under Law*, 221.

41. Biographers often lionize Douglas's efforts, but Martin H. Quitt astutely emphasizes his distress and desperation. Quitt, *Stephen A. Douglas*, 170, 173, 185.

42. Hyman and Wiecek, *Equal Justice under Law*, 221; Johannsen, *SAD*, 816–17.

43. Shelden, *Washington Brotherhood*, 144–66; Johannsen, *SAD*, 652–53, 814–39.

44. *CG*, 32nd Cong., 2nd Sess., 114 (December 18, 1860).

45. SAD to Charles H. Lanphier, December 25, 1860, *LSAD*, 504.

46. Potter, *Lincoln and His Party*, 171; Cooper, *We Have the War upon Us*, 50–51; Cooper, *JDA*, 319.

47. Holzer, *Lincoln President-Elect*, 163–66.

48. J. Davis, *Rise and Fall*, 1:199.

49. W. Freehling, *Road to Disunion*, 2:474–75.

50. J. Davis, *Rise and Fall*, 1:69.

51. *CG*, 36th Cong., 2nd Sess., appendix, 35–42 (January 3, 1861).

52. Nevins, *Emergence of Lincoln*, 2:386–404; David M. Potter, "Why the Republicans Rejected Both Compromise and Secession," in Knoles, *Crisis of the Union*, 90–106; McPherson, *Battle Cry of Freedom*, 252–54; Holzer, *Lincoln President-Elect*; Oakes, *Freedom National*, 73–74. For Lincoln's opposition to popular sovereignty, see Abraham Lincoln to Lyman Trumbull, December 10, 1860; Lincoln to William Kellogg, December 11, 1860; Lincoln to Elihu B. Washburne, December 13, 1860; Lincoln to Thurlow Weed, December 17, 1860; and Lincoln to John D. Defrees, December 18, 1860, *CWAL*, 4:149–50, 150, 151, 154, 155. The letters to Washburne and Weed mentioned Thayer by name.

53. *CG*, 36th Cong., 2nd Sess., appendix, 35–42 (January 3, 1861).

54. *CG*, 36th Cong., 2nd Sess., 586 (January 28, 1861), 1388, 1403 (March 2, 1861); Johannsen, *SAD*, 819–39; Crofts, *Lincoln and the Politics of Slavery*.

55. JD to George Lunt, January 17, 1861, *PJD*, 7:14–15.

56. JD to F. W. Pickens, January 13, 1861, *JDC*, 5:36–37.

57. JD to Edwin De Leon, January 8, 1861, *PJD*, 7:6 (quotation); JD to J. J. Pettus, January 4, 1861, *JDC*, 4:564–65.

58. *CG*, 36th Cong., 2nd Sess., 487 (January 21, 1861).

59. J. Davis, *Inaugural Address of President Davis*, 6.

60. JD to F. W. Pickens, January 13, 1861, *JDC*, 5:36–37; JD to Franklin Pierce, January 20, 1861, *JDC*, 5:37–38.

61. Current, "Confederates and the First Shot"; Cooper, *JDA*, 339–40.

62. On the hat anecdote, see Crofts, *Secession Crisis Enigma*, 111–13.

63. *CG*, 36th Cong., 2nd Sess., 1436–38 (March 6, 1861).

64. Edwin M. Stanton to James Buchanan, March 12, 1861, in J. B. Moore, *Works of James Buchanan*, 11:166 (quotation); J. C. Greene to SAD, March 7, 1861, box 39, folder 15, and Joseph Knox to SAD, March 10, 1861, box 39, folder 19, SADP.

65. Johannsen, *SAD*, 841–54.

66. Forney, *Anecdotes of Public Men*, 1:224–25.

67. Forney, 1:225–27; Johannsen, *SAD*, 858–60.

68. "Statement" [April 14, 1861], *LSAD*, 509–10.

69. *CG*, 36th Cong., 2nd Sess., 28 (December 10, 1860).

70. A. Withers to SAD, April 16, 1861, box 40, folder 19, SADP.

71. R. M. Foster to SAD, May 10, 1861, box 40, folder 21, SADP.

72. D. B. Martin to SAD, April 18, 1861, box 40, folder 20; V. Hickox to SAD, May 4, 1861, box 40, folder 21, SADP. Rumors of secessionist plots in southern Illinois—Egypt—abounded; see Pease and Randall, *Diary of Orville Hickman Browning*, 465.

73. Egerton, *Year of Meteors*, 3, 330; Johannsen, *SAD*, 862–70.

74. Pease and Randall, *Diary of Orville Hickman Browning*, 465–66.

75. Douglas, *Speech of Senator Douglas, before the Legislature of Illinois*.

76. Cochran, *Dream of a Northwestern Confederacy*; Hess, "Mississippi River and Secession"; Gazaway B. Lamar to Howell Cobb, February 22, 1861, in U. Phillips, "Correspondence of Robert Toombs," 546.

77. Thomas S. Drew to SAD, May 13, 1861, box 41, folder 1, SADP; Catton and Catton, *Two Roads to Sumter*, 67; Egnal, *Clash of Extremes*.

78. Douglas, *Speech of Senator Douglas, before the Legislature of Illinois*, 7.

79. Robert Smith to SAD, May 17, 1861, box 41, folder 1, SADP. Emphasis original.

80. [J. B. Tanner] to SAD, May 23, 1861, box 41, folder 1, SADP. See also "Stephen Arnold Douglas," *Portland (Maine) Daily Advertiser*, June 4, 1861, in Perkins, *Northern Editorials on Secession*, 2:1028–30.

81. Johannsen, *SAD*, 870–72.

82. Committee of the Regiment, *Story of the Fifty-Fifth Regiment*, 18–19.

83. Quoted in J. Lander, *Lincoln and Darwin*, 99.

84. "Speech from President Davis of the Southern Confederacy," *Richmond Enquirer*, February 19, 1861.

85. Quoted in Alfriend, *Life of Jefferson Davis*, 243.

86. Quoted in Alfriend, 350.

87. For incisive analysis of Confederate dreams of perfect solidarity, see McCurry, *Confederate Reckoning*, esp. pp. 11–84. On ruptures across previously masked fault lines, see Levine, *Fall of the House of Dixie*, 287–89.

88. Quoted in Williams, Williams, and Carlson, *Plain Folk*, 94; Levine, *Fall of the House of Dixie*, 79–81, 83–86; Escott, *After Secession*, 94–134; Wesley, *Collapse of the Confederacy*, 74–104; Durrill, *War of Another Kind*.

89. Quoted in Levine, *Fall of the House of Dixie*, 242.

90. Quoted in Williams, Williams, and Carlson, *Plain Folk*, 94.

91. Robinson, *Bitter Fruits of Bondage*, 283.

92. For a critique of binary approaches to the question of Confederate defeat, see Gallagher, "Disaffection, Persistence, and Nation," 352. On efforts to mitigate class conflict, see Blair, *Virginia's Private War*.

93. Williams, *Rich Man's War*, 61, 103–6.

94. McCurry, *Confederate Reckoning*, 85–217.

95. D. Hamilton, *Limits of Sovereignty*; Dirck, "Posterity's Blush."

96. Quoted in Levine, *Fall of the House of Dixie*, 82.

97. Quoted in Robinson, *Bitter Fruits of Bondage*, 106.

98. Levine, *Fall of the House of Dixie*, 81–82; Williams, Williams, and Carlson, *Plain Folk*, 53; Martinez, *Confederate Slave Impressment*.

99. Quoted in Levine, *Fall of the House of Dixie*, 198.

100. Levine, 250–58.

101. Abraham Lincoln to Henry Asbury, November 19, 1858, *CWAL*, 3:339. Emphasis original.

Bibliography

MANUSCRIPT COLLECTIONS

Amherst, Mass.
    University of Massachusetts Amherst, Special Collections and University Archives
        W. E. B. Du Bois Papers (digital)
Ann Arbor, Mich.
    University of Michigan, William L. Clements Library
        Lewis Cass Papers
Blacksburg, Va.
    Virginia Polytechnic Institute and State University, Special Collections
        Cochran Family Letters
Boston, Mass.
    Massachusetts Historical Society
        Theodore Parker Papers
Cambridge, Mass.
    Harvard University, Houghton Library
        Charles Sumner Papers (microfilm)
Chicago, Ill.
    University of Chicago Library, Special Collections Research Center
        Douglas Family Collection
        Stephen A. Douglas Papers
Columbus, Ohio
    Ohio Historical Society
        Joshua R. Giddings Papers
        Jesse Spangler Correspondence
Durham, N.C.
    Duke University, David M. Rubenstein Rare Book and Manuscript Library
        Jefferson Davis Papers

Houston, Tex.
    Rice University, Fondren Library, Woodson Research Center
        Papers of Jefferson Davis
        Papers of Jefferson Davis (digital)
        William Harrison Hamman Papers
Indianapolis, Ind.
    Indiana State Library
        Schuyler Colfax Papers
Jackson, Miss.
    Mississippi Department of Archives and History
        Charles-Crutcher-McRaven Papers
        Cooke (H. A.) Letters
        Jefferson Davis and Family Papers
        Fontaine (Charles D.) and Family Papers
        Lamar (L. Q. C.) and Edward Mayes Papers
        McRaven (W. H.) Papers
        Mississippi Governor (1859–1863: Pettus) Correspondence and Papers
           (microfilm)
        Quitman (John A.) Papers
        Quitman (John A.) and Family Papers
        Walker (Robert J.) Papers
Lebanon, Tenn.
    Cumberland University
        Papers of Martin Van Buren (digital)
Lexington, Ky.
    Transylvania University, Special Collections and Archives
        Jefferson Davis Papers
Montgomery, Ala.
    Alabama Department of Archives and History
        Hall Family Papers
        Lewis E. Parsons Papers
Philadelphia, Pa.
    Historical Society of Pennsylvania
        William Bigler Papers
        James Buchanan Papers (microfilm)
        Democratic Douglas Arthur Association Minute Book (1858–1860)
Portland, Ore.
    Oregon Historical Society
        J. W. Bend Letter to William G. Bend, June 9, 1861
        Asahel Bush Letters
        Matthew Paul Deady Papers
        Joseph Lane Papers
        James Willis Nesmith Papers
Springfield, Ill.
    Abraham Lincoln Presidential Library
        Sidney Breese Papers
        Sidney Breese Papers re: Election of 1858
        Letter, R. B. Carpenter to James Buchanan, June 23, 1858

Stephen A. Douglas Incoming Correspondence and Papers
Stephen A. Douglas Papers
Augustus C. French Papers
Joseph Gillespie Papers
O. M. Hatch Papers
Charles H. Lanphier Papers
John A. McClernand Papers
Lyman Trumbull Family Papers
Hezekiah M. Wead Diary
Yates Family Papers
St. Louis, Mo.
Missouri History Museum Archives
Kennett Family Papers
Samuel Treat Papers
Washington, D.C.
Library of Congress, Manuscript Division
Jeremiah Sullivan Black Papers (microfilm)
Abraham Lincoln Papers (digital)
Papers of Lyman Trumbull (microfilm)

DIGITAL COLLECTIONS

The American Presidency Project, University of California, Santa Barbara, https://www.presidency.ucsb.edu/.
Kansas Memory, Kansas Historical Society, https://www.kansasmemory.org/.
Legal Information Institute, Cornell Law School, https://www.law.cornell.edu/.
Mississippi History Now, Mississippi Historical Society, http://www.mshistorynow.mdah.ms.gov/.

NEWSPAPERS AND PERIODICALS

Abbeville (S.C.) Independent Press
Albany Evening Journal
Alexandria Gazette (Washington, D.C.)
Alton (Ill.) Telegraph
Anti-Slavery Bugle (New Lisbon, Ohio)
Ashtabula (Ohio) Weekly Telegraph
Athens (Tenn.) Post
Buchanan County Guardian (Iowa)
Cass County Republican (Dowagiac, Mich.)
Chicago Press and Tribune
Cincinnati Daily Enquirer
Clarksville (Tenn.) Chronicle
Clearfield (Pa.) Republican
Cleveland Morning Leader
Daily Southern Confederacy (Atlanta)
Daily Vicksburg Whig
Dallas Herald
DeBow's Review

Detroit Free Press
Edgefield (S.C.) Advertiser
Feliciana Democrat (Clinton, La.)
Flag of the Union (Jackson, Miss.)
Franklin (La.) Planters' Banner
Glasgow (Mo.) Weekly Times
Gonzales (Tex.) Inquirer
Grand River Times (Grand Haven, Mich.)
Harper's New Monthly Magazine
Harper's Weekly
Harrisburg (Pa.) Morning Herald
Highland Weekly News (Hillsborough, Ohio)
Illinois Free Trader and LaSalle County Commercial Advertiser (Ottawa)
Illinois State Journal (Springfield)
Illinois State Register (Springfield)
Indianapolis Locomotive
Jersey City (N.J.) Daily Telegraph
LaGrange (N.C.) Sentinel
The Liberator (Boston)
Madison (Miss.) Whig Advocate
Marshall County Democrat (Plymouth, Ind.)
M'Arthur (Ohio) Democrat
Memphis Daily Appeal
Middlebury (Vt.) Register
Mississippian (Jackson)
Mississippi Creole (Canton)
Mississippi Free Trader (Natchez)
Monroe (Miss.) Democrat
Nashville Patriot
Nashville Union and American
Natchez (Miss.) Daily Courier
National Era (Washington, D.C.)
National Intelligencer (Washington, D.C.)
New Hampshire Patriot (Concord)
New Orleans Daily Delta
New Orleans Daily Picayune
New York Evangelist
New York Evening Post
New York Herald
New York Sunday Atlas
New York Times
New York Tribune
North Carolina Standard (Raleigh)
North-Carolinian (Fayetteville)
Ohio Cultivator
Okolona (Miss.) Prairie News
Opelousas (La.) Courier
Ottawa (Ill.) Free Trader

Oxford (Miss.) Intelligencer
Penn-Yan (N.Y.) Democrat
Philadelphia Press
Port Gibson (Miss.) Daily Southern Reveille
Republican Times (La Porte, Ind.)
Richmond (Va.) Daily Dispatch
Richmond (Va.) Enquirer
Ripley (Miss.) Advertiser
Sacramento Daily Union
Semi-Weekly Mississippian (Jackson)
Southern Cultivator
Southern Literary Messenger
Southern Press (Washington, D.C.)
Southern Quarterly Review
Southron (Jackson, Miss.)
Texas Planter (Brazoria)
Texas State Gazette (Austin)
Thibodaux (La.) Minerva
Times Dispatch (Richmond, Va.)
Tri-Weekly Sentinel (Vicksburg)
True Democrat (Paulding, Miss.)
United States Magazine and Democratic Review
Vermont Phoenix (Brattleboro)
Vicksburg Sentinel and Expositor
Vicksburg Weekly Whig
Wabash Express (Terre Haute, Ind.)
Washington (D.C.) Daily Union
Washington (D.C.) Evening Star
Washington (D.C.) Republic
Washington (D.C.) Sentinel
Washington (D.C.) Union
Weekly Mississippian (Jackson)
Weekly North Carolina Standard (Raleigh)
Weekly North Iowa Times (McGregor)
West Baton Rouge (La.) Sugar Planter
Wheeling (Va.) Daily Intelligencer
Wilmington (N.C.) Journal
Woodville (Miss.) Republican
Yazoo Democrat (Yazoo City, Miss.)

GOVERNMENT DOCUMENTS

Congressional Globe
The Covode Investigation Report: Report of the Select Committee on Alleged Corruptions in Government. Washington, D.C.: Government Printing Office, 1860.
Public Acts of the Thirty-Third Congress of the United States. In *The Statutes at Large and Treaties of the United States of America. From December 1, 1851, to March 3, 1855 . . .*, edited by George Minot. Vol. 10. Boston: Little, Brown, 1855.

Register of Debates

Report of the Committee on Territories, on "A Bill to Authorize the People of the Ter-ritory of Kansas to Form a Constitution and State Government, Preparatory to Their Admission into the Union, When They Have the Requisite Population," etc. Also, the Views of the Minority of Said Committee. Washington, D.C.: A. O. P. Nich-olson, 1856.

Reports of Explorations and Surveys: To Ascertain the Most Practicable and Econom-ical Route for a Railroad from the Mississippi River to the Pacific Ocean, Made under the Direction of the Secretary of War, in 1853–5 . . . 12 vols. Washington, D.C.: A. O. P. Nicholson, 1855–60.

Senate Report No. 15, 33rd Cong., 1st Sess. (January 4, 1854). In *The Reports of the Committees of the Senate of the United States for the First Session, Thirty-Third Congress, 1853-'54, Volume I.* Washington, D.C.: Beverley Tucker, 1854.

PRINTED PRIMARY SOURCES

American Colonization Society. *Forty-Fourth Annual Report of the American Coloni-zation Society.* N.p., 1861.

———. *Forty-Second Annual Report of the American Colonization Society, with the Proceedings of the Board of Directors and of the Society: January 18, 1859.* Wash-ington, D.C.: C. Alexander, Printer, 1859.

———. *Forty-Third Annual Report of the American Colonization Society, with the Pro-ceedings of the Board of Directors and of the Society. January 17, 1860.* Washington, D.C.: C. Alexander, Printer, 1860.

Aughey, John H. *Tupelo.* Lincoln, Neb.: State Journal, 1888.

[Baird, Robert]. *View of the Valley of the Mississippi, or the Emigrant's and Travel-ler's Guide to the West.* 2nd ed. Philadelphia: H. S. Tanner, 1834.

Bartlett, John Russell. *Personal Narrative of Explorations and Incidents in Texas, New Mexico, Sonora, and Chihuahua* . . . 2 vols. New York: D. Appleton, 1854.

Basler, Roy P., ed. *The Collected Works of Abraham Lincoln.* 8 vols. New Brunswick, N.J.: Rutgers University Press, 1953–55.

Biographical and Historical Memoirs of Mississippi. 2 vols. Chicago: Goodspeed, 1891.

Biographical Sketch of Stephen A. Douglas, of Illinois. N.p., Towers, 1853.

Black Hawk. *Life of Ma-Ka-Tai-Me-She-Kia-Kiak or Black Hawk.* Edited by J. B. Patterson. Boston: n.p., 1834.

[Black, Jeremiah S.]. *Observations on Senator Douglas's Views of Popular Sover-eignty, as Expressed in Harpers' Magazine, for September, 1859.* 2nd ed. Washing-ton: Thomas McGill, 1859.

Blaine, James G. *Twenty Years of Congress: From Lincoln to Garfield.* 2 vols. Norwich, Conn.: Henry Bill, 1886.

Bremer, Fredrika. *The Homes of the New World; Impressions of America.* 2 vols. New York: Harper and Brothers, 1853.

Brooks, R. P., ed. "Howell Cobb Papers." *Georgia Historical Quarterly* 5 (June 1921): 29–52.

———. "Howell Cobb Papers." *Georgia Historical Quarterly* 6 (March 1922): 35–84.

———. "Howell Cobb Papers." *Georgia Historical Quarterly* 6 (June 1922): 147–73.

————. "Howell Cobb Papers." *Georgia Historical Quarterly* 6 (September 1922): 233–64.

Bunkers, Suzanne L., ed. *The Diary of Caroline Seabury, 1854–1863*. Madison: University of Wisconsin Press, 1991.

"Calhoun and Secession." In *Publications of the Southern History Association, Volume 6*, 415–16. Washington, D.C.: Southern History Association, 1902.

Claiborne, J. F. H. *Life and Correspondence of John A. Quitman*. 2 vols. New York: Harper and Brothers, 1860.

Cluskey, M. W., ed. *Speeches, Messages, and Other Writings of the Hon. Albert G. Brown, a Senator in Congress from the State of Mississippi*. 2nd ed. Philadelphia: Jas. B. Smith, 1859.

A Committee of the Regiment. *Story of the Fifty-Fifth Regiment Illinois Volunteer Infantry in the Civil War, 1861–1865*. Clinton, Mass.: W. J. Coulter, 1887.

Cooper, William J., Jr., ed. *Jefferson Davis: The Essential Writings*. New York: Modern Library, 2003.

Crallé, Richard K., ed. *The Works of John C. Calhoun*. 6 vols. New York: D. Appleton, 1883.

Crist, Lynda Lasswell, et al., eds. *The Papers of Jefferson Davis*. 14 vols. Baton Rouge: Louisiana State University Press, 1971–2015.

Cutts, J. Madison. *A Brief Treatise upon Constitutional and Party Questions, and the History of Political Parties . . .* New York: D. Appleton, 1866.

Davis, Jefferson. *Inaugural Address of President Davis, Delivered at the Capitol, Monday, February 18, 1861, at 1 o'clock, P.M.* Montgomery, Ala.: Shorter and Reid, Printers, 1861.

————. *The Rise and Fall of the Confederate Government*. 2 vols. New York: D. Appleton, 1881.

————. *A Short History of the Confederate States of America*. New York: Belford, 1890.

————. *Speeches of the Hon. Jefferson Davis, of Mississippi, Delivered during the Summer of 1858*. Baltimore: John Murphy, 1859.

Davis, Reuben. *Recollections of Mississippi and Mississippians*. Boston: Houghton, Mifflin, 1890.

[Davis, Varina Howell]. *Jefferson Davis, Ex-President of the Confederate States of America, a Memoir*. 2 vols. New York: Belford, 1890.

Declaration of the Immediate Causes Which Induce and Justify the Secession of South Carolina from the Federal Union: and the Ordinance of Secession. Charleston, S.C.: Evans and Cogswell, 1860.

Dew, Thomas R. *Review of the Debate in the Virginia Legislature of 1831 and 1832*. Richmond: T. W. White, 1832.

Dixon, Mrs. Archibald. *The True History of the Missouri Compromise and Its Repeal*. Cincinnati: Robert Clarke, 1899.

Douglas, Stephen A. *Atlantic & Pacific Railroad. A Letter, from the Hon. S. A. Douglass, to A. Whitney, Esq., N.Y.* Quincy, Ill.: Woods and Flagg, [1845].

————. *Non-intervention—Popular Sovereignty. Speech of Hon. S. A. Douglas, of Illinois . . .* Washington, D.C.: Lemuel Towers, 1859.

————. *Remarks of the Hon. Stephen A. Douglas, on Kansas, Utah, and the Dred Scott Decision. Delivered at Springfield, Illinois, June 12th, 1857*. Chicago: Daily Times Book and Job Office, 1857.

——. *Removal of Judge Douglas by the Senate as Chairman of the Committee on Territories. Letter of Judge Douglas in Reply to the Speech of Dr. Gwin at Grass Valley, Cal.* N.p., 1859.

——. *River and Harbor Improvements. Letter of Senator Douglas to Governor Matteson of Illinois.* N.p., 1854.

——. *Speeches of Mr. Douglas, of Illinois, at the Democratic Festival at Jackson Hall, January 8, 1852. And at the Congressional Banquet to Kossuth, January 7, 1852.* [Washington, D.C.]: Towers, [1852].

——. *Speeches of Senator S. A. Douglas, on the Occasion of His Public Receptions by the Citizens of New Orleans, Philadelphia, and Baltimore.* Washington, D.C.: Lemuel Towers, 1859.

——. *Speech of Hon. S. A. Douglas, of Illinois, Delivered in the City of Petersburg, Virginia, August 28, 1860.* Washington, D.C.: L. Towers, 1860.

——. *Speech of Hon. Stephen A. Douglas, on the "Measures of Adjustment," Delivered in the City Hall, Chicago, October 23, 1850.* Washington, D.C.: Gideon and Co., Printers, 1851.

——. *Speech of Senator Douglas, before the Legislature of Illinois, April 25, 1861, in Compliance with a Joint Resolution of the Two Houses.* N.p., 1861.

The Dred Scott Decision: Opinion of Chief Justice Taney, with an Introduction by Dr. J. H. Van Evrie . . . New York: Van Evrie, Horton, 1859.

Dumond, Dwight Lowell., ed. *Southern Editorials on Secession.* 1931. Gloucester, Mass.: P. Smith, 1964.

Estes, Matthew. *A Defence of Negro Slavery, as It Exists in the United States.* Montgomery: Press of the "Alabama Journal," 1846.

Fabens, J. W. *The Camel Hunt: A Narrative of Personal Adventure.* New ed. New York: George P. Putnam, 1853.

[Flint, Henry Martin]. *Life of Stephen A. Douglas, United States Senator from Illinois, with His Most Important Speeches and Reports.* New York: H. Dayton, 1860.

Foote, Henry S. *Casket of Reminiscences.* Washington, D.C.: Chronicle, 1874.

Forney, John W. *Anecdotes of Public Men.* 2 vols. New York: Harper and Brothers, 1873.

Fry, William Henry. *Republican "Campaign" Text-Book, for the Year 1860.* New York: A. B. Burdick, 1860.

Fulkerson, H. S. *Random Recollections of Early Days in Mississippi.* Vicksburg: Vicksburg Printing and Publishing, 1885.

Genoways, Ted, and Hugh H. Genoways, eds. *A Perfect Picture of Hell: Eyewitness Accounts by Civil War Prisoners from the 12th Iowa.* Iowa City: University of Iowa Press, 2001.

Gihon, John H. *Geary and Kansas: Governor Geary's Administration of Kansas . . .* Philadelphia: J. H. C. Whiting, 1857.

Gordon, John B. *Reminiscences of the Civil War.* New York: Charles Scribner's Sons, 1903.

Graf, Leroy P., Ralph W. Haskins, and Paul Bergeron, eds. *The Papers of Andrew Johnson.* 16 vols. Knoxville: University of Tennessee Press, 1967–99.

Greeley, Horace. *Recollections of a Busy Life.* New York: J. B. Ford, 1868.

Greenhow, Robert. *The History of Oregon and California, and the Other Territories of the North-West Coast of North America . . .* Boston: Charles C. Little and James Brown, 1844.

Halstead, M. *Caucuses of 1860. A History of the National Political Conventions of the Current Presidential Campaign* . . . Columbus, Ohio: Follett, Foster, 1860.

Heap, Gwin Harris. *Central Route to the Pacific, from the Valley of the Mississippi to California* . . . Philadelphia: Lippincott, Grambo, 1854.

Helper, Hinton Rowan. *The Impending Crisis of the South: How to Meet It.* New York: Burdick Brothers, 1857.

Herndon, William H., and Jesse William Weik. *Herndon's Lincoln.* Edited by Douglas L. Wilson and Rodney O. Davis. Galesburg, Ill.: Knox College Lincoln Studies Center, 2006.

History of Sangamon County, Illinois. Chicago: Inter-State Publishing, 1881.

[Ingraham, Joseph Holt]. *The South-West.* 2 vols. New York: Harper and Brothers, 1835.

Jaffa, Harry V., and Robert W. Johannsen, eds. *In the Name of the People: Speeches and Writings of Lincoln and Douglas in the Ohio Campaign of 1859.* Columbus: Ohio State University Press, 1959.

[Jennings, Dudley S.]. *Nine Years of Democratic Rule in Mississippi: Being Notes upon the Political History of the State, from the Beginning of the Year 1838, to the Present Time.* Jackson, Miss.: Thomas Palmer, 1847.

Johannsen, Robert W., ed. *The Letters of Stephen A. Douglas.* Urbana: University of Illinois Press, 1961.

———, ed. *The Lincoln-Douglas Debates of 1858.* New York: Oxford University Press, 1965.

Jones, J. William. *The Davis Memorial Volume; or our Dead President, Jefferson Davis, and the World's Tribute to His Memory.* Richmond, Va.: B. F. Johnson, 1890.

Journal of the Convention of the People of South Carolina, Held in 1860–'61 . . . Charleston: Evans and Cogswell, 1861.

Journal of the Proceedings of the South-Western Convention, Began and Held at the City of Memphis, on the 12th November, 1845. Memphis: n.p., 1845.

Journal of the State Convention, and Ordinances and Resolutions Adopted in March, 1861. Jackson, Miss.: E. Barksdale, 1861.

Kirke, Edmund. *Down in Tennessee, and Back by Way of Richmond.* New York: Carleton, 1865.

Laws of the State of Mississippi, Passed at a Regular Session of the Mississippi Legislature, Held in the City of Jackson, November, 1857. Jackson: E. Barksdale, 1858.

Manning, Edward. *Six Months on a Slaver: A True Narrative.* New York: Harper and Brothers, 1879.

Marsh, Edward S., ed. *Stephen A. Douglas, a Memorial* . . . Brandon, Vt.: privately printed for the Committee of Arrangements, 1914.

Marsh, George P. *The Camel: His Organization Habits and Uses Considered with Reference to His Introduction into the United States.* Boston: Gould and Lincoln, 1856.

Mayes, Edward. *Lucius Q. C. Lamar: His Life, Times, and Speeches, 1825–1893.* Nashville: Publishing House of the Methodist Episcopal Church, South, 1896.

McConnell, George Murray. "Recollections of Stephen A. Douglas." In *Transactions of the Illinois State Historical Society for the Year 1900,* 40–50. Springfield, Ill.: Phillips Bros., 1900.

Montgomery, Frank A. *Reminiscences of a Mississippian in Peace and War.* Cincinnati: Robert Clarke, 1901.

Moore, John Bassett, ed. *The Works of James Buchanan, Comprising His Speeches,*

State Papers, and Private Correspondence. 12 vols. Philadelphia: J. B. Lippincott, 1908–11.

Nevins, Allan, and Milton Halsey Thomas, eds. *The Diary of George Templeton Strong*. 4 vols. New York: Macmillan, 1952.

Official Proceedings of the National Democratic Convention, Held in Cincinnati, June 2–6, 1856. Cincinnati: Enquirer, 1856.

Olmsted, Frederick Law. *A Journey in the Back Country*. London: Sampson Low, 1860.

———. *A Journey through Texas; or, a Saddle-Trip on the Southwestern Frontier*. New York: Dix, Edwards, 1857.

Pease, Theodore Calvin, and James G. Randall, eds. *The Diary of Orville Hickman Browning: Volume 1, 1850–1864*. Springfield: Trustees of the Illinois State Historical Library, 1925.

Perkins, Howard Cecil, ed. *Northern Editorials on Secession*. 2 vols. New York: Appleton-Century, 1942.

Perry, James R., Richard H. Chused, and Mary DeLano, eds. "Spousal Letters of Samuel R. Thurston, Oregon's First Territorial Delegate to Congress: 1849–1851." *Oregon Historical Quarterly* 96 (Spring 1995): 4–79.

Phillips, Ulrich Bonnell, ed. "The Correspondence of Robert Toombs, Alexander H. Stephens, and Howell Cobb." *Annual Report of the American Historical Association for the Year 1911, Vol. 2*. Washington, D.C.: Government Printing Office, 1913.

Pollard, Edward A. *Life of Jefferson Davis, with a Secret History of the Southern Confederacy, Gathered "Behind the Scenes in Richmond."* Philadelphia: National Publishing Company, 1869.

———. *The Lost Cause: A New Southern History of the War of the Confederates*. New York: E. B. Treat, 1867.

Proceedings of the Conventions at Charleston and Baltimore. Published by Order of the National Democratic Convention, (Maryland Institute, Baltimore,) and under the Supervision of the National Democratic Executive Committee. Washington, D.C.: n.p., 1860.

Proceedings of the Democratic National Convention, Held at Baltimore, June, 1852. Washington, D.C.: Buell and Blanchard, Printers, 1852.

The Pro-slavery Argument, as Maintained by the Most Distinguished Writers of the Southern States . . . Philadelphia: Lippincott, Grambo, 1853.

Quaife, Milo Milton, ed. *The Diary of James K. Polk during His Presidency, 1845 to 1849*. 4 vols. Chicago: A. C. McClurg, 1910.

Register of the Debates and Proceedings of the Va. Reform Convention. Richmond: R. H. Gallaher, 1851.

"Reminiscences of Stephen A. Douglas." *Atlantic Monthly* 8 (August 1861): 205–13.

Roberts, Daniel. "A Reminiscence of Stephen A. Douglas." *Harper's New Monthly Magazine*, November 1893, 957–59.

Rowland, Dunbar, ed. *Jefferson Davis, Constitutionalist: His Letters, Papers, and Speeches*. 10 vols. Jackson: printed for the Mississippi Department of Archives and History, 1923.

Seraiah the Scribe. *Chronicles of the Fire-Eaters of the Tribe of Mississippi*. Brandon, Miss.: Republican Office, 1853.

Shanks, Henry Thomas, ed. *The Papers of Willie Person Mangum*. 5 vols. Raleigh: State Department of Archives and History, 1950–56.

Sheahan, James W. *The Life of Stephen A. Douglas.* New York: Harper and Brothers, 1860.

"Some Papers of Franklin Pierce, 1852–1862. (First Installment.)" *American Historical Review* 10 (October 1904): 110–27.

A Southern Citizen [Reverdy Johnson]. *Remarks on Popular Sovereignty, as Maintained and Denied Respectively by Judge Douglas, and Attorney-General Black.* Baltimore: Murphy and Co., 1860.

Strode, Hudson, ed. *Jefferson Davis: Private Letters, 1823–1889.* New York: Harcourt, Brace and World, 1966.

Stuart, A. A. *Iowa Colonels and Regiments: Being a History of Iowa Regiments in the War of the Rebellion; and Containing a Description of the Battles in Which They Have Fought.* Des Moines: Mills, 1865.

[Tucker, Beverley]. *The Partisan Leader: A Tale of the Future.* 2 vols. Washington, D.C.: D. Green, 1836.

Van Evrie, J. H. *Negroes and Negro "Slavery," the First, an Inferior Race—the Latter, Its Normal Condition.* Baltimore: John D. Toy, Printer, 1853.

Waddell, James D., ed. *Biographical Sketch of Linton Stephens, (Late Associate Justice of the Supreme Court of Georgia,) Containing a Selection of His Letters, Speeches, State Papers, Etc.* Atlanta: Dodson and Scott, 1877.

Walker, Robert J. *Letter of Mr. Walker, of Mississippi, Relative to the Annexation of Texas . . .* Washington, D.C.: Globe Office, 1844.

Wilson, Henry. *History of the Rise and Fall of the Slave Power in America.* 3 vols. Boston: J. R. Osgood, 1872–77.

SECONDARY SOURCES

Books

Abzug, Robert H., and Stephen E. Maizlish., eds. *New Perspectives on Race and Slavery in America: Essays in Honor of Kenneth M. Stampp.* Lexington: University Press of Kentucky, 1986.

Adams, Sean Patrick, ed. *A Companion to the Era of Andrew Jackson.* Malden, Mass.: Blackwell, 2013.

Alfriend, Frank H. *The Life of Jefferson Davis.* Cincinnati: Caxton, 1868.

Allen, Felicity. *Jefferson Davis, Unconquerable Heart.* Columbia: University of Missouri Press, 1999.

Anderson, Gary Clayton. *The Conquest of Texas: Ethnic Cleansing in the Promised Land, 1820–1875.* Norman: University of Oklahoma Press, 2005.

Ankrom, Reg. *Stephen A. Douglas: The Political Apprenticeship, 1833–1843.* Jefferson, N.C.: McFarland, 2015.

Arenson, Adam. *The Great Heart of the Republic: St. Louis and the Cultural Civil War.* Cambridge, Mass.: Harvard University Press, 2011.

Ashworth, John. *"Agrarians" and "Aristocrats": Party Political Ideology in the United States, 1837–1846.* Atlantic Highlands, N.J.: Humanities Press, 1983.

———. *Slavery, Capitalism, and Politics in the Antebellum Republic.* 2 vols. New York: Cambridge University Press, 1995–2007.

Atchison, R. Jarrod. *A War of Words: The Rhetorical Leadership of Jefferson Davis.* Tuscaloosa: University of Alabama Press, 2017.

Auer, J. Jeffery, ed. *Antislavery and Disunion, 1858–1861: Studies in the Rhetoric of Compromise and Conflict*. New York: Harper and Row, 1963.

Baker, Jean H. *Affairs of Party: The Political Culture of Northern Democrats in the Mid-Nineteenth Century*. New York: Fordham University Press, 1998.

———. *James Buchanan*. New York: Times Books, 2004.

Baptist, Edward E. *Creating an Old South: Middle Florida's Plantation Frontier before the Civil War*. Chapel Hill: University of North Carolina Press, 2002.

———. *The Half Has Never Been Told: Slavery and the Making of American Capitalism*. New York: Basic Books, 2014.

Barr, Alwyn. *Black Texans: A History of African Americans in Texas, 1528–1995*. 2nd ed. Norman: University of Oklahoma Press, 1996.

Bartlett, Irving H. *John C. Calhoun: A Biography*. New York: W. W. Norton, 1993.

Beard, Charles A. *An Economic Interpretation of the Constitution of the United States*. New York: Macmillan, 1913.

Beatty, Jack. *Age of Betrayal: The Triumph of Money in America, 1865–1900*. New York: Alfred A. Knopf, 2007.

Beckert, Sven. *Empire of Cotton: A Global History*. New York: Alfred A. Knopf, 2014.

Bell, W. Scott. *The Camel Regiment: A History of the Bloody 43rd Mississippi Volunteer Infantry, 1862–65*. Gretna, La.: Pelican, 2017.

Benson, Lee. *The Concept of Jacksonian Democracy: New York as a Test Case*. Princeton: Princeton University Press, 1961.

Bergeron, Paul H. *The Presidency of James K. Polk*. Lawrence: University Press of Kansas, 1987.

Berwanger, Eugene H. *The Frontier against Slavery: Western Anti-Negro Prejudice and the Slavery Extension Controversy*. Urbana: University of Illinois Press, 1967.

Bicknell, John. *Lincoln's Pathfinder: John C. Frémont and the Violent Election of 1856*. Chicago: Chicago Review Press, 2017.

Billington, Ray Allen. *Westward Expansion: A History of the American Frontier*. New York: Macmillan, 1949.

Bilotta, James D. *Race and the Rise of the Republican Party, 1848–1865*. New York: P. Lang, 1992.

Birkner, Michael J., ed. *James Buchanan and the Political Crisis of the 1850s*. Selinsgrove, Pa.: Susquehanna University Press, 1996.

Blair, William Alan. *Virginia's Private War: Feeding Body and Soul in the Confederacy, 1861–1865*. New York: Oxford University Press, 1998.

Blue, Frederick J. *The Free Soilers: Third Party Politics, 1848–54*. Urbana: University of Illinois Press, 1973.

Bolton, Charles C. *Poor Whites of the Antebellum South: Tenants and Laborers in Central North Carolina and Northeast Mississippi*. Durham, N.C.: Duke University Press, 1994.

Bond, Bradley G. *Political Culture in the Nineteenth-Century South: Mississippi, 1830–1900*. Baton Rouge: Louisiana State University Press, 1995.

Bonner, Robert E. *Mastering America: Southern Slaveholders and the Crisis of American Nationhood*. New York: Cambridge University Press, 2009.

Bouton, Terry. *Taming Democracy: "The People," the Founders, and the Troubled Ending of the American Revolution*. New York: Oxford University Press, 2007.

Bowes, John P. *Land Too Good for Indians: Northern Indian Removal.* Norman: University of Oklahoma Press, 2016.

Brands, H. W. *American Colossus: The Triumph of Capitalism, 1865–1900.* New York: Anchor Books, 2011.

Breen, Patrick H. *The Land Shall Be Deluged in Blood: A New History of the Nat Turner Revolt.* New York: Oxford University Press, 2015.

Brooks, Corey M. *Liberty Power: Antislavery Third Parties and the Transformation of American Politics.* Chicago: University of Chicago Press, 2016.

Brown, David. *Southern Outcast: Hinton Rowan Helper and "The Impending Crisis of the South."* Baton Rouge: Louisiana State University Press, 2006.

Buley, R. Carlyle. *The Old Northwest: Pioneer Period, 1815–1840.* 2 vols. Indianapolis: Indiana Historical Society, 1950.

Burin, Eric. *Slavery and the Peculiar Solution: A History of the American Colonization Society.* Gainesville: University Press of Florida, 2005.

Burlingame, Michael. *Abraham Lincoln: A Life.* 2 vols. Baltimore: Johns Hopkins University Press, 2008.

Burt, John. *Lincoln's Tragic Pragmatism: Lincoln, Douglas, and Moral Conflict.* Cambridge, Mass.: Belknap Press of Harvard University Press, 2013.

Campbell, Randolph B. *An Empire for Slavery: The Peculiar Institution in Texas, 1821–1865.* Baton Rouge: Louisiana State University Press, 1989.

Capers, Gerald M. *Stephen A. Douglas, Defender of the Union.* Boston: Little, Brown, 1959.

Carey, Anthony Gene. *Parties, Slavery, and the Union in Antebellum Georgia.* Athens: University of Georgia Press, 1997.

Carrigan, William D. *The Making of a Lynching Culture: Violence and Vigilantism in Central Texas, 1836–1916.* Urbana: University of Illinois Press, 2004.

Carroll, Charles C. *The Government's Importation of Camels: A Historical Sketch.* U.S. Department of Agriculture, Bureau of Animal Husbandry—Circular No. 53. Washington, D.C.: Government Printing Office, 1904.

Cashin, Joan E. *First Lady of the Confederacy: Varina Davis's Civil War.* Cambridge, Mass.: Belknap Press of Harvard University Press, 2006.

Catton, William, and Bruce Catton. *Two Roads to Sumter: Abraham Lincoln, Jefferson Davis and the March to Civil War.* New York: McGraw-Hill, 1963.

Chadwick, Bruce. *The Two American Presidents: A Dual Biography of Abraham Lincoln and Jefferson Davis.* Secaucus, N.J.: Carol Publishing Group, 1999.

Childers, Christopher. *The Failure of Popular Sovereignty: Slavery, Manifest Destiny, and the Radicalization of Southern Politics.* Lawrence: University Press of Kansas, 2012.

Cochran, William C. *The Dream of a Northwestern Confederacy.* [Madison]: State Historical Society of Wisconsin, 1916.

Cohen, Nancy L. *The Reconstruction of American Liberalism, 1865–1914.* Chapel Hill: University of North Carolina Press, 2002.

Cole, Arthur Charles. *The Era of the Civil War, 1848–1870.* 1919. Freeport, N.Y.: Books for Libraries Press, 1971.

Cole, Donald B. *Martin Van Buren and the American Political System.* Princeton: Princeton University Press, 1984.

Cooper, William J., Jr. *Jefferson Davis, American.* New York: Alfred A. Knopf, 2000.

———. *Jefferson Davis and the Civil War Era*. Baton Rouge: Louisiana State University Press, 2008.

———. *The South and the Politics of Slavery, 1828–1856*. Baton Rouge: Louisiana State University Press, 1978.

———. *We Have the War upon Us: The Onset of the Civil War, November 1860–April 1861*. New York: Vintage Books, 2013.

Craven, Avery. *The Growth of Southern Nationalism, 1848–1861*. Baton Rouge: Louisiana State University Press, 1953.

Crofts, Daniel W. *Lincoln and the Politics of Slavery: The Other Thirteenth Amendment and the Struggle to Save the Union*. Chapel Hill: University of North Carolina Press, 2016.

———. *A Secession Crisis Enigma: William Henry Hurlbert and "The Diary of a Public Man."* Baton Rouge: Louisiana State University Press, 2010.

Cronon, William. *Nature's Metropolis: Chicago and the Great West*. New York: W. W. Norton, 1991.

Davis, William C. *Jefferson Davis: The Man and His Hour*. New York: HarperCollins, 1991.

Dean, Adan Wesley. *An Agrarian Republic: Farming, Antislavery Politics, and Nature Parks in the Civil War Era*. Chapel Hill: University of North Carolina Press, 2015.

Deslandes, Karine, Fabrice Mourlon, and Bruno Tribout, eds. *Civil War and Narrative: Testimony, Historiography, Memory*. Cham, Switz.: Palgrave Macmillan, 2017.

Deyle, Steven. *Carry Me Back: The Domestic Slave Trade in American Life*. New York: Oxford University Press, 2005.

Dirck, Brian R. *Abraham Lincoln and White America*. Lawrence: University Press of Kansas, 2012.

———. *Lincoln and Davis: Imagining America, 1809–1865*. Lawrence: University Press of Kansas, 2001.

Diouf, Sylviane A. *Dreams of Africa in Alabama: The Slave Ship* Clotilda *and the Story of the Last Africans Brought to America*. New York: Oxford University Press, 2008.

Dodd, William E. *Jefferson Davis*. Philadelphia: G. W. Jacobs, 1907.

Donald, David Herbert. *Lincoln*. New York: Simon and Schuster, 1995.

———, ed. *Why the North Won the Civil War*. Baton Rouge: Louisiana State University Press, 1960.

Doyle, Don Harrison. *The Social Order of a Frontier Community: Jacksonville, Illinois, 1825–70*. Urbana: University of Illinois Press, 1978.

Du Bois, W. E. B. *The Suppression of the African Slave-Trade to the United States of America, 1638–1870*. 1896. New York: Dover, 1970.

Dubay, Robert W. *John Jones Pettus, Mississippi Fire-Eater: His Life and Times, 1813–1867*. Jackson: University Press of Mississippi, 1975.

Dumond, Dwight Lowell. *The Secession Movement, 1860–1861*. New York: Macmillan, 1931.

Durden, Robert Franklin. *The Self-Inflicted Wound: Southern Politics in the Nineteenth Century*. Lexington: University Press of Kentucky, 1985.

Durrill, Wayne K. *War of Another Kind: A Southern Community in the Great Rebellion*. New York: Oxford University Press, 1990.

Dusinberre, William. *Slavemaster President: The Double Career of James Polk.* New York: Oxford University Press, 2003.

Earle, Jonathan H. *Jacksonian Antislavery and the Politics of Free Soil, 1824–1854.* Chapel Hill: University of North Carolina Press, 2004.

Eaton, Clement. *Jefferson Davis.* New York: Free Press, 1977.

Egerton, Douglas R. *Year of Meteors: Stephen Douglas, Abraham Lincoln, and the Election That Brought on the Civil War.* New York: Bloomsbury, 2010.

Egnal, Marc. *Clash of Extremes: The Economic Origins of the Civil War.* New York: Hill and Wang, 2009.

Ellis, Richard E. *The Union at Risk: Jacksonian Democracy, States' Rights, and the Nullification Crisis.* New York: Oxford University Press, 1987.

Ely, James W., Jr. *The Guardian of Every Other Right: The Constitutional History of Property Rights.* New York: Oxford University Press, 1992.

Emmett, Chris. *Texas Camel Tales: Incidents Growing Up around an Attempt by the War Department of the United States to Foster an Uninterrupted Flow of Commerce through Texas by the Use of Camels.* San Antonio: Naylor Printing, 1932.

Ericson, David F. *Slavery in the American Republic: Developing the Federal Government, 1791–1861.* Lawrence: University Press of Kansas, 2011.

Escott, Paul D. *After Secession: Jefferson Davis and the Failure of Confederate Nationalism.* Baton Rouge: Louisiana State University Press, 1978.

Etcheson, Nicole. *Bleeding Kansas: Contested Liberty in the Civil War Era.* Lawrence: University Press of Kansas, 2004.

———. *The Emerging Midwest: Upland Southerners and the Political Culture of the Old Northwest, 1787–1861.* Bloomington: Indiana University Press, 1996.

Evans, David. *Sherman's Horsemen: Union Cavalry Operations in the Atlanta Campaign.* Bloomington: Indiana University Press, 1996.

Everett, Frank E., Jr. *Brierfield: Plantation Home of Jefferson Davis.* Hattiesburg: University and College Press of Mississippi, 1971.

Eyal, Yonatan. *The Young America Movement and the Transformation of the Democratic Party, 1828–61.* New York: Cambridge University Press, 2007.

Faragher, John Mack. *Sugar Creek: Life on the Illinois Prairie.* New Haven: Yale University Press, 1986.

Faulk, Odie B. *The U.S. Camel Corps: An Army Experiment.* New York: Oxford University Press, 1976.

Fehrenbacher, Don E. *The Dred Scott Case: Its Significance in American Law and Politics.* New York: Oxford University Press, 1978.

———. *Prelude to Greatness: Lincoln in the 1850s.* Stanford: Stanford University Press, 1962.

———. *The Slaveholding Republic: An Account of the United States Government's Relations to Slavery.* Completed and edited by Ward M. McAfee. New York: Oxford University Press, 2001.

———. *The South and Three Sectional Crises.* Baton Rouge: Louisiana State University Press, 1980.

Fiege, Mark. *The Republic of Nature: An Environmental History of the United States.* Seattle: University of Washington Press, 2012.

Finkelman, Paul, ed. *Slavery and the Law.* Lanham, Md.: Rowman and Littlefield, 2002.

Finkelman, Paul, and Donald R. Kennon, eds. *Congress and the Crisis of the 1850s.* Athens: published for the United States Capitol Historical Society by Ohio University Press, 2012.

Foner, Eric. *Free Soil, Free Labor, Free Men: The Ideology of the Republican Party before the Civil War.* 1970. New York: Oxford University Press, 1995.

Foote, Shelby. *The Civil War, a Narrative.* 3 vols. 1958–74. New York: Vintage Books, 1986.

Ford, Lacy K. *Deliver Us from Evil: The Slavery Question in the Old South.* New York: Oxford University Press, 2009.

Fornell, Earl Wesley. *The Galveston Era: The Texas Crescent on the Eve of Secession.* Austin: University of Texas Press, 1961.

Fox-Genovese, Elizabeth, and Eugene D. Genovese. *Slavery in White and Black: Class and Race in the Southern Slaveholders' New World Order.* New York: Cambridge University Press, 2008.

Francaviglia, Richard V., and Douglas W. Richmond, eds. *Dueling Eagles: Reinterpreting the U.S.-Mexican War, 1846–1848.* Fort Worth: Texas Christian University Press, 2000.

Fredrickson, George M. *Big Enough to Be Inconsistent: Abraham Lincoln Confronts Slavery and Race.* Cambridge, Mass.: Harvard University Press, 2008.

——. *The Black Image in the White Mind: The Debate on Afro-American Character and Destiny, 1817–1914.* New York: Harper and Row, 1971.

——. *White Supremacy: A Comparative Study in American and South African History.* New York: Oxford University Press, 1981.

Freehling, Alison Goodyear. *Drift toward Dissolution: The Virginia Slavery Debate of 1831–1832.* Baton Rouge: Louisiana State University Press, 1982.

Freehling, William W. *Prelude to Civil War: The Nullification Controversy in South Carolina, 1816–1836.* New York: Harper and Row, 1966.

——. *The Reintegration of American History: Slavery and the Civil War.* New York: Oxford University Press, 1994.

——. *The Road to Disunion.* 2 vols. New York: Oxford University Press, 1990–2007.

——. *The South vs. the South: How Anti-Confederate Southerners Shaped the Course of the Civil War.* New York: Oxford University Press, 2001.

Freeman, Joanne B. *The Field of Blood: Violence in Congress and the Road to Civil War.* New York: Farrar, Straus and Giroux, 2018.

Frymer, Paul. *Building an American Empire: The Era of Territorial and Political Expansion.* Princeton: Princeton University Press, 2017.

Fuller, A. James, ed. *The Election of 1860 Reconsidered.* Kent: Kent State University Press, 2013.

Ganaway, Loomis Morton. *New Mexico and the Sectional Controversy, 1846–1861.* Albuquerque: University of New Mexico Press, 1944.

Gara, Larry. *The Presidency of Franklin Pierce.* Lawrence: University Press of Kansas, 1991.

Gardner, William. *Life of Stephen A. Douglas.* Boston: Roxburgh Press, 1905.

Gates, Paul W. *The Illinois Central Railroad and Its Colonization Work.* Cambridge, Mass.: Harvard University Press, 1934.

Genovese, Eugene D. *The Slaveholders' Dilemma: Freedom and Progress in Southern Conservative Thought, 1820–1860.* Columbia: University of South Carolina Press, 1992.

Gerring, John. *Party Ideologies in America, 1828–1996*. New York: Cambridge University Press, 1998.

Gienapp, William E. *The Origins of the Republican Party, 1852–1856*. New York: Oxford University Press, 1987.

Gleeson, David T. *The Green and the Gray: The Irish in the Confederate States of America*. Chapel Hill: University of North Carolina Press, 2013.

Goldman, Ralph Morris. *Search for Consensus: The Story of the Democratic Party*. Philadelphia: Temple University Press, 1979.

Graebner, Norman A. *Empire on the Pacific: A Study in American Continental Expansion*. New York: Ronald Press, 1955.

Gray, A. A., Francis P. Farquhar, and William S. Lewis. *Camels in Western America*. San Francisco: California Historical Society, 1930.

Green, Fletcher Melvin. *Democracy in the Old South, and Other Essays*. Edited by J. Isaac Copeland. Nashville: Vanderbilt University Press, 1969.

Greenberg, Amy S. *A Wicked War: Polk, Clay, Lincoln, and the 1846 U.S. Invasion of Mexico*. New York: Alfred A. Knopf, 2012.

Gross, Ariela J. *Double Character: Slavery and Mastery in the Antebellum Southern Courtroom*. Princeton: Princeton University Press, 2000.

Guasco, Suzanne Cooper. *Confronting Slavery: Edward Coles and the Rise of Antislavery Politics in Nineteenth-Century America*. DeKalb: Northern Illinois University Press, 2013.

Gudmestad, Robert. *Steamboats and the Rise of the Cotton Kingdom*. Baton Rouge: Louisiana State University Press, 2011.

Guelzo, Allen C. *Lincoln and Douglas: The Debates That Defined America*. New York: Simon and Schuster, 2008.

Hahn, Steven. *A Nation without Borders: The United States and Its World in an Age of Civil Wars, 1830–1910*. New York: Viking, 2016.

Hahn, Steven, and Jonathan Prude, eds. *The Countryside in the Age of Capitalist Transformation: Essays in the Social History of Rural America*. Chapel Hill: University of North Carolina Press, 1985.

Hamilton, Daniel W. *The Limits of Sovereignty: Property Confiscation in the Union and the Confederacy during the Civil War*. Chicago: University of Chicago Press, 2007.

Hamilton, Holman. *Prologue to Conflict: The Crisis and Compromise of 1850*. New York: W. W. Norton, 1966.

——. *The Three Kentucky Presidents: Lincoln, Taylor, Davis*. 1978. Lexington: University Press of Kentucky, 2003.

Hammond, John Craig. *Slavery, Freedom, and Expansion in the Early American West*. Charlottesville: University of Virginia Press, 2007.

Hammond, John Craig, and Matthew Mason, eds. *Contesting Slavery: The Politics of Bondage and Freedom in the New American Nation*. Charlottesville: University of Virginia Press, 2011.

Harden, Edward J. *The Life of George M. Troup*. Savannah, Ga.: E. J. Purse, 1859.

Harris, William C. *Lincoln's Rise to the Presidency*. Lawrence: University Press of Kansas, 2007.

Harrold, Stanley. *The Abolitionists and the South, 1831–1861*. Lexington: University Press of Kentucky, 1995.

Hattaway, Herman, and Richard E. Beringer. *Jefferson Davis, Confederate President*. Lawrence: University Press of Kansas, 2002.

Haynes, Robert V. *The Mississippi Territory and the Southwest Frontier, 1795–1817*. Lexington: University Press of Kentucky, 2010.

Heerman, M. Scott. *The Alchemy of Slavery: Human Bondage and Emancipation in the Illinois Country, 1730–1865*. Philadelphia: University of Pennsylvania Press, 2018.

Hermann, Janet Sharp. *The Pursuit of a Dream*. New York: Oxford University Press, 1981.

Hettle, Wallace. *The Peculiar Democracy: Southern Democrats in Peace and Civil War*. Athens: University of Georgia Press, 2001.

Hietala, Thomas R. *Manifest Design: Anxious Aggrandizement in Late Jacksonian America*. Ithaca: Cornell University Press, 1985.

Hine, Robert V., and John Mack Faragher. *Frontiers: A Short History of the American West*. New Haven: Yale University Press, 2007.

Hofstadter, Richard. *The American Political Tradition and the Men Who Made It*. New York: Vintage Books, 1948.

Holt, Michael F. *The Election of 1860: "A Campaign Fraught with Consequences."* Lawrence: University Press of Kansas, 2017.

——. *Franklin Pierce*. New York: Times Books, 2010.

——. *The Political Crisis of the 1850s*. New York: W. W. Norton, 1978.

——. *The Rise and Fall of the American Whig Party: Jacksonian Politics and the Onset of the Civil War*. New York: Oxford University Press, 1999.

Holton, Woody. *Unruly Americans and the Origins of the Constitution*. New York: Hill and Wang, 2007.

Holzer, Harold. *Lincoln President-Elect: Abraham Lincoln and the Great Secession Winter, 1860–1861*. New York: Simon and Schuster, 2008.

Howard, Warren S. *American Slavers and the Federal Law, 1837–1862*. Berkeley: University of California Press, 1963.

Huston, James L. *The British Gentry, the Southern Planter, and the Northern Family Farmer: Agriculture and Sectional Antagonism in North America*. Baton Rouge: Louisiana State University Press, 2015.

——. *Calculating the Value of the Union: Slavery, Property Rights, and the Economic Origins of the Civil War*. Chapel Hill: University of North Carolina Press, 2003.

——. *The Panic of 1857 and the Coming of the Civil War*. Baton Rouge: Louisiana State University Press, 1987.

——. *Stephen A. Douglas and the Dilemmas of Democratic Equality*. Lanham, Md.: Rowman and Littlefield, 2007.

Hyman, Harold M., and William M. Wiecek. *Equal Justice under Law: Constitutional Development, 1835–1875*. New York: Harper and Row, 1982.

Jaffa, Harry V. *Crisis of the House Divided: An Interpretation of the Issues in the Lincoln-Douglas Debates*. 1959. Chicago: University of Chicago Press, 2009.

Jennings, Thelma. *The Nashville Convention: Southern Movement for Unity, 1848–1851*. Memphis: Memphis State University Press, 1980.

Jentz, John B., and Richard Schneirov. *Chicago in the Age of Capital: Class, Politics, and Democracy during the Civil War and Reconstruction*. Urbana: University of Illinois Press, 2012.

Johannsen, Robert W. *Frontier Politics and the Sectional Conflict: The Pacific Northwest on the Eve of the Civil War.* Seattle: University of Washington Press, 1955.

———. *The Frontier, the Union, and Stephen A. Douglas.* Urbana: University of Illinois Press, 1989.

———. *Lincoln, the South, and Slavery: The Political Dimension.* Baton Rouge: Louisiana State University Press, 1991.

———. *Stephen A. Douglas.* 1973. Urbana: University of Illinois Press, 1997.

Johannsen, Robert W., et al. *Manifest Destiny and Empire: American Antebellum Expansionism.* Edited by Sam W. Haynes and Christopher Morris. College Station: Texas A&M University Press, 1997.

Johansen, Dorothy O., and Charles M. Gates. *Empire of the Columbia: A History of the Pacific Northwest.* New York: Harper and Row, 1957.

Johnson, Michael P. *Toward a Patriarchal Republic: The Secession of Georgia.* Baton Rouge: Louisiana State University Press, 1977.

Johnson, Walter. *River of Dark Dreams: Slavery and Empire in the Cotton Kingdom.* Cambridge, Mass.: Belknap Press of Harvard University Press, 2013.

———. *Soul by Soul: Life inside the Antebellum Slave Market.* Cambridge, Mass.: Harvard University Press, 1999.

Jordan, Winthrop D. *Tumult and Silence at Second Creek: An Inquiry into a Civil War Slave Conspiracy.* Baton Rouge: Louisiana State University Press, 1993.

Jung, Patrick J. *The Black Hawk War of 1832.* Norman: University of Oklahoma Press, 2007.

Karp, Matthew. *This Vast Southern Empire: Slaveholders at the Helm of American Foreign Policy.* Cambridge, Mass.: Harvard University Press, 2016.

Kelley, Sean M. *Los Brazos de Dios: A Plantation Society in the Texas Borderlands, 1821–1865.* Baton Rouge: Louisiana State University Press, 2010.

Kennedy, Roger G. *Cotton and Conquest: How the Plantation System Acquired Texas.* Norman: University of Oklahoma Press, 2013.

Kiser, William S. *Borderlands of Slavery: The Struggle over Captivity and Peonage in the American Southwest.* Philadelphia: University of Pennsylvania Press, 2017.

Klein, Philip Shriver. *President James Buchanan, a Biography.* University Park: Pennsylvania State University Press, 1962.

Knoles, George Harmon, ed. *The Crisis of the Union, 1860–1861.* Baton Rouge: Louisiana State University Press, 1965.

Kovel, Joel. *White Racism: A Psychohistory.* 1971. New York: Columbia University Press, 1984.

Krug, Mark M. *Lyman Trumbull, Conservative Radical.* New York: A. S. Barnes, 1965.

Lamar, Howard Roberts. *The Far Southwest, 1846–1912: A Territorial History.* New Haven: Yale University Press, 1966.

Lander, Ernest McPherson, Jr. *Reluctant Imperialists: Calhoun, the South Carolinians, and the Mexican War.* Baton Rouge: Louisiana State University Press, 1979.

Lander, James. *Lincoln and Darwin: Shared Visions of Race, Science, and Religion.* Carbondale: Southern Illinois University Press, 2010.

Landis, Michael Todd. *Northern Men with Southern Loyalties: The Democratic Party and the Sectional Crisis.* Ithaca: Cornell University Press, 2014.

Larson, John Lauritz. *Internal Improvement: National Public Works and the Promise of Popular Government in the Early United States.* Chapel Hill: University of North Carolina Press, 2001.

Leichtle, Kurt E., and Bruce G. Carveth. *Crusade against Slavery: Edward Coles, Pioneer of Freedom*. Carbondale: Southern Illinois University Press, 2011.

Leonard, Gerald. *The Invention of Party Politics: Federalism, Popular Sovereignty, and Constitutional Development in Jacksonian Illinois*. Chapel Hill: University of North Carolina Press, 2002.

Leuchtenburg, William E. *The Supreme Court Reborn: The Constitutional Revolution in the Age of Roosevelt*. New York: Oxford University Press, 1995.

Levine, Bruce C. *The Fall of the House of Dixie: The Civil War and the Social Revolution that Transformed the South*. New York: Random House, 2013.

Link, William A. *Roots of Secession: Slavery and Politics in Antebellum Virginia*. Chapel Hill: University of North Carolina Press, 2003.

Litwack, Leon F. *Trouble in Mind: Black Southerners in the Age of Jim Crow*. New York: Alfred A. Knopf, 1998.

MacLeod, Duncan J. *Slavery, Race and the American Revolution*. New York: Cambridge University Press, 1974.

Mahoney, Barbara S. *The Salem Clique: Oregon's Founding Brothers*. Corvallis: Oregon State University Press, 2017.

Maizlish, Stephen E. *A Strife of Tongues: The Compromise of 1850 and the Ideological Foundations of the American Civil War*. Charlottesville: University of Virginia Press, 2018.

Malavasic, Alice Elizabeth. *The F Street Mess: How Southern Senators Rewrote the Kansas-Nebraska Act*. Chapel Hill: University of North Carolina Press, 2017.

Mann, Charles W. *The Chicago Common Council and the Fugitive Slave Law of 1850*. Chicago: n.p., 1903.

Marques, Leonardo. *The United States and the Transatlantic Slave Trade to the Americas, 1776–1867*. New Haven: Yale University Press, 2016.

Martinez, Jaime Amanda. *Confederate Slave Impressment in the Upper South*. Chapel Hill: University of North Carolina Press, 2013.

Mason, Matthew. *Apostle of Union: A Political Biography of Edward Everett*. Chapel Hill: University of North Carolina Press, 2017.

May, Robert E. *John A. Quitman: Old South Crusader*. Baton Rouge: Louisiana State University Press, 1985.

———. *Manifest Destiny's Underworld: Filibustering in Antebellum America*. Chapel Hill: University of North Carolina Press, 2002.

———. *Slavery, Race, and Conquest in the Tropics: Lincoln, Douglas, and the Future of Latin America*. New York: Cambridge University Press, 2013.

———. *The Southern Dream of a Caribbean Empire, 1854–1861*. Baton Rouge: Louisiana State University Press, 1973.

Mayfield, John. *Rehearsal for Republicanism: Free Soil and the Politics of Antislavery*. Washington, N.Y.: Kennikat Press, 1980.

McCardell, John. *The Idea of a Southern Nation: Southern Nationalists and Southern Nationalism, 1830–1860*. New York: W. W. Norton, 1979.

McCurry, Stephanie. *Confederate Reckoning: Power and Politics in the Civil War South*. Cambridge, Mass.: Harvard University Press, 2010.

McDonough, Daniel, and Kenneth W. Noe, eds. *Politics and Culture of the Civil War Era: Essays in Honor of Robert W. Johannsen*. Selinsgrove, Pa.: Susquehanna University Press, 2006.

McElroy, Robert. *Jefferson Davis: The Real and the Unreal.* 1937. New York: Kraus Reprint, 1969.

McLemore, Richard Aubrey, ed. *A History of Mississippi.* 2 vols. Hattiesburg: University and College Press of Mississippi, 1973.

McMaster, John Bach. *A History of the People of the United States, from the Revolution to the Civil War.* 8 vols. New York: D. Appleton, 1901–14.

McPherson, James M. *Battle Cry of Freedom: The Civil War Era.* New York: Oxford University Press, 1988.

———. *Embattled Rebel: Jefferson Davis as Commander in Chief.* New York: Penguin Press, 2014.

McPherson, James M., and William J. Cooper Jr., eds. *Writing the Civil War: The Quest to Understand.* Columbia: University of South Carolina Press, 1998.

Merk, Frederick. *Manifest Destiny and Mission in American History: A Reinterpretation.* New York: Alfred A. Knopf, 1963.

Merritt, Keri Leigh. *Masterless Men: Poor Whites and Slavery in the Antebellum South.* New York: Cambridge University Press, 2017.

Miles, Edwin A. *Jacksonian Democracy in Mississippi.* Chapel Hill: University of North Carolina Press, 1960.

Miller, John Chester. *The Wolf by the Ears: Thomas Jefferson and Slavery.* New York: Free Press, 1977.

Miller, William Lee. *Arguing about Slavery: John Quincy Adams and the Great Battle in the United States Congress.* New York: Alfred A. Knopf, 1995.

Milner, II, Clyde A., Carol A. O'Connor, and Martha A. Sandweiss, eds. *The Oxford History of the American West.* New York: Oxford University Press, 1994.

Milton, George Fort. *The Eve of Conflict: Stephen A. Douglas and the Needless War.* Boston: Houghton Mifflin Company, 1934.

Monroe, Dan. *The Republican Vision of John Tyler.* College Station: Texas A&M University Press, 2003.

Moore, John Hebron. *The Emergence of the Cotton Kingdom in the Old Southwest: Mississippi, 1770–1860.* Baton Rouge: Louisiana State University Press, 1988.

Morris, Christopher. *Becoming Southern: The Evolution of a Way of Life, Warren County and Vicksburg, Mississippi, 1770–1860.* New York: Oxford University Press, 1995.

———. *The Big Muddy: An Environmental History of the Mississippi and Its Peoples, from Hernando de Soto to Hurricane Katrina.* New York: Oxford University Press, 2012.

Morris, Roy. *The Long Pursuit: Abraham Lincoln's Thirty-Year Struggle with Stephen Douglas for the Heart and Soul of America.* New York: Collins, 2008.

Morris, Thomas D. *Southern Slavery and the Law, 1619–1860.* Chapel Hill: University of North Carolina Press, 1996.

Morrison, Chaplain W. *Democratic Politics and Sectionalism: The Wilmot Proviso Controversy.* Chapel Hill: University of North Carolina Press, 1967.

Morrison, Michael A. *Slavery and the American West: The Eclipse of Manifest Destiny and the Coming of the Civil War.* Chapel Hill: University of North Carolina Press, 1997.

Nedelsky, Jennifer. *Private Property and the Limits of American Constitutionalism: The Madisonian Framework and Its Legacy.* Chicago: University of Chicago Press, 1990.

Neely Jr., Mark E. *Lincoln and the Democrats: The Politics of Opposition in the Civil War*. New York: Cambridge University Press, 2017.

Nevins, Allan. *The Emergence of Lincoln*. 2 vols. New York: Charles Scribner's Sons, 1950.

Nichols, Roy Franklin. *The Democratic Machine, 1850–1854*. New York: Columbia University Press, 1923.

——. *The Disruption of American Democracy*. 1948. New York: Free Press, 1967.

Niven, John. *Martin Van Buren: The Romantic Age of American Politics*. New York: Oxford University Press, 1983.

Oakes, James. *Freedom National: The Destruction of Slavery in the United States, 1861–1865*. New York: W. W. Norton & Co., 2013.

——. *The Radical and the Republican: Frederick Douglass, Abraham Lincoln, and the Triumph of Antislavery Politics*. New York: W. W. Norton & Co., 2007.

——. *The Ruling Race: A History of American Slaveholders*. New York: Vintage Books, 1982.

Obadele-Starks, Ernest. *Freebooters and Smugglers: The Foreign Slave Trade in the United States after 1808*. Fayetteville: University of Arkansas Press, 2007.

Olsen, Christopher J. *Political Culture and Secession in Mississippi: Masculinity, Honor, and the Antiparty Tradition, 1830–1860*. New York: Oxford University Press, 2000.

Pacheco, Josephine F. *The* Pearl*: A Failed Slave Escape on the Potomac*. Chapel Hill: University of North Carolina Press, 2005.

Parrish, William Earl. *David Rice Atchison of Missouri, Border Politician*. Columbia: University of Missouri Press, 1961.

Paul, James C. N. *Rift in the Democracy*. Philadelphia: University of Pennsylvania Press, 1951.

Paulus, Carl Lawrence. *The Slaveholding Crisis: Fear of Insurrection and the Coming of the Civil War*. Baton Rouge: Louisiana State University Press, 2017.

Pease, Theodore Calvin. *The Frontier State, 1818–1848*. Chicago: A. G. McClurg and Co., 1922.

Peck, Graham A. *Making an Antislavery Nation: Lincoln, Douglas, and the Battle over Freedom*. Urbana: University of Illinois Press, 2017.

Perman, Michael. *Pursuit of Unity: A Political History of the American South*. Chapel Hill: University of North Carolina Press, 2009.

Peterson, Merrill D. *The Jefferson Image in the American Mind*. 1960. Charlottesville: University Press of Virginia, 1998.

Pfau, Michael. *The Political Style of Conspiracy: Chase, Sumner, and Lincoln*. East Lansing: Michigan State University Press, 2005.

Phillips, Christopher. *The Rivers Ran Backward: The Civil War and the Remaking of the American Middle Border*. New York: Oxford University Press, 2016.

Pierce, Bessie Louise. *A History of Chicago*. 3 vols. New York: Alfred A. Knopf, 1937–1957.

Pletcher, David M. *The Diplomacy of Annexation: Texas, Oregon, and the Mexican War*. Columbia: University of Missouri Press, 1973.

Ponce, Pearl T. *To Govern the Devil in Hell: The Political Crisis in Territorial Kansas*. DeKalb: Northern Illinois University Press, 2014.

Pooley, William Vipond. *The Settlement of Illinois from 1830 to 1850*. Madison, WI: n.p., 1908.

Potter, David M. *The Impending Crisis, 1848–1861*. Completed and edited by Don E. Fehrenbacher. New York: Harper Torchbooks, 1976.

———. *Lincoln and His Party in the Secession Crisis*. New Haven: Yale University Press, 1942.

Quinn, Arthur. *The Rivals: William Gwin, David Broderick, and the Birth of California*. New York: Crown Publishers, 1994.

Quist, John W., and Michael J. Birkner, eds. *James Buchanan and the Coming of the Civil War*. Gainesville: University Press of Florida, 2013.

Quitt, Martin H. *Stephen A. Douglas and Antebellum Democracy*. New York: Cambridge University Press, 2012.

Rable, George C. *The Confederate Republic: A Revolution Against Politics*. Chapel Hill: University of North Carolina Press, 1994.

Rainwater, Percy Lee. *Mississippi: Storm Center of Secession, 1856–1861*. Baton Rouge: O. Claitor, 1938.

Ranck, James Byrne. *Albert Gallatin Brown, Radical Southern Nationalist*. New York: D. Appleton Century Company, 1937.

Rawley, James A. *Race & Politics: "Bleeding Kansas" and the Coming of the Civil War*. Lincoln: University of Nebraska Press, 1969.

Ray, P. Orman. *The Repeal of the Missouri Compromise, Its Origin and Authorship*. Cleveland: Arthur H. Clark, 1909.

Rayback, Joseph G. *Free Soil: The Election of 1848*. Lexington: University Press of Kentucky, 1970.

Read, James H. *Majority Rule Versus Consensus: The Political Thought of John C. Calhoun*. Lawrence: University Press of Kansas, 2009.

Rediker, Marcus. *The* Amistad *Rebellion: An Atlantic Odyssey of Slavery and Freedom*. New York: Viking, 2012.

Remini, Robert V., ed. *The Age of Jackson*. Columbia: University of South Carolina Press, 1972.

Remini, Robert V. *Martin Van Buren and the Making of the Democratic Party*. New York: Columbia University Press, 1959.

Rhodes, James Ford. *History of the United States from the Compromise of 1850 to the McKinley-Bryan Campaign of 1896*. New ed. 8 vols. New York: The Macmillan Company, 1920.

Richards, Kent D. *Isaac I. Stevens: Young Man in a Hurry*. Provo, UT: Brigham Young University Press, 1979.

Richards, Leonard L. *The California Gold Rush and the Coming of the Civil War*. New York: Alfred A. Knopf, 2007.

———. *"Gentlemen of Property and Standing": Anti-Abolition Mobs in Jacksonian America*. New York: Oxford University Press, 1970.

———. *The Slave Power: The Free North and Southern Domination, 1780–1860*. Baton Rouge: Louisiana State University Press, 2000.

Richardson, Heather Cox. *The Greatest Nation of the Earth: Republican Economic Policies during the Civil War*. Cambridge, MA: Harvard University Press, 1997.

Riley, Padraig. *Slavery and the Democratic Conscience: Political Life in Jeffersonian America*. Philadelphia: University of Pennsylvania Press, 2016.

Roberts, Alasdair. *America's First Great Depression: Economic Crisis and Political Disorder after the Panic of 1837*. Ithaca, NY: Cornell University Press, 2012.

Robinson, Armstead L. *Bitter Fruits of Bondage: The Demise of Slavery and the Collapse of the Confederacy, 1861–1865.* Charlottesville: University of Virginia Press, 2005.

Rodriguez, Junius P., ed. *Slavery in the United States: A Social, Political, and Historical Encyclopedia.* 2 vols. Santa Barbara, CA: ABC-CLIO, 2007.

Roediger, David, and Martin H. Blatt, eds. *The Meaning of Slavery in the North.* New York: Garland Publishing, Inc., 1998.

Rogers, Brent M. *Unpopular Sovereignty: Mormons and the Federal Management of Early Utah Territory.* Lincoln: University of Nebraska Press, 2017.

Rothman, Adam. *Slave Country: American Expansion and the Origins of the Deep South.* Cambridge, MA: Harvard University Press, 2005.

Rothman, Joshua D. *Flush Times and Fever Dreams: A Story of Capitalism and Slavery in the Age of Jackson.* Athens: University of Georgia Press, 2012.

Rugemer, Edward Bartlett. *The Problem of Emancipation: The Caribbean Roots of the American Civil War.* Baton Rouge: Louisiana State University Press, 2008.

Russel, Robert R. *Improvement of Communication with the Pacific Coast as an Issue in American Politics, 1783–1864.* Cedar Rapids, IA: Torch Press, 1948.

Rutland, Robert Allen. *The Democrats, from Jefferson to Carter.* Baton Rouge: Louisiana State University Press, 1979.

Saler, Bethel. *The Settlers' Empire: Colonialism and State Formation in America's Old Northwest.* Philadelphia: University of Pennsylvania Press, 2015.

Salzmann, Joshua A. T. *Liquid Capital: Making the Chicago Waterfront.* Philadelphia: University of Pennsylvania Press, 2018.

Schlesinger Jr., Arthur M., ed. *History of U.S. Political Parties.* 4 vols. New York: Chelsea House Publishers, 1973.

Schlesinger Jr., Arthur M. *The Age of Jackson.* Boston: Little, Brown and Company, 1945.

Schoen, Brian. *The Fragile Fabric of Union: Cotton, Federal Politics, and the Global Origins of the Civil War.* Baltimore: Johns Hopkins University Press, 2009.

Schouler, James. *History of the United States of America under the Constitution.* 7 vols. New York: Dodd, Mead & Company, 1894–1913.

Schwantes, Carols A. *The Pacific Northwest: An Interpretive History.* Lincoln: University of Nebraska Press, 1989.

Sellers, Charles. *The Market Revolution: Jacksonian America, 1815–1846.* New York: Oxford University Press, 1991.

Sewell, Richard H. *John P. Hale and the Politics of Abolition.* Cambridge, MA: Harvard University Press, 1965.

Shelden, Rachel A. *Washington Brotherhood: Politics, Social Life, and the Coming of the Civil War.* University of North Carolina Press, 2013.

Siegel, Stanley. *A Political History of the Texas Republic, 1836–1845.* Austin: University of Texas Press, 1956.

Silbey, Joel H. *Martin Van Buren and the Emergence of American Popular Politics.* Lanham, MD: Rowman & Littlefield, 2002.

———. *The Partisan Imperative: The Dynamics of American Politics before the Civil War.* New York: Oxford University Press, 1985.

———. *Storm over Texas: The Annexation Controversy and the Road to Civil War.* New York: Oxford University Press, 2005.

Silver, James W. *Mississippi: The Closed Society*. New York: Harcourt, Brace & World, 1964.

Simeone, James. *Democracy and Slavery in Frontier Illinois: The Bottomland Republic*. DeKalb: Northern Illinois University Press, 2000.

Sinha, Manisha. *The Counterrevolution of Slavery: Politics and Ideology in Antebellum South Carolina*. Chapel Hill: University of North Carolina Press, 2000.

———. *The Slave's Cause: A History of Abolition*. New Haven: Yale University Press, 2016.

Smith, Adam I. P. *The Stormy Present: Conservatism and the Problem of Slavery in Northern Politics, 1846–1865*. Chapel Hill: University of North Carolina Press, 2017.

Smith, Elbert B. *The Presidency of James Buchanan*. Lawrence: University Press of Kansas, 1975.

Smith, Gene Allen. *The Slaves' Gamble: Choosing Sides in the War of 1812*. New York: Palgrave Macmillan, 2013.

Smith, Stacey L. *Freedom's Frontier: California and the Struggle over Unfree Labor, Emancipation, and Reconstruction*. Chapel Hill: University of North Carolina Press, 2013.

Smith, Timothy B. *The Mississippi Secession Convention: Delegates and Deliberations in Politics and War, 1861–1865*. Jackson: University Press of Mississippi, 2014.

Stewart, James Brewer. *Holy Warriors: The Abolitionists and American Slavery*. New York: Hill and Wang, 1976.

Striner, Richard. *Lincoln and Race*. Carbondale: Southern Illinois University Press, 2012.

Strode, Hudson. *Jefferson Davis*. 3 vols. New York: Harcourt, Brace, 1955–1964.

Summers, Mark W. *The Plundering Generation: Corruption and the Crisis of the Union, 1849–1861*. New York: Oxford University Press, 1987.

Sydnor, Charles S. *The Development of Southern Sectionalism, 1819–1848*. Baton Rouge: Louisiana State University Press, 1948.

———. *A Gentleman of the Old Natchez Region: Benjamin L. C. Wailes*. Durham, NC: Duke University Press, 1938.

Tadman, Michael. *Speculators and Slaves: Masters, Traders, and Slaves in the Old South*. Madison: University of Wisconsin Press, 1996.

Takaki, Ronald T. *A Pro-slavery Crusade: The Agitation to Reopen the African Slave Trade*. New York: Free Press, 1971.

Tate, Allen. *Jefferson Davis: His Rise and Fall, a Biographical Narrative*. New York: Minton, Balch, 1929.

Taylor, Alan. *The Internal Enemy: Slavery and War in Virginia, 1772–1832*. New York: W. W. Norton & Co., 2013.

Tise, Larry E. *Proslavery: A History of the Defense of Slavery in America, 1701–1840*. Athens: University of Georgia Press, 1987.

Torget, Andrew J. *Seeds of Empire: Cotton, Slavery, and the Transformation of the Texas Borderlands, 1800–1850*. Chapel Hill: University of North Carolina Press, 2015.

Towers, Frank. *The Urban South and the Coming of the Civil War*. Charlottesville: University of Virginia Press, 2004.

Tutorow, Norman E. *Texas Annexation and the Mexican War: A Political Study of the Old Northwest*. Palo Alto, CA: Chadwick House, 1978.

Unruh, John David. *The Plains Across: The Overland Emigrants and the Trans-Mississippi West, 1840–60.* Urbana: University of Illinois Press, 1978.

Utley, Robert M. *Frontiersmen in Blue: The United States Army and the Indian, 1848–1865.* New York: Macmillan, 1967.

Van Cleve, George William. *A Slaveholders' Union: Slavery, Politics, and the Constitution in the Early American Republic.* Chicago: University of Chicago Press, 2010.

Varon, Elizabeth R. *Disunion! The Coming of the American Civil War, 1789–1859.* Chapel Hill: University of North Carolina Press, 2008.

Von Holst, H. *The Constitutional and Political History of the United States.* 8 vols. Chicago: Callaghan and Company, 1881–1892.

Walters, Ronald G. *The Antislavery Appeal: American Abolitionism after 1830.* Baltimore: Johns Hopkins University Press, 1976.

Walther, Eric H. *William Lowndes Yancey and the Coming of the Civil War.* Chapel Hill: University of North Carolina Press, 2006.

Weiner, Dana Elizabeth. *Race and Rights: Fighting Slavery and Prejudice in the Old Northwest, 1830–1870.* DeKalb: Northern Illinois University Press, 2013.

Wells, Damon. *Stephen Douglas: The Last Years, 1857–1861.* Austin: University of Texas Press, 1971.

Werstein, Irving. *Abraham Lincoln versus Jefferson Davis.* New York: T. Y. Crowell, 1959.

Wesley, Charles H. *The Collapse of the Confederacy.* Washington: Associated Publishers, Inc., 1937.

White, Richard. *"It's Your Misfortune and None of My Own": A New History of the American West.* Norman: University of Oklahoma Press, 1991.

Wilentz, Sean. *The Rise of American Democracy: Jefferson to Lincoln.* New York: W. W. Norton & Co., 2005.

Williams, David. *Rich Man's War: Class, Caste, and Confederate Defeat in the Lower Chattahoochee Valley.* Athens: University of Georgia Press, 1998.

Williams, David., Teresa Crisp Williams, and David Carlson. *Plain Folk in a Rich Man's War: Class and Dissent in Confederate Georgia.* Gainesville: University Press of Florida, 2002.

Wills, Jocelyn. *Boosters, Hustlers, and Speculators: Entrepreneurial Culture and the Rise of Minneapolis and St. Paul, 1849–1883.* St. Paul: Minnesota Historical Society Press, 2005.

Wilson, Major L. *The Presidency of Martin Van Buren.* Lawrence: University Press of Kansas, 1984.

Winders, Richard Bruce. *Panting for Glory: The Mississippi Rifles in the Mexican War.* College Station: Texas A&M University Press, 2016.

Wingerd, Mary Lethert. *North Country: The Making of Minnesota.* Minneapolis: University of Minnesota Press, 2010.

Woods, Michael E. *Emotional and Sectional Conflict in the Antebellum United States.* New York: Cambridge University Press, 2014.

Woodworth, Steven E. *Davis and Lee at War.* Lawrence: University Press of Kansas, 1995.

——. *Jefferson Davis and His Generals: The Failure of Confederate Command in the West.* Lawrence: University Press of Kansas, 1990.

————. *Manifest Destinies: America's Westward Expansion and the Road to the Civil War*. New York: Alfred A. Knopf, 2010.

Worster, Donald. *Under Western Skies: Nature and History in the American West*. New York: Oxford University Press, 1992.

Zarefsky, David. *Lincoln, Douglas, and Slavery: In the Crucible of Public Debate*. Chicago: University of Chicago Press, 1990.

Articles

Addis, Cameron. "The Whitman Massacre." *Journal of the Early Republic* 25 (Summer 2005): 221–58.

Albin, Ray R. "The Perkins Case: The Ordeal of Three Slaves in Gold Rush California." *California History* 67 (December 1988): 215–27.

Auchampaugh, Philip G. "The Buchanan-Douglas Feud." *Journal of the Illinois State Historical Society* 25 (April 1932): 5–48.

Barker, Eugene C. "The African Slave Trade in Texas." *Quarterly of the Texas State Historical Association* 6 (October 1902): 145–58.

Bean, W. G. "Anti-Jeffersonianism in the Ante-bellum South." *North Carolina Historical Review* 12 (April 1935): 103–24

Bestor, Arthur. "State Sovereignty and Slavery: A Reinterpretation of Proslavery Constitutional Doctrine, 1848–1860." *Journal of the Illinois State Historical Society* 54 (Summer 1961): 117–80.

Bleser, Carol K. "The Marriage of Varina Howell and Jefferson Davis: 'I Gave the Best and All My Life to a Girdled Tree.'" *Journal of Southern History* 65 (February 1999): 3–40.

Broussard, Albert S. "Slavery in California Revisited: The Fate of a Kentucky Slave in Gold Rush California." *Pacific Historian* 29 (Spring 1985): 17–21.

Brown, David. "Slavery and the Market Revolution: The South's Place in Jacksonian Historiography." *Southern Studies* 4 (Summer 1993): 189–207.

Brown, Richard H. "The Missouri Crisis, Slavery, and the Politics of Jacksonianism." *South Atlantic Quarterly* 65 (Winter 1965): 55–72.

Carter, John D. "Henry Stuart Foote in California Politics, 1854–1857." *Journal of Southern History* 9 (May 1943): 224–37.

Childers, Christopher. "Interpreting Popular Sovereignty: A Historiographical Essay." *Civil War History* 57 (March 2011): 48–70.

Clinton, Anita Watkins. "Stephen Arnold Douglas—His Mississippi Experience." *Journal of Mississippi History* 50 (June 1988): 56–88.

Collins, Bruce. "The Ideology of the Ante-Bellum Northern Democrats." *Journal of American Studies* 11 (April 1977): 103–21.

————. "The Lincoln-Douglas Contest of 1858 and Illinois' Electorate." *Journal of American Studies* 20 (December 1986): 391–420.

Collins, Bruce W. "The Democrats' Electoral Fortunes during the Lecompton Crisis." *Civil War History* 24 (December 1978): 314–31.

Crane, J. Michael. "Controlling the Night: Perceptions of the Slave Patrol System in Mississippi." *Journal of Mississippi History* 61 (June 1999): 119–36.

Crist, Lynda Lasswell. "A 'Duty Man': Jefferson Davis as Senator." *Journal of Mississippi History* 51 (December 1989): 281–95.

———. "Jefferson Davis and Abraham Lincoln: A Comparison." *Journal of Mississippi History* 70 (March 2008): 27–40.

Current, Richard N. "The Confederates and the First Shot." *Civil War History* 7 (December 1961): 357–69.

Curti, M. E. "Young America." *American Historical Review* 32 (October 1926): 34–55.

Danbom, David B. "The Young America Movement." *Journal of the Illinois State Historical Society* 67 (September 1974): 294–306.

Davis, Granville D. "Douglas and the Chicago Mob." *American Historical Review* 54 (April 1949): 553–56.

Dean Jr., Eric T. "Stephen A. Douglas and Popular Sovereignty." *Historian* 57 (Summer 1995): 733–48.

Dennison, George M. "An Empire of Liberty: Congressional Attitudes toward Popular Sovereignty in the Territories, 1787–1867." *Maryland Historian* 6 (June 1975): 19–40.

Derry, Linda. "Camels in Cahawba." *Alabama Heritage* 112 (Spring 2014): 28–35.

Dickerson, O. M. "Stephen A. Douglas and the Split in the Democratic Party." *Proceedings of the Mississippi Valley Historical Association* 7 (1913–1914): 196–211.

Dirck, Brian R. "Posterity's Blush: Civil Liberties, Property Rights, and Property Confiscation in the Confederacy." *Civil War History* 48 (September 2002): 237–56.

Egerton, Douglas R. "Averting a Crisis: The Proslavery Critique of the American Colonization Society." *Civil War History* 43 (June 1997): 142–56.

Escott, Paul D. "Jefferson Davis and Slavery in the Territories." *Journal of Mississippi History* 39 (June 1977): 97–116.

Etcheson, Nicole. "'A Living, Creeping Lie': Abraham Lincoln on Popular Sovereignty." *Journal of the Abraham Lincoln Association* 29 (Summer 2008): 1–26.

Eyal, Yonatan. "With His Eyes Open: Stephen A. Douglas and the Kansas-Nebraska Disaster of 1854." *Journal of the Illinois State Historical Society* 91 (June 1998): 175–217.

Ezell, John. "Jefferson Davis Seeks Political Vindication, 1851–1857." *Journal of Mississippi History* 26 (December 1964): 307–21.

Feller, Daniel. "A Brother in Arms: Benjamin Tappan and the Antislavery Democracy." *Journal of American History* 88 (June 2001): 48–74.

Finkelman, Paul. "Slavery and the Northwest Ordinance: A Study in Ambiguity." *Journal of the Early Republic* 6 (Winter 1986): 343–70.

Fleming, Walter L. "Jefferson Davis's Camel Experiment." *The Popular Science Monthly* 74 (February 1909): 141–52.

Fletcher, Randol B. "Oregon or the Grave." *Columbia: The Magazine of Northwest History* 20 (Winter 2006/2007): 37–43.

Foner, Eric. "The Wilmot Proviso Revisited." *Journal of American History* 56 (September 1969): 262–79.

Formisano, Ronald P. "Toward a Reorientation of Jacksonian Politics: A Review of the Literature, 1959–1975." *Journal of American History* 63 (June 1976): 42–65.

Gallagher, Gary W. "Disaffection, Persistence, and Nation: Some Directions in Recent Scholarship on the Confederacy." *Civil War History* 55 (September 2009): 329–53.

Gara, Larry. "Slavery and the Slave Power: A Crucial Distinction." *Civil War History* 15 (March 1969): 5–18

Gates, Paul W. "The Struggle for Land and the 'Irrepressible Conflict.'" *Political Science Quarterly* 66 (June 1951): 248–71.

Gonzales, John Edmond. "Henry Stuart Foote: A Forgotten Unionist of the Fifties." *Southern Quarterly* 1 (Winter 1963): 129–39.

Guasco, Suzanne Cooper. "'The Deadly Influence of Negro Capitalists': Southern Yeomen and Resistance to the Expansion of Slavery in Illinois." *Civil War History* 47 (March 2001): 7–29.

Hamilton, Holman. "Democratic Senate Leadership and the Compromise of 1850." *Mississippi Valley Historical Review* 41 (December 1954): 403–18.

Hansen, Vagn K. "Jefferson Davis and the Repudiation of Mississippi Bonds: The Development of a Political Myth." *Journal of Mississippi History* 33 (June 1971): 105–32.

Harmon, George D. "Douglas and the Compromise of 1850." *Journal of the Illinois State Historical Society* 21 (January 1929): 453–99.

Hearon, Cleo. "Mississippi and the Compromise of 1850." *Publications of the Mississippi Historical Society* 14 (1914): 7–229.

———. "Nullification in Mississippi." *Publications of the Mississippi Historical Society* 12 (1912): 37–71.

Hess, Earl J. "The Mississippi River and Secession, 1861: The Northwestern Response." *Old Northwest* 10 (Summer 1984): 187–207.

Hodder, Frank Heywood. "Genesis of the Kansas-Nebraska Act." *Proceedings of the State Historical Society of Wisconsin* (1912): 69–86.

———. "The Railroad Background of the Kansas-Nebraska Act." *Mississippi Valley Historical Review* 12 (June 1925): 3–22.

Hubbart, Henry Clyde. "Revisionist Interpretations of Stephen A. Douglas and Popular Sovereignty." *The Social Studies* 25 (March 1934): 103–7.

Huston, James L. "Democracy by Scripture versus Democracy by Process: A Reflection on Stephen A. Douglas and Popular Sovereignty." *Civil War History* 43 (September 1997): 189–200.

Jeffrey, Kirk, Jr. "Stephen Arnold Douglas in American Historical Writing." *Journal of the Illinois State Historical Society* 61 (September 1968): 248–68.

Johannsen, Robert W. "The Douglas Democracy and the Crisis of Disunion." *Civil War History* 9 (September 1963): 229–47.

———. "Stephen A. Douglas and the South." *Journal of Southern History* 33 (February 1967): 26–50.

———. "Stephen A. Douglas, 'Harper's Magazine,' and Popular Sovereignty." *Mississippi Valley Historical Review* 45 (March 1959): 606–31.

———. "Stephen A. Douglas' New England Campaign, 1860." *New England Quarterly* 35 (June 1962): 162–86.

Johnson, Ludwell H. "Jefferson Davis and Abraham Lincoln as War Presidents: Nothing Succeeds Like Success." *Civil War History* 27 (March 1981): 49–63.

Jordan, Daniel P. "Mississippi's Antebellum Congressmen: A Collective Biography." *Journal of Mississippi History* 38 (June 1976): 157–82.

Kelley, Donald Brooks. "Harper's Ferry: Prelude to Crisis in Mississippi." *Journal of Mississippi History* 27 (December 1965): 351–72.

Kelley, Sean. "Blackbirders and *Bozales*: African-Born Slaves on the Lower Brazos River of Texas in the Nineteenth Century." *Civil War History* 54 (December 2008): 406–23.

———. "'Mexico in His Head': Slavery and the Texas-Mexico Border, 1810–1860." *Journal of Social History* 37 (Spring 2004): 709–23.

Lack, Paul D. "Slavery and Vigilantism in Austin, Texas, 1840–1860." *Southwestern Historical Quarterly* 85 (July 1981): 1–20.

Lammons, Frank Bishop. "Operation Camel: An Experiment in Animal Transportation in Texas, 1857–1860." *Southwestern Historical Quarterly* 61 (January 1957): 20–50.

Latner, Richard B. "A New Look at Jacksonian Politics." *Journal of American History* 63 (March 1975): 943–69.

Learned, Henry Barrett. "The Relation of Philip Phillips to the Repeal of the Missouri Compromise in 1854." *Mississippi Valley Historical Review* 8 (March 1922): 303–17.

Lee, R. Alton. "Slavery and the Oregon Territorial Issue: Prelude to the Compromise of 1850." *Pacific Northwest Quarterly* 64 (Fall 1973): 112–19.

Lesley, Lewis B. "The Purchase and Importation of Camels by the United States Government, 1855–1857." *Southwestern Historical Quarterly* 33 (July 1929): 18–33.

Liles, Debbie. "Slavery and Cattle in East and West Texas." *East Texas Historical Journal* 52 (Fall 2014): 29–38.

Luthin, Reinhard H. "The Democratic Split during Buchanan's Administration." *Pennsylvania History* 11 (January 1944): 13–35.

Lynch, Daniel. "Southern California Chivalry: Southerners, Californios, and the Forging of an Unlikely Alliance." *California History* 91 (Fall 2014): 60–62.

Malin, James C. "The Motives of Stephen A. Douglas in the Organization of Nebraska Territory: A Letter Dated December 17, 1853." *Kansas Historical Quarterly* 19 (November 1951): 321–53.

May, Robert E. "A 'Southern Strategy' for the 1850s: Northern Democrats, the Tropics, and Expansion of the National Domain." *Louisiana Studies* 14 (Winter 1975): 333–59.

McAfee, Ward M. "California's House Divided." *Civil War History* 33 (June 1987): 115–30.

McFaul, John M. "Expediency vs. Morality: Jacksonian Politics and Slavery." *Journal of American History* 62 (June 1975): 24–39.

McKee Jr., James W. "William Barksdale and the Congressional Election of 1853 in Mississippi." *Journal of Mississippi History* 34 (June 1972): 129–58.

McMahon, Edward. "Stephen A. Douglas: A Study of the Attempt to Settle the Question of Slavery in the Territories by the Application of Popular Sovereignty—1850–1860." *Washington Historical Quarterly* 2 (April 1908): 209–32.

———. "Stephen A. Douglas: A Study of the Attempt to Settle the Question of Slavery in the Territories by the Application of Popular Sovereignty—1850–1860 (Continued)." *Washington Historical Quarterly* 2 (July 1908): 309–32.

Meerse, David E. "Buchanan, the Patronage, and the Lecompton Constitution: A Case Study." *Civil War History* 41 (December 1995): 291–312.

———. "The Northern Democratic Party and the Congressional Elections of 1858." *Civil War History* 19 (June 1973): 119–37.

———. "Origins of the Buchanan-Douglas Feud Reconsidered." *Journal of the Illinois State Historical Society* 67 (June 1974): 154–74.

Miles, Edwin A. "The Mississippi Slave Insurrection Scare of 1835." *Journal of Negro History* 42 (January 1957): 48–60.

Nevins, Allan. "Stephen A. Douglas: His Weaknesses and His Greatness." *Journal of the Illinois State Historical Society* 42 (December 1949): 385–410.

Nichols, James David. "The Line of Liberty: Runaway Slaves and Fugitive Peons in the Texas-Mexico Borderlands." *Western Historical Quarterly* 44 (Winter 2013): 413–33.

Nichols, Roy F. "The Kansas-Nebraska Act: A Century of Historiography." *Mississippi Valley Historical Review* 43 (September 1956): 187–212.

Parish, John C. "A Project for a California Slave Colony in 1851." *Huntington Library Bulletin* 8 (October 1935): 171–75.

Peck, Graham A. "New Records of the Lincoln-Douglas Debate at the 1854 Illinois State Fair: The *Missouri Republican* and the *Missouri Democrat* Report from Springfield." *Journal of the Abraham Lincoln Association* 30 (Summer 2009): 25–80.

———. "Was Stephen A. Douglas Antislavery?" *Journal of the Abraham Lincoln Association* 26 (Summer 2005): 1–21.

Persinger, Clark E. "The 'Bargain of 1844' as the Origin of the Wilmot Proviso." *Quarterly of the Oregon Historical Society* 15 (September 1914): 137–46.

Peterson, Owen. "Ethelbert Barksdale in the Democratic National Convention of 1860." *Journal of Mississippi History* 14 (October 1952): 257–78.

Phillips, Christopher. "'The Crime against Missouri': Slavery, Kansas, and the Cant of Southernness in the Border West." *Civil War History* 48 (March 2002): 60–81.

Pratt, Harry E. "Stephen A. Douglas, Lawyer, Legislator, Register and Judge: 1833–1843." *Lincoln Herald* 115 (Fall 2013): 155–65.

———. "Stephen A. Douglas, Lawyer, Legislator, Register and Judge: 1833–1843 [Part 2]." *Lincoln Herald* 115 (Winter 2014): 232–41.

Rawson, Donald M. "Democratic Resurgence in Mississippi, 1852–1853." *Journal of Mississippi History* 26 (March 1964): 1–27.

Roberson, Jere W. "The South and the Pacific Railroad, 1845–1855." *Western Historical Quarterly* 5 (Summer 1974): 163–86.

Russel, Robert R. "The Issues in the Struggle over the Kansas-Nebraska Bill, 1854." *Journal of Southern History* 29 (May 1963): 187–210.

———. "What Was the Compromise of 1850?" *Journal of Southern History* 22 (August 1956): 292–309.

Sansing, David. "A Happy Interlude: Jefferson Davis and the War Department, 1853–1857." *Journal of Mississippi History* 51 (December 1989): 297–312.

Sellers, Charles Grier, Jr. "Andrew Jackson versus the Historians." *Mississippi Valley Historical Review* 44 (March 1958): 615–34.

Shade, William G. "'The Most Delicate and Exciting Topics': Martin Van Buren, Slavery, and the Election of 1836." *Journal of the Early Republic* 18 (Autumn 1998): 459–84.

Silbey, Joel H. "The Southern National Democrats, 1845–1861." *Mid America* 47 (July 1965): 176–90.

Smith, Hal H. "Historic Washington Homes." *Records of the Columbia Historical Society* 11 (1908): 243–67.

Smith, Stacey L. "Beyond North and South: Putting the West in the Civil War and Reconstruction." *Journal of the Civil War Era* 6 (December 2016): 566–91.

———. "Remaking Slavery in a Free State: Masters and Slaves in Gold Rush California." *Pacific Historical Review* 80 (February 2011): 28–63.

St. John, Rachel. "State Power in the West in the Early American Republic." *Journal of the Early Republic* 38 (Spring 2018): 87–94.

Stegmaier, Mark J. "A Law that Would Make Caligula Blush? New Mexico Territory's Unique Slave Code, 1859–1861." *New Mexico Historical Review* 87 (Spring 2012): 209–42.

Stenberg, Richard R. "An Unnoted Factor in the Buchanan-Douglas Feud." *Journal of the Illinois State Historical Society* 25 (January 1933): 271–84.

Swan, Patricia B., and James B. Swan. "James W. Sheahan: Stephen A. Douglas Supporter and Partisan Chicago Journalist." *Journal of the Illinois State Historical Society* 105 (Summer-Fall 2012): 133–66.

Tingley, Donald Fred. "The Jefferson Davis–William H. Bissell Duel." *Mid America* 38 (July 1956): 146–55.

Towers, Frank. "Partisans, New History, and Modernization: The Historiography of the Civil War's Causes, 1861–2011." *Journal of the Civil War Era* 1 (June 2011): 237–64.

Tyler, Ronnie C. "Fugitive Slaves in Mexico." *Journal of Negro History* 57 (January 1972): 1–12.

Venable, Austin L. "The Conflict Between the Douglas and Yancey Forces in the Charleston Convention." *Journal of Southern History* 8 (May 1942): 226–41.

Waite, Kevin. "Jefferson Davis and Proslavery Visions of Empire in the Far West." *Journal of the Civil War Era* 6 (December 2016): 536–65.

Wilentz, Sean. "Jeffersonian Democracy and the Origins of Political Antislavery in the United States: The Missouri Crisis Revisited." *Journal of the Historical Society* 4 (September 2004): 375–401.

Winston, James E. "The Annexation of Texas and the Mississippi Democrats." *Southwestern Historical Quarterly* 25 (July 1921): 1–25.

——. "Mississippi and the Independence of Texas." *Southwestern Historical Quarterly* 21 (July 1917): 36–60.

——. "Texas Annexation Sentiment in Mississippi, 1835–1844." *Southwestern Historical Quarterly* 23 (July 1919): 1–19.

Woods, Michael E. "What Twenty-First-Century Historians Have Said about the Causes of Disunion: A Civil War Sesquicentennial Review of the Recent Literature." *Journal of American History* 99 (September 2012): 415–39.

Zimmerman, Charles. "The Origin and Rise of the Republican Party in Indiana from 1854 to 1860." *Indiana Magazine of History* 13 (December 1917): 349–412.

Zucconi, Adam J. "'Preserve Us From Such Democracy': Politics, Slavery, and Political Culture in Antebellum Northwest Virginia, 1850–1861." *Virginia Magazine of History and Biography* 123 (2015): 324–54.

Dissertations

Fehrenbacher, Don E. "Illinois Political Attitudes, 1854–1861." Ph.D. diss., University of Chicago, 1951.

Jenkins, Robert Louis. "The Gadsden Treaty and Sectionalism: A Nation Reacts." Ph.D. diss., Mississippi State University, 1978.

Lampton, Joan E. "The Kansas-Nebraska Act Reconsidered: An Analysis of Men, Methods, and Motives." Ph.D. diss., Illinois State University, 1979.

McGhee, Fred Lee. "The Black Crop: Slavery and Slave Trading in Nineteenth Century Texas." Ph.D. diss., University of Texas, 2000.

Rawson, Donald M. "Party Politics in Mississippi, 1850–1860." Ph.D. diss., Vanderbilt University, 1964.

Sanders, Phyllis Moore. "Jefferson Davis: Reactionary Rebel, 1808–1861." Ph.D. diss., University of California, Los Angeles, 1976.

Shelton, William Allen. "The Young Jefferson Davis, 1808–1846." Ph.D. diss., University of Kentucky, 1977.

Wynne, Benjamin Ray. "Politics and Pragmatism: Unionism in Antebellum Mississippi, 1832–1860." Ph.D. diss., University of Mississippi, 2000.

Index

223–26; and Crittenden Compromise, 218–19; on Cuba, 187; and Democratic Party, 2–3, 4, 64, 65–66, 80, 98, 110, 113, 118, 166–67, 175–76, 191, 193, 197, 201; on Douglas, 5, 6, 106, 110, 175, 186–87, 207; and *Dred Scott v. Sandford*, 150, 200; education of, 18, 21, 24–25, 79; and election of 1843, 65–66; and election of 1844, 66–68, 98; and election of 1845, 68–69; and election of 1848, 95–96; and election of 1851, 108–10, 175, 200, 205, 214, 217; and election of 1852, 4, 113, 115, 116, 118; and election of 1853, 114; and election of 1856, 4, 139, 146–48; and election of 1860, 6, 176, 191, 192–93, 194, 197, 199, 201–10; and filibustering, 180; on free soil, 88, 101, 175; and Fugitive Slave Act, 105, 106, 193; health problems of, 2, 4, 28, 108, 109, 163, 164, 200, 220; and Henry S. Foote, 91, 108–10, 114; in House of Representatives, 69–73; on internal improvements, 72–73, 95, 120–22, 127; and John Van Evrie, 153; and Kansas-Nebraska Act, 134; on Kansas Territory, 120, 157, 176; and land-grant colleges, 285n89; and Lecompton Constitution, 143–44, 153, 157–66; marriage (first) of, 27–29; marriage (second) of, 68; and Martin Van Buren, 65, 66, 67; military service of, 25–27, 78–80; on the Mississippi River, 12; northern tour (1858) by, 166–67; on nullification, 98; on Oregon Territory, 70–71, 86–87, 95; on Pacific railroad, 121–22, 128, 141, 183; plantation of (Brierfield), 11, 13, 28–29, 42, 79, 110, 189, 220, 239–40n88; on popular sovereignty, 2–3, 6, 90–91, 95–96, 99–100, 101, 102–3, 106, 116, 140, 150, 157, 175, 183, 185, 192–93, 200–202, 217; on property rights, 1–4, 86–87, 88, 91, 99–100, 101, 103–4, 108–9, 150, 152, 156, 164, 175, 179–80, 183, 187, 192–93, 200–202, 203, 217; public criticism of, 4, 6, 114, 142, 177, 188; public support for, 3, 79, 177; racism of, 21, 102–3, 108–9, 110, 119, 151–53, 155, 166–67, 227, 238n46; on repudiation of state debts, 66, 179; resignation from Senate, 4,

220; and secession, 88, 98, 99, 108, 113, 114, 117–18, 147, 162, 163, 176, 188, 201, 205, 212, 213–20; as secretary of war, 4, 5, 25, 26, 111–12, 116–25, 141, 153, 260n49; on slavery, 1–4, 12, 21, 36, 80, 85, 99–100, 101–2, 108–9, 119, 120, 150, 151–52, 156, 157, 163, 175–76, 179–80, 186–87, 192, 224, 238n46; and states' rights, 7, 69; strips Douglas of Territorial Committee chair, 181; on territorial slave code, 2–3, 179–80, 183–84, 187, 192–93, 200–202; on Texas annexation, 4, 66–67, 68; on tonnage duties, 127; and U.S.-Mexican War, 4, 12, 24, 78–80, 98, 112; and War of 1812, 21–22; westward migration of, 4, 7, 12, 15; on Wilmot Proviso, 88, 89, 91, 92, 95, 101, 140, 185

Davis, Joseph, 19–20, 21, 22, 25, 27, 28–29, 65, 78, 189, 237n37; influence over Jefferson Davis, 23–24, 64

Davis, Reuben, 18, 217

Davis, Samuel, 15, 17, 18, 20–21, 23

Davis, Sarah Knox Taylor, 27–29, 31, 64

Davis, Varina, 5, 63–64, 65, 66, 67, 68–69, 78, 85, 106, 108, 117, 148, 162, 167, 189, 239–40n88

Davis Bend (Miss.), 19–20, 21, 28–29, 43

Deavenport, James J., 119

Deere, John, 30

Democratic Party: antislavery criticism of, 53; doughfaces in, 8, 47, 112, 162, 187–88, 199; early history of, 46–54; 1860 division of, 6, 8, 143, 177–78, 197–99, 202–3, 209–10; formation of, 46–47; historians' views of, 8, 45, 235n17, 242n4; in Illinois, 35, 55–56, 62, 96, 113, 114, 126, 137, 138, 142, 156, 161, 170, 181, 222–23; in Mississippi, 22–23, 42, 48, 65–66, 67, 96, 108, 113–14, 117, 142, 175, 181, 187, 194; northern wing of, 50, 52, 53, 71–73, 87, 96, 104, 105, 112, 115–16, 117–18, 135, 138, 140, 141, 142, 143, 145, 146, 147, 148, 155, 156, 159, 160, 163, 164, 165–66, 174–76, 177–78, 184, 185–86, 188, 193, 194–96, 199, 215, 221–23; platform (1844) of, 70, 71, 73; platform (1848) of, 94; platform (1852) of, 115, 186; platform (1856) of, 146–47,

Democratic Party (*continued*)
159, 186, 191, 198, 200, 202; platform
(1860) of, 188, 191, 193, 194, 196–98, 202,
203; proslavery criticism of, 48–49,
50, 53, 162–63, 174; and racism, 8, 9,
47, 53, 87, 144, 151–55, 159, 166–67, 173,
188, 192; sectional divisions within,
7–8, 44–45, 47–49, 53–54, 61–62, 71–74,
76–77, 82, 85–87, 94, 96–97, 104, 105,
110, 117–18, 126, 127, 130, 134, 135,
140–41, 142, 143–44, 146–47, 149–50,
154–55, 159, 165–66, 170, 174–76, 177–78,
181, 183, 184, 185–86, 188–89, 190–91,
194–99, 201–3, 209–10, 226–27; southern wing of, 49, 52, 53, 72–73, 87, 96,
97–98, 104, 105, 112, 115, 117–18, 121, 127,
130, 131, 133–35, 140, 143, 146, 147, 148,
154, 155, 156, 157, 159, 162, 163, 165–66,
167, 171, 173, 174–76, 178, 179–80, 181,
184, 188–89, 193, 195–97; and states'
rights, 8, 9, 48; "Young Americans" in,
114–16, 126, 146
Democratic-Republican Party, 46–47
Dew, Thomas, 153–54
Dickinson, Daniel S., 90, 151, 169
Dill, Benjamin F., 115
Dixon, Archibald, 133–34, 140
Dobbin, James C., 91, 134
Dodge, Augustus C., 132
Dorr, Joseph B., 186
Douglas, Adele Cutts, 54, 59, 62, 148, 208
Douglas, Martha Martin, 81, 125
Douglas, Stephen A.: on abolitionists
and abolitionism, 9, 85–86, 92, 94,
116, 141, 144, 172, 227; on African slave
trade, 179, 186, 280n10; and American Colonization Society, 152; and
Andrew Jackson, 30, 54–55, 56, 61,
72, 206; background of, 4, 29–41, 167;
on Bank War, 54, 55, 56; on Brooks-
Sumner incident, 146; and California
statehood, 97, 107, 110, 135, 162, 204;
and Chicago, 7, 31, 58, 81–84, 100,
107, 111, 126, 129, 136, 147, 189–90;
on Committee of Thirteen, 217–19;
on common-property doctrine, 89,
132, 161; and Compromise of 1850, 6,
100–106, 107, 110, 114, 132, 134, 186, 200,
218; and convention system, 55–56;

and Crittenden Compromise, 218–19;
death of, 4, 223; and Democratic Party,
2, 7, 54–55, 125, 129, 130, 155, 158, 162,
165, 170, 173, 180, 185, 186, 191, 200–201;
Dorr letter of, 186–87, 193; and *Dred
Scott v. Sandford*, 150, 172, 187; education of, 30–31; and election of 1836,
55–56; and election of 1838, 57–58; and
election of 1840, 59; and election of
1843, 60; and election of 1844, 67–68;
and election of 1846, 78; and election
of 1848, 91–92, 94–95; and election of
1852, 114–16, 186; and election of 1854,
137–38; and election of 1856, 54, 111,
139, 146–48, 186; and election of 1858, 5,
29–30, 39, 63, 92, 161, 167–74, 194, 223;
and election of 1860, 30, 53, 147, 158,
177–78, 186–87, 191, 194–99, 202–10;
and English Compromise, 165; on free
soil, 88–89, 92, 94, 95, 96, 102, 114,
132; Freeport Doctrine of, 171–72, 178,
180, 183, 184, 185; and Fugitive Slave
Act, 105, 107, 126, 127, 133, 141, 161,
168, 220; on the Greater Northwest,
61–63, 73, 74, 80–84, 92–93, 98–99, 100,
125–29, 141, 162, 181, 182–83, 190–91,
199; *Harper's* essay by, 187–89; health
problems of, 4, 101, 141–42, 148, 201,
223; on homestead legislation, 61, 84,
88, 100, 126, 130, 132, 135, 176, 190–91;
in House of Representatives, 60–63,
69–73; on Illinois, 31, 33, 80–84; and
Illinois Central Railroad, 100, 126–27;
in Illinois legislature, 56–57, 168; on
Illinois supreme court, 59–60; on
internal improvements, 56–57, 61–63,
72–73, 81–84, 100, 125–29, 130, 145,
190; and John Brown's raid, 189; and
Kansas-Nebraska Act, 111, 129–42,
145, 147, 158, 159, 160, 161, 186, 200; and
Kansas Territory, 144–46, 155, 176, 184;
and land-grant colleges, 285n89; land
speculation by, 30, 34, 41, 57, 82, 100,
189–90; on Latin American expansion,
180; as lawyer, 40–41; and Lecompton
Constitution, 143–44, 152, 153, 156–66,
168, 170, 172, 179, 218; marriage (first)
of, 81, 125; marriage (second) of, 54,
148; on Mexican Cession, 87, 88, 90,

Printed in the USA
CPSIA information can be obtained
at www.ICGtesting.com
LVHW090812081223
765923LV00003B/285